AS/400
POWER TIPS & TECHNIQUES

by Steve Bisel

MIDRANGE COMPUTING

DISCLAIMER

First Edition, June 1995

This book is a collection of AS/400 tips and techniques collected and compiled by the author into a single reference source. It is designed to provide information about the AS/400, the Operating System, and several IBM Licensed Program Products. Every effort has been made to make the information in this book as complete and as accurate as possible.

Much of the information contained in this book, such as IBM phone numbers, is oriented toward users in the continental United States and may not apply to users outside the U.S. Users outside the U.S. should consult with their local IBM office for information that may be unique to a particular country.

The information contained in this book does not constitute a recommendation, and the author does not guarantee the accuracy or assume responsibility for its contents. The information contained herein has not been submitted to any formal test and is distributed on an "as-is" basis, without any warranty either expressed or implied.

Copyright © 1995 by Midrange Computing
ISBN: 1-883884-13-6
First Edition, Rev. 2, V3R1

Midrange Computing
5650 El Camino Real, Suite 225
Carlsbad, CA 92008
(619) 931-8615
FAX (619) 931-9935

For comments to the author,
refer to the Reader Comment Form at the back of this book.

TABLE OF CONTENTS

PREFACE

AS/400 Power Tips & Techniques started as an informal IBM document in 1989. Then, it was merely a collection of notes that I had compiled while supporting the AS/400. These notes were just little tips on how to perform specific functions or little "gotchas" that go with the territory. Some of my colleagues requested copies of my notes, and it was soon evident that others could benefit from this collection. I began distributing the notes as a document within IBM titled, ***AS/400 Tips and Techniques***, and, through five revisions, it grew from a 12-page "cheat sheet" to a 160-page document distributed worldwide. This book is an extensively revised edition of the previous IBM internal book and incorporates many new tips and corrects errors that I found in the previous edition.

ABOUT THE AUTHOR

Steve Bisel is an IBM AS/400 System Operations Services Specialist. He has supported the AS/400 as an IBM Systems Engineer since its introduction in 1988. Prior to 1988, Steve worked in the IBM Rochester, Minnesota, facility as a development and manufacturing engineer. Besides the AS/400, he works on a variety of other products including personal computer platforms. Steve's current responsibilities include providing internal technical marketing support, product defect support, and AS/400 consulting and operations services.

You can reach Steve at Midrange Computing. Refer to the Reader Comment Form at the back of this book, or send an electronic note via the Internet to:

Steve Bisel
75771.1123@compuserve.com

ABOUT THE BOOK

This edition of ***AS/400 Power Tips & Techniques*** applies to Version 2, Release 1, and all subsequent releases of the Operating System. Updates that apply to Version 3, Release 1, have been incorporated and are indicated as such in the text.

WHAT THIS BOOK IS

AS/400 Power Tips & Techniques is designed to help you with many routine tasks that you might perform on the AS/400. I have found that there are many tasks that are simple but, because they are performed infrequently, you tend to forget exactly how to do them. A reminder is sometimes all that is needed.

Some tasks seem never to get documented in the manuals — or they are documented, but hard to find. Some of the tips in this book fall into these categories. Including the tips here makes for a handy reference.

Many tips in this book are little things that I have run across in my work. I don't know if they are documented in other locations or not. But, they seemed like good ideas, so I included them.

I hope that, as you read this book, you are able to better understand a few of the subtleties of housekeeping, backup, security, and operational concepts on the AS/400 and some of the IBM application programs. I have tried to make the overall tone general in nature rather than an in-depth discussion of every subject.

WHAT THIS BOOK IS NOT

AS/400 Power Tips & Techniques does not intend to replace other documentation and is not a complete discussion of the subjects. You should have your IBM AS/400 manuals or CD-ROM disk at hand for specific and unique situations. Where appropriate, I have included references to the IBM AS/400 publications where you can find additional information. The tips in this book are informal, and they do not necessarily constitute a recommendation. Users should use their own judgment in determining the applicability in their own environment.

BIBLIOGRAPHY

As this is not intended to be your single source for AS/400 operations, readers are advised to refer to the IBM AS/400 manuals and Redbooks. The titles and publication numbers are valid as of Version 3, Release 1, of the Operating System.

Publication Title	IBM Publication Number
AS/400 System Handbook	GA19-5486
AS/400 PC Support Under DOS	GG24-3255
AS/400 Office Application Programming Interfaces	GG24-3306
AS/400 Application Recovery	GG24-3441
AS/400 Communication Definitions Examples	GG24-3449
IBM AS/400 Printing	GG24-3452
AS/400 Security and Auditing Considerations	GG24-3501

Publication Title	IBM Publication Number
Managing Multiple AS/400s in a Peer Network	GG24-3614
PC Support/400 Coexistence with Novell and Windows	GG24-3637
IBM AS/400 Printing II	GG24-3704
AS/400 Performance Management, V2R2	GG24-3723
AS/400 Communications Definitions Examples II	GG24-3763
AS/400 Performance Capacity Planning, V2R2	GG24-3908
OfficeVision/400 Version 2 Technical Tips and Techniques	GG24-3937
Using DOS PC Support/400 with Novell NetWare 3.11 and NetWare for SAA 1.3	GG24-4013
IBM AS/400 Printing III	GG24-4028
An Implementation Guide for AS/400 Security and Auditing	GG24-4200
V2R3 PC Support/400 and Microsoft Windows 3.1 Advanced Topics	GG24-4253
AS/400 Communication Definition Examples III	GG24-4386
IBM AS/400 Printing IV	GG24-4389
Inside Client Access/400 for Windows 3.1	GG24-4429
Managing Your AS/400 Tape Library	GR31-1146
Physical Planning Reference	SA41-3109
ASCII Work Station Reference	SA41-3130
ADTS/400: Application Development Manager/400 User's Guide	SC09-1808
System Reference Summary	SC21-8104
InfoSeeker — Use	SC41-3002
AS/400 Software Installation	SC41-3120

Publication Title	IBM Publication Number
AS/400 Softcopy Library Installation from Tape	SC41-3127
System Operation for New Users	SC41-3200
AS/400 System Operation	SC41-3203
System Startup and Problem Handling	SC41-3206
AS/400 Security — Basic	SC41-3301
AS/400 Security — Reference	SC41-3302
AS/400 Backup and Recovery — Basic	SC41-3304
AS/400 Backup and Recovery — Advanced	SC41-3305
AS/400 Work Management	SC41-3306
Distributed Data Management	SC41-3307
AS/400 Communications Configuration	SC41-3401
TCP/IP Configuration and Reference	SC41-3420
Client Access/400 for DOS Extended Memory — Setup	SC41-3500
Client Access/400 for DOS Extended Memory User Guide	SC41-3501
Client Access/400 for Windows 3.1 — Getting Started	SC41-3530
Client Access/400 for DOS and OS/2 Technical Reference	SC41-3563
Integrated File System Introduction	SC41-3711
AS/400 Printer Device Programming	SC41-3713
AS/400 CL Programming	SC41-3721
AS/400 CL Reference	SC41-3722
OS/400 Server Concepts and Administration	SC41-3740
System API Programming	SC41-3800

Publication Title	IBM Publication Number
System API Reference	SC41-3801
Planning for and Setting Up OfficeVision/400	SH21-0695
AS/400 Managing OfficeVision/400	SH21-0699
AS/400 Office Services Concepts and Programmer's Guide	SH21-0703
AS/400 Softcopy Library (CD-ROM)	SK2T-2171
AS/400 Redbook Softcopy Library (CD-ROM)	SK2T-2172
AS/400 System Upgrade Road Map	SX41-3135
Programming Reference Summary	SX41-3720
Twinaxial Cabling Troubleshooting Guide	SY31-0703

ACKNOWLEDGMENTS

It seems unfair that one person should get all of the credit for completing a book such as this. I have received tips and suggestions from many sources, and I wish to take this opportunity to acknowledge those people who have provided tips, techniques, or their time in helping me compile this book. The following is a partial list of the many people to whom I am indebted.

Marco Soberanes
Ed Seghers
Richard Thies
Joe Lindsey
Ken Ray
Gary Seigal
Raymond Lee
Jean Johnson
Dave Prescott
Bob McDonald
Roy Birdsong
Sarah Cloud
Val Kaliszewski
George Lee
Yolanda Kinnerup
Joel Sewald

I also wish to express my gratitude to my wife, Pauline. She has put up with my idiosyncrasies for 25 years, and, more recently, my preoccupation with completing this book. Her patience and support have been a great help to me over the years.

I owe a lot to Anita Craig, the new book editor at Midrange Computing. Anita is the reincarnation of my high school English teacher who predicted that, someday, I would be grateful for doing those writing compositions and grammar drills. If only I had been paying attention. Anita reviewed every word of this book and made it more readable.

INTRODUCTION

I have written this book to help users of the AS/400, new and old. The AS/400 has the most advanced architecture of any computer system. It is the easiest multi-user system to manage, has outstanding interactive performance, and provides the lowest cost of operation of any multi-user environment. With over 300,000 installed systems worldwide, it is also the most widely used multi-user computer system.

As with any computer system, the AS/400 requires care and feeding. Your job in managing the system becomes much easier as your knowledge grows. Strive to expand your knowledge by enrolling in the many educational offerings that are available, and by becoming familiar with the manuals and various periodicals devoted to the AS/400.

There are several other sources of information that you can refer to besides the IBM manuals. Three popular periodicals are:

- *Midrange Computing*
- *AS/400 Magazine*
- *NEWS 3X/400*

NEW FUNCTIONS IN VERSION 3, RELEASE 1 (V3R1)

$\boxed{V3R1}$ IBM announced V3R1 in May 1994, and began shipping it in December 1994. There are several new functions and enhancements unique to V3R1. Where appropriate, new features are indicated with this symbol.

Unless otherwise indicated, all other functions in this book refer to earlier versions of the Operating System, although they are still applicable to V3R1.

BEFORE YOU USE THE AS/400

Before you begin using the AS/400, you need to understand a few of the concepts and to review the documentation that comes with the AS/400. I expect that, if you are new to the AS/400, you will do this as a matter of course.

If you are familiar with the AS/400, and performing a new installation or an upgrade, you may want to review the topics in this chapter before you start.

ACCESS TO IBM MANUALS

Before you access the AS/400, you should understand where to go for additional information. The logical choice, of course, would be the AS/400 manuals.

A current trend in the computer industry is to reduce the amount of paper or hardcopy manuals shipped with a computer system. In the past, IBM provided hardcopy manuals that filled a bookcase. Today, you can obtain hard copies of the system manuals, but, unless you specifically order them, IBM only ships a few basic manuals. However, all of the AS/400 system manuals are available in softcopy form. These soft copies are on either a CD-ROM or on a tape, your choice, and are provided at no charge with every license of the Operating System. Presuming that you have at least one PC attached using Client Access/400 or PC Support/400, I recommend you choose the CD-ROM version as this gives you the most flexibility for access. With the CD-ROM, you can access the manuals using:

- A PC with CD-ROM drive.
- A PC on a network where the CD-ROM is a shared resource on a server.
- A PC user on the AS/400 using Client Access/400 (or PC Support/400). Manuals are accessed using the shared folders function.

$\boxed{V3R1}$
- A terminal user on the AS/400 accessing the manuals using InfoSeeker (V3R1 only).

If you have the manuals on tape, then you can only load the manuals into shared folders for access via PCs or terminals.

INSTALLING SOFTCOPY MANUALS ON THE AS/400

The term "softcopy" is IBM's nomenclature for documents delivered electronically (e.g., on tape or CD-ROM). These manuals are in BookManager format, which, when used with the BookManager READ software, provides the capabilities for reading, printing, navigating, and searching through the softcopy documents.

If you have an interest in creating your own BookManager documents using either WordPerfect, Microsoft Word for Windows, or ASCII text files as the source, call IBM and ask for information about *IBM BookManager BUILD/2*, IBM Announcement Number 293-739.

Installing Softcopy Manuals from Tape

 If you have received your softcopy manuals on magnetic tape (V3R1 or later), you install manuals using the Restore Bookshelf (RSTSHF) command. You are offered several options:

- Select the bookshelves to install from a list of bookshelves on the tape.
- Install only those bookshelves for the products you have installed on your AS/400.
- Install a specific bookshelf or a list of bookshelves by name.
- Install all bookshelves on the media.
- Select whether to install just bookshelves. The default is to install the books with their bookshelves. Installing only the bookshelves allows greater flexibility in installing only the books you want on your system.

For more information, refer to the *AS/400 Softcopy Library Installation from Tape* manual.

Installing Softcopy Manuals from CD-ROM

If you have your manuals on CD-ROM, you can install the softcopy manuals on the AS/400 using the SCRT function provided on the CD-ROM. You must use a PC running Client Access/400 that is attached to the AS/400. The procedure is:

1. Initiate a connection to the AS/400 using Client Access/400.
2. Start the shared folders function.
3. Insert the CD-ROM disk into the CD-ROM reader.
4. Start a full-screen DOS session on the PC, and change to the CD-ROM drive (e.g., D drive).
5. Enter the command STARTCD, and follow the instructions on the screen. You are given three options:

   - Install the IBM Library READ program on your PC.
   - Copy bookshelves and books to the AS/400.
   - Run online demonstrations.

For more information, refer to the *AS/400 Softcopy Library* instruction manual that comes with your CD-ROM.

Options for CD-ROM Softcopy Manuals

IBM offers the Version 3, AS/400 softcopy manuals on two different CD-ROMs.

- *AS/400 Softcopy Library, Version 3:* SK2T-2171.
  Contains all the books for the Operating System and most of the books for other licensed programs.
- *AS/400 Redbook Softcopy Library, Version 3:* SK2T-2172.
  Contains everything on previous CD-ROM plus most of the AS/400-related Redbooks.

You have the option of getting the first CD-ROM with your software instead of receiving the manuals on tape. However, the Redbooks version must be ordered separately. For information on ordering publications (including CD-ROMS), refer to Frequently Called IBM Telephone Numbers on page 321.

If InfoSeeker Cannot Access Softcopy Books

You can access books on the AS/400 using:

- A PC running IBM BookManager or IBMRead.
- An AS/400 terminal using InfoSeeker on the AS/400.

If you are accessing the softcopy books using a PC running IBM BookManager or IBMRead, you only need the book, shelf, and index files on the AS/400 shared folders.

If you are accessing the softcopy books using InfoSeeker, then the structure is more rigid. Presuming you are using the defaults, you need to have a shared folder called QBKBOOKS with the following subfolders:

- BOOKS
- SHELVES
- SRCHTMP
- UNITABLE

The QBKBOOKS\UNITABLE shared folder should contain several EPHU* files.

If you get an error when using InfoSeeker stating something on the order that books cannot be opened, try doing the following:

```
CRTFLR FLR(SRCHTMP) INFLR(QBKBOOKS)
RSTDLO DLO(*ALL) SAVFLR(QBKBOOKS) DEV(*SAVF) SAVF(QSYS/QSBMGTBL)
```

This creates the necessary shared folders and restores the EPHU* files that InfoSeeker needs to access the softcopy books.

INFORMATION ASSISTANT

When you access the AS/400, the Information Assistant provides one-stop shopping for all of your information needs. You can use the Information Assistant to get information about the AS/400, the Operating System, even tools in QUSRTOOL; provide personal feedback to IBM; discover what is new with the latest release of the Operating System; plus a few other options.

To access the Information Assistant, enter the command **GO INFO**.

```
INFO                    Information Assistant Options
                                                   System:    AS400
To select one of the following, type its number below and press Enter:


     1. Where do I look for information?
     2. How can I comment on information?

    10. What's new this release?
    11. What's coming in the next release?

    20. Start search index (InfoSeeker)
    21. Start online education
    22. Start question and answer
    23. Work with problems


Type a menu option below
    __

F1=Help   F3=Exit   F9=Command line   F12=Cancel   F14=Access IBMLink
(C) COPYRIGHT IBM CORP. 1980, 1993.
```

Using option 20 (InfoSeeker), you can explore the AS/400 to find information on many topics. The first time you enter InfoSeeker, you will be presented with a screen similar to the one below:

```
                               InfoSeeker

Type options, press Enter.  (+ indicates an expandable topic)
  5=Display topic   6=Print topic   7=Expand topic   8=Compress topic

Opt   Topic
 __   AS/400 System Information
 __   + AS/400 Query Management
 __   + AS/400 Structured Query Language (SQL)
 __   + Communication and connectivity
 __   + Customer support and education
 __   + Debug topics
 __   + Glossary
 __   + Interactive Data Definition Utility (IDDU)
 __   + Operating System/400 CL commands
 __   + Questions and Answers
 __   + REXX
                                                         More...
Or type search words and press Enter.  (* indicates a topic match)
_____

F3=Exit help   F5=All topics   F6=Main topics   F11=Hide structure
F12=Cancel     F13=Information Assistant   F18=More indexes   F24=More keys
```

On this screen, you can expand or compress topics (the + indicates that a topic is expandable), or you can search for a topic by entering key words on the command line. Other features are available such as creating search profiles. For additional information, enter the search word **infoseeker** on the command line and press Enter. Then display and read the topic on InfoSeeker. Refer to the *System Operation for New Users* manual for additional information on InfoSeeker.

REVIEW ANY PRE-INSTALLATION INSTRUCTIONS

If you are preparing to install or upgrade an AS/400, ensure that ANY and ALL pre-installation instructions outlined in the documentation shipped with your system have been completed. Once you have completed those steps, install your system or software. If you see documentation with the words **READ ME FIRST**, or something similar, then do what it says. Don't skip a step because you are in a hurry.

So, presuming you have read all the instructions and performed the pre-installation steps, you are ready to install or upgrade the system.

If this is an initial system installation, then attach only the system console to the AS/400. The system console is one of following:

- A twinaxial-attached terminal on port 0, address 0, on the first work station controller (WSC).
- A PC running 5250 Emulation (not Client Access or PC Support) attached on port 0, address 0, on the first WSC.
- An ASCII terminal attached to the ASCII WSC.
- A PC running ASCII terminal emulation attached to the ASCII WSC.
- An Apple Macintosh PC attached to the AppleTalk controller.

AS/400 SMOOTHSTART

For a nominal fee, IBM provides a program called **AS/400 SmoothStart** (or something similar, depending on your area) to its customers. This is a total system implementation that includes customer setup and installation, software installation, system level verification, operator training, and recovery management. If you are new to the AS/400, this service can get you up and running faster than you are likely to achieve on your own. Generally, the cost is low and the value is high. You can obtain more information from your friendly IBM Marketing Representative or Systems Engineer.

SmoothStart may not be available in all countries. Contact your local IBM Support Center to discuss what services IBM provides in your area.

IBM HARDWARE AND SOFTWARE SUPPORT

If you are going to be involved with the AS/400, a time will come when you will likely need hardware or software support. This support is available from a variety of sources, IBM being one them. I am somewhat biased in my belief that IBM is the best source.

Most users are familiar with IBM's and other vendors' offerings for hardware support. Hardware support typically is provided via a hardware maintenance agreement. IBM provides hardware maintenance at no cost during the warranty period. Once the warranty period expires, you have to enter into an agreement to obtain hardware maintenance.

Software support is also provided at no cost during the software warranty period. As with hardware support, you have to enter into an agreement to continue software support. In recent years, IBM's policy toward software support has gone through some significant changes. This is not of consequence to new IBM customers, but long-term IBM customers should be aware of these changes. Fundamentally, these changes are:

- Software defect support is provided at no cost.
- Software usability support is only provided for a fee.
- Access to all software support can be obtained via:
    - Telephone voice support
    - Electronic Customer Support (ECS)
    - FAX
    - Mail
- Users must have a software service agreement to obtain telephone voice support.

The most pervasive change is that users must have a software support agreement to obtain telephone voice support for *any* software support.

IBM's vehicle for providing AS/400 software support is called AS/400 SupportLine. This service is provided as a monthly or hourly subscription. I strongly recommend you obtain a SupportLine agreement. You can get additional information on this service from your IBM Representative, or you can call the Support Family services directly (refer to Frequently Called IBM Telephone Numbers on page 321).

INSTALLATION CHECKLIST

I created a simple checklist to help first-time users install an AS/400. The checklist is in Appendix A: Initial Installation Checklist on page 323, and is meant to be a bare minimum of activities you should complete before placing your AS/400 into operation.

CONFIRM DELIVERY

Before you begin to install or upgrade your system, you should confirm that the system is complete and that all hardware and IBM Program Products are installed. Also, check that the program temporary fixes (PTFs) are at the current cumulative tape level. If you do not know the current PTF level, call IBM Support, 1-800-237-5511, and ask the support personnel. The media description report that comes with your system indicates the PTF level shipped with your system.

SYSTEM PASSWORD

When installing or upgrading the AS/400, you may be prompted to enter the System Password. IBM uses the system password to detect hardware movement and allow IBM an opportunity to validate the software license for the system and the customer. The system password is entered only once; therefore, IBM says, there is no need to have the ability to view the password. Review the documentation that ships with your system. You should find a document with the System Password (e.g., you are installing a new software license or hardware upgrade). Record the password somewhere for safekeeping, just in case.

If ownership of the hardware has changed, you are obliged to purchase a new software license. If the system determines that ownership has changed, then it is possible that the system will set the password to "expired." If this occurs, then you must contact an IBM Marketing Representative to order the AS/400 System Password RPQ (Request for Price Quotation). Refer to System Password on page 185 for additional information.

MULIC/FULIC TAPE

One of the first things you should do before installing or upgrading an AS/400 is verify that you have a MULIC or FULIC tape. Although this sounds like something that you cough up when you have the flu, it is in fact the Model (or Feature) Unique Licensed Internal Code tape. The MULIC tape is associated with the AS/400 B-F model. The FULIC tape is associated with the new Advanced Series Models (i.e., the black boxes).

> *The FULIC or MULIC tape contains information that is unique to your system, and it remains the property of IBM. Do not lose the tape. Do not record over it. Under normal circumstances, you will never need this tape, but it may be required for system upgrades or other abnormal circumstances.*

You need to verify that your MULIC or FULIC tape is labeled with your system type, model, and serial number. The tape media should be compatible with your system's alternate IPL tape device. If it is not, you need to obtain a new one. If the label does not match your system type, model, or serial number, notify your local IBM Representative as soon as possible.

If you need to obtain a new MULIC or FULIC tape, you must order the tape from IBM. There may be a nominal charge incurred. The following steps should be helpful.

1. Have your IBM Marketing Representative verify that your system administrative records are correct with respect to AS/400 type/model, Alternate-IPL device, and media type.

2. Place an order for an RPQ for your new tape. The RPQ number varies according to system and tape media type.

RPQ Number	AS/400 Model and Tape Media
S40302	9406 Bxx - Fxx models, MULIC tape, all media types except 8mm on B models
S40347	9406 Bxx models, MULIC tape with 8mm media
S40370	9402/9404 Bxx - Fxx models, MULIC 1/4" tape cartridge
S40371	9404 Bxx - Fxx models, MULIC 1/2" cartridge
S40372	9402/9404 Bxx - Fxx models, MULIC 1/2" reel
S40373	9402/9404 Bxx - Fxx models, MULIC 8mm cartridge
843819	9402/9404 2xx models, FULIC 1/2" cartridge
843820	9402/9404 2xx models, FULIC 1/2" reel
843818	9402/9404 2xx models, FULIC 1/4" cartridge
843821	9402/9404 2xx models, FULIC 8mm cartridge
843817	9404/6 3xx models, FULIC all media types

3. Complete and sign a certification form. Your IBM Representative can print a copy of this form, called AS400CRT, from AEFORMS.

If you have any questions, you can send an IBMLink note to RCHVMP(ENTITLE). Refer to Sending E-mail on IBMLink on page 302 for instructions on sending IBMLink notes.

PREPARING FOR NEW RELEASE OF OPERATING SYSTEM ONLY

If you are only going to install a new release of the Operating System, then the following three subsections outline the recommended minimum actions that you should perform in preparation for that activity. This is not to say that this is all you should do. You may also want to go through the actions that you would perform to install a brand new system.

Software Upgrade Checklist

Refer to Appendix B: Software Upgrade Checklist on page 325 for a checklist of activities that you should perform to prepare for upgrading your system software.

Prepare for New Release

As you prepare for installation of a new release of the Operating System, perform the following preparatory actions in advance.

- Make sure that your current release is at a high enough level for the release you are installing. With few exceptions, you cannot skip more than one full release.

- Read the new release planning manual(s) appropriate to the release that you intend to install.

- Read the *Read This First* and the *Memo to User* documentation provided with new release tapes.

- Understand the importance of the IBM Print Services Facility/400. Refer to Advanced Function Printing to IPDS Printers on page 141. If you need this function, make sure you have ordered it and it is on your upgrade tapes.

- Perform thorough research to determine if there are any changes that may affect your applications. For example:

  - OfficeVision/400 changes.

  - Third party software compatibility with new release.

- Download the Preventive Service Planning Information, PTF SF98vrm. Refer to PTF Information on page 124.

- Confirm that you have all necessary upgrade tapes. Plan to install the entire new release, not a partial installation.

- Verify that your media is compatible with your system and that the tapes are readable. Use the CHKSAVTAP command available as part of QUSRTOOLs.

- Make sure you have enough DASD space. If you don't, you are probably a good candidate for additional DASD.

- Plan for ample time to install the new release. The documentation that ships with the software provides installation time estimates. Make sure you include enough time in your plan to re-install the old version or release should something go wrong.

- Approximately one week before you plan to install the new release, order the latest cumulative PTF package for the release of the software you intend to install (not your current release). Refer to PTF Information on page 124.

- Notify all of the users of your intention to install a new release. If there are any changes that will affect the end users, you must make sure that they are informed and educated.

Check/Verify Software Distribution Tapes

Before installing a new release of the Operating System, IBM advises you to verify that your distribution tapes are OK. A good method to verify that your save tapes, and especially your version/release upgrade distribution tapes, are readable and in good condition is to use the tool CHKSAVTAP, which is part of the QUSRTOOLs. Refer to QUSRTOOL Library on page 307 for additional information.

VERIFY ALL HARDWARE AND SOFTWARE COMPLETE

Before upgrading a system, make sure that your current hardware and software are correct.

- The installed hardware and software should match the records IBM used to configure your upgrade.
- All installed IBM software should all be at the same version and release.
- Make sure IBM is aware of any non-IBM hardware such as third-party memory or adapter cards.

After performing the upgrade, the following system commands are useful to determine that your system is complete. Of course, you should keep this short list in mind for any occasion that you wish to verify hardware or software resources.

GO LICPGM   Menu for working with licensed programs

GO PTF   Menu for working with PTFs.

GO CMDPTF   Another menu for working with PTFs.

DSPSFWRSC   The Display Software Resources command shows, prints, or writes to an output file the list of installed software resources.

DSPHDWRSC   The Display Hardware Resources command displays, prints, or saves in an output file the various types of System Resource Management (SRM) information.

WRKHDWPRD   The Work with Hardware Product command aids in determining if all features are correct for your system.

Once you have determined that the configuration is correct, save the configuration by using option 3 to replace the rack configuration in the file QUSRSYS/QASURACK (this is the default file when using option 3 of the WRKHDWPRD command). Perform this task each time a change is made to the rack configuration (e.g., adding memory, upgrading processor). The configuration file is for back-up purposes — if the primary system configuration file becomes damaged, you have a backup, which should be saved with library QUSRSYS.

Print a copy of the rack configuration for your records. Use option 1 of the WRKHDWPRD command, then F17 to print.

Related Topics

Refer to System Management on page 119, which lists additional tips that you should become familiar with prior to initial installation. Start a good policy of system management now and this task is much easier later.

PERFORMING NEW INSTALLATIONS AND UPGRADES

The following installation tips are general in nature. You will likely have to customize your system to fit in with your unique requirements.

> Before you continue, I recommend that you review the topics in
> *Before You Use the AS/400* beginning on page 3.

The steps discussed in this section apply to both an initial installation and when upgrading your system software. This, of course, does not replace the special instructions that you receive with your system or with your new version or release of software. It does serve as fairly complete, step-by-step instructions to get your AS/400 ready for productive use.

Experienced users find these installation tips to be a good refresher for reviewing tasks such as initial system setup and security. You can use these installation steps to review many of the objects (e.g., System Values) that control the operation of the AS/400.

> If you are installing a new AS/400, go through this section in the
> order presented. When you have completed these steps, your
> AS/400 will be ready to go into production mode or ready to load
> application software.
>
> If you are upgrading your AS/400, it is a good idea to go through
> these installation steps to be sure that system objects have not
> changed.

PREPARATION FOR UPGRADE OF SOFTWARE

If you are installing a new version or release of the software, refer to Preparing for New Release of Operating System Only on page 10.

CHANGE LIBRARY (CHGSYS)

One of the first steps to installing a new AS/400 is creating a library to contain an original copy of any IBM-supplied objects that you may be changing. Save a copy of any IBM-supplied objects in this library before making any changes to the original object. I suggest that you create a library on the system called CHGSYS (or something similar):

```
CRTLIB CHGSYS TEXT('Changed System Objects Library')
```

Then create a duplicate object of the original IBM object:

```
CRTDUPOBJ OBJ(objectname) FROMLIB( libraryname) OBJTYPE(type)
    TOLIB(CHGSYS)
```

> *It is important to do this (or keep accurate records) so you can recover the original object if something goes wrong. New releases of the operating system or PTFs might replace existing IBM objects. Any changes you may have made to an IBM object may be lost. Make a note of your changes so you can put things back if an IBM object is replaced. Using the CHGSYS library for this purpose is an easy way to maintain the original copy of the IBM object.*

Related Topics

Refer to Changing IBM Commands on page 316 for information about using a user library to hold all user commands and all changed IBM commands.

CHANGE CONTROLLING SUBSYSTEM TO QCTL

Before proceeding much further, change the controlling subsystem to QCTL. Refer to description of system value QCTLSBSD under the topic System Control System Values on page 20.

```
CHGSYSVAL SYSVAL(QCTLSBSD) VALUE('QCTL QSYS')
```

The change will not take effect until after the next IPL.

SYSTEM STARTUP PROGRAM

When the controlling subsystem starts, the autostart job in the subsystem transfers control to the program specified in the system value QSTRUPPGM (refer to QSTRUPPGM on page 23). This is commonly referred to as the system autostart program.

If you are performing a new installation, you will want to tailor this program or create your own program and change the QSTRUPPGM system value to that program name. Use the shipped program QSTRUP in QSYS as a base to tailor or create your own program.

1. Make a copy of the original program. For example, you could call it QSTRUPBAK.

```
CRTDUPOBJ OBJ(QSTRUP) FROMLIB(QSYS) OBJTYPE(*PGM) NEWOBJ(QSTRUPBAK)
```

2. Retrieve the source of the shipped program using the RTVCLSRC command:

```
RTVCLSRC PGM(QSYS/QSTRUP) SRCFILE(YOURLIB/YOURFILE))
```

3. Change this program source code. For example, if OfficeVision/400 is installed, modify the startup program to start the subsystem QSNADS.

4. Create the program using the CRTCLPGM command, give it a name other than QSTRUP, and put it into the QSYS library. For example, you could call it STARTUP.

5. Test the program to ensure that it works.

6. Change the system value QSTRUPPGM to the program name and library you specified on the CRTCLPGM command.

> *If you are upgrading your software to a new version or release, there may be changes that are expected or required. For example, when you upgrade to V3R1, the name of the subsystem for Client Access changes from QXFPCS to QSERVER. The upgrade process may create a new startup program, QSYS/QSTRUP. After upgrading, follow the above instructions to modify the new QSTRUP program or make any necessary changes to your customized program.*

SOFTWARE UPGRADES AND SYSTEM OBJECTS

Any changes you have made to IBM-supplied objects in libraries other than QGPL and QUSRSYS are not saved when you install a new release. For example:

*   Changes to subsystem descriptions.

*   Changes to the QPJOBLOG printer file in the QSYS library for values such as lines per inch or page size.

*   Changes or duplicates to any IBM-supplied objects such as commands.

You have to make these changes again when you have completed the installation process.

If you duplicated IBM-supplied product libraries, delete them before you install your new release. The automatic installation process fails and the new release does not install until duplicated IBM-supplied libraries are deleted.

If you have created logical files over IBM-supplied physical files in QSYS, the logical files are deleted during the installation process.

Refer to the **AS/400 Software Installation** manual for further information.

AUXILIARY STORAGE POOLS (ASP) AND CHECKSUM

If you plan to have user-defined auxiliary storage pools (User ASPs) or initiate CHECKSUM, configure the hardware now. If you need help with this task, confer with your IBM Systems Engineer or Customer Engineering Representative. It is far easier to set up user ASPs and CHECKSUM before you customize your system. This avoids a potential complete reload of the system after you have loaded it with your own applications. When configuring multiple

ASPs on your AS/400, there are some special considerations of which you should be aware. Refer to Setting Up and Managing User Auxiliary Storage Pools on page 202 for additional information.

When you configure a user ASP, consider making it larger (by maybe double) than you think you really need. You can always make the user ASP smaller. With earlier releases of the Operating System, any time a disk unit is removed from any ASP (system or user), that ASP is destroyed and objects in that ASP must be restored. The save/restore operation for the system ASP is likely to take a lot longer than for a user ASP. With later versions/releases of the Operating System, you can add/remove disk units without destroying the ASP objects. Make sure you verify which level of the Operating System you have before doing something you may regret.

INITIAL SYSTEM VALUES

Pay attention to the list of system values that follows — particularly during a system installation. This is not a comprehensive list of the system values. Refer to the **AS/400 Work Management** manual for a complete discussion of all system values and their significance.

> *Some of the system values that I have commented on here can also be set using the Operational Assistant. However, when the Operational Assistant makes the changes to the system values, it is not obvious that a system value is actually being changed. You can use the Operational Assistant to change the system values that I have noted, or you can use the method described here. I recommend using this "manual" method because it gives you a better understanding of what is taking place. I like the Operational Assistant, but when performing certain tasks you are better off using other methods.*
>
> *For explanation and discussion of the Operational Assistant, refer to Operational Assistant on page 83.*

When you are working with system values, the two most common tasks are displaying and changing the values. If you use the command WRKSYSVAL, you can do either, and you can prompt the command to obtain a full or partial listing of the system values.

> *You can also use the Set Up Your System option (part of the Operational Assistant). To access this menu, enter the command **GO SETUP**. Take option 1 to change system values. I have indicated which values can be changed is this manner by including an asterisk enclosed in parentheses (*).*

Printing a Listing of System Values

Print a copy of all of the system values with their current and default (shipped) values. This makes a handy "quick reference" for inclusion in your system control book. Enter the command:

```
WRKSYSVAL OUTPUT(*PRINT)
```

Date and Time System Values

The date-and-time system values allow you to control the date and time on your system.

QDATE (*)   Set the current date.

QTIME (*)   Set the current time.

QUTCOFFSET   The difference in time between Coordinated Universal Time (Greenwich Mean Time) and local time. This probably has significance at locations outside the United States or U.S. locations with international operations. This is the number of hours and minutes that need to be added or subtracted from local time to obtain UTC (or GMT). The value is five characters long. The default value is *+0000*. The format is:

shhmm   where: *s* = "+" to add or "-" to subtract.
hh = hours (00 to 24).
mm = minutes (00 to 59).

Editing System Values

The editing system values allow you to control the format used for displaying currency symbols, dates, and decimal values on your system.

QCURSYM   Currency symbol. The initial value is set at "$". You may prefer a different value.

QDATFMT (*)   Allows you to set the system date format. Default value is MDY (Month Day Year). You can set to DMY, YMD, MDY, or JUL (Julian format).

| | **QDATSEP (*)** | Specify the character separator for dates. The default value is "/". You may want "," or "." depending on the convention in your country. |

QDATSEP (*)   Specify the character separator for dates. The default value is "/". You may want "," or "." depending on the convention in your country.

QDECFMT   This value determines the type of zero suppression, the decimal point character, and the three-digit grouping character.

Value	Decimal Point	Three-Digit Separator	Zero Suppression
blank	.	,	Left of decimal point
J	,	.	2nd position left of decimal point
I	,	.	Left of decimal point

System Control System Values

The system control system values allow you to control or display information specific to your system.

QASTLVL   The assistance level available to users on the system. If you are new to the AS/400, you may want to leave this value at the default value *BASIC. More experienced users may prefer *INTERMED or *ADVANCED. This value can be overridden two ways:

- By the user, when using CL commands that allow a change in the assistance level.
- By changing the assistance level field in the user profile.

Refer to Using Assistance Levels on page 95.

QAUTOCFG   Initial setting is ON. Leave it on to simplify configuration of devices unless you specifically want device names other than those in the AS/400 naming convention. After your system has stabilized, you may want to turn QAUTOCFG OFF.

QCMNRCYLMT   The system value for communications recovery limits; consists of two parts. The first part is the number of recovery attempts to be made by the system before an inquiry message is sent to the system operator. If the count limit is set to zero, then no recovery is attempted.

The second part is the time period (in minutes) before the system sends an inquiry message to the system operator if the count limit is reached. If the time interval is set to zero, then there is infinite recovery.

The initial (shipped) value is set to 0 0, which equates to "no recovery." IBM recommends that you initially set this to 2 5.

QCTLSBSD

I recommend changing this to QCTL. The initial value is QBASE, which is OK for smaller, less complex systems. System management tasks are much easier if this value is set to QCTL. For a discussion of what this does, refer to the *AS/400 Work Management* manual. Change this value to QCTL QSYS.

QDEVNAMING (*)

Set this to the S/36 naming convention only if you plan to run the S/36 environment predominantly and have some reason to want your devices named using that convention. Otherwise, I recommend setting it to *DEVADR (then the auto-configured device names are derived from the device address). If you set it to *NORMAL, the devices are named in numerical sequence. Here are some examples:

Value	Display	Printer
*S36	W1, W2	P1, P2
*NORMAL	DSP01, DSP02	PRT01, PRT02
*DEVADR	DSP010403	PRT030006

When you don't want device names to follow the above conventions, you can configure the devices manually, or allow the system to auto-configure them, and then you can rename them. Refer to Renaming Device, Controller, or Line Descriptions on page 315.

QKBDBUF

Specifies whether type-ahead feature and attention key option should be used. Initial value is *TYPEAHEAD, which sets type ahead on and Attention key off.

QIPLDATTIM

Date and time to automatically IPL the system. Refer to Automatic IPL After System Shutdown on page 238.

QPFRADJ

Permits the system to do automatic performance adjustments. Initially, the value is set to 2, which allows the system to make performance adjustments at every IPL and dynamic adjustments during system operation. You can change the value to 0 for no adjustments, 1 to make adjustments only at IPL, or 3 to make adjustments dynamically but not at IPL. You should only set this system value to 0 or 3.

Do not use 1 or 2. Option 1 was provided before there was an option 2 or 3. It makes no sense to allow the system to make performance adjustments during an IPL and not allow for dynamic tuning. Option 2 is not recommended because it is unnecessary to make adjustments during IPL as well as dynamic adjustments.

For new system installations, I recommend using 3, which allows for automatic performance adjustments but does not cause a reset upon an IPL. For most smaller systems (Model 45 and Model 200s and below), I believe that dynamic tuning is best. However, larger systems and all systems with more complex mixes of interactive and batch work may benefit using manual tuning.

If you plan to tune the system manually, then set this value to 0. Refer to Storage System Values on page 25, and Work Management and Performance on page 199, for additional information.

QPRTDEV (*)   The default printer device description. Initially, this is set to PRT01. If your default printer is going to be something else, you should change this; otherwise, leave it alone.

QPWRRSTIPL   This system value sets whether the system should automatically start (IPL) when power is restored after a power failure. Set it to 0 (do not do an automatic IPL), or 1 (do an automatic IPL).

QSPCENV (*)   This is the system value for special environment (i.e., S/36 Environment).

Verify that the factory setting is what you want (i.e., S/36 Environment or AS/400 Native mode).

S/36 execution environment studies recommend that you use the Special Environment parameter in the user profiles to put user(s) in the S/36 environment rather than setting a special environment with this system value.

QSTRUPPGM   The startup program default name is QSTRUP in library QSYS. You may want to change this to a different program or you may want to modify the default program. To modify the default program, refer to System Startup Program on page 16.

QUPSDLYTIM   Specifies UPS delay time value — how long the system operates using the UPS battery power after normal utility power is lost. The value of QUPSDLYTIM depends on the model. For a 9404 system with a built-in battery feature, set the value to the default *CALC so the system calculates the wait time. For larger models with the UPS attachment, calculate the value according to the guidelines outlined in the *AS/400 Backup and Recovery — Advanced* manual.

Library List System Values

The library list system values allow you to control or display the system and user parts of the library list.

QSYSLIBL   This is the system part of the library list. The shipped value is:

`'QSYS QSYS2 QHLPSYS QUSRSYS'`

QUSRLIBL   This is the user part of the library list. The shipped value is:

`'QGPL QTEMP'`

Allocation System Values

The allocation system values allow you to control the number of jobs and storage sizes on your system.

QACTJOB   Sets the initial number of active jobs for which auxiliary storage is allocated during IPL. The amount allocated is approximately 110K. The initial value is 20. A reasonable assigned value is your estimate of the number of active jobs on a typical heavy-use day. Estimate the number by viewing the Active Jobs field on the active jobs display (WRKACTJOB command). Consider both user and system jobs when assigning a value to QACTJOB.

A good method to estimate this value is:

1. Execute WRKACTJOB several times during a busy day.

2. Pick the highest number of active jobs observed.

3. Increase that number by 10 to 15 percent.

4. Use this value for QACTJOB.

QRCLSPLSTG Specifies the number of days to keep unused spooled storage. The default value is 8, which is probably fine. Unused spool storage (which is not the same as spool files) is deleted if the storage space is not used within the specified time.

You can specify any number of days (1 to 366), *NONE, or *NOMAX. If you specify *NONE, then all unused spool storage is deleted. Programs producing spooled files must slow down long enough to create storage space for the spooled file. If you specify *NOMAX, then the system does not automatically delete unused spool storage space. You have to do it using the RCLSPLSTG command. Refer to Reclaim Unused Spool Storage on page 105. This alternative has advantages. You can schedule the reclaim procedure during periods of low activity (e.g., nightly backup).

Some system overhead is required to perform reclaim spool storage, so you may want to investigate allowing the system to handle the task versus performing it yourself.

QTOTJOB Total number of jobs for which auxiliary storage is allocated during IPL. The amount of storage allocated is the sum of the QJOBSPLA and QJOBMSGQSZ system values (refer to the *AS/400 Work Management* manual for more discussion). The initial value for QTOTJOB is 30. A reasonable value is two to seven times the value used for QACTJOB — depending on how often you clear your output queues (smaller values if you keep them cleared frequently, larger if you don't). Values exceeding 300 may affect the time to perform an IPL.

Here is an estimating technique you might try:

1. Execute WRKSYSSTS several times during a busy day.

2. Pick the highest observed number of total jobs shown on the display.

3. Increase that value by 25 percent and use this as the value for QTOTJOB.

Remember that the system keeps track of all jobs from the time they enter the system until they leave — this includes jobs that are active, in the job queues, and in the output queues. Keeping spooled files hanging around too long in output queues means that your system must keep track of them.

Storage System Values

The storage system values allow you to control storage size and activity levels on your system.

QTSEPOOL This value specifies whether interactive jobs should be moved to another main storage pool when they reach time slice end. The shipped value is *NONE — jobs are not moved. If you are allowing IPL adjustments to tune the system (QPFRADJ = 1, 2, or 3), then you may want to change the value of QTSEPOOL to *BASE. Also refer to Tips to Improve Memory/CPU Utilization on page 214 for additional information.

There is a "gotcha" ... if jobs are moved to *BASE, they compete with jobs already running in *BASE. The moved jobs continue to run at interactive priority, which may adversely affect any batch jobs that might be running in *BASE.

Security System Values

The security system values allow you to control security measures on your system.

> *If you are new to the AS/400, then I strongly recommend that you refer to Security on page 171 for additional security tips.*

V3R1 **QALWOBJRST** Determines whether objects that are security-sensitive may be restored to your system. Use it to prevent anyone from restoring a system state object or an object that adopts authority.

> **CAUTION:** Do not change from the default setting of *ALL until you understand the significance of this value. Refer to *Restoring Security-Sensitive Objects* on page 173.

QAUTOVRT
Controls the number of virtual devices automatically configured for pass-through. The initial value is 0. Change this value to the maximum number likely to be used. Of course, if you are not going to use pass-through or you intend to configure the virtual devices manually, you can leave it at 0.

QDSPSGNINF
Controls the display of sign-on information when a user signs on to the system. Default value 0 suppresses sign-on information. I prefer to display the sign-on information (set the value to 1). If you have a lot of remote users, the extra time required for this screen may be annoying. Choose the value you prefer.

QINACTITV
Controls the inactive job time-out interval. The initial value is *NONE. You can change this to any interval from 5 to 300 minutes.

QINACTMSGQ
The subsystem sends a message to the designated message queue when a job has been inactive for a time specified by QINACTITV. Refer to the *AS/400 Work Management* manual for more information.

QLMTDEVSSN
Controls ability to limit concurrent device sessions. Initial value 0 allows users to sign on to more than one device. A value of 1 limits users to only one session.

QLMTSECOFR (*)
Default value is 1. This limits users with *ALLOBJ or *SERVICE special authority to specific work stations. The default restricts them from signing on to auto-configured displays unless specifically granted authority to that display. You may wish to change this value to 0.

QMAXSGNACN
This specifies the action taken when the maximum number of invalid sign-on attempts is reached. The initial value is 3, which disables the user profile and the device. Other values are 1 (disable the device only), and 2 (disable the user profile only).

QMAXSIGN
The maximum number of invalid sign-on attempts allowed by the system. Initially set to 15. When the

number of invalid sign-on attempts is reached, the system performs the action specified by the system value QMAXSGNACN. I recommend resetting this to 4 or 5.

QPWDEXPITV The password expiration interval. The initial value is *NOMAX. To force users to change their passwords at a specific interval, change this to the number of days you want passwords to be valid.

You can override the password change interval by changing the user profile. For example, you may have a particularly sensitive user profile and want to force more frequent change intervals (e.g., QSECOFR). Some profiles may require no change (e.g., a profile for multiple users in training). Also, keep in mind that IBM service personnel need to know the password for the service user profile — QSRV.

```
CHGUSRPRF USRPRF(username)
    PASSWORD(userpassword) PWDEXP(*YES or
    *NO) PWDEXPITV(*NOMAX or password-
    expiration-interval)
```

Other system values can be used to further refine the selection of user passwords. Refer to the **AS/400 Work Management** manual for more information.

QRMTSIGN Remote sign-on control.

*FRCSIGNON — Default value, normal sign-on required.

*SAMEPRF — Source and target user profile are the same.

*REJECT — No remote sign-on allowed.

*VERIFY — Verify that user has access to system. Use this value if you want to eliminate the second sign-on information when using PC Support.

QSECURITY (*) Initially 10. There are five security levels: 10, 20, 30, 40, and 50. For a complete discussion of security levels, refer to the **AS/400 Security — Basic** or **AS/400 Security — Reference** manuals.

Level 10 offers no security at all. Level 20 provides password protection, but all users have access to all objects. Level 30 provides password and resource protection. Levels 40 and 50 provide integrity protection and enhanced integrity protection. I do not recommend running your system at security levels 10 or 20. If you start running your system at security level 10 or 20, you will have problems if you switch to level 30, 40, or 50 later. IBM recommends running at security level 30 or above as these levels offer the greatest level of security.

For newly installed systems, I recommend starting at level 30. If you intend to run your system at level 40 or 50, start the security audit journal and monitor for security violations before going to those levels. If your system is already at level 40 or 50 and you are installing a new application, you may want to switch to level 30 and monitor the security journal for violations associated with the new application. When you are satisfied that the new application can exist in the higher security environment, switch back. Refer to Auditing Security Using System-Provided Journals on page 183 for additional information about the security audit journal.

Message and Logging System Values

The message-and-logging system values allow you to control messages and how they are logged on your system.

QACGLVL (*)	Specifies the accounting information that is written to a journal. The shipped value is *NONE. When the QACGLVL system value is changed to other than *NONE, the system accounting journal QSYS/QACGJRN must exist. Valid values are *NONE, *JOB (job resource use is written to a journal), and *PRINT (print file resource use is written to a journal).
QPRBHLDITV	Specifies the hold interval (in days) for the problem log. After this time interval, problems can be deleted using the Delete Problem (DLTPROB) command. Default value is 30.
QPRTTXT	Used to print up to 30 characters of text on the bottom of listings and separator pages.

VERIFY THAT ELECTRONIC CUSTOMER SUPPORT IS SET UP

As part of an installation, you should verify that Electronic Customer Support (ECS) is set up. Your IBMLink Welcome Pack (if you received one) has telephone numbers for service and support. If you did not receive a Welcome Pack and you purchased your system from IBM, then call your IBM Marketing

Representative to be sure that you are enrolled in ECS. If you are not enrolled, then you are unable to access ECS to obtain PTFs or to report problems.

To verify and update the telephone numbers used in ECS, enter the following commands:

To Update	*Enter Command*
Service System Telephone Numbers	CALL QESPHONE *(updates data area QUSRSYS/QESTELE)*
Support System Telephone Numbers	CALL QTIPHONE *(updates data area QUSRSYS/QTITELE)*

If you precede the phone numbers with **SST-**, you engage the audio tone on the modem.

Use the command **WRKCNTINF** and take each option in turn to verify and update the ECS Contact Information.

> *The following information is valid only for the United States. AS/400 customers outside the continental U.S. should verify the phone numbers and contact information for your locality.*

A recent addition to the AS/400 is a program that you can call to update the phone numbers. Follow these steps:

1. Enter the command:

   ```
   CALL QSCBMKTE
   ```

2. On the first screen, you are asked if you have a Welcome Package. Select "Yes," even if you don't. Fill in the fields on the next screen and press Enter. An example is shown below.

```
          Specify IBM Remote Marketing Parameters
                                              System: APACHE
Type information, press Enter.


Connection numbers
 Primary telephone number  . . . . . .   1-800-327-0949
 First alternate number . . . . . . . .   _____
 Second alternate number  . . . . . . .   _____
 Third alternate number . . . . . . . .   _____


Connection number prefix
 Number required to obtain
   outside line . . . . . . . . . . . .   9
 Turn modem speaker on  . . . . . . . .   Y      Y=Yes, N=No
 Select tone or pulse dialing . . . . .   1      1=Tone, 2=Pulse



   F3=Exit    F5=Refresh   F12=Cancel
```

The primary telephone number is:

- 1-800-527-8207 — if your ZIP code begins with 0, 1, 2, or 3.
- 1-800-327-0949 — if your ZIP code begins with 4, 5, 6, 7, 8, or 9.

If you need a number to access an outside line, put in that number.

3. A screen displaying the phone number information you just entered appears. Press Enter to confirm.

4. The Work Contact Information screen appears. Take option 2 to work with, and then change, the Local Contact Information. Fill in the information as shown below:

```
          Change Service Contact Information System:
                                                    APACHE
Type changes, press Enter.

     Company . . . . . . . . .   ACME Rocket Shoe Company
     Contact . . . . . . . . .   Wile Coyote
     Contact telephone numbers:
       Primary . . . . . . . .   (602) 555-1212
       Alternative . . . . . .   _____
     Fax telephone numbers:
       Primary . . . . . . . .   (602) 555-1211
       Alternative . . . . . .   _____
     Mailing address:
       Street address  . . . .   Route 1

                                 _____

       City/State  . . . . . .   Painted Desert, Arizona
       Country . . . . . . . .   U.S.A.
       Zip code  . . . . . . .   85200

                                               More...
F3=Exit   F4=Prompt   F5=Refresh   F12=Cancel
```

Before pressing Enter, page down to the next screen and make sure that the national language version and the PTF media type are correct. The default for media type is AUTOMATIC selection. Change this to the type of media you use to ensure that you receive your PTF tapes on the proper media.

5. After completing the previous step, press F12 to return to the Work with Support Contact Information screen. Take option 3 to work with, and then change, the IBM product information. Fill in the fields as shown below:

```
                 Change Product Contact Information
                                               System:   APACHE
Type changes, press Enter.

   Remote source:
     Name . . . . . . . .    IBM Corporation
     Address . . . . . . .   4111 Northside Parkway
                            Atlanta, Georgia  30327
                            _____


   Telephone number . . . .  1-800-543-3912
   3270 printer emulation    Y.          N=No, Y=Yes
   SNA DBCS 3270PC Emulation N           N=No, Y=Yes




 F3=Exit  F5=Refresh  F12=Cancel
```

Press Enter when complete, then F12 to return to the Work with Support Contact Information menu.

6. Select option 4 to work with, and then change, the Technical Information Exchange (TIE) information. Fill in the fields as shown below:

```
                 Change TIE Contact Information
                                               System:   APACHE
Type changes, press Enter.

   Remote source:
     Name . . . . . . . .    IBM Corporation, Dept C7V
     Address . . . . . . .   1 East Kirkwood Blvd.
                            Roanoke, Texas 76299-0015
                            _____


     Telephone number . . .  1-800-543-3912
   Host connection information:
     Account number . . . .  LNK1    (see the IBMLink Welcome Packet)
     Use connect code . . .  Y            Y=Yes, N=No
   Mail box information:
     Support system account
       number . . . . . . .  MKST
     Support system user ID  DSCFIE



                                                      Bottom
 F3=Exit  F5=Refresh  F12=Cancel
```

Press Enter when you have updated the fields. Press F12. This completes the setup for ECS.

AUTOSTART JOB ENTRY FOR OFFICEVISION/400

If OfficeVision/400 is installed, make the activation of the calendar alarm program automatic. Refer to the *Planning for and Setting Up OfficeVision/400* manual for discussion.

> *If you intend to run the alarm program in subsystem QBATCH, make sure that the value for maximum active jobs for QBATCH is at least two. The user profile used to start the QALARM job must be enrolled in the system directory and MUST NOT BE QSECOFR.*

SELECT SPELLING AID DICTIONARY

If OfficeVision/400 is installed, define the spelling aid dictionaries used in OfficeVision/400. This saves time later and avoids many phone calls from confused office users. Follow these steps:

1. WRKTXTPRF (Work with Text Profiles) — press Enter.
2. Select option 2 (Revise Text Profiles) — press Enter.
3. Confirm revise the SYSTEM profile — press Enter.
4. Select option 6 (Dictionary Options) — press Enter.
5. On the Specify Dictionary Options screen, specify the dictionaries you wish to use in the order you want them searched. For a list of all dictionaries, put the cursor on the Dictionary column and press the Help key. All dictionaries are in the QDCT library. For example, you might specify:

Order	Dictionary	Library
1	US	QDCT
2	MEDICAL	QDCT
3	LEGAL	QDCT

   If you are in England, you would probably choose the UK dictionary as the first choice; or choose GERMAN for Germany, SHEEP for Australia.
6. Exit (use the F3 or F12 key) and save the profile.

NETWORK ATTRIBUTES

When first installing an AS/400, check and make the appropriate modifications to the network attributes listed below. Do this now, before configuring any devices or using any applications that reference the network attributes, such as Client Access. If you wait until after you enroll users and configure your AS/400 as part of a network, any changes you make to the network attributes are much more difficult to accomplish.

SYSNAME	The System Name default is based on the system serial number. Now is the time to change it. Make it something meaningful to the users.

```
CHGNETA SYSNAME('new system name')
```

You can also use the Operational Assistant to change the system name. Enter the command **GO SETUP**. The only problem with using the Operational Assistant is that you cannot change the three network attributes that follow. I recommend using the command CHGNETA.

LCLNETID(APPN)	Normally, the Local Network ID is set to APPN. However, there are occasions where you may have to set it to something different. Determine the correct value and set it now, before defining the network to which your AS/400 belongs.
LCLCPNAME	The Local Control Point Name for the system is normally the same as the System Name. It could be different, but to do so sometimes adds confusion when you configure communications. If you do not have a good reason to use a different name, keep it the same as the System Name.
LCLLOCNAME	The Local Location Name for the system is normally the same as the System Name. The same advice applies as with the Local Control Point Name.

For other network attributes, refer to the *AS/400 Work Management* manual. Also refer to Preventing Remote DDM Commands on page 187.

SERVICE ATTRIBUTES

 Service attributes are new with V3R1. They allow you to specify the following:

- Whether problem analysis routines should run automatically when a failure occurs.
- How the specified service provider should be notified of problems.
- When PTFs should be installed.
- Where critical system messages are sent.

Automated Problem Management and Reporting

 In Version 3, Release 1, new problem management functions are available on the AS/400 system. They provide automated problem analysis, as well as automated problem reporting. To run these functions, the appropriate service attributes must be set to *YES. You may display the service attributes by using the Display Service Attribute (DSPSRVA) command, or change the service attributes by using the Change Service Attributes (CHGSRVA) command.

> *Of particular interest is the ability to notify a list of user classes or specific users of critical system messages by sending a break message.*

The CHGSRVA command is used to specify:

- Whether problem analysis routines are run automatically when a failure occurs.
- How the specified service provider is notified of problems.
- When a PTF is installed.
- Where critical system messages are sent. Refer to Critical System Messages on page 39 for a discussion on setting up a critical message queue and a list of critical system messages.

I recommend setting the service attributes as follows:

```
CHGSRVA  ANZPRBAUTO(*YES)  RPTPRBAUTO(*YES)  +
    RPTSRVPVD(*IBMSRV)  +
    CRITMSGUSR(*SYSOPR/*SECOFR/*SECADM/user_name)
```

The optional parameters and their purposes are:

ANZPRBAUTO Specifies whether problem analysis routines run automatically at the time of failure. Problem analysis routines are programs that attempt to isolate or correct the problem. If problem analysis routines are run automatically, they are run at the time of failure as a background batch job. If problem analysis routines are not run automatically at the time of failure, they can be run manually from the QSYSOPR message queue, or by using the Work with Problems (WRKPRB) command.

RPTPRBAUTO Specifies whether notification of problems that have been analyzed automatically are sent to the service provider specified on the RPTSRVPVD parameter.

If automatic problem notification is specified, it is run as a background batch job at the time of failure. If automatic problem notification is not specified, problems can be reported manually to a service provider from the QSYSOPR message queue, or by using the WRKPRB command.

RPTSRVPVD Specifies the name of the service provider to receive automatic notification of problems.

Problem notification is automatically sent to the service provider specified on this parameter when

RPTPRBAUTO(*YES) is specified. This service provider must be in the list of service providers. Use the Work with Service Providers (WRKSRVPVD) command to see the service providers defined for your system.

PTFINSTYP Specifies when a PTF is applied. The value specified on this parameter is used when applying a PTF using either the Install Program Temporary Fix (INSPTF) command or the Program Temporary Fix (PTF) menu (option 7 or 8).

SNDDTAPKT Specifies whether additional data collected by the program that detects the problem is sent to the service provider when a problem is reported.

CRITMSGUSR Specifies users, or classes of users, that can receive a break message when the system detects a critical condition, such as a direct-access storage device (DASD) failure.

The values specified in this parameter should be specified sequentially, in order of priority (highest to lowest). If the system detects a critical condition, it attempts to send a break message indicating the nature of the problem to the user, or class of users. Notification messages are sent in the same priority sequence that you list the users or class of users.

If none of the users indicated by the value are currently signed on, the next value specified is checked. This process continues until either a break message can be sent, or the last value is checked.

> *This parameter is valid only if ANZPRBAUTO(*YES) is specified.*

The user classes that can be specified are:

- *SYSOPR
- *SECOFR
- *SECADM
- *PGMR
- *USER
- user-name

CUSTOMIZED SIGN-ON DISPLAY

If you wish to customize the sign-on display, refer to Appendix C: Customizing Your Sign-On Display on page 327.

When you customize your sign-on display, you may want to include a news line to notify users of special events, messages, or other information. Refer to Appendix D: Adding a "News Line" to the Sign-on Screen on page 329.

SET UP OPERATIONAL ASSISTANT

If you are installing a new AS/400 or upgrading the software, and you wish to set up the Operational Assistant, proceed with the section Operational Assistant on page 83. Then return to this point to proceed with the remainder of the tasks for initial installation. You are especially encouraged to review the procedure for setting up the backup-tasks part of the Operational Assistant (refer to Using the BACKUP Menu on page 90).

ROUTING FOR JOB LOGS, PROGRAM AND SERVICE DUMPS

Initially, all logs/dumps are sent to the default printer output queue for printing. You probably do not want this to happen.

> *I recommend using the Operational Assistant, and skipping this section. Unlike the setting of System Values, there is little benefit to doing these steps manually. The instructions included here are for:*
>
> - *Systems using older versions of the Operating System (V1).*
> - *Users who do not want to use the Operational Assistant naming conventions for the logs and outqueues,*
> - *Users who wish to be more precise in routing all job logs by category in one output queue.*

Refer to Operational Assistant on page 83 for instructions on using the Operational Assistant.

> *If you enable the cleanup options in the Operational Assistant, output queues called QEZJOBLOG and QEZDEBUG are created for you in library QUSRSYS. Refer to the* **AS/400 System Operation** *manual for more information. All job logs go to the QEZJOBLOG output queue and all dumps go to the QEZDEBUG output queue.*

If you want to create your own outques for job logs, program dumps, and service dumps, use the following procedure:

1. Create an output queue for job logs and program and service dumps in the QUSRSYS library by keying in:

```
CRTOUTQ OUTQ(QUSRSYS/JOBLOGQ) TEXT('OUTQ for Joblogs')
CRTOUTQ OUTQ(QUSRSYS/PGMDMPQ) TEXT('OUTQ for Pgm Dumps')
CRTOUTQ OUTQ(QUSRSYS/SRVDMP) TEXT('OUTQ for Service Dumps')
CRTOUTQ OUTQ(QUSRSYS/CSMPRTQ) TEXT('OUTQ for SST')
```

2. Place the output queues into the HOLD status:

```
HLDOUTQ OUTQ(QUSRSYS/JOBLOGQ)
HLDOUTQ OUTQ(QUSRSYS/PGMDMPQ)
HLDOUTQ OUTQ(QUSRSYS/SRVDMPQ)
HLDOUTQ OUTQ(QUSRSYS/CSMPRTQ)
```

3. Create duplicate objects of the following print files in the CHGSYS library and refer to Change Library (CHGSYS) on page 15:

```
CRTDUPOBJ OBJ(QPJOBLOG) FROMLIB(QSYS) OBJTYPE(*FILE)
    TOLIB(CHGSYS)
CRTDUPOBJ OBJ(QPPGMDMP) FROMLIB(QSYS) OBJTYPE(*FILE)
    TOLIB(CHGSYS)
CRTDUPOBJ OBJ(QPSRVDMP) FROMLIB(QSYS) OBJTYPE(*FILE)
    TOLIB(CHGSYS)
CRTDUPOBJ OBJ(QPCSMPRT) FROMLIB(QSYS) OBJTYPE(*FILE)
    TOLIB(CHGSYS)
```

4. Modify the print files in QSYS to direct output to the new output queues:

```
CHGPRTF QPJOBLOG OUTQ(QUSRSYS/QPJOBLOG) HOLD(*YES)
CHGPRTF QPPGMDMP OUTQ(QUSRSYS/QPPGMDMP) HOLD(*YES)
CHGPRTF QPSRVDMP OUTQ(QUSRSYS/QPSRVDMP) HOLD(*YES)
CHGPRTF QPCSMPRT OUTQ(QUSRSYS/QPCSMPRT) HOLD(*YES)
```

ELIMINATING OR MINIMIZING JOB LOGS

After the system stabilizes, you may want to change the IBM-supplied job descriptions to eliminate job logs. This determination is made based on customer requirements. Also refer to Print Writer Job Logs on page 154 for information about print writer job logs.

> *IBM-supplied objects usually begin with the letter* **Q**. *For example, if you wish to see a list of all the IBM-supplied job descriptions, enter the command* **WRKJOBD Q***.

1. To stop the generation of job logs entirely:

```
CHGJOBD JOBD(jobdname) LOG(0 *SAME *SAME)
```

2. To allow job logs for unsuccessful completion only:

```
CHGJOBD JOBD(jobdname) LOG(4 0 *NOLIST)
```

3. To allow job logs for unsuccessful completion only and log commands issued in a CL program:

```
CHGJOBD JOBD(jobdname) LOG(4 0 *NOLIST) LOGCLPGM(*YES)
```

> *This is the recommended value for logging level. I recommend that you use this level of logging unless you need additional logging for security reasons. See recommended changes for IBM-supplied job descriptions below.*

4. To force job log generation for all jobs:

```
CHGJOBD JOBD(jobdname) LOG(4 0 *SECLVL)
```

> *The SIGNOFF command default parameter is LOG(*NOLIST). When you sign off, the *NOLIST logging parameter ignores the logging level set for the job.*

You can see a list of the IBM-supplied job descriptions by entering:

```
WRKOBJ OBJ(QGPL/Q*) OBJTYPE(*JOBD)
WRKOBJ OBJ(QSYS/Q*) OBJTYPE(*JOBD)
```

For additional discussion on job logs and their management, refer to Appendix E: AS/400 Job Logs and Output Queue Utility on page 331.

RECOMMENDED LOGGING LEVEL FOR IBM-SUPPLIED JOB DESCRIPTIONS

Consider changing the following IBM-supplied job description logging levels to capture detailed information in the job logs.

```
CHGJOBD   JOBD(QBATCH)    LOG(4 0 *NOLIST)   LOGCLPGM(*YES)
CHGJOBD   JOBD(QINTER)    LOG(4 0 *NOLIST)   LOGCLPGM(*YES)
CHGJOBD   JOBD(QPGMR)     LOG(4 0 *NOLIST)   LOGCLPGM(*YES)
CHGJOBD   JOBD(QSPLPRTW)  LOG(4 0 *NOLIST)   LOGCLPGM(*YES)
CHGJOBD   JOBD(QDFTJOBD)  LOG(4 0 *NOLIST)   LOGCLPGM(*YES)
```

> *Be very cautious when making changes to any of the IBM-supplied job descriptions. With the exception of changing the logging levels, or possibly the printer or output queue names, I recommend not making any other changes — at least not until you are very familiar with job routing and work management. The consequences can be severe — such as the inability to sign on to the AS/400. For additional information, refer to Job Descriptions on page 238.*

MESSAGE ROUTING

By default, the AS/400 routes messages to the QSYSOPR message queue. You may want to redefine the delivery of these messages to the BREAK mode:

```
CHGMSGQ QSYSOPR *BREAK
```

One of the more common message types sent to the QSYSOPR message queue is a printer message. The default message queue for all printer devices is the QSYSOPR message queue. You can create different message queues for printers so printer messages don't clutter up the QSYSOPR queue. Train users in how to respond to the messages. You may not want to do this, but it can make life a bit easier for the system operator if users are instructed to respond to printer messages. Also, you may wish to have the system automatically respond to some printer messages such as, "Check that forms are aligned." When you see these messages in the QSYSOPR message queue, press the Help key to view the entire message. Look for the message ID and write it down. Typically, you respond to messages with the same ID with the same response. Once you know which message-response combinations you want to automate, you can set them up in the system. Use the following command to see the existing replies:

```
WRKRPYLE
```

View the existing entries, then use F6 to add more. Use the Help key to understand the field entries.

Refer to Printer Management on page 141 and Annoying Printer Messages on page 141 for additional information on setting up and managing printers on the AS/400.

CRITICAL SYSTEM MESSAGES

If you have V2R3 or later, then you can create the optional QSYSMSG message queue in the QSYS library. The QSYSMSG message queue can monitor specific system messages that indicate potentially severe system conditions. Only messages that require immediate action are sent to the QSYSMSG message queue. If you have a QSYSMSG message queue, monitor it to be aware of critical messages related to your system. If you do not have a QSYSMSG message queue, consider creating one. Otherwise, important system messages are sent to the QSYSOPR message queue where they reside with other sundry messages, most of them of a noncritical nature. The chance that an important system-related message will go unnoticed increases when the message resides in the QSYSOPR message queue.

To create the QSYSMSG message queue, enter the following command:

```
CRTMSGQ QSYS/QSYSMSG TEXT('Optional MSGQ to receive
    important system messages')
```

Once the QSYSMSG message queue is created, certain specific system messages are directed there. The following is a partial list of the important system messages sent to the QSYSMSG message queue.

Message ID	Message Text
CPF0907	Serious storage condition may exist. Press Help.
CPF111C	System scheduled to power down.
CPF111D	System is powering down.
CPF1269	Program Start request received on communications device was rejected with reason codes.
CPF1393	User profile disabled because maximum number of sign-on attempts reached.
CPF1397	Subsystem varied off work station.
CPI0920	Error occurred on disk unit &1.
CPI0953	ASP storage threshold reached.
CPI0954	ASP storage limit exceeded.
CPI0955	System ASP unprotected storage limit exceeded.
CPI0956	Mirrored protection is suspended on disk unit &1.
CPI0964	Weak battery condition exists.
CPI0965	Failure of battery power unit feature in system unit.
CPI0966	Failure of battery power unit feature in expansion unit.
CPI0970	Disk unit &1 not operating.
CPI0988	Mirrored protection resuming on disk unit &1.
CPI0992	Error occurred on disk unit &1.
CPI0997	Nearly all available machine addresses used.

Message ID	Message Text
CPI1117	Damaged job schedule &1 in library &2 deleted.
CPI0998	Error occurred on disk unit &1.
CPI1153	System password bypass period ended.
CPI1154	System password bypass period will end in &5 days.
CPI1393	Subsystem &1 disabled user profile &2 on device &3.
CPI2209	User profile &1 deleted because it was damaged.
CPI8A13	QDOC library nearing save history limit.
CPI8A14	QDOC library exceeded save history limit.
CPI9014	Password received from device not valid.
CPI94CE	Error detected in bus expansion adapter or bus extension adapter.
CPI94CF	Main storage card failure detected.
CPP0DD9	A system processor failure detected.
CPP29B8	Device parity protection suspended on device &25.
CPP29B9	Power protection suspended on device &25.
CPP29BA	Hardware error on device &25.

For a complete listing and description of these messages, refer to the *AS/400 CL Programming* manual.

You can write a break-handling program that monitors messages sent to the QSYSMSG message queue and takes action on specific messages you identify. Instructions and a sample program to receive messages from the QSYSMSG message queue are included in the *AS/400 CL Programming* manual.

You might consider having two consoles (or one console with two sessions). One console or session would be for a system operator with the QSYSOPR message allocated in break mode, the other for a second operator with the QSYSMSG message queue allocated in break mode.

TAPE AND DISKETTE NAMES

Check the names of the tape and diskette devices. If you want to change the names, use WRKDEVD or RNMOBJ commands. Refer to Renaming Device, Controller, or Line Descriptions on page 315.

RENAMING SYSTEM PRINTER

You may wish to rename the system printer from the default PRT01 (P1 if you are using the S36 Environment). Maybe something like SYSPRT, or something more meaningful to you. Enter the following commands:

```
ENDWTR PRT01
VRYCFG CFGOBJ(PRT01) OJBTYPE(*DEV) STATUS(*OFF)
RNMOBJ OBJ(QSYS/PRT01) OBJTYPE(*DE
VD) NEWOBJ(newname)
VRYCFG CFGOBJ(newname) OJBTYPE(*DEV) STATUS(*ON)
STRPRTWTR newname
```

Now change the System Value that defines the system printer:

```
CHGSYSVAL SYSVAL(QPRTDEV) VALUE('newname')
```

CREATING A PROGRAMMER ENVIRONMENT

If programmers use the system, I recommend that you create a special environment for them:

1. Sign on as QPGMR.
2. Create user(s) library:

    ```
    CRTLIB LIB(username) TYPE(*TEST) TEXT('username Library')
    ```

3. Change current library:

    ```
    CHGCURLIB LIB(username)
    ```

4. Create user source files in library 'username':

    ```
    CRTSRCPF username/QDDSSRC TEXT('DDS Source File')
    CRTSRCPF username/QCBLSRC TEXT('COBOL Source File')
    CRTSRCPF username/QRPGSRC TEXT('RPG Source File')
    CRTSRCPF username/QBASSRC TEXT('BASIC Source File')
    CRTSRCPF username/QCLSRC  TEXT('CL Source File')
    CRTSRCPF username/QCMDSRC TEXT('CMD Source File')
    ```

5. Create user output queue:

    ```
    CRTOUTQ username/username TEXT('username Output Queue')
    ```

6. Sign on as QSECOFR (or with SECOFR authority).

7. Create user profile(s) for programmer(s):

```
CRTUSRPRF USRPRF(username) USRCLS(*PGMR) +
    CURLIB(username) GRPPRF(QPGMR) OWNER(*GRPPRF)
    OUTQ(username/username) +
    TEXT ('username User Profile')
```

> *This user is part of the QPGMR group profile. All objects created by the user are owned by the group profile QPGMR. The current library is the one just created (USERNAME), and printed output goes to the outpu queue USERNAME in library USERNAME.*

8. Place the programmers in their own subsystem; their jobs run at priority 30 rather than the usual priority 20 for interactive users. This minimizes the impact that programmers can sometimes have on the rest of the interactive users. IBM has created a subsystem description for this purpose called QPGMR.

   a. Sign on as the security officer and add subsystem QPGMR to the startup program. Refer to the section System Control System Values on page 20.

   b. Add work station entries to the subsystem description (the work stations that the programmers use). Refer to Allocating Devices to Subsystems on page 230.

   You may prefer to use routing entries in the default subsystem description (normally QINTER) with appropriate details to transfer the job to the QPGMR subsystem if there is a match on the compare value. Refer to the **AS/400 Work Management** manual for a discussion on using routing entries in this manner.

   ```
   ADDWSE SBSD(QGPL/QPGMR) WRKSTN(devname)
   ```

   c. Add job description QGPL/QPGMR to the user profiles of the programmers:

   ```
   CHGUSRPRF   USRPRF(name) JOBD(QGPL/QPGMR)
   ```

   d. Now go back and add this subsystem to your startup program, QSTRUP, so that it starts-up automatically when you IPL the system. Refer to System Startup Program on page 16. If you don't, then you must start the subsystem manually at system startup, which you may prefer.

CONSIDER REMOVING BATCH JOBS FROM THE *BASE MEMORY POOL

Batch jobs generally run better if they are removed from the *BASE memory pool. Refer to Moving Batch Jobs Out of *BASE Memory Pool on page 216.

This topic covers the procedures that you should perform to establish basic security on your system. Do not skip over this section during an initial installation. This topic may also be useful as a review at any time.

Set System Security

> *If this is an initial installation (or new application), you should not set security at level 40 or 50 until you review the security audit journal.*

If you haven't set security to level 30, do it now, before you create user profiles. This saves time later when you want to modify the object authorizations based on user authorities:

```
CGHSYSVAL QSECURITY(30)
```

The change takes effect after the next IPL.

Set the Special Environment of IBM-Supplied User Profiles

Regardless of which mode of operation you are using (i.e., S/36 Environment or native AS/400), change the following IBM-supplied user profiles to set the SPCENV parameter to *NONE. *Refer to QSPCENV on page 22 for information regarding special environments.*

- QPGMR
- QSECOFR
- QSRV
- QSYSOPR

Use the following command:

```
CHGUSRPRF USRPRF(QPGMR) SPCENV(*NONE)
```

Repeat for other three profiles.

This puts these profiles in native mode when signing on, thus making system maintenance easier.

Set Up Group Profiles

Review and gain an understanding of Group Profiles. Group Profiles are very useful for easing administration and control of access. Try to create group profiles before you create user profiles. But don't worry too much, you can come back later to make changes. Group profiles should have the password set to *NONE. Refer to Group Profiles on page 176 for additional information.

Create User Profiles and Grant Authorities

Create user profiles and grant proper authorities. You should create at least one profile with QSECOFR authority. Use the IBM-supplied profile QSECOFR only when absolutely required.

To create user profiles, become familiar with the parameter USROPT (user options). In particular the options:

*CLKWD   Presents the CL key word list when in CL prompting.

*EXPERT   Gives user additional information on the display when adjusting certain system parameters.

When creating user profiles, you can use up to 10 characters. However, if you intend to use OfficeVision/400, then limit the length of user profiles to eight characters or less. Review Recommendations for Naming User Profiles on page 173.

Change Passwords for IBM-Supplied User Profiles

 If your system came installed with V3R1, or later, of the OS/400 licensed program, QSECOFR is the only IBM-supplied profile that ships with a password. Earlier versions of the operating system have additional IBM-supplied profiles that ship with passwords. Changing the password for the QSECOFR profile immediately after installation is essential to prevent unauthorized people from signing on your system.

Regardless of the version of your operating system, sign on to the system using the QSECOFR profile. Change the passwords for QSECOFR and QSRV. Leave or set the passwords for the other IBM-supplied profiles to *NONE. If your system has an earlier version of the operating system, or if you upgraded to V3R1, then consider setting the passwords for all remaining IBM-supplied user profiles to *NONE. In previous versions, the default passwords for those IBM-supplied user profiles are the same as the user profile.

You should not set the QSRV user profile password to *NONE because this profile is routinely used by IBM Service Representatives to perform diagnostic chores.

After you have changed the passwords for QSECOFR and QSRV, record the passwords and keep them in a safe place. The QSECOFR password should be kept sealed and safeguarded. Only a limited number of people should have access to the QSECOFR user profile (e.g., Director of IS, CEO, CFO). If the password is required for any reason, breaking the seal is your clue to change it.

Keep the password for QSRV in a safe place, but make sure that it is available for IBM Service Personnel. The QSRV user profile has most of the authorities that service personnel need to perform service work.

An easy way to change the passwords for IBM-supplied user profiles is to use the Operational Assistant Setup menu. Type the command **GO SETUP**, take option 2.

> *If you lose the password for QSECOFR, you can reset it by performing a manual (or attended) IPL and bringing up DST (Dedicated Service Tools). Enter the DST Master Security Password and reset the Operating System QSECOFR password to the shipped value. If you don't know the DST Master Security Password, you are SOL.*
>
> *IBM Service Personnel need access to the QSRV user profile. Make sure that the password is available to them.*
>
> *You can force user passwords to expire within a specified interval with the system value QPWDEXPITV. You can override the system value with the user profile also. Refer to Initial System Values on page 18.*
>
> *With the exception of the password, do not change anything else on the IBM-supplied user profiles. Some system functions may be affected. For example, Performance Tools may be affected if you change the QPGMR user profile and you may not be able to perform service functions if you change the QSRV user profile.*

Change Password for Dedicated Service Tools Security

You may want to change the DST security officer profile. The DST profiles differ from the Operating System user profiles in that they are available for use only when you start Dedicated Service Tools. The functions you can perform are limited to those available in DST. The master security officer profile used in DST can be used to reset the Operating System QSECOFR password. This is a security risk if an individual knows how to execute DST and uses the shipped value for the DST security officer. To change the DST security officer profile, you must perform a manual IPL and, when prompted, take the option to start DST. The DST security profile is QSECOFR (the same name as the Operating System profile), and the default shipped password is QSECOFR. Once you have signed on, reset the Operating System Security Officer Password to the shipped default. You may want to change the DST Security Officer password.

> **CAUTION:** *If you change the DST Security Officer Password, do not lose it. Some critical system diagnostic functions require use of the DST security functions. This is also your fallback password should you ever have to reset the Operating System QSECOFR password.*

Once you have reset the Operating System security officer password in DST, you can resume the IPL. Upon completion of the IPL, you can sign on to the system using the QSECOFR password.

If you know either the QSECOFR password or the DST security capability password, you can reset the other one. You can also change the DST full capability password and the DST basic capability password if you know the DST security capability password.

Verify Public Authority to IBM-Supplied Libraries

Check authorities of *PUBLIC to the IBM-supplied libraries. Users should have read-only access to these libraries and the objects in them. The exception is QGPL.

Establish Rights of Users with *ALLOBJ Authority to Display Devices

If you want users with *ALLOBJ authority to sign on to auto-configured devices, grant specific authority to each auto-configured device:

```
GRTOBJAUT OBJ(objectname) USER(userprofilename)
```

or you can change the system value **QLMTSECOFR** (refer to Initial System Values on page 18).

Restrict Use of System Commands

To limit use of certain commands to a few users, use the GRTOBJAUT command. You can exclude users or allow use of objects with this command.

After the initial installation, there are further security considerations to take into account. Refer to Security on page 171.

UNINTERRUPTIBLE POWER SUPPLY CONSIDERATIONS

If you have a rack-mounted AS/400 (9406), I recommend acquiring an UPS. If you already have an UPS, set up the system with an UPS handling program. Refer to Uninterruptible Power Supplies (UPS) on page 139 for additional information.

APPLY CUMULATIVE PTF PACKAGE

At this point in the installation, you should apply the latest the cumulative PTF package. Refer to PTF Management on page 122 and the **AS/400 System Operation** manual for information on obtaining and installing PTFs.

Select the option to automatically perform an IPL.

SAVE THE ENTIRE SYSTEM

Now save the entire system. Use option 21 from the SAVE menu. Make sure
that you have placed the QSYSOPR message queue in the *BREAK mode
before running the save.

```
CHGMSGQ QSYSOPR DELIVERY(*BREAK)
GO SAVE
```

(Take option 21.)

IPL THE SYSTEM

Changes made to system parameters, such as system values, network
attributes, and job descriptions, may not take effect until you IPL the system.
For example, a change to the System Name only takes effect during the first IPL
after the name change. If you did not perform an IPL as part of Applying
Cumulative PTFs, then do so now. You can perform an IPL using either of these
two methods:

- PWRDWNSYS *IMMED RESTART(*YES) IPLSRC(B)
- Access the POWER menu by entering **GO POWER,** and take option 4.

> *If you have loaded PTFs and marked them for delayed apply,
> then do not use this method. The IPL performed from the
> POWER menu does not perform the exact same functions as a
> PWRDWNSYS. If you use the POWER menu to perform an
> IPL, PTFs marked for delayed apply are not applied.*

TEST THE ALTERNATE IPL DEVICE

Something that many users never do until it is required is test the alternate IPL
device. A little explanation may be in order here. The primary IPL device is the
load source disk drive. This is the disk unit designated as unit number 1 if you
run the WRKDSKSTS command. When you IPL the system, the required
objects to get your system up and running are located on the source drive. This
is similar to booting up your PC from the hard disk.

The alternate IPL device is one of your tape drives. Like a personal computer,
this gives you the capability to boot up from a different source should the need
arise. Generally, a PC uses the first floppy diskette drive as an alternative to
booting off the hard drive. The AS/400 uses a designated tape drive.

When you perform a SAVSYS to tape, all the necessary objects are saved to
allow you to IPL from tape. You should perform a test to ensure that you can
successfully IPL from tape. Do the following:

1. Notify users you plan to IPL the system.

2. End all system activity.

```
ENDSBS SBS(*ALL) OPTION(*IMMED)
```

3. Place your SAVSYS tape in the designated alternate IPL tape device and make the tape drive ready.

4. Perform an IPL from the tape drive: Make sure you designate the IPL source as D.

```
PWRDWNSYS OPTION(*IMMED) RESTART(*YES) IPLSRC(D)
```

The IPL will take longer than normal. The test is successful if the system is able to IPL from tape. If you get an error, perform an IPL from the control panel using the load source disk drive as your source. (Refer to Performing an IPL from the System Control Panel on page 311.) This gets your system back online. Then, call your IBM Service Representative to correct the problem.

DOCUMENT YOUR SYSTEM

Make sure you review the section Documenting Your System on page 119. Many installations are poorly documented, yet I cannot stress how important this is. Your job is a lot easier if you maintain a good habit of documenting your system, which in turn leads to better system management.

MISCELLANEOUS REVIEW ITEMS

After performing the above steps, the system is ready to begin loading the customer's code. Make sure all personnel with system responsibilities have reviewed and understand the following:

- User profiles.
- Group profiles.
- Security.
- Programmer function and libraries needed.
- Keeping a master source library that programmers can copy but cannot update.
- Testing procedures.
- IBM software support structure:
  - Level 1: 1-800- 237-5511 (U.S.A.)
  - Level 2: Access via Level 1 or directly via ECS
  - Industry Application Hotlines (e.g., DMAS, MAPICS)
- Backup and recovery procedures, journaling, commitment control, CHECKSUM, etc.

- If you intend to write your own applications, understand the design considerations on AS/400 performance. Get the Rochester videotapes by John Sears called *Application Design for Performance*. You can order these tapes from Mechanicsburg:

    - Tape 1 of 3: SV32-0644

    - Tape 2 of 3: SV32-0645

    - Tape 3 of 3: SV32-0646

- Use of user tools in the QUSRTOOL library (refer to QUSRTOOL Library on page 307).

- Application and use of Performance Tools, if installed. If not installed, consider getting it, especially if you have a larger system or one that you believe is running in a complex environment. If you do not intend to get Performance Tools, you can still collect performance data and have it analyzed on a system with Performance Tools.

- How to use ECS, IBMLink, Help functions on the system, Q&A Database.

- How to analyze problems with the Problem Handling menus and the command WRKPRB.

- The features of the Operational Assistant (refer to Operational Assistant on page 83).

- System configuration and cabling system. Do not exceed recommended cable lengths. Make sure you understand recognized cable standards. Use the appropriate cable type required for your installation. Stress the importance of good electrical installation. Consider asking an IBM Installation Planning Representative to visit your site.
Education. IBM offers classroom instruction and seminars. IBM Education catalogs and schedules are available by calling 1-800-IBM-TEACh (1-800-426-8322).

BACKUP

Each user's backup situation is different. This book does not attempt to cover all situations or suggest that any one strategy is better than another. All users should evaluate their risks, develop a backup strategy to address those risks, and develop a written procedure for managing disk space. This includes backing up IBM products and documents as well as user applications and data.

If you are managing an AS/400 system, become familiar with the following references:

AS/400 Backup and Recovery — Basic manual
AS/400 Backup and Recovery — Advanced manual
The Redbook, **AS/400 Application Recovery**
AS/400 Office Services Concepts and Programmer's Guide

There are many users who blissfully run their information systems with incomplete backup procedures. Your business depends on your information system and the data it contains. If you are not taking adequate steps to protect the system, then you are placing your business' very survival at risk. I cannot over emphasize how important it is to back up. Learn all you can about backup and recovery. I have touched on some of the aspects of backup and recovery in this book, but it is not the definitive source. I cannot cover the entire subject here. So get out those manuals that I reference. If you use only this document to develop your backup procedures, you are short changing yourself, and you may end up with an inadequate procedure. That's my lecture. I hope the little bit here helps you understand AS/400 backup procedures and their importance.

CONSIDERATIONS WHEN USING V3R1

If you are using V3R1 of OS/400, several changes affect your save and restore strategy:

- New Integrated File System (IFS) incorporated as part of the Operating System.
- Additional SAV and RST commands added to support the IFS.
- Document Library Objects (DLOs) in user Auxiliary Storage Pools (ASPs).
- Database enhancements (Referential Constraints and Triggers) affect save/restore strategy.
- A new system value, QALWOBJRST, may affect your restore procedure.

- InfoSeeker bookshelves are stored in folders.
- Changes to the Operational Assistant backup procedures.
- Changes to the SAVE menu.

Integrated File System

V3R1   The most significant change to V3R1 is the IFS within the Operating System. Before V3R1, objects on the AS/400 were seen from the perspective of libraries or Document Library Objects (DLOs). With the IFS, there are several different ways to store and access objects using five file systems:

- The "root" file system supports hierarchical directories with characteristics of the DOS and OS/2 file systems.
- The QSYS.LIB file system supports the AS/400 library structure.
- The QDLS file system is used for document library objects. It supports a hierarchical structure of documents within folders.
- The QLANSrv file system has a directory structure and supports the LAN Server/400 licensed program.
- The QOpenSys file system and the "root" file system also support a directory structure and provide compatibility with systems such as UNIX**.

The IFS acts like an umbrella over all of these file systems. It provides a means for accessing objects in any file system.

Use the SAV command to save objects in directories and the RST command to restore them. You can also use the SAV and RST commands for objects in any file system. Options 21 and 23 on the SAVE menu also save objects in directories.

LAN Server/400 Licensed Program

Personal systems can be attached to an AS/400 using the File Server I/O Processor. The File Server I/O Processor provides the personal systems with fast access to information that is stored on the AS/400 system in the QLANSrv file system. The LAN Server/400 licensed program provides the interface to manage the QLANSrv file system.

The procedure for saving and restoring LAN Server/400 data is different than the procedure for normal AS/400 objects. If you have the File Server I/O Processor (FSIOP) and LAN Server/400, refer to the *AS/400 Backup and Recovery — Basic* manual for additional information.

PREPARE FOR BACKUPS AND SAVES

Before backing up the system or performing a major save of objects or libraries, take the following steps:

1. Change the QSYSOPR message queue to the break mode:

```
CHGMSGQ MSGQ(QSYSOPR) DLVRY(*BREAK)
```

2. Clean the tape drive.

3. Initialize enough of the backup media (e.g., tapes, cartridges, diskettes).

4. If you are saving objects or libraries, and the system is active, you need to allocate the object(s). Also, to avoid impacting the interactive performance of the system, run the save in batch mode by using the Submit Job command (enter SBMJOB and prompt with the F4 key).

> *To save an object, the system must be able to allocate it. Take the necessary measures to assure that there are no locks on the object being saved. The easiest way to accomplish this is to perform a complete system save, to the extent that you can, by placing the system in a restricted state. A restricted state is accomplished by signing on to the system console using a user profile with job control authority and ending all subsystems. This ends all user jobs. When you have accomplished this, the system console is the only active terminal on the system and all non-IBM jobs have ended.*

BACKING UP THE ENTIRE SYSTEM USING THE SAVE MENU

The main problem with AS/400 backups is that users either do not back up OS/400 and other products, or are doing so in an incomplete manner because they do not understand the interdependencies of various libraries.

The simplest and safest way to back up IBM products is to use option 21 (Save the Entire System) on the SAVE menu. Option 21 does a SAVSYS; SAVLIB *NONSYS; SAVDLO; and, if using V3R1, a SAV of all directories. Before saving, option 21 places the system into a restricted state that provides two benefits:

- The Save runs faster.
- Ensures that all objects are saved by making sure no one is using any of them.

V3R1

The SAVE menu actually consists of three parts, or screens. Although you are referred to options 21, 22, and 23 most frequently (options 22 and 23 are new to V3R1), there are others.

Options 21, 22, and 23 are designed for backing up the entire system, system data only, and user data. These are the most commonly used options when users wish to back up the entire system.

The menu screens are reproduced below.

```
SAVE                          Save
                                       System:   NAVAJO
 Select one of the following:

    Save Data
       1. Files
       2. Libraries
       3. Documents and folders
       4. Programs
       5. Other objects
       6. Changed objects only
       7. Licensed programs
       8. Security data
       9. Storage
      10. Configuration
      11. Objects in directories

                                                      More...
 Selection or command
 ===>  _____

 F3=Exit   F4=Prompt   F9=Retrieve   F12=Cancel   F13=Information Assistant
 F16=AS/400 Main menu
 (C) COPYRIGHT IBM CORP. 1980, 1994.
```

```
SAVE                          Save
                                       System:   NAVAJO
 Select one of the following:

    Save System and User Data
      21. Entire system
      22. System data only
      23. All user data

    Save Office Data
      30. All documents, folders, and mail
      31. New and changed documents, new folders, all mail
      32. Documents and folders
      33. Mail only
      34. Calendars



                                                      More...
 Selection or command
 ===>  _____

 F3=Exit   F4=Prompt   F9=Retrieve   F12=Cancel   F13=Information Assistant
 F16=AS/400 Main menu
```

```
SAVE                          Save
                                              System:   NAVAJO
Select one of the following:

  Save Libraries
     40. All libraries other than system library
     41. All IBM libraries other than system library
     42. All user libraries
     43. All changed objects in user libraries

  Save for Different Systems
     50. Save in System/36 format

  Related Commands
     70. Related commands


                                                         Bottom
Selection or command
===>

F3=Exit   F4=Prompt   F9=Retrieve   F12=Cancel   F13=Information Assistant
F16=AS/400 Main menu
```

BACKING UP THE ENTIRE SYSTEM USING THE SAVSTG COMMAND

You can perform a complete system backup using SAVSTG. But if this is the first time you have ever saved the system (e.g., initial installation), then DO NOT use the SAVSTG command at this time. Refer to Save Storage Command on page 60 for a description of this procedure and its limitations.

BACKING UP THE SYSTEM FROM REMOTE LOCATIONS

When you back up the system using the SAVSYS command, you have to use a display device that is in the controlling subsystem (QBASE or QCTL) and does not rely on any communications subsystem(s) (e.g., QCMN). This rules out any display device that relies on a communications router such as Client Access/400. System saves require that the system be placed in a restricted state.

In order to initiate the necessary commands to perform system saves from a remote location, you must have:

- An ASCII WSC installed and a remote device description configured.
- Either an ASCII terminal or a personal computer with ASCII emulation software.
- A tape drive with enough capacity so you do not need to change tapes.

To issue commands that place the system into a restricted state, your work station must be under the control of the system controlling subsystem. If the work station you intend to use is not under the control of the system controlling subsystem, then add a work station entry (ADDWSE) to the controlling subsystem. Refer to Remote Console Using ASCII Work Station Controller on page 231.

Now when you dial in to the AS/400, you can perform functions that require placing the system into a restricted state, including running the SAVSYS command.

> *A dialed-up connection via public phone lines is not the most stable connection in the world. If you lose the connection while you are performing functions such as SAVSYS, your job ends.*

SAVING DOCUMENTS AND FOLDERS

The only way to save documents and folders is with the SAVDLO (Save Document Library Objects) command. Immediately before SAVDLO, perform the following steps:

1. CHGJRN (Change Journal)

   So you can delete the detached journal receivers after saving them or use the STG(*FREE) option when you save the journals.

   Refer to Journals on page 106 and Operational Assistant on page 83 for additional information.

2. SAVLIB QUSRSYS (Save Library QUSRSYS)

   Save this library to save the journaling information and other distribution objects (see the **AS/400 Backup and Recovery — Basic** manual). **DO NOT** use the STG(*FREE) option when you save library QUSRSYS.

   If you are also saving distribution objects, then perform a SAVSYS or a SAVSECDTA MAIL(*YES).

   Execute SAVDLO. Refer to the **AS/400 Backup and Recovery — Basic** manual for options when using this command.

   Delete the journal receivers from library QUSRSYS, which have been saved. Use the command WRKJRNA and press F15. Refer to Journals on page 106.

Consider variations such as saving the journal receivers in QUSRSYS often (maybe daily) and doing a SAVDLO less often; or perhaps doing a SAVDLO more often (maybe daily) in which you save only the documents that have changed since the last SAVDLO.

Refer to Save and Restore Figures on page 79 for a diagram of save and restore commands. Refer to the **AS/400 Backup and Recovery — Basic** manual for a list of IBM-supplied journals used for documents or folders.

OFFICEVISION/400 BACKUP CONSIDERATIONS

If you are an OfficeVision/400 user, then you should be aware of the following when developing a backup strategy. Refer to the **AS/400 Backup and Recovery — Basic** and **AS/400 Backup and Recovery — Advanced** manuals and the **AS/400 Office Service Concepts and Programmer's Guide** for additional information.

Journals	Journals must be managed and saved. Refer to Journals on page 106.
Documents	Documents and folders are in library QDOC. However, the only way to save documents and folders is with the SAVDLO command. Refer to Saving Documents and Folders on page 56.
Security Data	Users in an office environment frequently change authorization lists, document classifications, and the like, thereby, changing the security data on the system. Therefore, users should be saving the security data using SAVSECDTA or SAVSYS.
Mail	Mail objects can be saved with SAVSYS. Often users do not wish to perform a SAVSYS on, say, a daily basis, but do want to save their mail objects. If you save mail, but do not want to do a SAVSYS, then refer to Saving OfficeVision/400 Data on a Daily Basis on page 64 for a suggested method to avoid SAVSYS. This method includes the command SAVSECDTA, which saves all security information without requiring a dedicated system, and saves:

- User profiles
- Authorization lists
- Authority holders
- Internal office distribution objects

Library QUSRSYS	QUSRSYS is important for OfficeVision/400 users. Among other objects, the following information is stored in this library:

- System Distribution Directory files
- Distribution Lists files
- Document and Folder Search Index files
- Access Code Definition files
- User Permission file
- Nickname file
- Office Services Journal
- Journal receivers
- Distribution objects
- Distribution documents
- Dictionary files

The easiest way to save these objects is to save the library. Also consider using the SAVCHGOBJ command.

Library QGPL   QGPL contains additional information that is important for OfficeVision/400 users. Although there are no OfficeVision-specific objects in QGPL, users should be saving QGPL as a part of their routine backup operation.

Refer to Save and Restore Figures on page 79 for a diagram that illustrates saving objects associated with OfficeVision/400. Refer to the *AS/400 Office Services Concepts and Programmer's Guide* for additional information.

SAVING PROGRAM PRODUCTS

When individually saving program products (other than OS/400), be sure to use the SAVLICPGM (Save Licensed Program) command (or the appropriate menu option) because program products sometimes place objects in libraries other than their primary library.

> *The SAVLICPGM command is not for backup purposes, but can be useful for distributing licensed programs to other systems. Refer to Save and Restore Figures on page 79 for a diagram showing save and restore commands.*

A technique to use as part of a save strategy is to create a distribution tape. Use option 40 on the Work with Licensed Programs menu (GO LICPGM). This saves licensed internal code, the operating system (OS/400), and the licensed program products.

SAVING CONFIGURATION OBJECTS

A little known (or used) command that is really useful is RTVCFGSRC. This command retrieves all of the configuration objects (or a subset of them) such as line descriptions and device descriptions, and a create CL program in a source file that you can then use to restore the configuration. The source file serves as an excellent reference and backup in case you change something. If you view the source file after it is created, you see that it contains all the necessary commands to recreate the configuration objects (e.g., line, controller, and device descriptions).

```
CRTSRCPF FILE(QGPL/CFGSRC)
RTVCFGSRC CFGD(*ALL) CFGTYPE(*ALL) SRCFILE(QGPL/CFGSRC)
    TEXT('Configuration Source of All Objects')
```

SAVING THE SYSTEM

An important tip to remember when saving the system is to use the tape device that is defined as the Alternate IPL Device. This is important because, when you perform system save, it is analogous to creating a boot diskette on a personal computer. Your first tape created during the system save contains data that allows you to IPL the system from tape.

When you do a SAVSYS, be sure to do a SAVLIB *NONSYS (i.e., save all the libraries on the system other than QDOC), or save the rest of the libraries with OS/400 individually. These libraries are:

- #LIBRARY
- QGPL
- QQALIB
- QUSRSYS
- QSSP
- #DSULIB
- #CGULIB
- QUSRTOOL
- QFNTCPL
- GDDM
- QHLPSYS
- QSDE
- QMGU
- #DFULIB
- #SDALIB
- QSYS38
- QSYSPRV

Refer to Saving User Libraries and IBM-Supplied Libraries on page 60 for additional information on saving IBM and non-IBM libraries.

Two libraries you may want to take notice of are QRPLOBJ and QRCL. QRPLOBJ is used for REPLACE(*YES) processing when doing compiles. QRCL is used as a repository for objects without libraries following the Reclaim Storage (RCLSTG) command. You have to decide if you want to save these libraries.

There may be a few more. It is hard to pin them all down. IBM Rochester is operating under the assumption that everybody who does a SAVSYS is also doing a SAVLIB *NONSYS and a SAVDLO. You should save all of these libraries because the library QSYS (saved by the SAVSYS command) contains PTF information for all portions of OS/400, not just the portions in QSYS. You can skip saving them if you are sure there have been no OS/400 PTFs installed since they were saved. Before V1R3, you were advised to save the library QGPL to assure that some miscellaneous PTF information was saved. With the exception of PTF save files, that is no longer the case. These save files are created when you order PTFs using ECS. If you have not yet loaded or applied these PTFs, then you might want to save the library QGPL to pick up these PTF Save Files. Refer to PTF Management on page 122 and PTF Save Files on page 113. If you do not save all the libraries listed above, I believe you should still save QGPL and save QUSRSYS because these libraries contain important information that concerns system users (like message queues).

The easiest and most sure way to save the system is to perform the system save from the SAVE menu. This ensures that the entire system and all libraries are saved.

Saving Security Data

If the only reason you are doing a SAVSYS is to backup your security information (e.g., user profiles, authorization lists), you can use the command SAVSECDTA (Save Security Data). This backs up only the security data, thus saving a lot of time.

Save Storage Command

The Save Storage command (SAVSTG) can also be used to quickly save all of the storage. This is faster and more efficient than SAVSYS; however, you cannot restore individual objects from the SAVSTG tape — you can only restore the entire storage. Therefore, this command is normally used for disaster recovery purposes and not for routine saves.

Refer to the AS/400 Backup and Recovery Guide, Chapter 11, for a description of the Save Storage process.

> *Make sure the keylock switch is in the NORMAL position before you begin SAVSTG.*

> *If you have changed the system configuration since the last SAVSTG, you cannot restore the system using the Restore Storage Procedure. If the configuration has changed (e.g., addition of disk drives, change to the ASPs) run another SAVSTG.*

Refer to Save and Restore Figures on page 79 for a diagram of save and restore commands.

SAVING USER LIBRARIES AND IBM-SUPPLIED LIBRARIES

When using the Save Library (SAVLIB) or the Save Changed Object (SAVCHGOBJ) commands, you can specify the following for the LIB parameter:

SAVLIB LIB(xxx)   Save from 1 to 300 libraries of name specified.

SAVLIB LIB(*NONSYS)	Save all libraries with a few specific exceptions.
SAVLIB LIB(*IBM)	Save all IBM-supplied libraries and any libraries that begin with the letter Q (with a few specific exceptions). One important exception is that this command does not save QGPL.
SAVLIB LIB(*ALLUSR)	Save all user-created libraries and IBM-supplied libraries that contain user data.
SAVCHGOBJ LIB(*ALLUSR)	Saves changed objects in all user-created libraries and IBM-supplied libraries that contain user data.

The following chart (taken from the ***AS/400 Backup and Recovery — Basic*** manual) is a list of the libraries that support the SAVLIB LIB(*NONSYS), (*IBM), and (*ALLUSR) values.

Library Name	*NONSYS	*IBM	*ALLUSR
QDOC (1)			
QDOCnnnn (1)			
QDSNX	X		X
QGPL	X		X
QGPLTEMP	X	X	
QGPL38	X		X
QPFRDATA	X		X
QRCL	X		X
QRECOVERY (3)			
QRPLOBJ (3)			
QSPL (3)			
QSRV (3)			
QSSP	X	X	
QSYS (2)			
QSYS2	X	X	
QS36F	X		X
QTEMP (3)			
QUSER38	X		X
QUSRSYS	X		X
QUSRTEMP	X	X	
QUSRVxRxMx (4)	X		X
QXZ1	X	X	
Qxxxxxx (5)	X	X	

Library Name	*NONSYS	*IBM	*ALLUSR
#LIBRARY	X		X
#CGULIB	X	X	
#COBLIB	X	X	
#DFULIB	X	X	
#SDALIB	X	X	
#DSULIB	X	X	

The following notes refer to the table above:

V3R1

(1) Prior to V3R1, all DLOs were in library QDOC in the system ASP. Beginning with V3R1, a QDOCnnnn library exists for each user ASP that contains DLOs. The library for DLOs in the system ASP remains as QDOC (same as in versions prior to V3R1). The library for DLOs in other ASPs is:

QDOCnnnn   where: *nnnn* = 0001, 0002, etc.,

which designates the user ASP number. Use the SAVDLO command to save DLOs in the QDOCnnnnn libraries.

(2) Use the SAVSYS command to save information in the QSYS library.

(3) The libraries contain temporary information. They are not saved or restored.

(4) A different library name using the format QUSRVxRxMx may have been created for each previous release supported by IBM. This library contains user commands to be compiled in a CL program for a previous release. The format VxRxMx is the version, release, and module level of a previous release that IBM continues to support.

(5) Qxxxxxx refers to any other library that starts with the letter Q. These libraries are intended to contain IBM-supplied objects. They are not saved when you specify *ALLUSR. For a complete list of IBM libraries that start the character Q, see the *AS/400 CL Reference* manual.

SAMPLE BACKUP STRATEGIES

I have included two examples that you may wish to use for developing your own backup plans. The two example environments are:

- IBM program products and associated data, but without OfficeVision/400.
- OfficeVision/400 save strategy.

Example of IBM Program Products and Associated Data

A simple and feasible strategy for backing up IBM program products and associated data follows.

- Keep a log of PTFs received and applied, including:
  - How you received them (so you can get them again if necessary).
  - The PTF numbers.

- The products to which they apply.
- When applied.

- After permanently applying a cumulative PTF package, save all the licensed programs and all of the affected libraries. This is a SAVSYS and a Save Licensed Programs, and I recommend saving libraries QGPL and QUSRSYS. See PTF Management on page 122.

- Keep a log of configuration changes including a printout of each changed configuration object.
    - System directory
    - Line, controller, and device descriptions
    - Date of the change

- You can also run the RTVCFGSRC command. Refer to Saving Configuration Objects on page 58.

- Do a SAVSECDTA often, since it is easy — **at least weekly**.

- Do a complete system save (using option 21 on the SAVE menu) at least monthly, or whenever enough PTFs have been applied and enough configuration changes have been made so that it is more painful to reapply them manually than to do the backup.

- Do a SAVDLO often — or work out a more sophisticated approach if necessary and feasible. Some users are exposed to catastrophe in the area of document recovery. Frequent saves of your DLOs will minimize your risk of loss.
    - When you do a SAVDLO, also save library QUSRSYS to save the appropriate journal receivers. Then you can delete the detached receivers from the system.
    - Refer to Operational Assistant on page 83 and Journals on page 106 for additional information.

- Develop a strategy for backing up non-IBM program products and user data. Aspects to consider are:
    - Changes to customer application products.
    - Changes to programmers' source code.
    - Changes within OfficeVision/400. Refer to OfficeVision/400 Backup Considerations on page 56.
    - Saving only objects that have changed since the last save. The command SAVCHGOBJ is ideal for source files and other multi-member files.
    - Saving the access paths (use the ACCPTH parameter), depending on the files you are saving. This increases the save time but greatly reduces the restore time.
    - Change journal receivers, if applicable.
    - Risk assessment evaluation.

- On any system, you should keep more than one set of backup media in case the most recent set is unusable. To make the best use of the second-to-the-last backup, have the most current journal receivers saved as of the most recent backup. This implies that, when you do backups, the receivers should be saved onto a separate tape than the data files.

There are two AS/400 backup and recovery guides. At no extra cost, you get the standard equipment: **AS/400 Backup and Recovery — Basic** manual (SC41-3304). This is packaged along with your **AS/400 System Operation** manual. For a modest fee, you can get the optional equipment: turbo-charged edition of the **AS/400 Backup and Recovery — Advanced** manual.

So, what do you get for your extra money if you buy the turbo-charged edition? You get more information on disk recovery, mirroring, checksumming, journaling, and commitment control. You also get information on uninterruptible power supplies. The information on save and restore procedures is the same in both manuals.

These manuals have some good information on planning a save and restore strategy. I recommend that you familiarize yourself with this information. Read Chapters 1 through 3 in either manual.

Example Save Strategy — OfficeVision/400

If you have OfficeVision/400, you must make sure that your save strategy includes those objects that are unique to OfficeVision/400.

Saving OfficeVision/400 Data on a Daily Basis

Perform the following in the sequence specified in the following table.

Command	What It Saves	Comments

CHGJRN
  QAOSDIAJRN
  JRNRCV(*GEN)
	Not applicable.	Detaches current office journal and generates a new one.

SAVCHGOBJ
  OBJ(*ALL)
  LIB(QUSRSYS)
  OBJTYPE(*ALL)
  OBJJRN(*YES)
  ACCPTH(*YES)
	Office database file changes since last complete SAVLIB command was run:
	
	• System distribution directory files
	• Distribution list files
	• Document and folder search files
	• Access code definition files
	• User permission files
	• Nickname files
	• Calendar files
	• QAOSDIAJRN Office Journal
		Cumulative effect. If you run a SAVLIB or SAVSYS on Monday, changes made on Tuesday are saved when SAVCHGOBJ is run on Tuesday. Same again on Wednesday and Thursday because the date stamp on the file is when the last system or library save occurred.
		
		If you specified OBJJRN(*YES), the office files that changed since last complete save are saved along with their journal receivers.
		
		If you specified OBJJRN(*NO), the journaled office files are not saved; only their journal receivers

Command	What It Saves	Comments
		are saved. This is not recommended as it creates more steps during the restore procedure.
WRKJRNA QAOSDIAJRN	Not applicable.	Use F15, option 4, to delete detached receiver(s). You saved the journal receiver in the previous step...you don't need it now.
SAVSECDTA MAIL(*YES)	All of the distribution objects from the QUSRSYS library: • Dist. Recipient Queues • Dist. Tracking Objects	If mail is an important part of your operation, save it daily.
SAVDLO DLO(*SEARCH) SRCHTYP(*ALL) OWNER(*ALL) REFCHGDATE(date)	All filed documents created or changed since last complete save. Newly created folders since last complete save.	System saves changed documents and folders that meet specifications.
SAVDLO DLO(*MAIL)	All distribution documents from library QUSRSYS and all filed documents in library QDOC that are referenced by a distribution.	If you are running the SAVSECDTA MAIL(*YES) command, the SAVDLO command must be run at least daily to ensure documents, referenced by the saved distribution objects are also saved.

Saving Office Vision/400 Data on a Weekly Basis

Perform the following in the sequence specified in the table.

Command	What It Saves	Comments
SAVLIB LIB(*NONSYS)	All Licensed Program Libraries, all user created libraries, and IBM-supplied libraries that contain user data (e.g., QUSRSYS).	You may want to modify this and specify each library, but this command makes it easy to hit all the non-system libraries.
SAVDLO DLO(*ALL) FLR(*ANY)	All documents and folders in QDOC and all distribution documents in QUSRSYS. This includes all the Client Access files in the system folders and all other PC files	

Command	What It Saves	Comments
	that may be stored in shared folders.	
SAVSECDTA MAIL(*YES)	User profiles, authorization lists, authority holders, and distribution objects.	

Saving OfficeVision/400 Data on a Monthly Basis

You can go to the SAVE menu by entering **GO SAVE**. Then take option 21. Or perform the following sequence.

Command	What It Saves	Comments
CHGMSGQ MSGQ(QSYSOPR) DLVRY(*BREAK)	Not applicable.	Sets QSYSOPR message queue in break mode so you can receive all messages immediately. Useful in case you have to respond to a message.
ENDSBS SBS(*ALL) OPTION(*IMMED)	Not applicable.	Places the system into a restricted state.
SAVSYS	The following: • LIC and OS/400 objects • User profiles • Authorization lists • Authority holders • Distribution objects • Device configurations	
SAVLIB LIB(*NONSYS)	See weekly save.	
SAVDLO DLO(*ALL) FLR(*ANY)	See weekly save.	

Refer to Save and Restore Figures on page 79 for a diagram of save and restore commands.

> *Take the time to read through the chapter on Data Backup and Storage Management in the* **Office Service Concepts and Programmer's Guide**, *and the* **AS/400 Backup and Recovery Guide**. *These manuals have good detail on the concepts, and several tips on how to set up procedures for performing backups and restores of OfficeVision/400 objects. A little time spent now saves you lots of work later.*

UNATTENDED BACKUPS

Users may be interested in performing unattended backups during offpeak hours, typically at night or on weekends. A good discussion of this subject is available in the Redbook, *Managing Multiple AS/400s in a Peer Network*.

Unless you have a tape drive with the capacity for unattended backup, the unattended backup uses save files to save data. For greatest efficiency and security, consider using a separate user ASP for your save files. This provides better performance and minimizes risk of disk failure. After you have saved your data and you return to the office, transfer the save file data to tape. When doing so, you must use the SAVSAVFDTA (Save Save File Data) command.

Refer to Save and Restore Figures on page 79 for a diagram of save and restore commands.

HISTORICAL SAVE INFORMATION

When an object is saved, the system updates the object description with information about the save and restore process. Display this information using the Display Object Description (DSPOBJD) command and specify DETAIL(*FULL).

There are also six data areas in library QSYS that contain save and restore history information; they do not contain data. The system uses the object descriptions of the data areas to record the save and restore information. Use the DSPOBJD command to view this information, not the DSPDTAARA command.

- QSAVLIBALL contains information for the SAVLIB LIB(*NONSYS) operation.
- QSAVALLUSR contains information for the SAVLIB LIB(*ALLUSR) operation.
- QSAVIBM contains information for the SAVLIB LIB(*IBM) operation.
- QSAVUSRPRF contains the last use of SAVSYS, SAVSECDTA, and RSTUSRPRF commands.
- QSAVSYS contains information on the last use of the SAVSYS command.
- QSAVSTG contains information on the last use of the SAVSTG command.

The following is an example:

```
DSPOBJD OBJ(QSYS/data-area-name) OBJTYPE(*DTAARA) DETAIL(*FULL)
```

AUTOMATED BACKUP USING THE BACKUP MENU

Use the BACKUP functional portion of the Operational Assistant to set up automated backups of your system. Refer to Using the BACKUP Menu on page 90 for additional information.

RESTORING YOUR AS/400

> *If you do not have a hard copy of the* **Basic** *and* **Advanced Backup and Recovery Guides**, *get one of each. These manuals are extremely important and they should be a part of every AS/400 installation library.*

Just as with each user's backup, restoration for each user is likely to be unique. Refer to the **AS/400 Backup and Recovery — Basic** manual for a discussion on developing a good recovery strategy.

Simply put, restoration is the reverse of backup. Restoring single objects is straightforward. However, restoration of groups of objects, like OfficeVision/400 objects or SYSTEM objects, may require special considerations. Users are advised to refer to the manuals.

RESTORING THE ENTIRE SYSTEM

There is no command to restore the entire system. The following procedure is a suggested guideline. It does not consider journaling or checksum.

> *The steps are listed in the order you needed to completely restore the system. These instructions are abbreviated and the user should refer to the* **AS/400 Backup and Recovery — Basic** *manual before proceeding.*

> *If you have experienced a power failure or any problems with DASD, do not run a RCLSTG (Reclaim Storage) until AFTER you have restored your system and your mail items have been restored. If you do a RCLSTG before you have restored mail, mail items not on Distribution Recipient Queues are deleted.*

> *If you have been doing daily saves, DO NOT run the RSTAUT command until AFTER you have restored the latest daily save tape from the RSTDLO command.*

> *I recommend that you carefully review the* **AS/400 Backup and Recovery — Basic** *manual if you are performing any system restoration. The actual procedures used to restore system objects depend on the type of failure from which you are recovering.*

The following procedure takes you through the restore process using the restore commands. These steps presume that you have a complete set of system save tapes available. It does not take into account save strategies that use SAVCHGOBJ commands or apply journal changes.

If you created your save tapes using the SAVE menu (option 21), then, after the first three steps, you could complete the restoration process by using the RESTORE menu. Enter **GO RESTORE** to get to the RESTORE menu and then take option 21.

System Restoration Procedure

The following table summarizes the steps for system restoration. Also refer to Save and Restore Figures on page 79 for save and restore diagram.

Command	What It Restores	Comments
Prepare for restore	Not applicable.	Clean the tape drive and, at first opportunity, change the QSYSOPR message queue delivery to *BREAK.
Restore LIC	Restore the Licensed Internal Code.	Mount the SAVSYS tape and perform a D IPL from the system control panel. (Refer to Performing an IPL from the System Control Panel on page 311.) Select option 23 or 24 at the A6xx 6001 halt. The option you use depends on the type of failure from which you are recovering. Refer to the *AS/400 Backup and Recovery — Basic* manual.
Install OS/400	Restores the operating system.	This is performed during a manual IPL. Follow instructions in the *AS/400 Backup and Recovery — Basic* manual for restoring OS/400.
ENDSBS SBS(*ALL) OPTION(*IMMED)	Not applicable.	The system needs to be in a restricted state during a restore of the system.

Command	What It Restores	Comments
CHGMSGQ MSGQ(QSYSOPR) DLVRY(*BREAK) SEV(60)	Places the QSYSOPR message queue into break mode and places the system into a restricted state.	With the QSYSOPR message queue in break mode, all messages are displayed immediately.
V3R1 RCLSTG	Recover addressability of lost or damaged objects. Refer to Reclaiming Storage (RCLSTG) on page 73.	To reclaim storage: 1. If at V3R1, make sure QRCL library is included in the system value QALWUSRDMN. 2. Enter command RCLSTG.
V3R1 CHGSYSVAL SYSVAL(QALWOBJRST) VALUE(*ALL)	Not applicable.	If you are at V3R1, the QALWOBJRST system value must be set to *ALL for correct restoration of many system objects.
RSTUSRPRF USRPRF(*ALL) MAIL(*YES)	Restores user profiles, authorization lists, authority holders, and office distribution objects.	User profiles must be restored before restoring nonsystem libraries. Mail cannot be restored until library QUSRSYS is restored. Before V2R1, you had to do this step twice, once with MAIL(*NO) and once with MAIL(*YES). Don't perform an IPL between the RSTUSRPRF and the RSTAUT (last step, below).
RSTCFG OBJ(*ALL)	Restores device configurations, communications objects, and other device-related objects.	Use the tapes from most recent SAVSYS. The file with configuration objects is labeled QFILEIOC. Use the DSPTAP to locate the correct file.

Command	What It Restores	Comments
RSTLIB SAVLIB(*NONSYS)	Restores user-created libraries, IBM-supplied libraries with user date (e.g., QUSRSYS), and Licensed Program libraries.	If you saved libraries using the SAVLIB LIB(*NONSYS), then you can restore using this command. Otherwise, you must specifically name each library.
RSTDLO DLO(*ALL) SEQNBR(beg end)	Restore objects in library QDOC.	If you are restoring daily saves, then you must run this three (yes, three) times. (If you are restoring a complete save, then you only run it once.) First, for weekly SAVDLO DLO(*ALL) FLR(*ANY) tape to restore all folders and documents in QDOC. Second, for the daily SAVDLO DLO(*SEARCH) tape to restore new folders and new or changed documents since the weekly save tape. Third, for the daily SAVDLO DLO(*MAIL) tape to restore all distribution documents.
RSTOBJ OBJ(*ALL) SAVLIB(QUSRSYS)	Restores all daily objects that were saved. Issue this command once for each library that was saved from the save examples.	This step is required if you are doing a daily restore. If you are doing a complete restore, skip to next step. If you used OBJJRN(*NO) when you saved the SAVCHGOBJ command in your daily save, you then apply the journal changes now to all the office files EXCEPT the search index files. You do not restore changes to these files (QAO*) as they are

Command	What It Restores	Comments
		synchronized by the RCLDLO command.
APYJRNCHG JRN(QUSRSYS/ QAOSDIAJRN) FILE(QUSRSYS/file)	Applies journaled changes to QAO* files.	This step required only if doing a daily restore. If you are doing a complete restore, skip to next step. Run this for all QAO* files EXCEPT the files QAOSSH10 to 19. They are updated with the RSTDLO command.
RSTAUT USRPRF(*ALL)	Restore users' authorities to objects.	If you leave this step out, the users' authority is no longer what it was.

RECLAIMING STORAGE (RCLSTG)

Objects can become lost or damaged because of power failures, equipment failures, or other types of system problems. (Refer to the *AS/400 Backup and Recovery — Basic* manual) By using the Reclaim Storage (RCLSTG) command, you can correct some of these conditions, delete objects, or remove pieces of objects that cannot be made usable. There are several situations described in the *AS/400 Backup and Recovery — Basic* manual that suggest performing RCLSTG. Many users have implemented procedures to run RCLSTG on a routine schedule to keep their auxiliary storage cleaned up. Consider the following:

- RCLSTG requires auxiliary storage to run. The command could fail if there is not enough storage available for it to run.
- Every object in auxiliary storage is checked.
- RCLSTG can take a long time to complete.

> *I have had occasion to talk with some administrators who have indicated that the RCLSTG takes such a long time to run that they prefer to perform a complete scratch installation of their system (i.e., complete system restore). The complete restore actually cleans up your system better than a RCLSTG. You may want to consider this alternative method.*

- The system must be in a restricted state to run RCLSTG.
- If at V3R1, make sure QRCL library is included in the system value QALWUSRDMN.

V3R1
Prior to Version 2 of the Operating System, the RCLSTG command sent status messages to inform you of current processing. These messages are sent to the QSYSOPR message queue in the break mode. So, unless you are there to answer the messages, the RCLSTG command suspends operation until the message is answered. Most users don't really care about the status — they just want the command to end. If you are running Version 1 software, you can check QSYSOPR message queue or the history log (QHST) for a record of what was done. It is possible to run the RCLSTG command as an unattended function. A simple CL Program, such as the following, should do the job. If at V3R1, make sure QRCL library is included in the system value QALWUSRDMN.

```
ENDSBS *ALL
DLYJOB delay long enough to end the subsystems
CHGJOB BRKMSG(*HOLD)
RCLSTG
PWRDWNSYS OPTION(*IMMED) RESTART(*YES)
```

> *When performing a RCLSTG, the system deletes unusable objects, assigns unowned objects to user QDFTOWN, and places objects without libraries into library QRCL. Therefore, before and after running RCLSTG, make note of the objects in library QRCL and objects owned by QDFTOWN. If you see any changes, you may have to perform some object authority or library changes to get things back to where they should be. After processing objects in QRCL, you may want to go ahead and delete the objects, or the library itself, so it doesn't continue to use up disk storage space.*

Refer to the *AS/400 Backup and Recovery — Basic* manual for additional information.

RECLAIM DOCUMENTS AND FOLDERS

When users have problems working with documents and folders, you may have to run the Reclaim Document Library Objects (RCLDLO) command. For example, use RCLDLO when trying to restore a document into a damaged folder or when there might be other internal errors. Check the online information for the RCLDLO command.

The format for the command is:

```
RCLDLO DLO(*ALL)
```

RESTORE LICENSED INTERNAL CODE

To restore the Licensed Internal Code (LIC) you must manually IPL from tape. Refer to the *AS/400 System Operation* manual for instructions.

DISK RECOVERY ACTIONS

The following table is a summary of the recovery actions that may be performed by an IBM Service Representative and the AS/400 system administrator or operator.

> *This summary applies only if your AS/400 system ASP is **NOT** protected using checksum, mirroring, or device parity (RAID-5) protection. Refer to the **AS/400 Backup and Recovery — Basic** manual for additional information.*

> *If a disk unit fails, the Service Representative determines if data loss has occurred. You and the Service Representative may decide that it is not practical to save and restore the data onto a replacement device (sometimes referred to as "pumping" the drive).*
>
> *During the "drive pump," the Service Representative saves data from the failed disk unit to tape. Data from unreadable sectors is not saved. If you then restore the data from the tape back to the system, and then perform an IPL, you may have some damaged objects on the system.*
>
> *If the unreadable sector is part of a damaged object description, the object may be unusable. If the sector is part of a data file, the file may still be usable, except for the records on the damaged sector. You may have to restore the entire the system. If, after discussion with your Service Representative, you decide to use this save media as part of a recovery, you must assume the risk of doing so.*

Type of Disk Failure	Service Representative Actions	AS/400 System Administrator Actions
Load source unit failure with no data loss.	1. Save the disk unit data. 2. Attach new disk unit. 3. Install LIC using function code 24 (install) to the load source unit. 4. Restore the disk unit data. 5. Perform an IPL.	1. If journaling is used on the system, recovery may be required after abnormal system end. Refer to the **AS/400 Backup and Recovery — Advanced** manual for additional information.

Type of Disk Failure	Service Representative Actions	AS/400 System Administrator Actions
Load source unit failure with some unreadable sectors.	1. Save the disk unit data. 2. Attach the new disk unit. 3. Install LIC using function code 24 (install) on the load source unit. 4. Restore the disk unit data. 5. Perform an IPL.	1. Restore the operating system. 2. End all subsystems. 3. Reclaim storage. 4. If damaged objects are found, restore them from the most recent save media.
Load source unit failure with all sectors unreadable.	1. Attach the new disk unit. 2. Install the LIC using function code 24 (install). 3. Recover the configuration using the Recover Configuration option on the Work with Disk Units display. 4. Perform an IPL.	1. Restore the operating system. 2. Restore user profiles. 3. Restore device configurations. 4. Restore the user libraries. 5. Restore the DLOs. 6. If you have changed objects to restore, continue with step 7; otherwise, go to step 11. 7. Restore changed objects. 8. Apply journaled changes. 9. If you have DLOs that you saved daily, restore them; otherwise, go to step 11. 10. Apply journaled changes to the DLOs. 11. Restore authority.
Non-load source unit failure with no data loss.	1. Attach new disk unit. 2. Restore data to the new disk unit. 3. Perform an IPL.	If journaling is used on the system, recovery may be required after abnormal system end. Refer to the *AS/400 Backup and Recovery — Advanced* manual for additional information.

Type of Disk Failure	Service Representative Actions	AS/400 System Administrator Actions
Failure of a non-load source disk unit in the system ASP with SOME unreadable sectors.	1. Save the disk unit data. 2. Attach the new disk unit. 3. Restore the disk unit data. 4. Restore the LIC using function code 23 (restore). 5. Perform an IPL.	1. Restore the operating system. 2. End all subsystems. 3. Reclaim storage. 4. If damaged objects are found, restore them from the most recent save media.
Failure of a non-load source disk unit in the system ASP with ALL sectors unreadable.	1. Attach the new disk unit. 2. Delete the ASP data. 3. Restore the LIC using function code 23 (restore). If user ASPs are configured, they remain intact.	1. Restore the operating system. 2. End all subsystems. 3. Reclaim storage. 4. Restore user profiles. 5. Restore user libraries. 6. Restore the DLOs. 7. If you have changed objects to restore, continue with step 8; otherwise, go to step 12. 8. Restore changed objects. 9. Apply journaled changes. 10. If you have DLOs that you saved daily, restore them; otherwise go to step 12. 11. Apply journaled changes to the DLOs. 12. Restore authority.
Failure of a disk unit in a user ASP with SOME unreadable sectors.	1. Save the disk unit data. 2. Attach the new disk unit. 3. Restore the disk unit data. 4. Perform an IPL.	1. End all subsystems. 2. Reclaim storage. 3. If damaged objects are found, restore them from the most recent save media.

Type of Disk Failure	Service Representative Actions	AS/400 System Administrator Actions

Failure of disk unit in a user ASP with ALL sectors unreadable.	1. Attach the new disk unit.
	2. Delete the ASP data.
	3. Perform an IPL.
		A. ASP was in overflowed status:
		  1. End all subsystems.
		  2. Reclaim storage.
		  3. Restore user profiles.
		  4. Delete objects in the ASP.
		  5. Restore objects to the ASP.
		  6. Restore authority.
		B. ASP was not in overflowed status:
		  1. Restore user profiles.
		  2. Restore objects to the ASP.
		  3. Restore authority.

SAVE AND RESTORE FIGURES

The following figures are graphical representations of system and OfficeVision/400 save and restore procedures.

SYSTEM SAVE FIGURE

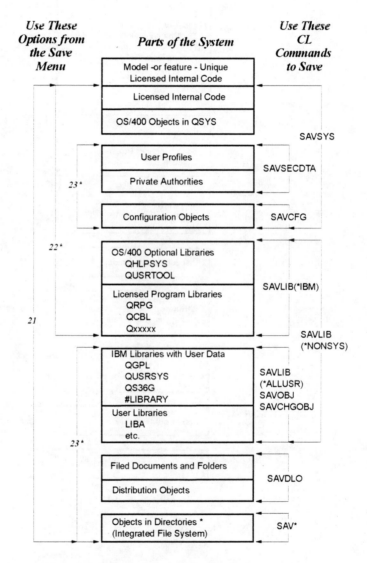

*NOTE: Items denoted with * are new with V3R1. Does not apply to prior versions/releases.*

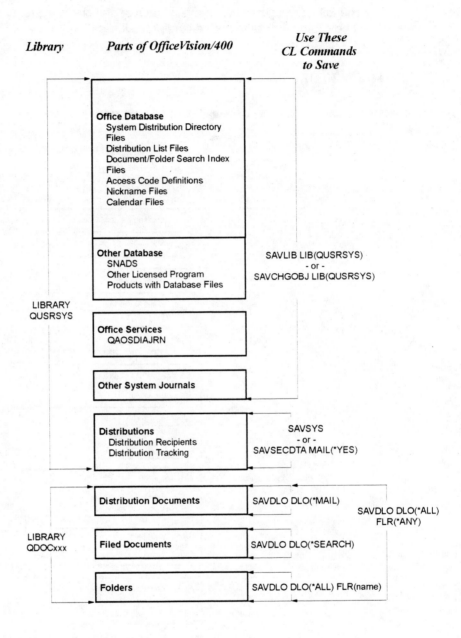

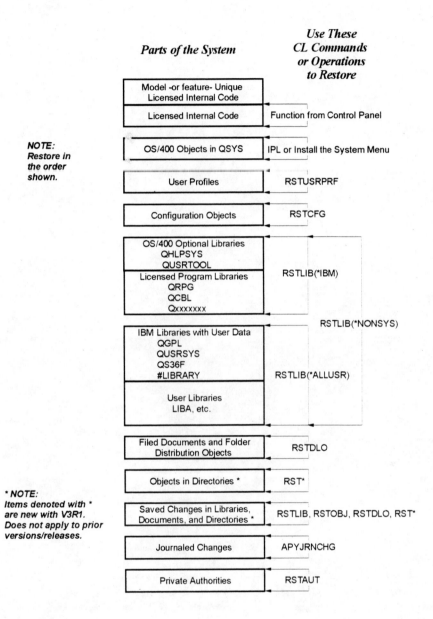

NOTE:
Restore in
the order
shown.

Parts of the System

Use These
CL Commands
or Operations
to Restore

Parts of the System	CL Commands or Operations to Restore
Model -or feature- Unique Licensed Internal Code	
Licensed Internal Code	Function from Control Panel
OS/400 Objects in QSYS	IPL or Install the System Menu
User Profiles	RSTUSRPRF
Configuration Objects	RSTCFG
OS/400 Optional Libraries QHLPSYS QUSRTOOL	RSTLIB(*IBM)
Licensed Program Libraries QRPG QCBL Qxxxxxxx	
IBM Libraries with User Data QGPL QUSRSYS QS36F #LIBRARY	RSTLIB(*ALLUSR)
User Libraries LIBA, etc.	
Filed Documents and Folder Distribution Objects	RSTDLO
Objects in Directories *	RST*
Saved Changes in Libraries, Documents, and Directories *	RSTLIB, RSTOBJ, RSTDLO, RST*
Journaled Changes	APYJRNCHG
Private Authorities	RSTAUT

RSTLIB(*NONSYS)

* NOTE:
Items denoted with *
are new with V3R1.
Does not apply to prior
versions/releases.

OPERATIONAL ASSISTANT

The Operational Assistant is a menu-driven interface that allows users to perform common system tasks quickly and easily. Users can access many familiar functions (e.g., the SAVE menu), as well as some newer menus and functions (e.g., the POWER and CLEANUP menus). As with so many other menus and functions on the AS/400, you can access all of the Operational Assistant functions and menus via the GO menu commands, or by using a fast-path command.

Beginning with V2R1, less emphasis has been placed on the term Operational Assistant. I believe this is because IBM does not want users to think of the Operational Assistant so much as a unique function, but rather as a methodology to make the AS/400 easier for users to deal with.

Besides entering the command **GO ASSIST**, users can access the Operational Assistant by pressing the Attention key. Review how the Attention Key handling program works. When you "enroll" users in the Operational Assistant, the Attention Key brings up the initial Operational Assistant menu (this is the same menu accessed when entering the command GO ASSIST). From this menu, pressing the F9 key brings up a command line. As the system administrator, you may not want all users to have this access — or you may permit only limited access.

> *Refer to the* **AS/400 Operator's Guide**, *Chapter 3, for additional information on setting up your system and administrating the functions of the Operational Assistant.*

The following information is provided as a reference to help you with your choices for implementation.

SETTING UP THE OPERATIONAL ASSISTANT

Enter the command **GO ASSIST**. Several options are available for your use. Acquaint yourself with them. The easiest way to review the options is to use the Help key and review the associated Help text. After entering the GO ASSIST command, you are presented with the menu below.

```
ASSIST                AS/400 Operational Assistant (TM) Menu
                                                        System:   APACHE
To select one of the following, type its number below and press Enter:


        1. Work with printer output
        2. Work with jobs
        3. Work with messages
        4. Send messages
        5. Change your password

       10. Manage your system, users, and devices
       11. Customize your system, users, and devices

       75. Information and problem handling

       80. Temporary sign-off



Type a menu option below

     __

 F1=Help   F3=Exit   F9=Command line   F12=Cancel
```

Options 1 through 5 are self explanatory. Option 10 opens the MANAGESYS menu providing you with various system-related tasks such as running backups, working with jobs and messages, and working with signed-on users. The following example shows the MANAGESYS menu.

```
MANAGESYS           Manage Your System, Users, and Devices
                                                        System:   APACHE
To select one of the following, type its number below and press Enter:


        1. Display system status
        2. Run a backup
        3. Work with system operator messages

       10. Work with printer output
       11. Work with jobs
       12. Work with signed-on users

       20. Device status tasks

       60. Customize your system, users, and devices




Type a menu option below



 F1=Help   F3=Exit   F9=Command line   F12=Cancel
```

If you take option 11 from the main ASSIST menu, you are presented with the system SETUP menu. As with all AS/400 system menus, you can access the SETUP menu directly by using the **GO *menu_name*** command. The example below shows the SETUP menu.

```
SETUP                Customize Your System, Users, and Devices
                                              System:   APACHE
To select an option, type its number below and press Enter:

     1. Change system options
     2. Cleanup tasks
     3. Power on and off tasks
     4. Disk space tasks
     5. Backup tasks

    10. Work with user enrollment
    11. Change passwords for IBM-supplied users

    20. Communications configuration tasks




Type a menu option below


F1=Help   F3=Exit   F9=Command line   F12=Cancel
```

Option 2 from the SETUP menu takes you to the CLEANUP menu to guide you through setting up system cleanup tasks. Take this option to go through the automatic cleanup options. When you set up automatic cleanup, the Operational Assistant adds STRCLNUP to the QCTL autostart program QSYS/QSTRUP. The job STRCLNUP is submitted to QCTL with a delayed start time.

Option 5 takes you to the BACKUP menu. (See Using the BACKUP Menu on page 90.)

STARTING THE OPERATIONAL ASSISTANT

Enter **GO ASSIST** to initiate the Operational Assistant menu. The system administrator should first set up the Operational Assistant with the appropriate options before users are allowed to use the Operational Assistant.

Several CL commands are available to start the various functions of the Operational Assistant. These can be useful to include from within user application programs.

CALL QEZOUTPT	Work with Printer Output
CALL QEZBCHJB	Work with Jobs
CALL QEZMSG	Work with Messages
CALL QEZUSRCLNP	CL Program to be customized for user cleanup
CALL QEZSNDMG	Send Message

| **STRCLNUP** | Start Automatic Cleanup |
| **ENDCLNUP** | End Automatic Cleanup |

> *The STRCLNUP command is included in the startup program QSYS/QSTRUP that runs at every IPL. If you have changed the startup program or the system value QSTRUPPGM, you may want to verify that the start cleanup command is included with each IPL. Otherwise, you must restart the cleanup manually after every IPL.*

FUNCTIONS

The following table summarizes the Operational Assistant functions.

Operational Assistant Function	Comments
Control Printing	Lists user's printed output, where it is, and current status. If authorized, allows user to start or change printer, select number of copies, specify pages to print, and other printing options. Type **GO ASSIST**, option 1.
Control Jobs	Provides a list of the user's jobs and allows user to control those jobs. Includes spooled files in output queues. Type **GO ASSIST**, option 2.
Messages	Provides options related to messages sent to user and allows user to send messages. Type **GO ASSIST**, option 3.
Documentation and Problem Handling	Displays a list of AS/400 publications. Saves the information about a user's session necessary for a technical support person to do problem analysis later. Stores information in output queue QUSRSYS/QEZDEBUG. Refer to the *AS/400 System Operation* manual for a list of the information collected.
Technical Support	Displays system operator messages. Work with system problems. Work with PTFs. Start/stop copy screen function. Connect/disconnect remote support sessions.

Operational Assistant Function	Comments
Temporary Sign Off	Disconnects user from current job and returns work station to a sign-on display. If user signs on again at the same display station within a specified length of time (default is four hours), then session picks up where it left off. This is useful to save system resource of signing off and on. Same as command DSCJOB.
Auto-cleanup	Runs at specified time every day. Cleans up user messages, system messages, job logs, system journals (except the security journal QAUDJRN), history logs, problem logs, alerts, and old calendar entries. Also cleans up PTF save files unless SystemView SystemManager/400 is installed on the system. Type **GO CLEANUP**.
Backup List	Allows you to back up objects using a predefined list, which you can customize. Backup jobs can be submitted to batch with a delay time. You can access this option at any time by going to the BACKUP menu directly with the command **GO BACKUP**. Refer to the *AS/400 System Operation* manual for additional information.
Communications Configuration	Provides fast and easy way to configure communications for remote work stations, other AS/400s, and System/36s. Type **GO CMNCFG**.
Disk Space Information	The OA has a tool to collect disk space information and organize it into an easy-to-read report. Type **GO DISKTASKS**.
Signed On Users	You can see what users are doing on the system. Using this function, the user, activity, and display station information are displayed. You can sign a user off and send messages. Type **GO MANAGESYS**, option 12.
System Setup, User Enrollment	Type **GO SETUP** and you can: • Change passwords for IBM-supplied user profiles • Change cleanup options • Change power on/off schedule • Create user profiles • Enroll users in the OfficeVision/400 and the directory

Operational Assistant Function	Comments
Power Schedule	Menu-driven interface to schedule power off and power on (IPLs) and to immediately power off a system. Type **GO POWER** to access. Refer to Power Off and On Schedule on page 96.

DETERMINING CLEANUP OPTIONS

The Operational Assistant cleanup options shown in the following table are also in the *AS/400 System Operation* manual. The Automatic Cleanup column in the table describes the cleanup option performed by the Operational Assistant. You must remember to cleanup items in the Manual Cleanup column.

Automatic Cleanup	What It Does	Default	Manual Cleanup
Messages	Deletes messages older than number of days specified in: • User message queues • Work station message queues • System operator message queues	7 days	All other message queues.
System Messages	Every message sent to QSYSOPR is also sent to QHST. QHST is a history log. If messages are deleted from QSYSOPR that are needed for debugging or for other reasons, they can still be found in QHST through the DSPLOG command. By default, any messages in QSYSOPR and the work station message queues older than one day are deleted.	1 day	Maintain (cleanup) user-created objects: • Delete database files that are no longer needed. • Reorganize database files. • Delete programs no longer needed (e.g., Query/400 programs).
Job Logs and Other System Output	System-generated output is placed into separate output queues (see above). These output queues (QEZJOBLOG and QEZDEBUG) are checked for entries older than number of days specified. Any output older than number	7 days	Maintain all other output queues.

Automatic Cleanup	What It Does	Default	Manual Cleanup
	of days specified in these output queues is deleted.		
System Journals, System Logs, and PTF Files	The Operational Assistant changes (detaches) the attached journal receiver whenever it is greater than 5 megabytes (MB) or older than number of days specified. Deletes any journal receivers detached for more than the number of days specified. The following journals are maintained: • QAOSDIAJRN • QDSNX • QSNADS • QACGJRN *(if created by the Operational Assistant)* • QSXJRN • QPFRADJ The following logs are maintained: • QHST • Problem Log • Alerts Old PTF objects are deleted during cleanup of system journals and logs. This includes temporary objects, exit programs, and physical files associated with PTF. Old PTF Save Files are deleted if a library called QSMU DOES NOT exist.	30 days	Maintain: • Security journal • All user journals
OfficeVision Calendar Items	Deletes calendar items older than number of days specified. Also performs the following on Office objects: • Reorganizes folders. • Reorganizes Office database files. • Reorganizes mail log.	30 days	Perform the following: • Remove old mail log items. • Remove old documents and folders. • Remove outgoing mail status items.

USING THE BACKUP MENU

You can access additional save information on AS/400 objects by using the BACKUP menu that is part of the Operational Assistant. Start the Operational Assistant or enter the command **GO BACKUP**.

The following steps guide you through the screens to set up a simple, automated backup schedule using the BACKUP menu:

1. Enter **GO BACKUP**.

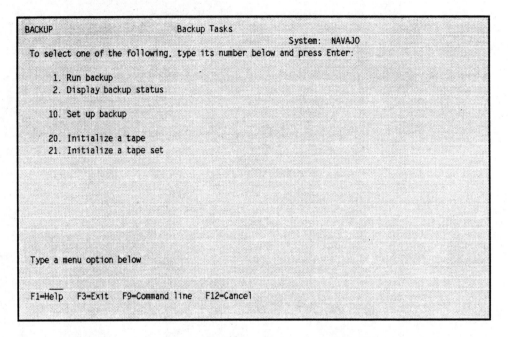

```
BACKUP                      Backup Tasks
                                        System:  NAVAJO
To select one of the following, type its number below and press Enter:

      1. Run backup
      2. Display backup status

     10. Set up backup

     20. Initialize a tape
     21. Initialize a tape set








Type a menu option below


F1=Help   F3=Exit   F9=Command line   F12=Cancel
```

2. Take option 2 to display the backup status. In the example below, the tape set used was *ANY, which indicates that there was no particular tape set specified in the backup options.

```
              Display Backup Status                    NAVAJO
                                              01/23/95  20:32:01
                                      Last
                                      Backup    Tape
What Was Backed Up                    Date      Set
User libraries:
  All  . . . . . . . . . . . . . . . . . :    01/17/95   *ANY
  All (changes only) . . . . . . . . . :
  From list . . . . . . . . . . . . . :
  From list (changes only) . . . . . . . :
Folders:
  All  . . . . . . . . . . . . . . . . . :    01/17/95   *ANY
  All (changes only) . . . . . . . . . :
  From list . . . . . . . . . . . . . :
Security data  . . . . . . . . . . . . :    01/17/95   *ANY
Configuration  . . . . . . . . . . . . :    01/17/95   *ANY
OfficeVision/400 calendars . . . . . . . :    01/17/95   *ANY
OfficeVision/400 mail  . . . . . . . . . :    01/17/95   *ANY


                                                        Bottom
Press Enter to continue.

F1=Help   F3=Exit   F12=Cancel   F22=Display backup history
```

3. Press F12 to return to the BACKUP menu, then take option 21 if you want to initialize a tape set. The example below shows preparation to initialize five tapes as part of tape set DAY1.

```
              Initialize a Tape Set
                                        System:   NAVAJO
Type choices below, then press Enter.

  Tape device . . . . . . . . . . . . . . TAP01    Name, F4 for list

  Tape set name  . . . . . . . . . . . . . day1    Name
    First tape to initialize . . . . . . .  01     01-99
    Last tape to initialize . . . . . . .   05     01-99

  Tape owner . . . . . . . . . . . . . . . BISEL

  Check tape for active files  . . . . . .  N      Y=Yes, N=No








F1=Help   F3=Exit   F5=Refresh   F12=Cancel
```

4. Press F12 to return to the BACKUP menu, then take option 10 to Set Up Backup.

```
SETUPBCKUP                    Set Up Backup
                                          System:   NAVAJO
To select one of the following, type its number below and press Enter:

        1. Change daily backup options
        2. Change weekly backup options
        3. Change monthly backup options

       10. Change library backup list
       11. Change folder backup list

       20. Change backup schedule







Type a menu option below
  _

F1=Help   F3=Exit   F9=Command line   F12=Cancel
```

5. In turn, take options 1, 2, and 3 to change the daily, weekly, and monthly backup options. There are two screens with options for daily, weekly, and monthly. Make sure you page down to see the second screens. The screens below show examples of information you can set.

```
                  Change Daily Backup Options
                                          System:   NAVAJO
Type choices below, then press Enter.

Where to back up:
  Backup device . . . . . . . . . . .  TAP01      Name, F4 for list
  Tape sets to rotate . . . . . . . .  DAY1       Name, *ANY




  Erase tape before backup . . . . . . .  Y        Y=Yes, N=No




                                                More...
F1=Help   F3=Exit   F5=Refresh   F12=Cancel  F16=Change library backup list
F17=Change folder backup list   F18=Change schedule
```

```
                  Change Daily Backup Options
                                            System:   NAVAJO
     Type choices below, then press Enter.

       What to back up:
         User libraries . . . . . . . . . . . .   2     1=Selected from list
                                                        2=All
                                                        3=None

         Folders  . . . . . . . . . . . . .       2     1=Selected from list
                                                        2=All
                                                        3=None
         Security data  . . . . . . . . . .       Y     Y=Yes, N=No
         Configuration  . . . . . . . . . .       Y     Y=Yes, N=No
         OfficeVision/400 mail  . . . . . .       Y     Y=Yes, N=No
         OfficeVision/400 calendars . . . .       Y     Y=Yes, N=No

       How to back up:
         Save changed objects only  . . ... . .   N     Y=Yes, N=No
         Submit backup as a batch job . . . . .   Y     Y=Yes, N=No
         Print detailed report  . . . . . . . .   Y     Y=Yes, N=No
                                                                     Bottom
     F1=Help  F3=Exit  F5=Refresh  F12=Cancel  F16=Change library backup list
     F17=Change folder backup list     F18=Change schedule
```

6. When you have finished setting the backup options for the daily, weekly, and
    monthly backups, press F12 to return to the SETUPBKUP menu. Take
    option 10, Change Library Backup List. All of the libraries are displayed in
    the list with the exception of QDOC and QSYS. As shown in the example
    below, all of the libraries are included in the daily, weekly, and monthly
    backups.

```
                    Change Library Backup List
                                            System:   NAVAJO
       Find library . . . . . .            Starting characters


     Type options below, then press Enter.
        2=Change backup   5=Display library contents   8=Display details


                        ---------Backup---------- Last
     Opt  Library    Daily   Weekly   Monthly   Backup    Changed
      ___  #LIBRARY   Yes     Yes      Yes      01/17/95   Yes
      ___  ACOMFILLIB Yes     Yes      Yes      01/17/95   Yes
      ___  ASN        Yes     Yes      Yes      01/17/95   Yes
      ___  ASYSWORDFL Yes     Yes      Yes      01/17/95   No
      ___  BFA        Yes     Yes      Yes      01/17/95   No
      2    BISEL      Yes     Yes      Yes      01/17/95   Yes
      ___  CARLISLE   Yes     Yes      Yes      01/17/95   No
      ___  CASTYA     Yes     Yes      Yes      01/17/95   Yes
      ___  QDSNX      Yes     Yes      Yes      01/17/95   No
      ___  QGPL       Yes     Yes      Yes      01/17/95   Yes
      ___  QPFRDATA   Yes     Yes      Yes      01/17/95   No
                                                                More...
     F1=Help    F3=Exit    F5=Refresh    F11=Display descriptions F12=Cancel
     F14=Select other libraries          F15=Change all
```

Using option 2 or the F15 key, you can change the libraries that are backed
up in each option, as the subsequent example screen shows. This screen
also appears if objects in the library changed since last saved.

> *When you create new libraries, they are added automatically to the daily, weekly, and monthly backup lists. New libraries are automatically added to the list to minimize the risk of omitting them when you run the backups. When you create a new library, make it a habit to check the backup list. Especially if you do not want it included in your regular backups.*

```
                        Change Library Backup List
.......................................................................
:                         Change Backup                               :
:                                                                     :
: Library . . . . . . . . . . :    BISEL                              :
: Description:                                                        :
:   Steve Bisel's Library                                            :
:                                                                     :
: Type choices below, then press Enter.                              :
:                                                                     :
:    Back up . . . . . . . . .    1   1=Daily, weekly, and monthly    :
:                                     2=Weekly and monthly            :
:                                     3=Monthly                       :
:                                     4=No backup                     :
:                                                                     :
:                                                                     :
:                                                                     :
:                                                                     :
:                                                                     :
:                                                                     :
: F1=Help   F5=Refresh   F12=Cancel                                  :
:                                                                     :
.......................................................................
```

7. When you have completed setting the library backup list, you need to repeat the process for folders using option 11 at the SETUPBKUP menu. After setting up folders, return to the SETUPBKUP menu and take option 20 (Change backup schedule) to set the backup schedule. In the example below, a daily backup runs at 10:00 PM, Monday through Thursday. On Friday, a weekly backup runs, except on the fourth Friday of the month when a monthly backup runs. Before each backup, at 3:00 PM, a message is sent to the QSYSOPR message queue reminding the operator to insert a tape into the tape drive.

```
                      Change Backup Schedule

Type choices below, then press Enter. Press F4 for list of backups.

    Run backup using this schedule  . . . . . .   Y   Y=Yes, N=No


                               Backup         Backup Time
                                              _____
    Sunday . . . . . . . .      _____
    Monday . . . . . . . .      *DAILY        22:00:00
    Tuesday . . . . . . . .     *DAILY        22:00:00
    Wednesday . . . . . .       *DAILY        22:00:00
    Thursday . . . . . . .      *DAILY        22:00:00
    Friday . . . . . . . .      *WEEKMONTH    22:00:00
    Saturday . . . . . . .      _____      _____

    Occurrence of day in month to run monthly
      backup . . . . . . . . . . . . . . . . .      4      1-4, *LAST

    Hours before backup to send load tape
      message  . . . . . . . . . . . . . . . .      7      1-24, *NOMSG
                                                           Bottom
F1=Help    F3=Exit    F5=Refresh    F12=Cancel
```

A complete discussion on using the Operational Assistant in your backup plans is included in the **AS/400 Backup and Recovery — Basic** manual. Read through the manual to better understand backing up your system.

CONSIDERATIONS WITH SYSTEMVIEW SYSTEM MANAGER/400

If you have **SystemView System Manager/400** installed (Licensed Program 5763-SM1), then the Operational Assistant does not clean up the PTF Save Files on your system. This is because the Operational Assistant assumes that, if System Manager is on your system, then your system is a service provider to other systems. Therefore, the PTF Save Files may be required to load/apply PTFs on any remote systems that may exist. All other cleanup options of the Operational Assistant are alright.

USING ASSISTANCE LEVELS

There are three assistance levels available when interacting with the system:

- BASIC
- INTERMEDIATE
- ADVANCED

The level of assistance varies according to user understanding or requirements.

The assistance level is set as a system value (QASTLVL), but can be overridden in the user profile or at the command level for each user. This provides a lot of flexibility to satisfy individual preferences. Experiment with each level and choose the one you prefer.

The following commands allow you to change the assistance level for the command itself:

- Display Messages (DSPMSG)
- Display System Status (DSPSYSSTS)
- Work with Configuration Status (WRKCFGSTS)
- Work with Messages (WRKMSG)
- Work with Spool Files (WRKSPLF)
- Work with System Status (WRKSYSSTS)
- Work with User Jobs (WRKUSRJOB)
- Work with User Profiles (WRKUSRPRF)
- Work with Writers (WRKWTR)

Press F21 while using the command you want to change, and change the assistance level. Or type the command you want to run, followed by:

```
ASTLVL(*xxxx)          where:   *xxxx is the assistance level desired.
```

The system saves your selection.

Refer to the *AS/400 System Operation* manual for more information.

POWER OFF AND ON SCHEDULE

To set up an automatic system power on and off schedule (i.e., an IPL schedule), access the POWER menu by entering the command **GO POWER**. Take options 1 and 2.

> *Make sure that the automatic cleanup option is enabled or else the power on/off schedule will not work.*

When a time to power down the system is scheduled, the OA sends a message warning users of the pending power shutdown (message ID CPA1E01). Disable the message by specifying 0 as the time to send the message. This is done from the Change Power Off/On Defaults menu. The Operational Assistant waits for a reply to this message. If no reply is received within one hour, the system is powered down anyway. For example, assume you select 10 minutes as the time to send a message before powering down, and you do not respond to the message. The power down occurs 1 hour after the message is sent, or 50 minutes after the time you scheduled.

> *Do not use the Power Off/On scheduler to apply delayed PTFs.*
> *The underlying command issued by the Power Off/On scheduler*
> *is not the one needed to perform delayed application of PTFs.*

POTENTIAL REASONS WHY THE POWER SCHEDULER DOES NOT WORK

If the Power Scheduler does not work, one of the following conditions may be the cause:

- The QSYSSCD job isn't running on the system. Issue the WRKACTJOB command and look for QSYSSCD, User QPGMR, Type BCH, and function PGM - QEZSCNEP. It is usually running in the QBASE or QCTL subsystem. If you don't find it, then the most likely reason is that the automatic cleanup option is not started. Issue the STRCLNUP command or go to the CLEANUP menu and enable automatic cleanup.

- The program identified in the system value QSTRUPPGM does not issue the STRCLNUP command. The shipped value (from IBM) for QSTRUPPGM issues this command. If you are using a different startup program, make sure that you have included the STRCLNUP command.

- Make sure the job queue that the Start Cleanup (STRCLNUP) command is submitted to has the maximum jobs parameter set to *NOMAX or a number greater than 1. The QSYSSCD job always runs and other jobs that perform automatic cleanup and power off functions are able to start unless the maximum jobs is greater than 1.

- Someone has canceled the QSYSSCD job.

- Cleanup may be scheduled to run at the same time you scheduled a Power Off. If it is within 30 minutes of the next scheduled Power On, then the Power Off is not initiated. You should have an error message indicating that the Power Off was canceled.

- If none of the above solves the problem, look for messages that might lead you to the cause.

CUSTOMIZING THE OPERATIONAL ASSISTANT FUNCTIONS

The Operational Assistant allows for customization to meet your unique requirements. You can use built-in application program interfaces (APIs) or you can use the Operational Assistant exit programs. Refer to the *System API Reference* manual for additional information.

Operational Assistant APIs

Most functions on the AS/400 Operational Assistant menu can be accessed individually by calling APIs found in the QSYS library. These Operational Assistant APIs allow you to incorporate Operational Assistant functions into your application menus.

The Operational Assistant APIs are:

QEZLSGNU   List Signed-On Users. Generates a list of signed-on users and places the list in the specified user space.

QEZMAIN   Operational Assistant Attention-Key-Handling (group jobs). Creates a group job to display the AS/400 Operational Assistant menu.

QEZAST   Operational Assistant Attention-Key-Handling (nongroup jobs). Uses the GO ASSIST command to display the AS/400 Operational Assistant menu.

QEZSAVIN   Save Information. Displays the Save Information to Help Resolve a Problem display.

QEZSNDMG   Send Message. Sends a message to one or more users or display stations, and optionally shows the Operational Assistant Send a Message display before sending the message.

QEZBCHJB   Work with Jobs. Displays either the Work with Jobs panel or the Work with User Jobs panel.

QEZMSG   Work with Messages. Displays either the Work with Messages panel or the Display Messages panel.

QEZOUTPT   Work with Printer Output. Displays either the Work with Printer Output panel or the Work with All Spooled Files panel.

Tailoring Operational Assistant Using Exit Programs

IBM supplies exit programs with the Operational Assistant. You can incorporate your own programs into these exit programs.

Automatic Cleanup Exit Program

The Automatic Cleanup exit program, QEZUSRCLNP, is supplied by IBM and runs each time the Operational Assistant cleanup is performed. Initially, of course, this program does nothing except send a message to the QSYSOPR message queue stating that user cleanup started and completed. You may want to incorporate your own programs or statements into the QEZUSRCLNP job. Then, whenever the system runs automatic cleanup, it also runs your own cleanup options. The following describes how to do this.

Make a copy of the QEZUSRCLNP program:

1. Enter RTVCLSRC PGM(QSYS/QEZUSRCLNP) SRCFILE(library_name/source_file_name). This retrieves the CL source of the QEZUSRCLNP program and places it into the source file you specify.

2. Modify the source file by inserting statements that run your own cleanup options. This might be CL commands or calls to your own programs.

3. Compile your source code to create a new CL program. DO NOT replace the original QEZUSRCLNP program in library QSYS. Place the new program (of the same name) in a library that appears AHEAD of QSYS in the system library list. Refer to Changing IBM Commands on page 316 and Changing System and User Library List on page 238 for additional information.

Now when the system runs Automatic Cleanup, your version of QEZUSRCLNP also runs.

Backup and Power Off Exit Programs

Similar to the procedure described for tailoring the cleanup, you can tailor the backup and the power off functions in the Operational Assistant.

You can tailor the Operational Assistant automatic backup by specifying an exit program on the Change Backup (CHGBCKUP) command. If an exit program is specified, that program is called both before the Operational Assistant backup is run and after the backup is run. You specify within the exit program when you want your functions to run.

The Power-Off exit program (QEZPWROFFP) is shipped with the system and stored in the QSYS library. This exit program powers off the system according to the power on and off schedule by running the Power Down System command PWRDWNSYS OPTION(*IMMED). Use the Change Power Schedule Entry (CHGPWRSCDE) command or the Change Power Schedule (CHGPWRSCD) command to set the power on and off schedule.

You can tailor this program to change how you want the system powered off. For example, you could change the program so that the system would not power off immediately.

HOUSEKEEPING

This section is devoted to methods that keep your disk storage cleaned up. The AS/400 has a propensity for using disk space. If you do not keep its appetite for disk space under control, you may find yourself running out of space. That is likely to happen over time anyway, but you do not want space occupied by unnecessary objects. Review this chapter for activities that keep the disk space use under control.

> *Before the creation of the Operational Assistant, housekeeping was a manual procedure that required a certain amount of discipline. The OA performs much of the housekeeping tasks on the AS/400, and I recommend that you take advantage of this capability. I have kept this section for reference. The techniques described here are still valid. In the case of user-created objects such as database files, you may prefer manual cleanup operations. For your user objects, you may want to take advantage of the Automatic Cleanup included in the Operational Assistant. Refer to Customizing the Operational Assistant Functions on page 97.*

For additional information, there is a good section on housekeeping and system cleanup in the *AS/400 System Operation* manual.

DETERMINING HOW DISK SPACE IS USED

The following procedure provides a way to estimate disk space usage.

Use the following commands to learn the total amount of space used by each library on the system. There is also a program in QUSRTOOLS that you could use (refer to QUSRTOOL Library on page 307).

```
DSPLIB LIB(*ALL) OUTPUT(*PRINT)
```

— or —

```
DSPOBJD *ALL/*ALL OUTPUT(*PRINT)
```

The size of the library appears at the end of each library listing. Be sure that the person running these commands has authority to all of the objects on the system. Unauthorized objects are not displayed.

I wouldn't necessarily recommend printing the listings. They might be lengthy. You may want to view only the spooled output, or output the listings to an outfile, then create a CL program to scan the file and only look for the total size of objects in each library.

The Auxiliary Storage megabytes listing is different from the Main Storage megabytes listing because main storage is always shown as a power of 2. For example, 1KB of main storage is actually 1,024 bytes (2^{10}), and 1MB of main storage is actually 1,048,576 bytes (2^{20}). However, 1MB of auxiliary storage is 1,000,000 bytes. The AS/400 is a single-level storage system and all storage is represented as main storage. Therefore, values must be converted from Main Storage bytes to Auxiliary Storage bytes. The conversion factor is:

Main Storage MB x 1.0486 = Auxiliary Storage million bytes

To determine total auxiliary storage used, add:

- Storage used by all user profiles.
- Space allocated to temporary objects.
- Space used for IOP and DASD Licensed Internal Code on all DASD units.
- Main Storage size.
- Vertical Micro Code (VLIC) use.
- Storage space used by the Service Tools.
- Storage used by user profiles.
  - Use WRKUSRPRF *ALL, then use option 5 to display each profile. Scroll to the second screen to view space used. This total must be converted from Main Storage to Auxiliary Storage format. If you have a large number of user profiles, you may want to make a CL program to do this.
- Space allocated to temporary objects.
  - Take the CURRENT UNPROTECTED USED value from the WRKSYSSTS screen and subtract the size of the Load Source actuator. To get the size of the Load Source actuator, use WRKDSKSTS and the number under the SIZE (M) for unit 1. Example: 224 - 200 = 24. If the Load Source actuator is a 9332, do not convert this value.
  - There is also space allocated to permanent internal objects needed by the Operating System. The amount of space occupied by these objects is dependent upon information such as how the system is used and how big the system is. Therefore, the number can vary widely from system to system. Unfortunately, there is no way to determine how much is allocated to these types of objects.
- Input/output processor (IOP) and DASD Licensed Internal Code space.
  - There are 1.05MB reserved on each configured unit for IOP and DASD Licensed Internal Code loads. Multiply 1.05 by the number of configured units. DO NOT convert this value.
- Main storage size.
  - Space is allocated on the Load Source DASD to dump Main Storage when a failure occurs. This space is equal to the size of Main Storage. This total must be converted from Main Storage to Auxiliary Storage format.
- VLIC size.
  - VLIC takes up 100MB of disk space on the Load Source of a high-end system. For a low-end system, VLIC takes 75MB of disk space. Do not convert this value.

- Service Tools storage.
  - Use STRSST to approximate the amount used by the Service Tools, Error Log, and VLIC Log size, plus the approximate value given by the Trace tables. There is no way to get an exact value of space actually allocated by the Trace Tables. This total must be converted from Main Storage to Auxiliary Storage format.
- Total Storage.
  - Add the totals to get the amount of disk space used.

PERFORM FREQUENT IPLs

IPL as frequently as you can. Every time you IPL, the system goes through a process that includes some housekeeping chores. For example, on each IPL, the library QRPLOBJ is cleared and excess spool storage is deleted. If you cannot IPL your system frequently, then you must be even more diligent in your manual housekeeping duties.

CLEANUP OPTIONS IN THE OPERATIONAL ASSISTANT

It is important to understand and use the Operational Assistant cleanup functions. Refer to Operational Assistant on page 83 for a discussion of the Operational Assistant functions and setup.

REORGANIZING PHYSICAL FILE MEMBERS WITH OFFICEVISION/400

Files that are accessed frequently for updates may, over the course of time, have deleted records. Although deleted, a record still occupies disk space until it is purged. Purging is performed when you reorganize the physical file member.

If you have OfficeVision/400 installed, several files require reorganization to purge deleted records. This aids performance and uses less disk space. Do this during times of low activity on a monthly basis. You can use the DSPFD (Display File Description) command to see which files have many deleted records. The Operational Assistant performs file reorganization during automatic cleanup. I recommend using this feature. If you do not intend to use the Operational Assistant for automatic cleanup, monitor the physical files for deleted records.

OfficeVision/400 files beginning with QAO* are candidates for reorganization. These are database files for documents, mail, and calendars. Refer to the *Planning for and Setting Up OfficeVision/400* manual.

If you don't reorganize the files to purge deleted records, the database fills up and you get messages to that effect. You are then given an option to add additional records. If you find that reorganization is required too frequently, consider:

- Educating users to delete more of their unnecessary files.
- Changing the maximum records allowed in the database file.
- Changing the increment value for adding records.

After running RGZPFM, immediately save any files being journaled and start a new journal receiver. Refer to the box note on page 109 for more information.

Try using the following CL programs to reorganize OfficeVision/400 physical files. You can modify this program to perform file reorganization on user-created files too.

CL Program to Reorganize OfficeVision Files

```
        PGM    /*  CL Program to Reorganize Office Vision Files */

               DCLF        FILE(QSYS/QAFDMBR)
               DSPFD       FILE(QUSRSYS/QAO*) TYPE (*MBR) +
                             OUTPUT(*OUTFILE) FILEATR(*PF) +
                             OUTFILE(QUSRSYS/QAOFILES)
               OVRDBF      FILE(QAFDMBR) TOFILE(QUSRSYS/QAOFILES)

        BEGIN: RCVF

               MONMSG      MSGID(CPF0864) EXEC(GOTO CMDLBL(STOP))
               IF          COND(&MBNDTR *EQ 0) THEN(GOTO +
                             CMDLBL(BEGIN))
               RGZPFM      FILE(&MBLIB/&MBFILE) MBR(&MBNAME)
               MONMSG      MSGID(CPF2981) EXEC(GOTO CMDLBL(BEGIN))
               GOTO        CMDLBL(BEGIN)

        STOP:  DLTF        FILE(QUSRSYS/QAOFILES)
               MONMSG      MSGID(CPF2105)

        ENDPGM
```

REORGANIZE DOCUMENT LIBRARY OBJECTS (RGZDLO)

The RGZDLO command is designed to minimize the size of documents and folders. Documents may contain unused storage after being edited, paginated, or browsed. This is useful when the document is undergoing revision, but if the document is not likely to be used for a long time, use the RGZDLO command to reduce disk usage. There is a good description and some examples of its use in your OfficeVision/400 manuals.

Reclaim Unused Spool Storage

Prior to V1R3, the system reclaimed unused spool storage every seven IPLs. Beginning with V1R3.0, that function has been disabled and customers must reclaim unused spool storage by using the system value QRCLSPLSTG, which controls when the system reclaims unused spool storage (see QRCLSPLSTG System Value under Allocation System Values on page 23) or by using the CL command RCLSPLSTG.

It might help to understand why unused spool storage exists. Every time you create a spool file, the system must have storage space available to place that spool file or it creates the storage space. Once the file is printed, the storage is no longer needed, but it can be reused for other spool files. This is fine if your system creates spool files at a relatively constant rate. But let's say you have created several very long or many small reports. Because you have created a larger requirement for storage space than exists on the system, the system goes out and creates the required space. Once you print the reports, the members are cleared but not deleted. Unfortunately, the system no longer needs all this space for the normal spooling operations, and you can't use the space for anything else. So, the unused members hang around until the time period specified in the system value QRCLSPLSTG is reached, or until you clear the space manually with the RCLSPLSTG command.

If you want to manually reclaim unused spool storage, then use the command RCLSPLSTG. I suggest the following procedure:

1. Delete unwanted spool files. Use the command WRKOUTQ to see all the OUTQs. Use option 5 to display the files in the output queues and use option 4 to delete the unwanted files.
2. Use the RCLSPLSTG to remove the unused members.

> RCLSPLSTG does not delete your unwanted spool files — only the unused members of spool storage.

If you allow the system to perform the Reclaim Spool Storage using the system value QRCLSPLSTG, the job to perform this task runs when the time limit is reached. There is some system overhead required to clear the members, but I cannot predict how much. I recommend allowing the system to perform the Reclaim Spool Storage and monitor to see how much overhead is involved. If you believe the system overhead is excessive, then plan to clear the members manually. If you decide to perform manual reclaim, then set the system value to *NOMAX (which disables it) and run the reclaim as part of your routine backup.

I do not believe there is much to be gained by running this procedure frequently. The whole purpose of allowing users this manual procedure is to provide a means of clearing these empty spool files on systems that seldom do an IPL (e.g., hospitals and hotels). (See Periodically IPL the System on page 131 for information regarding periodic IPLs.) Running RCLSPLSTG every two to four weeks is adequate.

> *The following discussion on journals applies to all journaling on the AS/400, but is specific to IBM-supplied journals. If you are journaling any files on your system, you can substitute your own journal names for the IBM journal names indicated here.*

Prior to V1R3, all journal maintenance was user-initiated. The Operational Assistant, a V1R3 enhancement, has a function that maintains the IBM-supplied system journals without user intervention. The exception is the security journal QAUDJRN. This journal **IS NOT** maintained by the Operational Assistant. If you use this journal, you must maintain it yourself. (Refer to Auditing Security Using System-Provided Journals on page 183.)

> *If you plan to use the Operational Assistant, do not attempt to maintain the IBM-supplied system journals yourself. You may run into conflicts. You should, however, continue to save all journals that may be a part of your backup strategy. The Operational Assistant does not save any journals, it only changes the receivers and deletes the receivers after they have aged a while. However, you can use the technique that follows to maintain user journals. Substitute the IBM system journal names with your own application's journal names.*

There are two kinds of objects in journaling:

- The Journal
- The Journal Receivers (hereafter called Receivers)

The data (record image) is stored in the Receivers (they "receive" the data). The administrative detail is kept in the Journal. This includes the name of the current (attached) Receiver and the status of the Receiver. The Receivers fill up with data, are saved onto tape, and are deleted off the system. The Journal provides a stable place to maintain administrative information.

The IBM-supplied journals that you need to consider are:

Journal Name	Library Name	Description
QACGJRN	QSYS	Keeps job accounting information. The Work Management book describes using this optional journal.
QAOSDIAJRN	QUSRSYS	Provides recovery for the document files and the distribution files. Used by Client Access/400 and OfficeVision/400.

Journal Name	Library Name	Description
QAUDJRN	QSYS	Keeps an audit record of security-relevant activity on the system. The Security - Reference book describes using this optional journal.
QCQJMJRN	QSVMSS	Provides an audit trail for Managed System Services/400.
QDSNX	QUSRSYS	Provides an audit trail for DSNX activity.
QLYJRN	QUSRSYS	Keeps a log of transactions made to Application Development Manager/400 datastore files. Used by the system if recovery is necessary. The *ADTS/400: Application Development Manager/400 User's Guide* provides more information about this journal.
QLYPRJLOG	QUSRSYS	Keeps the project logs for the Application Development Manager/400 licensed program. Used by the system if recovery is necessary. The *ADTS/400: Application Development Manager/400 User's Guide* provides more information about this journal.
QLZALOG	QUSRSYS	Used by the licensed management program to log requests that exceed the usage limit of a license.
QPFRADJ	QSYS	Keeps a log of dynamic performance tuning information. The *AS/400 Work Management* manual describes using this optional journal.
QSNADS	QUSRSYS	Provides an audit trail for SNADS activity.
QSNMP	QUSRSYS	Provides an audit trail for network management information. The Network and Systems Management book describes using this journal.
QSXJRN	QUSRSYS	Provides a log of the activity that occurs in the database files for service-related activity. The information in this journal should be kept for 30 days.
QZMF	QUSRSYS	Provides an audit trail for the mail server framework.

There are a few other journals — refer to the *AS/400 System Operation* manual for more details.

The QACGJRN is outside the scope of this book. It exists only if a package is using job accounting and starts job accounting journaling. In this situation, that programmer or package has the responsibility to manage the QACGJRN journal, but you make sure it is managed.

The Operational Assistant (if you decide to use the Operational Assistant) manages most of the journals, except QAUDJRN.

The Receivers have the same name structure as the Journals with four digits appended to the end. These digits are numbered sequentially, starting with 0001.

As supplied by the system, the Receivers have a threshold size of *NONE, which means they grow in size until someone manually "detaches" the Receiver and "attaches" a new one. The old receiver may then be saved and deleted to free up space. Another aspect to consider is that, with a threshold value of *NONE, no indicator is ever sent stating that the Receiver has reached the threshold size. Therefore, you may wish to create a new Receiver with a threshold size so the system operator knows if the Receiver is getting too large. Refer to Appendix F: Automated Journal Management on page 339 for further discussion. To manage Receivers:

1. Create a new Receiver.
2. Detach the previous Receiver.
3. Attach the new Receiver.
4. Save the detached Receiver.
5. Delete the saved Receiver as required to free up disk space.

Steps 1, 2, and 3 are accomplished with the CHGJRN command. This command:

*   Creates a new Receiver with the same name as the current attached Receiver plus 1.
*   Detaches the current Receiver
*   Attaches the new Receiver.

This is accomplished without affecting any jobs currently running on the system other than to cause a few seconds of delay in some users' response time. The CHGJRN command you need are:

```
CHGJRN JRN(lib_name/journal_name) JRNRCV(*GEN)
```

Step 4 (Save the detached Receiver) could be accomplished as part of the periodic backup using the SAVLIB command or using the SAVOBJ command. Remember that you must save library QUSRSYS.

Step 5 (Delete the saved Receiver as required to free up disk space) could be accomplished with the DLTJRNRCV command. If this procedure is not put into a CL program, a more user-friendly way to handle the deletes is to use the Work Journal Attributes command (WRKJRNA):

```
WRKJRNA JRN(lib_name/journal_name)
```

The first screen that is displayed shows which Receiver is attached. Use F15 to display all the receivers on the system for that journal, and whether they are attached. On that F15 display, use option 4 to delete specific Receivers. This process is simple and intuitive enough for most system operators to use. The system does not allow an attached Receiver to be deleted and warns you if it has not been saved.

For a discussion on how to automate journal management and a sample CL program, refer to Appendix E of the Redbook, **AS/400 Office Application Programming Interfaces**. This program requires modification to work properly. Also refer to Appendix F: Automated Journal Management on page 339 for a discussion on automated journal management and a sample CL program that has been tested.

If you have not been doing any housekeeping of journals and receivers, the first step is to understand the current situation. You can do this with the following command:

```
DSPOBJD OBJ(QUSRSYS/*ALL) OBJTYPE(*JRNRCV)
```

This lists the names of the Receivers and their sizes so you can see the impact on the disk space. You can display each one to see if it has been backed up. If it has, consider deleting it, depending on how old it is or other considerations unique to your system. Consider doing a CHGJRN for all four journals (see above), then a SAVLIB(QUSRSYS), and then deleting all old Receivers. Refer to the **AS/400 Backup and Recovery — Basic** manual for some guidelines.

Do not run DLTJRN (Delete Journal) on any IBM-supplied journals such as the Office Journal. It causes Office to stop working because commitment control is programmed into the product and it requires journaling. Refer to the **Planning for and Setting Up OfficeVision/400** manual.

> *Journals and the related physical files must be synchronized in order for the journal to work. If not "in sync," the system operator is alerted at IPL time. After an IPL, the system operator should check the message queue for this message. One way that the physical file goes out of sync with the journal is when RGZPFM is run on that file. This purges "deleted" records; therefore, the relative record index in the file does not match the journal. The only way to correct this is to save the file immediately and start a new Receiver.*

Job Logs

If you have created an output queue to which all job logs are sent, you need to control how many spool files (logs) you accumulate there (refer to Routing for Job Logs, Program and Service Dumps on page 36). Clear the job logs out of the output queue periodically, probably weekly. The most efficient way to do this is with the CLROUTQ (Clear Output Queue) command. One problem with this command is that it clears all job logs from the named output queue, so do not use this command if there is a job log that you need to save because of an unresolved problem. Print or move any logs that you need to keep to another queue and then run CLROUTQ.

```
WRKOUTQ OUTQ(JOBLOGQ)
```

Change the spooled file with option 2. Either print or move the file to another output queue.

```
CLROUTQ OUTQ(JOBLOGQ)
```

> *If the output queue is large, it might take some time to clear it.*

You can also use the Operational Assistant to maintain your job logs and job log output queues. (Refer to Operational Assistant on page 83 for additional information.) The output queues QUSRSYS/QEZJOBLOG and QUSRSYS/QEZDEBUG are created and the system printer files are changed the first time you start the Operational Assistant. Output is placed into these queues even if you turn off the automatic cleanup of the Operational Assistant.

Refer to Appendix E: AS/400 Job Logs and Output Queue Utility on page 331 for a discussion and program to manage job log output queues.

HISTORY LOGS

As with journals and job logs, history logs can be managed using the Operational Assistant. (Refer to Operational Assistant on page 83.) However, this manual method is useful when developing methods to manage the logs yourself — and for general information, if you understand what is going on here, you are better armed for good system administration.

History logs can accumulate at a rapid rate and occupy a large amount of disk space. Users should delete old history (QHST) logs at least monthly. You can see the current situation by entering the command:

```
WRKF FILE(QSYS/QHST*)
```

This shows all the history log files. Only the last one is active. When you run the DSPLOG command, the system accesses any of the files still on the system to satisfy your request. Thus, if you want to see the history for several days or weeks ago, you need to leave the appropriate log files on the system. When you run the WRKF command, the description field contains the date and time each file was created and closed, so you can decide which ones to delete. These files are in the QSYS library. You probably backup QSYS at least monthly, so right after that backup is a good time to delete some of the files.

The dates and times in the description fields of the WRKF command are not very readable because they run together. The format is:

```
OYYMMDDHHMMSSOYYMMDDHHMMSS
```

The beginning date and time are first, followed by the ending date and time.

You might also want to use the command DLTQHST — which is part of QUSRTOOL. This command provides a simple method to clean up the QHST logs. The parameter is DAYS, which is the number of days to keep the QHST logs; the default is 5. If you are not familiar with QUSRTOOLs, refer to QUSRTOOL Library on page 307.

MESSAGE QUEUES

The AS/400 uses message queues to communicate with users and programs running on the system.

User Message Queues

Message queues generally are not a problem. However, if the system operator fails to clear the QSYSOPR message queue, it can get very large. Also, if users are in the habit of sending broadcast messages (e.g., to tell other users to get off the system), and users are not trained to clear old messages, their message queues become large. Perform a DSPOBJD to see the sizes of message queues. They should be about 8700 bytes apiece, except for QSYSOPR. If other queues are large, you need to educate your users to delete their messages. The messages can be cleared out of the queue using F13 while displaying messages.

Generally, the message queues are in either the QSYS or QUSRSYS libraries. You can display the sizes of these queues with the following two commands:

```
DSPOBJD OBJ(QSYS/*ALL) OBJTYPE(*MSGQ)
DSPOBJD OBJ(QUSRSYS/*ALL) OBJTYPE(*MSGQ)
```

Refer to Operational Assistant on page 83 for information on using the Operational Assistant to maintain message queues.

System Operator Message Queues

The system operator message queue is your general operations message queue. If errors occur anywhere on your system, they are generally recorded here. There can be a vast number of messages in this message queue, so it is a good idea to clear out these messages occasionally. This keeps storage requirements down and makes the logging of messages more efficient. The best way to do this is to use the DSPMSG command and clear them as appropriate.

You can also use the function keys to clear all, or only the unanswered, messages. You can also use the following CL command to clear all except the unanswered messages:

```
CLRMSGQ MSG(QSYSOPR) CLEAR(*KEEPUNANS)
```

PROBLEM LOGS

Once again, you need to keep in mind that the Operational Assistant keeps your problem logs cleaned up now, so the following program is not necessary. But, many system administrators prefer to do things for themselves rather than control the system automatically, so this CL program may be helpful. Refer to Operational Assistant on page 83.

Problems detected by the AS/400 System are recorded in the problem log. This log becomes large if not managed. Review the problem log and clear out problems that you don't need to save. The AS/400 does not allow you to clear any problem less than the value specified by the System Value QPRBHLDITV. The shipped value for QPRBHLDITV is 30 days. You may want to run the DLTPRB command every now and then.

```
DLTPRB STATUS(*ALL) DAYS(30)
```

After deleting old problems, purge the deleted records from the database files to free up disk space by running the Reorganize Physical File Member command (RGZPFM). There are actually eight underlying physical files that may need to be reorganized. Consider the following CL program.

CL Program to Reorganize Problem Log Files

```
RGZPRBLOG:      PGM
        MONMSG MSGID(CPF2981) /*File not reorganized /
        MONMSG MSGID(CPF2995) /* No member or data to
reorg */
/* Delete all problem records older than 30 days */
        DLTPRB STATUS(*ALL) DAYS(30)
/* Reorganize files to remove deleted records */
        RGZPFM FILE(QUSRSYS/QASXCALL)
        RGZPFM FILE(QUSRSYS/QASXFRU)
        RGZPFM FILE(QUSRSYS/QASXNOTE)
        RGZPFM FILE(QUSRSYS/QASXPROB)
        RGZPFM FILE(QUSRSYS/QASXPTF)
        RGZPFM FILE(QUSRSYS/QASXSYMP)
        RGZPFM FILE(QUSRSYS/QASXEVT)
        RGZPFM FILE(QUSRSYS/QASXDTA)
        RETURN
        ENDPGM
```

ALERT LOG ENTRIES

Monitor and keep your alert entries cleaned up. The WRKALR command and option 4 next to an alert entry delete the specific alert. Reorganize Physical File Member (RGZPFM) reduces the amount of space that the alert physical file QAALERT takes up. Clear Physical File Member (CLRPFM) deletes all the alerts in the alert physical file. As with other logs, alerts can be managed using the Operational Assistant.

LIMITING INDIVIDUAL USER STORAGE

The default maximum storage space that any user can use is *NOMAX (no maximum). You may want to limit the amount of space for each user. How do you decide on limits? (More for your friends and less for your enemies.) Maybe you want to start at 500MB per user. The command to do this is:

```
CHGUSRPRF  USRPRF(name)  MAXSTG(500000)
```

(The value for MAXSTG is expressed in kilobytes, so 500,000KB is 500MB.)

DELETING OLD OR OBSOLETE DOCUMENTS LIBRARY OBJECTS

If you use OfficeVision/400 on your system, it is a good idea to enforce a policy of deleting documents when they become old or obsolete. Of course, this requires the cooperation of the users, but there are various methods you can employ to help enforce rules for keeping documents on your system. Review the various OfficeVision/400 manuals for help in this area. Also, see Archiving Documents on page 293 for additional information.

DELETING UNUSED OBJECTS

This subsection describes some of the objects that may be unused on your system. You must determine the relevancy for keeping them around. If you do not use or need them, then you can recover some disk space by deleting them. Make sure you save them first.

PTF Save Files

The PTF application process may produce save files on disk, depending on how you acquire the PTFs. After the PTFs are loaded, there is no need to keep these save files. The Operational Assistant automatically cleans up old save files (refer to Operational Assistant on page 83), but you can manage these PTF save files manually:

The Delete Program Temporary Fix (DLTPTF) command can be used to delete program temporary fix (PTF) save files, their associated cover letters, and the records of PTFs that have been ordered. The syntax for the command is:

```
DLTPTF PTF(ptf_number) LICPGM(program_number)
```

You can also use the Work with File (WRKF) command. PTF save files can be identified as:

Pxxxyyyy and Qxxxyyyy   where *xxx* is alphanumeric and *yyyy* is numeric.

Use one of the following commands:

```
WRKF FILE(QGPL/P*) FILEATR(SAVF)
```

    — or —

```
WRKF FILE(*LIBL/Q*) FILEATR(SAVF)
```

Generally the files have the following naming convention and an attribute of SAVF:

Paannnnn

    — or —

Qaannnnn   where *aannnnn* is the PTF designation (e.g., SF04718).

Use option 4 to delete the files you no longer need.

Student Enrollment Records

Another potential area to cleanup is unused student enrollment records. As the education administrator, you can perform this cleanup by entering the command STREDU and deleting student's enrollment.

Damaged Objects

Sometimes objects become damaged for reasons beyond our control. For example, users may turn off their terminal while in an active session, or your system may experience a power spike.

Perform a RCLSTG (Reclaim Storage) command once in a while, BUT BE CAREFUL. This command may run for a long time. It is best to perform a RCLSTG over a weekend. Refer to Reclaiming Storage (RCLSTG) on page 73 for additional information. After running RCLSTG, check the library QRCL. You need to analyze any objects found there, but, generally, you can delete them.

Delete Unnecessary Program Source Files

Program source files can take up unnecessary storage space on the AS/400. After you save these source files, consider deleting them from the system to help minimize storage use.

Library QUSRTOOL

If you do not need the library QUSRTOOL, then you may want to consider deleting it. Save it first, but be careful here. Sometimes there are applications that expect a particular tool in this library. If, after you delete this library, you suddenly discover that an object is missing, it may be in this library.

Libraries for Previous-Release Support

IBM includes libraries where objects are stored to allow software developers to compile programs for previous-release support. If you are not a programming site that requires this level of support, you can delete these libraries. Make sure you save the libraries before deleting them.

Look for libraries that have the format:

QSYSVxRyMz   where: x = Version number.
                       y = Release number.
                       z = Modification number of previous release(s).

You can search for these libraries by entering the command:

    WRKLIB LIB(QSYSV*)

Migration Aid

Library QMGU and other library names that start with QMGU are the migration aid utility programs. When the migration is complete and verified, you can delete these libraries. You can also delete migration objects from a S/36 such as

---

source files QS36LOD and Q36DDSSRC, and the DFU source members from the QS36SRC files. Generally, they are found in your application program libraries.

OfficeVision/400 Language Dictionaries

The OfficeVision/400 Language Dictionaries object installs all the language support. Review the list in the GO LICPGM menu and delete languages you do not need.

Remove Optional Parts of OS/400 and Client Access/400

Depending on your business needs, you may be able to delete some optional parts of the Operating System and Client Access that you do not use.

Before you delete any parts of IBM Licensed Program Products, you should make sure that you have saved everything. To save Licensed Program Products, perform the following:

1. Prepare enough tapes for the save operation.
2. Enter the command GO LICPGM, and take option 13 from the menu.
3. Select each Licensed Program Product you want to save.

You can restore any of the Licensed Program Products or optional parts that were deleted from these tapes by using the GO LICPGM command and taking option 11.

To delete unneeded optional parts, use GO LICPGM and take option 12. Then select the programs and optional parts you want to delete. You will only see the Licensed Program Products and optional parts that are installed on your system.

Use the Licensed Program Product Table and the Comment Key Table to help determine which programs or optional parts you want to remove. If you have products that are not in the table, you may also be able to remove some of the optional parts in those programs too. Just make sure that you have saved everything first.

Key(s)	Licensed Program and Optional Part Version 3, Release 1	Optional Part Number	Approx. Size (MB)
a	5763-SS1 OS/400		
q	OS/400 On-line Information (Help Text)	2	9.5 to 27.0
c	OS/400 S/36 and S/38 Migration	4	4.5 to 6.0
d	OS/400 S/36 and S/38 Environment	5, 6	2.0 to 9.0

Key(s)	Licensed Program and Optional Part Version 3, Release 1	Optional Part Number	Approx. Size (MB)
e	OS/400 Example Tools Library	7	10.0 to 35.5
f	OS/400 AFP Compatibility Fonts	8	6.5
g	OS/400 *PRV CL Compiler Support	9	9.9
c	OS/400 S/36 Migration Assistant	11	1.0
b, j	OS/400 Host Servers	12	4.7 to 7.0
e	OS/400 Openness Includes	13`	21.8
N/A	OS/400 GDDM	14	0.6
h	OS/400 Common Programming APIs Toolkit	15	0.6 to 1.2
i	OS/400 Ultimedia System Facilities	16	2.2 to 4.5
h	OS/400 Print Services Facility/400	17	1.0
h	OS/400 Media and Storage Extensions	18	0.1
j	5763-XA1 Client Access/400 Family - Base	Base	0.2
p	Client Access/400 - PC Tools Folder	1	7.8
k, l	5763-XB1 Client Access/400 for DOS with Extended Memory	Base	0.1 to 0.2
m	Client Access/400 - Extended DOS SBCS or DBCS	1 or 2	9.6 to 14.0
m	Client Access/400 - Extended DOS RUMBA SBCS or DBCS	3 or 4	5.0
i	Client Access/400 - Ultimedia Facilities	5	3.5
k, l	5763-XC1 Client Access/400 for Windows 3.1	Base	0.1 to 0.2
m	Client Access/400 - Windows 3.1 SBCS or DBCS	1 or 2	5.9 to 20.0
m, n	Client Access/400 - Windows 3.1 RUMBA SBCS or DBCS	3 or 4	3.1 to 5.5

Key(s)	Licensed Program and Optional Part Version 3, Release 1	Optional Part Number	Approx. Size (MB)
n	Client Access/400 - Windows 3.1 PC5250	5	7.4 to 10.0
o	Client Access/400 - Graphic Ops for Windows	6	0.1 to 11.0
i	Client Access/400 - Ultimedia Facilities	7	0.1 to 4.3
k, l	5763-XF1 Client Access/400 for OS/2	Base	0.1 to 0.2
m	Client Access/400 - OS/2 SBCS or DBCS	1 or 2	8.9 to 10.0
m	Client Access/400 - OS/2 RUMBA SBCS or DBCS	3 or 4	4.5 to 4.7
	Client Access/400 - OS/2 Communications Manager	5	5.5
o	Client Access/400 - Graphic Ops. for OS/2	6	14.1
i	Client Access/400 - Ultimedia Facilities for OS/2	7	7.4
k, l	5763-XG1 Client Access/400 Optimized for OS/2	Base	50.0
n	Client Access/400 - RUMBA Optimized for OS/2	1	7.0
n	Client Access/400 - PC5250 Optimized for OS/2	2	8.5
o	Client Access/400 - Graphic Ops for OS/2	3	14.0
i	Client Access/400 - Ultimedia Facilities	4	5.0
k, l	5763-XL1 Client Access/400 for DOS	Base	0.1 to 0.2
m	Client Access/400 - DOS SBCS or DBCS	1 or 2	6.3 to 10.0

Comment Key

a. You cannot delete the entire OS/400 Operating System. You can only delete optional parts.

b. Recommend that you **DO NOT** delete this part.

c. Delete this optional part if you are not migrating from an S/36 or S/36 to this AS/400, or you have finished migrating.

d. Delete this optional part if you are only running AS/400 applications.

e. This optional part is only needed by software developers.

f. **DO NOT** delete this optional part if you are using Print Services Facility/400. See Optional Part Number 17 in this table.

g. Delete this part if you do not need to compile CL programs destined for a previous-release system.

h. This option is ordered separately.

i. **DO NOT** delete this part if you have applications using the Ultimedia System Facilities.

j. **DO NOT** delete if you are using Client Access/400 products.

k. If you are not using this specific client (DOS, DOS with Extended Memory, Windows 3.1, or OS/2), you can delete the complete program for that client.

l. If you are using this specific client, **DO NOT** delete the base option.

m. If your system has the optional parts for both SBCS (Single-Byte Character Set) and DBCS (Double-Byte Character Set) installed, you may, depending on your national language needs, delete the optional part you are not using. Note that DBCS is generally used for Asian languages.

n. There are two 5250 emulators used in V3R1 (RUMBA and PC5250). You can delete the one you are not using.

o. Do not delete this optional part if you require the graphical user interface for system operations.

p. This optional part contains sample programs, migration tools, and debug tools. You should delete this optional part only after you have downloaded any tools used in your installation.

q. If you delete this optional part, you must first use the CHGSYSLIBL system command to remove QHLPSYS from the system library list.

SYSTEM MANAGEMENT

I wish to express my thanks to Dave Prescott for helping me to better understand system management. Good system management techniques are vital to the business. New users in particular, or those coming from a small environment, have not had experience with comprehensive system management concepts. I hope this section introduces newer users to the concept and help more experienced users by refreshing their memories.

There are many good sources to help you with system management. Most of my experience has been with IBM, and I have found that there is wealth of documentation and classes available to help you with this subject. What I hope to accomplish here is to emphasize the importance of documentation and how it applies to good management of any computer system.

DOCUMENTING YOUR SYSTEM

The following commands are useful to help you document your system. Become familiar with the commands and their use. Print hard copies of your system information, such as device descriptions and configurations, to keep in your System Log Book (refer to System Log Book on page 121).

Prime Option Menu From any display with a sign-on screen, press the Alt and Test keys simultaneously to get to the Prime Option Menu (on older 5250 devices, Cmd and the left arrow keys simultaneously). Take option 3 to get a list of all devices attached to the controller, complete with Controller Number, Port Number, Device Address, Logical ID, and Device Description — all this without even signing on.

WRKHDWPRD This command allows you to print the rack configuration. Run this and place the output in the log book each time your rack configuration changes. Also, copy the rack configuration each time the configuration is changed. After copying the rack configuration, attempt to run the REPLACE option. This way, you know immediately if your new copy is "REPLACE-able." If the REPLACE attempt results in a message about incompatibility between the file being copied and the system itself, **DO NOT** take the override. Instead, contact your CE to find out why it does not allow you to REPLACE. Usually, there is some information missing. Refer to Confirm Delivery on page 8.

WRKHDWRSC	This command, Work with Hardware Resource, displays and allows you to manage the various configuration objects. Enter the command and press F4 to prompt. One really nice feature of this command is that you can display all the communication resources (e.g., communication lines) and all the object descriptions (e.g., line descriptions) that use these resources. You can see at a glance the resources that do not have line descriptions configured for them and if any resources have multiple line descriptions. Refer to Using the WRKHDWRSC Command on page 167.
DSPLCLHDW	Allows you to display or print all the local hardware resources — and in the order in which they are attached (e.g., local devices are listed under the controller to which they are attached).
PRTDEVADR	This command prints a table of all devices attached to any local work station controller. You should have a listing of each controller on the system in your log book.
WRKLIND	Allows you to print out a listing of each line description. Keep a copy of each in the log book.
WRKCTLD	Same as WRKLIND.
WRKDEVD	Same as WRKLIND.
DSPSFWRSC	The Display Software Resources command allows you to display or print a complete list of all IBM Licensed Programs installed on your system.
RTVCFGSRC	This command creates a CL source file of various configuration objects such as line and controller descriptions. Refer to Saving Configuration Objects on page 58.
WRKSYSVAL	If you enter the command: `WRKSYSVAL SYSVAL(*ALL) OUTPUT(*PRINT)` you get a printed output of all system values with a description of each, the default values, and the current values.

Include the following in your system documentation:
- Cabling diagrams for your building
- Network configuration
- PTF status

- Changes to IBM-supplied objects
- Security topics
- Electronic Customer Support
- System Analysis report
- Backup and Recovery Plan

The remainder of this section provides tips on how to collect this information and how to manage it.

SYSTEM LOG BOOK

With accurate system documentation, users have — in a single source — the information they need to manage a computer system. Information such as hardware and software configurations, security, backup, and housekeeping tasks associated with the AS/400 should be documented. Consider keeping a 3-ring notebook (call it your log book) with the system. Label section tabs as follows:

Change Log
PTFs, new releases, changes to software applications.

Problem Log
Problem determination and resolution procedures, dates and resolutions of system problems.

System Configuration
Hardware and software installed, cable diagrams, security information.

Cabling Plan
You should have schematics and complete labeling information for all your cables and networks. This includes phone numbers, office numbers, or any other means of identifying location of all devices.

Backup Plan
Keep a plan of your backup and recovery plan in your log book. The backup plan includes instructions as well as routine backups performed.

Recovery Plan
Procedures for disaster recovery, power failure, storage of backup tapes.

Maintenance Calendar
Backup and housekeeping procedures and routine schedules, routine hardware maintenance (e.g., cleaning tape heads).

Support Information
IBM Customer Number (sometimes called ACCESS CODE), Customer and IBM Support Personnel contact information, Level 1 and Level 2 Software Support phone number, service information.

You are not limited to these subjects — feel free to add any sections you like. The important thing to remember is that establishing good, disciplined systems management procedures is important to the general management of I/S departmental resources. Consider this a mandatory requirement.

LICENSED INTERNAL CODE (LIC)

IBM's definition of the Licensed Internal Code (LIC) is:

> "The layered architecture below the machine interface (MI) and above the machine, consisting of the model-independent and the model-unique Licensed Internal Code. The Licensed Internal Code is a proprietary system design that carries out many functions including, but not limited to, storage management, pointers and addressing, program management functions, exception and event management, data functions, I/O managers, and security."

The system maintains two copies of the LIC. One copy is considered a permanent copy and is referred to as the *A side.* The other copy is a duplicate of the permanent copy and includes any PTFs that have been applied temporarily. This copy is referred to as the *B side.* When the system is running, it uses the copy you select prior to the IPL. Unless you change this, the same copy (A side or B side) is used each time an IPL occurs. To change the copy used when you IPL, use the control panel buttons to select either A or B. As an alternative, select either A or B when you use the CL command PWRDWNSYS (Power Down System). For example, if want to perform an immediate IPL and use the A side (permanent copy) of the LIC, then issue the command:

```
PWRDWNSYS OPTION(*IMMED) RESTART(*YES) IPLSRC(A)
```

> The default IPL Source for this command is **IPLSRC(*PANEL)**, which uses the LIC specified in the control panel window.

Normally, the AS/400 operates using the temporary copy, or B side, of the LIC. There are a few reasons to use the A side, such as recovering from a damaged PTF or performing special system tasks. It is not likely that, in your day-to-day operations, you will have reason to use the A side.

PTF MANAGEMENT

Program temporary fixes are created in response to problems that occur with the AS/400 and the Licensed Programs. IBM creates the PTFs — but it is the user's responsibility to obtain and apply them to their system.

Develop a good PTF management scheme for each AS/400 system. Acquaint yourself with the *AS/400 System Operation* manual. Use the following recommendations for setting up a PTF management policy:

- In a stable environment, consider installing the most recent cumulative PTF package every 3 to 4 months.

- Consider installing the most recent cumulative PTF package before making major changes to your system (hardware or software).

- If you require an excessive number of Corrective Service fixes, consider installing cumulative PTF packages more frequently.

I recommend that you read through the *System Startup and Problem Handling* manual for a more complete discussion of PTFs.

Temporary Versus Permanent PTFs

PTFs can be applied to an IBM program on either a temporary or a permanent basis. If applied temporarily, a copy of the old version of the object being changed is saved. If the PTF is being applied permanently, then the old version of the object is destroyed. Thus, permanently applied PTFs cannot be removed.

Delayed Versus Immediate PTFs

The PTF cover letter indicates immediate or delayed application. Some system functions are active whenever the system is active. Examples of this are Licensed Internal Code objects and many of the Operating System objectives. Any PTFs that need to be applied to these functions must be delayed until the next time the system is started. If you are applying PTFs to objects that are not in use whenever the system is active, then you may be able to apply the PTFs immediately. Examples are Client Access/400 objects and OfficeVision/400 objects. Make sure that no one is using the object.

Delayed PTFs must be identified and marked for application at the next unattended IPL. You can mark all PTFs (immediate and delayed) for application during an unattended IPL by issuing the command APYPTF prior to the IPL. Refer to Applying PTFs During an Unattended IPL on page 124 for additional information. For an explanation of the types of IPLs, refer to Types of IPLs on page 132.

If you perform an attended IPL (sometimes called a manual IPL), the Work with PTFs display is used to apply PTFs at system start. Some IPLs may take longer than others when PTFs are being applied. More information on applying PTFs is provided in the *AS/400 System Operation* manual.

Cumulative Versus Individual PTFs

Individual PTFs created in response to particular problems are gathered regularly into "cumulative packages" for mass distribution. These packages are recorded on tape and are available to customers on request through the Software Support Hotline or ECS. The tapes are distributed by mail, and, as of this writing, there is no charge for distribution. Individual PTFs can be ordered through the Software

Support hotline or ECS. If ordered from the Software Support hotline, the PTF is delivered by mail. If ordered from ECS, the PTF(s) is distributed electronically directly to the AS/400, if it's not too large; otherwise, distribution is by mail.

Displaying Cumulative PTF Level

To display the cumulative PTF level on your system, enter the following command:

```
DSPPTF LICPGM(5738SS1)
```

The cumulative PTFs appear at the beginning of the list and are identified as:

Tcyyddd   where: *yy* is the year.
                   ddd is the Julian date.

Applying PTFs During an Unattended IPL

After loading the cumulative PTF package (you can do this while the system is up and running), you can specify that you wish to perform an automatic IPL. If you do this, immediately after loading the PTF from the tape, the system does an IPL and all the PTFs that were loaded are applied. This is fine during a time of the day that you can afford to do so.

An alternative is to apply the PTFs during a scheduled, unattended IPL. (For an explanation of IPL types, refer to Types of IPLs on page 132.) This can be unattended and scheduled during a time of the day (e.g., nighttime or weekend) when you do not need to be in the office. If this is your choice, **DO NOT** specify an automatic IPL after loading the PTF package. I recommend the following steps:

1. To mark all PTFs to be applied during an unattended IPL, type the following command on any command line and press the Enter key:

```
APYPTF LICPGM(*ALL) SELECT(*ALL) APY(*TEMP) +
    DELAYED(*YES) IPLAPY(*YES)
```

2. When you are ready to perform the IPL, type the following command and press the Enter key:

```
PWRDWNSYS *IMMED RESTART(*YES) IPLSRC(B)
```

> *You cannot use the Power On and Off Tasks (POWER) menu to apply a PTF during an unattended IPL. The system will not run the appropriate PWRDWNSYS command. You must specify PWRDWNSYS RESTART(*YES) IPLSRC(B) to perform an IPL on the system.*

PTF Information

The following table lists the general types of PTFs that are available and the associated PTF numbers.

PTF Information	Description
Specific PTFs and cover letters PTF Number nnnnnnn	PTFs are issued for all licensed programs and Licensed Internal Code. Each PTF has its own unique identifying number. If you order an individual PTF electronically, and the file is too large for electronic transmission, then it will be delivered on magnetic tape.
PTF cover letter only	Issue the following command to receive a PTF cover letter only: SNDPTFORD nnnnnnn **(1)** PTFPART(*CVRLTR)
PTF cross-reference summary list V2R2M0 to V3R1M0 SF97062 V2R3M0 to V3R1M0 SF97071 V3R0M5 to V3R1M0 SF97080	Itemizes PTFs from an earlier release that are included in the current release. Use this list to make sure you order any PTFs for the new release that you had at the previous release. These PTFs will not have the same number, but they correct the same problems.
Cumulative PTF packages SF99vrm **(2)**	Cumulative PTF packages contain PTFs that affect the general system population. If a PTF provides a change for a limited set of users or requires special handling, it may not be included in the package. The entire cumulative PTF package should be installed after you first load or reload the operating system. Cumulative PTF packages can be ordered electronically or by telephone and are always sent by mail on a tape.
Preventive Service Planning (PSP) information for licensed programs SF98vrm **(2)**	This report provides information about major problems and information you need to determine if a PTF applies to your system and application. Order this report about every two weeks. In particular, review the report for any HIPER (High-Impact Pervasive) PTFs. If any applicable HIPER PTFs are listed that you have not installed, order the PTF(s) and apply at your earliest opportunity. HIPER PTFs fix the following problems: • Abnormal system termination • Data integrity problems • Work station hangs • DASD error handling

PTF Information	Description
PSP information for Licensed Internal Code MF98vrm **(2)**	Similar to the PSP information for licensed programs.
PTF summary listing SF97vrm **(2)**	This listing contains every PTF created for each particular release of software. It has the PTF number, the cumulative package ID (if it has been included in a cumulative package), a brief description, and a note indicating that it has been replaced by a later PTF (if applicable). Use this report to compare PTFs applied to your system and PTFs available on the latest cumulative package.
Informational PTFs II07641 **(3)**	This PTF contains a list of all available informational PTFs. For example, information on configuring Client Access/400 with Microsoft Windows. IBM tends to keep these up to date from release to release.

Notes:

(1) *nnnnnnn* is the PTF identifying number.

(2) *v* is the Version, *r* is the Release, and *m* is the Modification level of the system. For version 3, Release 1, this is **310**.

(3) Informational PTFs are not generally version or release dependent. You must read the PTF cover letter to determine applicability to your environment.

To order any PTF, issue the command SNDPTFORD, followed by the PTF number. For example, to order the latest cumulative PTF package for Version 3, Release 1, issue the command:

```
SNDPTFORD SF99310
```

Working with PTFs

You can work with PTFs from the PTF menu. Options are available to display, order, load, apply, and so forth. Enter one of these commands:

```
GO CMDPTF
```

— or —

```
GO PTF
```

You can also get the PTF menu from the Operational Assistant.

Loading Only the HIPER PTFs

Use the command **LODHIPER** to load only the HIPER PTFs on a cumulative PTF package. To use LODHIPER, follow the installation instructions included with the cumulative PTF package.

PTF Identification

PTFs are identified with two alpha characters followed by five numerals. This identifies all PTFs, and is used to identify and order the summary listing, preventive planning report, and cumulative packages:

SFnnvrm   *where*: if *nn* = 97, PTF summary listing.
                                   If *nn* = 98, PTF preventive service planning report.
                                   if *nn* = 99, PTF cumulative package.
                                   v = Version.
                                   r = Release.
                                   m = Modification.

For example, if you want the PTF summary listing for Version 3, Release 1, Modification 0, the identifier is SF97310. If you want the latest PTF cumulative package, the identifier is SF99310.

Viewing and Printing PTF Cover Letters

You can print the cover letter of any PTF by issuing the following command:

```
DSPPTF LICPGM(xxxxxxx) SELECT(yyyyyyy) COVERONLY(*YES)
    OUTPUT(*PRINT)
```

where: *xxxxxx* is the licensed program number

— and —

yyyyyy is the PTF identification number.

You can also DSPPTF command and select options to view or print PTF cover letters from the PTF status list. Enter the command:

```
DSPPTF LICPGM(program_number)
```

For example, if you use 57633SS1 for the program number, you would get a display similar to the following:

```
                              Display PTF Status
                                                      System:   APACHE
   Product ID . . . . . . . :   5763SS1
   IPL source . . . . . . :   ##MACH#B
   Release . . . . . . . . :   V3R1M0


   Type options, press Enter.
     5=Display PTF details   6=Print cover letter   8=Display cover letter


       PTF                                          IPL
   Opt ID      Status                               action
    _  TA94350 Superseded                           None
    _  TA94340 Superseded                           None
    _  TA94329 Superseded                           None
    _  TA94318 Superseded                           None
    _  TA94308 Superseded                           None
    _  TA94297 Superseded                           None
    _  SF98310 Cover letter only                    None
    _  SF22927 Save file only                       None
    _  SF22626 Temporarily applied                  None
                                                            More...
   F3=Exit   F11=Display alternate view   F12=Cancel
```

Then use option 6 to print the cover letter.

When individual PTFs are received from ECS, the PTF itself is placed in the QGPL library and the PTF cover letter is placed in a member of physical file QGPL/QAPZCOVER. There is a message in the job log showing the name of the member.

To display the cover letter of a PTF received electronically, enter the command:

```
DSPPFM FILE(QGPL/QAPZCOVER) MBR(Qnnnnnnnxx)
```

where: *nnnnnn* is the PTF number.
xx is the last two digits of the language code. (For cover letters in English, the language code does not appear.)

To print the cover letter of a PTF received electronically, enter the command:

```
CPYF FROMFILE(QGPL/QAPZCOVER) TOFILE(QGPL/QPRINT) FROMMBR(Qnnnnnnnxx)
```

*(Then do a WRKSPLF and look for a file name QPRINT in the **File** column. This is the cover letter.)*

If you have AS/400 Application Programming Development Manager installed on your AS/400, you can select from a list of PTF cover letters (members of the QAPZCOVER file) by entering:

```
WRKMBRPDM FILE(QGPL/QAPZCOVER)
```

You are presented with a display similar to the following screen.

```
                      Work with Members Using PDM              APACHE

File . . . . .   QAPZCOVER
  Library . . . .    QGPL                    Position to . . . . .

Type options, press Enter.
  3=Copy      4=Delete       5=Display  7=Rename    8=Display description
  9=Save     13=Change text  18=Change using DFU    25=Find string ...

Opt  Member     Date       Text
  _  QMF07122   07/27/94    PTF 5763999-MF07122 V3R0M5
  _  QMF07168   07/27/94    PTF 5763999-MF07168 V3R0M5
  _  QMF07174   07/27/94    PTF 5738999-MF07174 V2R2M0
  _  QMF07273   07/27/94    PTF 5763999-MF07273 V3R0M5
  _  QMF07326   07/27/94    PTF 5763999-MF07326 V3R0M5
  _  QMF07327   07/27/94    PTF 5763999-MF07327 V3R0M5
  _  QMF07331   07/27/94    PTF 5763999-MF07331 V3R0M5
  _  QMF07332   07/27/94    PTF 5763999-MF07332 V3R0M5
                                                             More...
Parameters or command
===>
F3=Exit          F4=Prompt          F5=Refresh         F6=Create
F9=Retrieve      F10=Command entry  F23=More options   F24=More keys
```

Yet another method to print the cover letter is to use the GET procedure to retrieve the physical file member into an office document, then print the document.

If the PTF is on tape, you receive a document describing the tape. To view or print the PTF cover letter(s), enter the following commands:

```
LODPTF LICPGM(lic_pgm_number) DEV(tape_dev_name) COVER(*ONLY)
   ENDOPT(*LEAVE)
```

Repeat for each PTF cover letter. For the last PTF, use *ENDOPT(*REWIND)*. To view or print the cover letter(s) received on tape, follow the instructions for viewing and printing cover letters of PTFs received from ECS.

> *Whenever you permanently apply new PTFs, save the system software (SAVSYS) and all affected licensed program libraries (SAVLICPGM). Refer to the **AS/400 Backup and Recovery — Basic** manual for more information.*

NEW VERSION OR RELEASE OF OPERATING SYSTEM

When you install a new version or release of the operating system, there are certain considerations to take into account. It is possible that IBM has made changes that could affect your system, especially if you have changed any system defaults.

System Object Changes

IBM periodically releases new versions or releases of the Operating System or program products. It is possible that IBM-supplied objects on the previous version or release that were modified by the user will be replaced with new objects when the Operating System or program product is updated. Any changes are lost. Examples of this are changes to:

- Printer files
- Message descriptions
- Subsystem descriptions
- Job descriptions
- The startup program

Before installing a new version or release, I recommend that you make note of the IBM-supplied objects that you may have modified. After you have installed a new version or release, go through the Performing New Installations and Upgrades on page 15, and pay special attention to those objects that you may have modified when you first installed your AS/400 or a previous version or release of the operating system. Check your system log — that you surely kept up to date — for documentation.

> *If you make changes to IBM system objects and wish to avoid the possibility of a new version or release overwriting your changes, place the changed object in a library other than the IBM library of the original object. Then modify the System Library List so that this library appears before IBM libraries. Refer to Changing IBM Commands on page 316 for additional information.*

Size of Error Log Files

After installing a new release, start Service Tools and check on the error log size. You may discover that the current size of the error log is too small.

STRSST   Select Option 1: *Start a Service Tool*
                   Select Option 1: *Work with Error Log*
                   Select Option 3: *Work with Error Log Sizes*

(Change the size of the error logs to the recommended size or larger.)

SYSTEM ANALYSIS REPORT

The PRTSYSANL command is part of QUSRTOOLs (refer to QUSRTOOL Library on page 307). It is a very long-running command, but provides extensive reporting of:

- System Summary
  - Last save dates
  - Number of QSYS/QHST* files

- Sizes of system journals
- Summary of OUTQs and spool files
- Cumulative PTF status
- Tape volume statistics
- System Values
  - Highlights each one changed from default
- System Hardware
  - Summary of local hardware
- History Log Analysis
  - Number of jobs by job type
  - Number of completions (normal or abnormal)
  - Analysis by CPU time
  - Job accounting information
  - QSYSOPR message analysis
- Library Analysis
  - List of libraries, size, number of files
  - Analysis by object owner
- Journal Summary
  - List of all journals and receivers on system
- Disk Status Report
  - List of all disk units and their utilization

PERIODICALLY IPL THE SYSTEM

Occasional IPLs are required on the AS/400 for proper operation. It is at IPL time that permanent and temporary addresses are regenerated, excess spool files are removed, PTFs are applied (for those PTFs that require an IPL in order to be applied), and changes to certain system values take effect.

Besides the need to IPL, there are other requirements that you must consider. For example:

- System subsystems such as QINTER must occasionally be ended in order to clear its job message queue. If a subsystem's job message queue reaches its maximum value, it ends abnormally.
- RCLSTG and release upgrades require a dedicated system.

I recommend that users perform an IPL at least monthly. Some additional guidelines can be found in the *AS/400 System Operation* manual. One indication that you should IPL on a more frequent interval is the percent of auxiliary storage used. Avoid running your system with a small amount of available disk storage. If you cannot avoid this, then IPL the system more frequently. Keep a record of auxiliary storage used before and after you IPL. The following shows the percentage used and the IPL frequency.

Percent Used	IPL Frequency
95	Daily
90	Weekly
Less than 90	Monthly

Types of IPLs

An IPL performs an Initial Program Load. This is the process of bringing the system to a ready state.

Attended IPL

The attended IPL, also known as the manual IPL, is used during the installation of the Operating System and for accessing Service Tools. The options available when you perform an Attended IPL are:

- Set system date and time
- Clear job queues
- Clear output queues
- Clear incomplete job logs
- Start print writers
- Start the console display device only
- Set other major system options
- Access Dedicated Service Tools (DST)
- Define or change the system at IPL

To perform an attended IPL:

1. Set the mode to manual using the keylock or keystick.
2. Power On the console device.
3. If the system is powered down, turn the power switch on. If the system is powered up, run the command:

```
PWRDWNSYS OPTION(*IMMED ) RESTART(*YES)
```

4. Follow directions on console. For example, you see options to start the IPL, change system options, and access Dedicated Service Tools.

Unattended IPL

The unattended IPL is sometimes referred to as a normal IPL. This brings the system to a ready status with minimum operator action. To perform an unattended IPL:

1. Set the mode to normal using the keylock or keystick.
2. Power On all devices to be used.

3. If the system is powered down, turn the power switch on. If the system is powered up, run the command:

```
PWRDWNSYS OPTION(*IMMED ) RESTART(*YES)
```

4. Wait for the sign-on screen.

SUGGESTED SYSTEM MAINTENANCE SCHEDULE

Use the following table as a guideline for performing routine system maintenance.

Task	Time Period	Comments
Back up entire system	Weekly and before new release or PTF package	Guards against loss of valuable data. Helps to quickly resume normal operation in case of system failure. Refer to the **AS/400 Backup and Recovery — Basic** manual.
IPL	2 to 4 weeks	Make more storage available. Delete temporary libraries. Compress work control blocks. Refresh address space.
Journal receiver management	60 days	Detach, save, and clear receivers. Refer to the **AS/400 Backup and Recovery — Basic** manual.
Message queue management	60 days	Review size of message queues. Clear outdated messages. Refer to the **AS/400 System Operation** manual.
OS/400 folder management	60 days	Review size and reduce very large folders.
Unused objects	60 days	Save to tape/diskette and delete unused objects.

Task	Time Period	Comments
User profiles	180 days and at time of any personnel action	Review user profiles and group profiles for accuracy, authority level, and security desired. Be aware of job changes and changes in levels of responsibility. Change passwords periodically. Refer to the *AS/400 Security — Basic* manual.
PTF Preventive Service Planning listing	14 days	Order the PSP report and review for HIPER PTFs. Order applicable HIPER PTFs not already applied.
Cumulative PTF management	90 days	Refer to the *AS/400 System Operation* manual. Order latest cumulative PTF tape. Apply temporary PTFs permanently. Remove PTF save files of permanently applied PTFs.
Reclaim storage	After IPL	Make more storage available. Deletes or stores lost or unnecessary objects in QRCL library. Long-running command.
Save file management	Daily	Save to tape and delete save files when they are not required. See PTF management (above).
Spooled file management	30 days	Spooled files can use large amounts of storage. Periodically remove spooled files not used within reasonable length of time. Use RCLSPLSTG command (or QRCLSPLSTG system value) to specify number of days spooled files are retained before they are automatically reclaimed (deleted).

Task	Time Period	Comments
Storage management	90 days	Check storage utilization. Delete unnecessary information from storage. This can easily occur in the various logs and queues maintained by the system. Optimal maximum for disk utilization is approximately 80 percent.
System logs management	60 days	System maintains job logs, history logs, error logs, problem logs, journal receivers, etc., to provide record of system performance and operation. Clear old, unnecessary information.

MONITOR ERROR LOG

It is a good idea to periodically monitor the system error log. The system maintains an error log — mostly for service personnel use — but you can display or print the log. Look for trends or obvious error conditions. A little common sense here avoids a bad situation later. If you have any questions, contact your IBM Service Representative.

> *Be cautious when using the following Service Tools function of the AS/400. You can mess things up here. If you do not understand a function within Service Tools, don't proceed.*

Use the following steps to monitor the error log:

1. Sign on as security officer.
2. Start System Service Tools:

   STRSST

3. Take option 1, Start a Service Tool.
4. Take option 1, Work with Error Log.
5. Take option 1, Display or Print Error Log.
6. On the Select Subsystem Data screen, select all error logs (option 1) and change the From and To date/time, if necessary.
7. On the Select Report Type for Subsystem screen, select option 1, Display Summary, and press Enter.
8. The first summary is displayed. Press the F11 key to go to the next summary or F10 to go to the previous summary. The summaries are:
   - Processor Entries
   - Magnetic Media Entries
   - Local Work Station Entries
   - Communication Entries

If you are at Version 2, Release 1 or later, of the Operating System, there is an easier way to print the error log:

```
GO CMDSRV
```

— or —

```
PRTERRLOG
```

Take the option to print the error log and fill in the details (e.g., date, time).

Look for trends and obvious problems. Ask your IBM Service Representative to help you spot errors or to answer your questions or concerns.

Program to Print Error Log Details

I wish to thank Ken Ray in Canberra, Australia, for this item.

It is good practice to regularly print the system error log, at least once per week. Examine it to determine if errors are increasing, particularly disk errors. This could lead to the early detection of possible DASD failure.

The program below automates this process. It uses a data area that recalls the last date and time it was run, and prints the log data from that time. This program can be scheduled weekly with the OfficeVision calendar function.

CL Program to Print Error Log Details

```
        PGM
/****************************************************************/
/*                                                            */
/*                                                            */
/* This program is used to print a summary of the system      */
/*   error log.                                               */
/*                                                            */
/* It uses a data area to record the date and time            */
/*    that it was last run, and if the data area cannot be     */
/*    found, it is created.  It is recommended that it be      */
/*    called at least once a week, and the output examined     */
/*    for any increase in errors.                             */
/*                                                            */
/*..........................................................*/
/****************************************************************/

        DCL     VAR(&PRTLOGDAT) TYPE(*CHAR) LEN(16)
        DCL     VAR(&PRTDAT)    TYPE(*CHAR) LEN(8)
        DCL     VAR(&PRTTIM)    TYPE(*CHAR) LEN(8)
        DCL     VAR(&QDATE)     TYPE(*CHAR) LEN(6)
        DCL     VAR(&QTIME)     TYPE(*CHAR) LEN(6)
        DCL     VAR(&SYSDAT)    TYPE(*CHAR) LEN(8)
        DCL     VAR(&SYSTIM)    TYPE(*CHAR) LEN(8)
/****************************************************************/
/*      Get current date and time                             */
/****************************************************************/
```

```
RTVSYSVAL        SYSVAL(QDATE) RTNVAR(&QDATE)
RTVSYSVAL        SYSVAL(QTIME) RTNVAR(&QTIME)
CHGVAR           VAR(&SYSDAT) VALUE(&QDATE)
CHGVAR           VAR(&SYSTIM) VALUE(&QTIME)
/*****************************************************************/
/*        Retrieve previous date and time                      */
/*****************************************************************/
RTVDTAARA        DTAARA(PRTLOGDAT) RTNVAR(&PRTLOGDAT)
MONMSG           MSGID(CPF0000) EXEC(DO)
/*****************************************************************/
/*        Create data area as it could not be found            */
/*****************************************************************/
CRTDTAARA        DTAARA(PRTLOGDAT) TYPE(*CHAR) LEN(16) +
                 VALUE(&SYSDAT *CAT &SYSTIM) TEXT('Last date and +
                 time PRTLOG was run')
CHGVAR           VAR(&PRTLOGDAT) VALUE('*CURRENT*AVAIL  ')
ENDDO      /* Data area not found */
/*****************************************************************/
/*        Unstring date and time                               */
/*****************************************************************/
CHGVAR           VAR(&PRTDAT) VALUE(%SST(&PRTLOGDAT 1 8))
CHGVAR           VAR(&PRTTIM) VALUE(%SST(&PRTLOGDAT 9 8))
/*****************************************************************/
/*        Print log and update data area                       */
/*****************************************************************/
PRTERRLOG        PERIOD((&PRTTIM &PRTDAT) (&SYSTIM &SYSDAT))
CHGVAR           VAR(&PRTLOGDAT) VALUE(&SYSDAT *CAT &SYSTIM)
CHGDTAARA        DTAARA(PRTLOGDAT) VALUE(&PRTLOGDAT)
RETURN
ENDPGM
```

TWINAXIAL TO TTP CABLING HUBS

Twinaxial cabling is the AS/400 standard for attaching terminals and printers. Although not the most convenient, its use stems from the older S/3X systems, and is very reliable. There is a 5,000-foot (1,524-meter) limitation for twinaxial cabling — the distance from AS/400 or 5394 to the end of the device string. However, many users now use telephone twisted pair (TTP) wiring and cabling hubs. Two such hubs from IBM, the 5299 Multi Terminal Connector and the 6299 Hub for Midrange Systems, can be used to convert twinaxial to TTP, which is a more flexible cabling scheme. If you plan to use TTP cabling, consult your IBM Service Representative for advice. TTP cabling is more prone to electrical noise than twinaxial cabling, and there are more stringent controls to consider. The following information on TTP cabling may be helpful to you in your planning.

- TTP cable

  - Type 3 or 4 cabling can be used, but Type 5 cable is recommended.

- Active and Passive Hubs

  - Passive hubs generally have one host input connector and seven output connectors. One hub, therefore, converts a single AS/400 twinaxial input port to seven TTP output ports. Somewhat prone to interference.

- Active hubs generally contain repeaters to increase reliability, and they provide longer cabling distances than passive hubs. May be able to convert more than one twinaxial input port to TTP output ports.
- Minimum device limitation
  - Many TTP hubs require at least two attached devices. Attaching only one device may cause a malfunction.
- Attach the TTPA (Telephone Twisted Pair Adapter), commonly referred to as the balun, directly to the work station. Do not use twinaxial cable to patch the balun to the work station.
- Do not mix TTPAs (baluns) from different manufacturers on any cable hub. There can be differences that can lead to unpredictable results.
- Avoid daisy-chaining work stations when using TTP cable. Use star topology wiring with the cabling hub.
- The following figure and accompanying table are recommended distances for Type 5 TTP cabling for the IBM 5299 and 6299 Cabling Hubs.

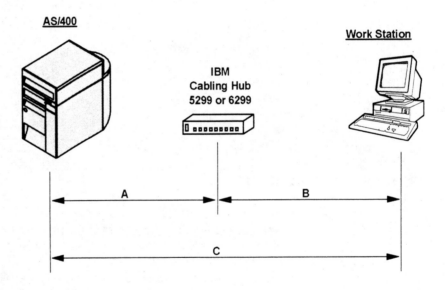

Refer to figure above. Dimension A is the maximum length of the connection from the AS/400 to the cabling hub. This can be either TTP or twinaxial cable. Dimension B is the maximum length of TTP cable from the cabling hub to the work station. Dimension C is the maximum cumulative length of the connection from the AS/400 to the hub and on to the work station.

IBM manufactures a passive hub (5299) and an active hub (6299). Active hubs typically provide greater reliability and connection distances. The table below shows the maximum distances supported using the specified cable types. Other manufacturers' specifications may differ.

Connection	5299 TTP Type 3	5299 TTP Type 5	5299 Twinax Cable	6299 TTP Type 3	6299 TTP Type 5	6299 Twinax Cable
AS/400 to Cabling Hub (Dimension A)	1,000 ft (305 m)	1,100 ft (335 m)	2,000 ft (610 m)	2,000 ft (610 m)	2,200 ft (671 m)	4,000 ft (1,220 m)
Cabling Hub to Work Station (Dimension B)	900 ft (275 m)	990 ft (302 m)	—	2,000 ft (610 m)	2,200 ft (671 m)	—
AS/400 to Work Station (Dimension C)	1,000 ft (305 m)	1,100 ft (335 m)	2,000 ft (610 m)	4,000 ft (1220 m)	4,400 ft (1341 m)	4,400 ft (1341 m)

UNINTERRUPTIBLE POWER SUPPLIES (UPS)

All AS/400s should be configured with an UPS. The 9404s can be equipped with internal battery packs. For these smaller systems, the internal battery backups are adequate. Usually the system is small enough that it runs IPL shortly after power is restored. The 9406s should have an external UPS (provided by the customer) installed to protect against power outages. Without an UPS, the AS/400 can take a long time to come back online after power is restored. All D series and higher of the 9406 have an internal battery backup, but this internal battery is not designed as an UPS. It is designed to allow the system to save a copy of main memory to the internal disk before the system quits for lack of external power. If your system has an internal battery, consider testing it from time to time. Refer to Testing the Internal Battery on 9402/9404 AS/400 Systems on page 312.

UPS HANDLING PROGRAMS AND UPS MESSAGE QUEUES

You may want to write an UPS Handling Program to perform an orderly shutdown of your AS/400 in the event that the main power is interrupted. Refer to the *AS/400 Backup and Recovery — Basic* manual for additional information on how to do this. You might want to send messages to a special message queue also. I have included a sample UPS handling program in Appendix G: Sample UPS Handling Program on page 349.

> *If the system is in a restricted state, then the UPS handling program is disabled. In case power goes out while the system is in this state, make sure your operators know how to end the system manually.*

SYSTEM MANAGEMENT AND OPERATIONS CHECKLIST

I have included a checklist that you might find useful for performing an audit of your system operations and management. I find this checklist to be particularly useful as an audit tool. It covers many of the aspects that you should be concerned with to efficiently manage any computer system — big or small. Refer to Appendix H: System Management and Operations Checklist on page 353 for the checklist. Feel free to copy this checklist for your own use.

MONITOR SYSTEM MESSAGES

Consider having two terminals set up as system consoles. One terminal is used as a system operator with the QSYSOPR message queue in break mode, and the other is used as a second system operator with the QSYSMSG message queue in break mode. Review the topics Automated Problem Management and Reporting on page 33, and Critical System Messages on page 39 for additional information.

PRINTER MANAGEMENT

Printer management and output management can be a bit confusing to new users. The following tips are not intended to be an all-encompassing discussion on printer and output management, but they should help you forge your way through an AS/400 system with multiple printers.

An excellent reference document for more complete information on AS/400 printing functions is the IBM Redbook, *IBM AS/400 Printing*.

ADVANCED FUNCTION PRINTING TO IPDS PRINTERS

If you are using V3R1, you must have installed Print Services Facility/400 (PSF/400). This software enables Advanced Function Printing (AFP) to IPDS (Intelligent Printer Data Stream) devices such as the IBM 4224, 3812, 3816, and 4028 printers. This also includes printing of FAX documents received by the AS/400.

Prior to V3R1, the ability to print to AFP documents was included in the Operating System. Beginning with V3R1, you must order this feature separately. If you are upgrading to V3R1, the cost is less than it would be to order after upgrading.

ANNOYING PRINTER MESSAGES

Users of newly installed systems may frequently see messages directed to the QSYSOPR message queue, alerting them to align forms to check that the proper forms are installed, or similar messages. You must, of course, respond to these messages. However, if you are sure that the response to these messages is constant, you can create automatic responses. Refer to Message Routing on page 39 for instructions on how to use the command WRKRPYLE.

For example, say you have a consistent reply to the Load Form Type message. The message is CPA3394 and the reply is G. (If you intend to use different form types on your printer, then do not add this particular reply.) The command used to add the reply is:

    WRKRPYLE

(You can view the replies and use F6 to add an entry.)

WHAT AFFECTS PRINTED OUTPUT

In order of highest to lowest priority, the system checks the following objects to determine printed output routing. Each system object takes precedence over the object that follows.

1. Printer file
2. Job description
3. User profile
4. Work station device description
5. System value (QPRTDEV)

Each of these objects has parameters that define the Print Device and the Spooled Output Queue. Whenever anything is printed, the printer file is searched first to determine routing. Unless otherwise specified, the default value in the print file designates the Job Description for routing. Similarly, unless otherwise specified, the job description designates the User Profile for routing. The User Profile, unless otherwise specified, designates the work station device description for routing; and the work station device description, by default, designates the system value. So, if the defaults are all in effect, printed output goes to the device specified by the system value QPRTDEV, which is normally PRT01 (refer to Initial System Values on page 18).

If you have several printers on your system, I recommend that you specifically select one of the printers for each user on the system and modify the user profile to use that printer. Alternatively, if you do not want the spooled output to print immediately, you can designate that the spooled output be sent to an output queue instead of a printer device. Then the printed output does not print until you view the output queue and select the "change" option to redirect the spooled file to a printer device. You can use the command WRKSPLF to find any user's output easily. To change the user profile, use the following command:

```
CHGUSRPRF USRPRF(username) PRTDEV(print-device-name) OUTQ(*DEV)
```

This is pretty simplistic. I suggest you review the references shown below for additional information. A simple example of printed output routing is shown in the Printed Output Routing Figure on page 148.

OUTPUT QUEUES, WRITERS, AND PRINTER DEVICES

It is common practice that each printer device has an output queue and a print writer of the same name. When a print device is created, an output queue and writer of the same name are created. The writer takes files one at a time from the output queue and prints them on the print device. There can only be one writer per printer device, but there can be multiple output queues, with or without an assigned writer.

To print anything, you must have the printer device "varied on" and the writer must be started.

```
VRYCFG CFGOBJ(printer-device-name) CFGTYPE(*DEV) +
    STATUS(*ON)
STRPRTWTR DEV(printer-device-name)
```

When you start print writer, the default output queue that is attached is the outque with the same name as the writer. You can attach a different output queue to a writer when you start the writer, or you can change the outque after the writer is already started.

When you start a print writer you can assign an outque:

```
STRPRTWTR DEV(writer_name)  OUTQ(lib_name/outq_name)
```

When the writer is already started, you can change the outque:

```
CHGWTR WTR(writer_name) OUTQ(lib_name/output_queue)
```

REMOTE SYSTEM PRINTING

The most common way to perform remote system printing is to send the spool file to the remote system. Prior to V3R1, this was a manual process that could be partially automated. With V3R1, more "automation" is enabled. Also with V3R1, you can perform remote system printing to some systems other than AS/400s. There are limitations. Refer to the manuals referenced below.

Remote Printing Prior to V3R1

If your AS/400s are at V3R0.5 or below, then the easiest way to perform remote system printing is to use the AS/400 Distribution Services function, which is part of the Operating System. Follow these steps:

1. Set up SNADS (System Network Architecture Distribution Services).

2. Define a user profile on the target system with the printer device specified in the user profile and a password of *NONE to prevent people from signing on with this profile.

```
CRTUSRPRF USRPRF(printername) PASSWRD(*NONE)
    PRTDEV(printername)
```

3. Add the new user profile to the system directory on the target system.

4. Make sure you have an entry in your source system SNADS table. This can be the user profile you created above or an entry of *ANY so you do not have to explicitly state the user on the target system.

5. Use the SNDNETSPLF command to send the spooled file to the user profile you just created on the target system. If the print writer is started on the target system, then your spooled file prints automatically.

    If you have a listing of the spool files on your display using either the WRKSPLF or the WRKOUTQ command, you see option 1, Send. (Refer to the figure under the heading How to Determine Which Print File was Used to Spool an Output on page 152 for an example of the WRKOUTQ display.)

Move the cursor to the spool file you wish to send, enter a 1 in the option field, and press Enter. You are then prompted for additional information.

Remote Printing Using V3R1

 If you are at V3R1, then you can use the Remote Printing feature that is part of V3R1. A full discussion of this topic is contained in the **AS/400 Printer Device Programming** manual and the IBM Redbook, **AS/400 Printing IV**.

The remote printing feature of V3R1 uses distribution services to "send" the spool file to a remote system. This is very similar to what is described in the preceding topic.

Example Configuration of V3R1 Remote System Printing

You can set up several configurations, depending on your underlying protocol and target systems. If you have multiple AS/400s all at V3R1, and your communication protocol is SNADS, you can configure remote system printing as shown below. (If the target system is not an AS/400, not at V3R1, or the protocol is TCP/IP, then the instructions are different and you should refer to the manuals referenced above.)

1. Configure distribution services (SNADS).

2. Create entries in the system directories on the target and the source AS/400.

   To send spool files, there must be entries in the respective system directories. On the target system, you must have an entry for user profile QNETSPLF. On the source system, you can either have an explicit user profile entry or an entry of *ANY.

   "Target" and "source" are dynamic terms. Their definitions depend on which way you are sending the spool file. You probably send files both ways, so you must perform the steps on all AS/400s.

3. Create an output queue for the remote system. For example, if the remote system name was NAVAJO and you wanted to give the OUTQ the same name:

   ```
   CRTOUTQ OUTQ(QUSRSYS/NAVAJO) RMTSYS(NAVAJO)
       CNNTYPE(*SNA) DESTTYPE(*OS400)
   ```

4. Start the remote printer writer.

   ```
   STRRMTWTR OUTQ(NAVAJO)
   ```

   (You can specify that you want to start the remote writers automatically when you create the remote OUTQ, above, using the AUTOSTRWTR parameter.)

5. Use the WRKWTR WTR(*ALL) command to work with all writers that have been started, including the remote writers.

> *When you want to work with remote writers, you must specify WRKWTR WTR(writername) or WRKWTR WTR(*ALL). If you specify *ALL, this shows all currently started writers including remote writers (type of *RMT). The default parameter WTR(*PRT) shows all of the writers on the system with a type of *PRT, including writers that have not been started — it does not show the remote writers.*

6. When a spool file arrives in the remote OUTQ, it is sent to the system specified. If using SNADS, confirmation messages are sent when received at the target system.

Remote Printing from OfficeVision/400

When you print from OfficeVision, you must specify a printer rather than an OUTQ. To enable the V3R1 feature for remote printing from OfficeVision/400, do the following:

1. Create a remote outque. Specify QUSRSYS as the library.

   ```
   CRTOUTQ OUTQ(QUSRSYS/outqname) RMTSYS(remotesysname) TEXT('whatever')
   ```

2. Create a virtual controller.

   ```
   CRTCTLVWS CTLD(remotectlrname) TEXT('whatever)
   ```

3. Create a virtual print device with the same name as the OUTQ that you used in step 1. Specify the virtual controller used in step 2.

   ```
   CRTDEVPRT DEVD(outqname) DEVCLS(*VRT)TYPE(3812) MODEL(1)
       CTL(remotectlrname) FONT(11) TEXT('whatever')
   ```

Now you have a virtual printer device description with the same name as the OUTQ. In your setup for OfficeVision/400, specify the name of the virtual device for printing on the remote system.

PRINTER LOAD BALANCING

Balancing your printer load can be accomplished using multiple print writers or limiting large spool files during times of heavy activity.

Multiple Print Writers

If you are using V3R1 or later, you can start multiple printer writers to a single output queue. The limit is 10. Up to 10 printers can print spooled output files from the same output queue. Using this technique, you can balance your workload between multiple printers. It also provides backup for printed jobs running unattended. For example, if one printer jams or runs out of paper, the others continue to print spooled output files from the associated output queue.

By using multiple printers, you can achieve a relatively high rate of printing with several, less-expensive printers rather than a single, high-speed (but more expensive) printer.

You can not route output to a specific printer. Therefore, you want to place the printers in the same location. If you don't, your users must go on a treasure hunt for their printed output.

To assign multiple writers (printers) to the same output queue, issue the STRPRTWTR command multiple times, specifying the same OUTQ. For example, if you want to start PRT01 and PRT02 to the same OUTQ, issue the commands:

```
STRPRTWTR DEV(PRT01) OUTQ(DEPTABC)
STRPRTWTR DEV(PRT02) OUTQ(DEPTABC)
```

Unless the OUTQ is on hold, when a spool file is ready to print, the OUTQ routes the output to the first available writer (printer).

You retain the ability to print spooled output on special forms. For example, if PRT02 in the above example had special forms, then, when you issue the STRPRTWTR command, you specify the form type. Then PRT02 only prints files that require that form. The remaining printed output is routed to the other printers assigned to the OUTQ.

Controlling Printing by Spooled File Size

V3R1

If you are at V3R1 or later, you can control printing of spool files using the MAXPAGES parameter on the CRTOUTQ or CHGOUTQ commands. This is accomplished using three elements of the MAXPAGES parameter:

- Spooled file size (pages)
- Starting time
- Ending time

> *The starting and ending times must be specified using the 24-hour method of measuring time. For example, 2:00 PM is entered as 1400.*

As an example, let's say that, between 10:00 AM and 2:00 PM, you want to restrict spooled files with more than 50 pages from printing on output queue DEPTABC. Also, between 12:00 PM and 1:00 PM you only want spooled files with 10 pages or less to print. Issue the following command:

```
CHGOUTQ OUTQ(DEPTABC) +
    MAXPAGES((50 1000 1400) (10 1200 1300))
```

(You can specify up to five different combinations of pages and start/stop times in the MAXPAGES parameter.)

Limitations

Keep in mind the following limitations when controlling printing by spool file size:

- If printed output is deferred because it exceeds the MAXPAGES parameter, it has a status of DFR when you display the OUTQ. If you need to print the file anyway (override the deferred status), then you must either redirect the file to another OUTQ or change the OUTQ MAXPAGES parameter.

- If the spooled file is of type *USERASCII, the system is unable to determine the number of pages in the file.

USEFUL PRINTER COMMANDS AND FUNCTIONS

The Operational Assistant ties a lot of the printer functions together so you don't have to remember so many printer commands. However, included below are some useful commands and functions that control printing.

GO PRINTER   Menu for various printer functions. From this menu, you can select options to control the print writer, to select output queue functions, etc. All of the following commands can be accessed from this menu.

WRKUSRJOB   Work with Job command. Take option 8 to work with the printed output for any listed job.

WRKOUTQ   Work with Output Queue command. Shows overall status of all output queues or the detailed status of a specific output queue. From this display, you can hold, release, display, change, or delete spooled files. The change option can be useful for moving output from one queue or device to another.

WRKSPLF   Work with Spooled Files command. Displays or prints all the spooled files you (or the user name specified if you prompt the command) have created on the system. Very useful for "finding" lost output.

WRKUSRJOB   Work with User Job command. Allows you to specify a user or users, and then gives you options to work with the jobs or their associated spooled files. This is useful for "finding" spooled output associated with a specific job.

WRKWTR   Shows all the printers configured to the system and status information. You can start, end, hold, release, or work with any printer from this display.

For additional information, refer to the following resources:

- *AS/400 System Operation* manual
- *AS/400 Work Management* manual
- *IBM AS/400 Printing* Redbooks

Printed Output Routing Figure

The following figure is a graphical representation of printed output routing.

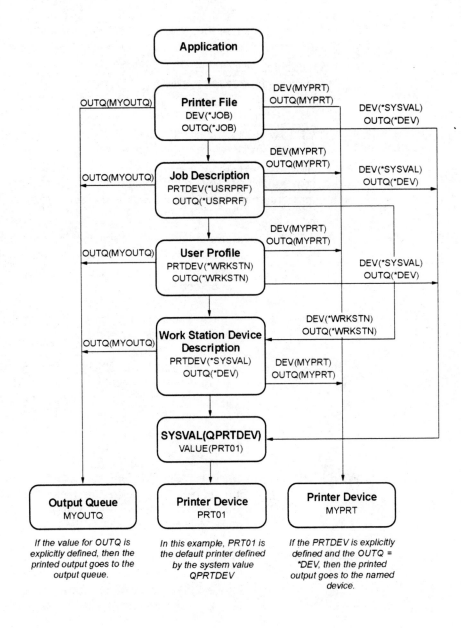

As an example of output routing, refer to the preceding figure. Say the system objects that control printing have the following values:

Printer File	DEV(*JOB) OUTQ(*JOB) — these are the default values for the printer file.
JOBD	PRTDEV(*WRKSTN) OUTQ(*WRKSTN)
USRPRF	PRTDEV(PRT02) OUTQ(*DEV)
Work Station Device Description	PRTDEV(PRT99) OUTQ(MYOUTQ)
SYSVAL (QPRTDEV)	PRT01

The printed output ends up going to the output queue MYOUTQ. Following the logic in the above figure, the values in the Printer File designate that the Job Description is used to route printed output. The job description designates the Work Station Description. The User Profile has no effect because it is bypassed by the values in the Job Description. The Work Station Description points to printer device PRT02, but the OUTQ is explicitly defined as MYOUTQ, so the value for Printer Device is ignored and the output goes to the MYOUTQ output queue. The system value QPRTDEV is also ignored because it has a lower precedence than all the preceding objects. The outque or printer device was designated in the one of preceding objects, so the system value was never referenced to determine the routing.

HOW TO TEMPORARILY CHANGE THE DEFAULT FOR YOUR PRINTED OUTPUT

If you want to temporarily redirect your printed output, you can use the Change Job (CHGJOB) command to reroute your printed output to an output queue or printer device.

The easiest way to use the CHGJOB command is to enter the command on the command line, then press the F4 (Prompt) key. The next screen is the CHGJOB screen. Press the F10 key (Additional parameters) to get to the screen shown below.

```
                        Change Job (CHGJOB)

Type choices, press Enter.

  Job name . . . . . . . . . . . .   *            Name, *
    User . . . . . . . . . . . . .                Name
    Number . . . . . . . . . . . .                000000-999999
  Job priority (on JOBQ) . . . . .   *SAME        0-9, *SAME
  Output priority (on OUTQ) . . .    5            1-9, *SAME
  Print device . . . . . . . . . .   prt15        Name, *SAME, *USRPRF...
  Output queue . . . . . . . . . .   *dev         Name, *SAME, *USRPRF, *DEV...
    Library . . . . . . . . . . .                 Name, *LIBL, *CURLIB
  Run priority . . . . . . . . . .   20           1-99, *SAME

                      Additional Parameters

  Job queue . . . . . . . . . . .    *SAME        Name, *SAME
    Library . . . . . . . . . . .                 Name, *LIBL, *CURLIB
  Print text . . . . . . . . . . .   *BLANK

                                                          More...
  F3=Exit   F4=Prompt   F5=Refresh   F12=Cancel   F13=How to use this display
  F24=More keys
```

In the example above, I am changing my job to send the printed output to
PRT15. I also specify that the output queue is the same as the print device by
entering *DEV.

When you sign off, the changes made are lost. The job operating parameters
revert back to the defaults.

HOW TO PRINT PART OF A SPOOL FILE

Occasionally there is a need to print part of a large document or spool file. You
can only do this if the spool file is still in the output queue (i.e., it was saved after
printing or has not yet printed). To print part of a spool file:

1. Find the document using WRKSPLF, WRKOUTQ, or the Operational
    Assistant.
2. Select the option to change the spool file.
3. If using Operational Assistant, enter the first and last page you wish to print.
    Otherwise, enter F10 for Additional Parameters and scroll down one page to
    enter the first and last page in the PAGERANGE parameter.
4. Select SAVE(*YES) to save the spooled file. Otherwise, it is lost after it
    finishes printing. If it hasn't finished printing, then you can still select
    SAVE(*YES).
5. Press Enter. The spool file reprints, starting with the page number you
    indicated.

DUPLICATING SPOOL FILES

The QUSRTOOL tool called DUPSPLF allows you to duplicate a spool file from
one OUTQ to another without reprinting it. It is easy to use from a CL program

and may be useful for printing several copies of a report by merely routing them to several printers rather than printing one report several times. Refer to QUSRTOOL Library on page 307 for additional information on QUSRTOOL.

ARCHIVING SPOOL FILES

Another QUSRTOOL, SPLCTL, supplied with the AS/400 provides a good way to save and retrieve OUTQs to or from save files or tape. Refer to QUSRTOOL Library on page 307 for additional information on QUSRTOOL.

ALLOWING USERS TO START PRINT WRITERS

If you want to allow users to start print writers without giving them job control or spool control special authorities, use the following procedure:

> *Giving job control or spool control authorities to users only so they can start print writers may violate your internal security authority or cause confusion if naive users inadvertently start and stop jobs unintentionally.*

1. On OUTQs for which you wish to allow users to start the print writers, set the object authority to *CHANGE. Do this for each user profile that needs to start print writers. If you want to allow all users to start the print writers, then grant *PUBLIC the *CHANGE authority.

2. Define your OUTQs as AUTCHK(*DTAAUT) and not as AUTCHK(*OWNER). Use the WRKOUTQ command to verify:

   ```
   CHGOUTQ OUTQ(outqname) AUTCHK(*DTAAUT)
   ```

> *The requester must have *READ, *ADD, and *DELETE data authority to the output queue.*

3. If the user profile has limited capability — LMTCPB(*YES) — then you must do the following:

   ```
   CHGCMD CMD(STRPRTWTR) ALWLMTUSR(*YES)
   ```

   (Refer to Changing IBM Commands *on page 316 for information about changing IBM commands.)*

SOME PRINTER CONTROL RECOMMENDATIONS

Here are some useful recommendations:

- Keep the Printed Output Routing Figure on page 148 in mind. Print files always take precedence over other objects that control printing. For example, if you are creating programs, the commands to create the program (e.g., CRTCBLPGM) use the print file QSYSPRT to direct the output. Check that print file. If it doesn't suit your needs, use the CHGCMDDFT command to change the CRTCBLPGM to use a print file of your choosing. *(Leave QSYSPRT alone because it is used by many different objects.)*

Refer to Changing IBM Commands *on page 316 for information about changing IBM commands.*

- Almost all commands have a print file associated with them. Refer to the **Programming Reference Summary** manual. If you modify system print files, then place a copy of the original object in the CHGSYS library.

- I recommend that you explicitly define a printer (or output queue) for each user on your system (not the system printer). Assign a printer or output queue in the user's profile or specify a printer or output queue with the device description.

- The WRKSPLF command is really good for finding "lost" spooled files. Educate your users on its use.

- Become familiar with and educate your users on the use of the Operational Assistant for controlling printing operations.

HOW TO DETERMINE WHICH PRINT FILE WAS USED TO SPOOL AN OUTPUT

Your printer characteristics may be such that you want to modify the printer file that controls physical output. For example, your page length may not be 66 lines per inch, which is the default for most of the IBM-supplied printer files.

To determine which printer file was used to control the physical spooled output of any spooled file, display the attributes of the spool file. From the Work with Spool Files or the Work with Output Queue screen, select option 8 to display the selected spool file attributes. This option causes the WRKSPLFA (Work with Spool File Attributes) command to run.

```
                          Work with Output Queue

 Queue:    BISEL        Library:    QUSRSYS        Status:    RLS

 Type options, press Enter.
   1=Send    2=Change    3=Hold    4=Delete    5=Display    6=Release    7=Messages
   8=Attributes          9=Work with printing status

 Opt  File        User       User Data    Sts    Pages    Copies  Form Type    Pty
  _   B1RESULTS   BISEL      SUNSTATE     SAV      19        1     *STD          5
  _   QPPTITVP    BISEL                   SAV      21        1     *STD          5
  _   QPPTSYSR    BISEL                   SAV       7        1     *STD          5
  _   QPPTITVJ    BISEL                   SAV      75        1     *STD          5
  _   QPPTITVR    BISEL                   SAV      12        1     *STD          5
  _   QPPTCPTR    BISEL                   SAV      38        1     *STD          5
  _   CRTBESTMDL  BISEL      SUNSTATE     SAV       2        1     *STD          5
  8   B1RESULTS   BISEL      SUNSTATE     SAV      19        1     *STD          5


                                                                         Bottom
 Parameters for options 1, 2, 3 or command
 ===>
 F3=Exit    F11=View 2    F12=Cancel    F22=Printers    F24=More keys
```

Scroll down one page. The printer file and library are shown as the Device File and Library.

```
                    Work with Spooled File Attributes

 Job . . . . . . . . . :   DSP02          File . . . . . . . . :   B1RESULTS
   User . . . . . . . :    BISEL          Number . . . . . . :     2
   Number . . . . . . :    135120

 Printer device type . . . . . . . . . :   *SCS
 Device file . . . . . . . . . . . . . :   QPCYBESTPF
   Library . . . . . . . . . . . . . . :     QPFR
 User-specified data . . . . . . . . . :   S: YSTATE
 Accounting code . . . . . . . . . . . :
 Program that opened file . . . . . . . :
   Library . . . . . . . . . . . . . . :
 Date file was opened . . . . . . . . . :   01/26/95
 Time file was opened . . . . . . . . . :   17:52:33
 User-defined file . . . . . . . . . . :   *NO


                                                              More...

 Press Enter to continue.

 F3=Exit   F5=Refresh   F12=Cancel   F13=Change
```

Now, if you want to change the printer file parameters to suit your preferences or situation, run the CHGPRTF (Change Printer File) command. In the example shown above, enter:

    CHGPRTF FILE(QPFR/QPCYBESTPF)

(Press the F10 key to display all the parameters that you can change.)

> *If you intend to change an IBM-supplied printer file, first copy the original file to another library or carefully document your changes. Keep in mind that, when you install a version or release upgrade, any IBM-supplied objects may be overwritten, thus negating any changes made to the original object.*

> *If you want to globally change all the print files for some reason (e.g., you want to change the lines per page), enter the command:*
>
>   CHGPRTF FILE(*ALL/*ALL) *then press F4 and F10.*

PRINT FILE SEPARATOR PAGES

You can enable (or disable) the insertion of separator pages between spooled output by using the FILESEP parameter in the printer files. For example, to enable separator pages on output that uses the QSYSPRT printer file:

```
CHGPRTF FILE(QSYS/QSYSPRT) FILESEP(1)
```

Insert one file separator page between spooled output with the following information:

- Job name
- User name
- Job number
- Data and time
- File name
- File number and copy number

Refer to Message and Logging System Values on page 28 for information on the use of the System Value QPRTTXT for placing text on separator pages.

PRINT WRITER JOB LOGS

If you find that each print writer produces a job log that you do not particularly want, you can prevent this with the command:

```
CHGJOBD JOBD(QSPLPRTW) LOG(0 99 *MSG)
```

This prevents data from being logged.

ROUTING WORK STATION SCREEN PRINTS

You can route the printed output of screen prints created at a work station to a particular printer, regardless of the print device defined in the user profile, by creating a print file and changing the display device description:

```
CRTDUPOBJ OBJ(QSYSPRT) FROMLIB(QSYS) OBJTYPE(*FILE) +
    TOLIB(QGPL) NEWOBJ(prtfname)
CHGPRTF FILE(QGPL/prtfname) DEV(prtr-dev-name)
CHGDEVDSP DEVD(devname) PRTFILE(QGPL/prtfname)
```

SAVING AND RESTORING SPOOL FILES

Use these steps to save and restore spool files on the source system or target system:

1. Create a physical file with a record length of 133. This supports a print length of 132.

```
CRTPF library/file RCDLEN(133)
```

2. Copy the spool file to the database file using the parameter CTLCHAR(*FCFC), which gives you carriage control in 0,1,blank format.

```
CPYSPLF FILE(spool_file) TOFILE(library/file) +
    CTLCHAR(*FCFC)
```

3. Save the database file to tape or diskette.

```
SAVOBJ OBJ(file) LIB(library) DEV(device) OBJTYPE(*FILE)
```

On the target system:

1. Restore the database file.

```
RSTOBJ OBJ(file) SAVLB(library) DEV(device) +
    OBJTYPE(*FILE)
```

2. Create a print file that expects the first character to be the forms control character. This requires the parameter CTLCHAR(*FCFC). If both the source and the target systems have PRTTXT footing, then you also need PRTTXT(*BLANK) or you get bad page breaks.

```
CRTPRTF FILE(QTEMP/MYPRINT) CTLCHAR(*FCFC) +
    PRTTXT(*BLANK)
```

3. Copy the file from the database file to the print file. This creates the printed output into any output queue you desire.

```
CPYF library/file QTEMP/MYPRINT
```

PRINTING SPOOL FILES ON PRINTER OF YOUR CHOICE

You can change where a spool file prints by selecting the spool file and using the CHANGE option to direct it to a different printer. Use the WRKSPLF or the WRKOUTQ command to get the listing of spool files, then use option 2 to change. Put in the printer device to which you want the spool file directed.

The example shown below is what you see when you use option 2 to change the printed output *if your Assistance Level is set to Basic.* If your Assistance Level is set to Intermediate or Advanced, the display looks different. Refer to QASTLVL on page 20 and Using Assistance Levels on page 95 for additional information.

```
                        Change Printer Output

User . . . . . . . . :  QSYSOPR       Date . . . . . . . . :  01/10/95
Printer output . . . :  QPSAVDLO      Time . . . . . . . . :  18:22:09
Pages . . . . . . . :  35
Status . . . . . . . :  Not assigned to printer

Type choices below, then press Enter.

  Printer to use . . . . . . . . . . .  _____       Name, F4 for list

  Copies and pages:
    Number of copies . . . . . . . . .  1_              1-255
    First page to print . . . . . . .   1_              Number
    Last page to print . . . . . . .    *LAST           Number, *LAST

  Type of forms . . . . . . . . . . .   *STD_____       Form type, *STD

  Print this output next . . . . . . .  N               Y=Yes, N=No

  Save printer output . . . . . . . . . N               Y=Yes, N=No

F1=Help   F3=Exit   F5=Refresh   F12=Cancel
```

If you want to change several spool files at once, put option 2 in front of the spool files you want to change, move the cursor to the command line, and enter the device to which you want the spool files directed. The device parameter is applied to all the spool files selected. An example is shown below. *This example uses the Intermediate assistance level.*

```
                        Work with Output Queue

Queue:  QPRINT       Library:  QGPL        Status:  RLS

Type options, press Enter.
  1=Send   2=Change   3=Hold   4=Delete   5=Display   6=Release   7=Messages
  8=Attributes        9=Work with printing status

Opt  File       User      User Data   Sts   Pages   Copies  Form Type   Pty
__   QPSAVOBJ   QSYSOPR                RDY     1       1     *STD         5
__   QPSAVOBJ   QSYSOPR                RDY     2       1     *STD         5
2    QPSAVOBJ   QSYSOPR                RDY    65       1     *STD         5
2    QPSAVDLO   QSYSOPR                RDY    35       1     *STD         5
2    QPEZBACK   QSYSOPR   DSPBCKSTS    RDY     1       1     *STD         5
2    QPSAVOBJ   QSYSOPR                RDY     1       1     *STD         5
2    QPSAVOBJ   QSYSOPR                RDY     2       1     *STD         5
__   QPSAVOBJ   QSYSOPR                RDY    65       1     *STD         5
__   QPSAVDLO   QSYSOPR                RDY    35       1     *STD         5
                                                                More...
Parameters for options 1, 2, 3 or command
===> dev(prt03)_____
F3=Exit   F11=View 2   F12=Cancel   F20=Writers   F22=Printers
F24=More keys
```

If you want all the files from an outque printed at a different printer, then attach the entire outque to the printer using the CHGWTR command. See Output Queues, Writers, and Printer Devices on page 142.

POOL SIZE IF USING ADVANCED FUNCTION PRINTING (AFP)

When you are using AFP, you should set the pool size for the spooling subsystem higher than you would otherwise. Refer to Spooling Performance of Advanced Function Printing on page 200.

COMMUNICATIONS

I highly recommend that you get the three IBM Redbooks, *AS/400 Communication Definition Examples, I, II, and III*. These books are indispensable when you are configuring communications. They are available in hardcopy or on CD-ROM. Refer to Bibliography on page xvi for product numbers.

QUICK AND DIRTY DISPLAY STATION PASS-THROUGH

The following procedure allows AS/400-to-AS/400 display station pass-through using the electronic customer support (ECS) lines. In the example shown in Pass-Through Using ECS Lines (AS/400 to AS/400) (below), type the commands that apply to either the target or the source system; type them exactly as shown. The parameters in lower case can be substituted with parameters of your choice. Note that some parameters have a line connecting one parameter to another. This means these parameters *must* match. If they do not match, you are unable to pass through.

An alternative method you may wish use is described in the topic, Providing Remote Support via the ECS Line, on page 161.

Pass-Through Using ECS Lines (AS/400 to AS/400)

Source System Commands	Target System Commands
CRTLINSDLC LIND(sourcelin)	CRTLINSDLC LIND(targetlin)
RSRCNAME(LIN011)	RSRCNAME(LIN011)
ONLINE(*NO)	ONLINE(*NO)
ROLE(*PRI)—①	④— ROLE(*SEC)
CNN(*SWTPP)	CNN(*SWTPP)
EXCHID(05600001)—②	③— EXCHID(05600002)
LINESPEED(2400)	LINESPEED(2400)
SWTCNN(*DIAL)	SWTCNN(*ANS)
AUTODIAL(*YES)	AUTODIAL(*NO)
DIALCMD(*V25BIS)	⑤— STNADR(FA)
DUPLEX(*FULL)	DUPLEX(*FULL)
CRTCTLAPPC CTLID(sourcectl)	CRTCTLAPPC CTLID(targetctl)
LINKTYPE(*SDLC)	LINKTYPE(*SDLC)
ONLINE(*NO)	ONLINE(*NO)
SWITCHED(*YES)	SWITCHED(*YES)
APPN(*NO)	APPN(*NO)
SWTLINLST(sourcelin)	SWTLINLST(targetlin)
RMTNETID(*NONE)	RMTNETID(*NONE)
EXCHID(05600002)—③	②— EXCHID(05600001)
INLCNN(*DIAL)	INLCNN(*ANS)
CNNNBR('SST9:9999999')	①— ROLE(*PRI)
ROLE(*SEC)—④	⑤— STNADR(FA)
STNADR(FA)—⑤	
CRTDEVAPPC DEVD(sourcedev)	CRTDEVAPPC DEVD(targetdev)
RMTLOCNAME(targetsys)—⑥	⑦— RMTLOCNAME(sourcesys)
ONLINE(*NO)	ONLINE(*NO)
LCLLOCNAME(sourcesys)—⑦	⑥— LCLLOCNAME(targetsys)
RMTNETID(*NONE)—⑧	⑧— RMTNETID(*NONE)
CTL(sourcectl)	CTL(targetctl)
MODE(BLANK)—⑨	⑨— MODE(BLANK)
APPN(*NO)	APPN(*NO)
VRYCFG CRTCTLVWS CTLD(targetctlvws)	
SOURCELIN *LIN *ON	ONLINE(*NO)
VRYCFG CRTDEVDSP DEVD(targetdevvrt)	
SOURCECTL *CTL *ON	DEVCLS(*VRT)
	TYPE(5251)
(Wait . . . Before you type	MODEL(11)
the next command, make sure	ONLINE(*NO)
all the commands have been	CTL(targetctlvws)
typed on both systems)	KBDTYPE(USB)
	VRYCFG
STRPASTHR	TARGETLIN *LIN *ON
RMTLOCNAME(targetsys)	
VRTCTL(targetctlvws)	VRCFG
MODE(BLANK)	targetctl *CTL *ON
	VRCFG
	targetctlvws *CTL *ON

NOTES:

1. *Control units describe both the local and the remote lines to the system on which they reside. They also contain the station address parameter.*
2. *CNNNBR is the phone number to dial. SST means turn on the modem's sound tone. 9: means dial 9 and wait for dial tone. If you don't want or need the SST or the 9:, then omit them.*
3. *The devices carry the locations, network identifiers, and mode for the conversation.*
4. *The virtual control unit and device are used instead of a physical device on the target system. If you need a different device than what is shown in this example, create the virtual device description using the appropriate MODEL and TYPE parameters.*
5. *The lines, control units, and devices must be varied on. To have the target system create the virtual device and controller descriptions automatically, set the System Value QAUTOVRT to 1. Refer to the **AS/400 Communications Configuration** manual for additional information.*

PROVIDING REMOTE SUPPORT VIA THE ECS LINE

Rochester Level 2 Support uses the built-in OS/400 command STRRMTSPT (Start Remote Support) to enable remote support on a customer's AS/400. This command creates the necessary line, controller, and device descriptions to enable a user on a remote system to access the AS/400 from the ECS line and modem.

The command ENDRMTSPT (End Remote Support) disables remote support. This command deletes the objects configured when the STRRMTSPT command was executed. Keep in mind that STRRMTSPT creates the necessary communication objects and ENDRMTSPT deletes them. This can be especially helpful when you need to access a remote system and your contact there does not know how to configure communications.

I have created a CL program and a CL user command called REMOTE, which uses the STRRMTSPT and the ENDRMTSPT CL commands. This CL program simplifies the entire operation by creating all the necessary communication devices on the source system while the command STRRMTSPT creates the communication devices on the target system. Refer to Appendix I: Using the ECS Line for Remote Support on page 363 for the CL source code. The program instructions are documented in the comments within the CL program source code.

SUBSYSTEMS FOR COMMUNICATION LINES AND REMOTE LOCATIONS

Many users create separate subsystems for their communication lines and remote locations. Some even create subsystems for each remote controller. Some reasons you may want to do this are:

* If there are line problems, it may be necessary to end and restart the subsystem to force the system to reset some pointers. If the communication

jobs are in the local work station subsystem, the local users are going to be very unhappy about getting knocked off the system.

- Having one subsystem per remote location saves some headaches when changing the devices at each location. If you have one line and three remote controllers in three separate locations, having three subsystems allows more flexibility. You can bring down one subsystem to make changes to the subsystem entries for the remote devices without disturbing other users of the line.

- You can create the individual subsystems and let them use *INTERACT for the memory pool. That way they won't be using memory unnecessarily.

The following is an example of setting up a subsystem running in the *INTERACT pool for a remote location.

1. Create a subsystem.

```
CRTSBSD SBSD(QGPL/SYDNEY) POOLS((1 *BASE) +
    (2 *INTERACT)) TEXT(Subsystem for Sydney)
```

2. Create a job description.

```
CRTJOBD JOBD(QGPL/SYDNEY) JOBQ(QGPL/SYDNEY) +
    OUTQ(QGPL/SYDNEY) +
    HOLD(*YES) TEXT(Job Description for Sydney)
```

3. Create an output queue.

```
CRTOUTQ OUTQ(QGPL/SYDNEY) TEXT(OUTQ for Sydney)
```

4. Create a job queue.

```
CRTJOBQ JOBQ(QGPL/SYDNEY)
```

5. Create a class with a run priority of 50.

```
CRTCLS CLS(QGPL/SYDNEY) RUNPTY(50)
```

   Note: The default value for RUNPTY is 50.

6. Add job queue entries.

```
ADDJOBQE SBSD(QGPL/SYDNEY) JOBQ(QGPL/SYDNEY) +
    MAXACT(*NOMAX) SEQNBR(10)
```

7. Add routing entries.

```
ADDRTGE SBSD(QGPL/SYDNEY) SEQNBR(10) CMPVAL(QCMDI) +
    PGM(QSYS/QCMD) CLS(QGPL/SYDNEY)
ADDRTGE SBSD(QGPL/SYDNEY) SEQNBR(20) CMPVAL(525XTEST) +
    PGM(QSYS/QARDRIVE) CLS(QGPL/SYDNEY)
ADDRTGE SBSD(QGPL/SYDNEY) SEQNBR(500) +
    CMPVAL(PGMEVOKE 29) PGM(*RTGDTA) CLS(QGPL/SYDNEY)
ADDRTGE SBSD(QGPL/SYDNEY) SEQNBR(9999) CMPVAL(*ANY) +
    PGM(QSYS/QCMD) CLS(QGPL/SYDNEY)
```

8. Add communications entries.

```
ADDCMNE SBSD(QGPL/SYDNEY) RMTLOCNAME(SYDNEY) +
    JOBD(QGPL/SYDNEY)
```

9. Add work station entries to subsystem SYDNEY.

```
ADDWSE SBSD(QGPL/SYDNEY) WRKSTN(SYDDSP*) AT(*SIGNON)
```

10. Start the subsystem.

```
STRSBS SYDNEY
```

ADDING COMMUNICATION ENTRIES TO SUBSYSTEMS

Make sure you understand how the subsystems allocate devices and communication devices, use the mode description, and use the routing entries in the job description. If you have the same communication entry in more than one subsystem, the order in which the subsystems start determines which subsystem allocates the communication device(s). Refer to the *AS/400 Work Management* manual for more information.

APPC PROGRAM RUN PRIORITY

The subsystem QCMN ships with a communication entry and routing details such that Advanced Program-to-Program (APPC) programs run at priority 50 (Class = QBATCH). For batch jobs, this is fine. But if you have interactive APPC applications, you may want to change this. Refer to the *AS/400 Work Management* and the APPC/Communication manuals for additional information.

One reason to change this may be starting Client Access communications (or router). At priority 50, you may experience delays in starting Client Access if several users attempt to sign on simultaneously during periods of high interactive use or periods of other batch-intensive jobs.

CREATING OBJECT CONFIGURATIONS FOR COMMUNICATIONS

When you are trying to create a communication environment, you frequently must create multiple objects such as line, controller, and device descriptions. During this process, you are likely to run into a few problems that will require modifying the objects that you create. In some cases, you have to delete an object and recreate it. This may not be a big deal if you are only creating a simple communication environment. Regardless, look over the following techniques to assist communications configuration.

Using a CL Program

The creation of communications objects usually involves several steps. For example, you must create line, controller, and device descriptions, and there are several matching parameters and other relationships that must be maintained. One way to help you visualize the relationships and help debug problems when creating these objects is to do your work using a CL program. The advantages are:

- You can review all of the commands required to create all of the objects (line, controller, and device) in one source file listing.

- You can debug problems more easily.
- You have a record of what you did so you can recreate it.

The steps to include in your CL program are shown below:

CL Program for Creating Communications Configurations

```
PGM  /* Program to create line, controller and device +
         descriptions   */

/* Vary off the line, which will in turn vary off the      */
/*  controller and the device associated with the line.    */
/*   Monitor for message which warns you that the line is  */
/*   already varied off.                                   */

     VRYCFG linename *LIN *OFF
     MONMSG MSGID(CPF9999)


/* Delete the device(s), controller(s) and the line. This  */
/* is done in so you can recreate them in the next step.   */
/* Monitor for message which warns you that the object does */
/* not exist.                                              */

     DLTDEVD devicename
     MONMSG MSGID(CPF9999)
     DLTCTLD controllername
     MONMSG MSGID(CPF9999)
     DLTLIND linename
     MONMSG MSGID(CPF9999)


/* Create the line, controller(s) & device(s) descriptions. */
/* The line, controller, and device here are an example     */
/*   only.                                                  */
/* Use the F4 key to prompt the command when creating your  */
/* CL source.                                               */

     CRTLINSDLC
     CRTCTLRWS
     CRTDEVDSP
     ENDPGM
```

Now, compile your program. If it doesn't compile, then correct your errors. After compiling, run your program. If it doesn't run to completion, then check your error messages and job log to determine why. Go back and correct your source, recompile, and run again. After successful completion, you have a record of what you did so you can recreate it in the future.

Even if you don't use a CL program to create the objects, certainly consider using the RTVCFGSRC command to create and save a copy of the necessary CL commands to recreate all communication objects on your system (see below).

Using Worksheets to Match Parameters

When creating communication objects, you generally have to match several parameters on the local and remote systems. Refer to Appendix J: Communication Matching Parameter Worksheets on page 369 for examples of these worksheets, which you can copy and use in your environment.

Example Use of RTVCFGSRC Command

Using the Retrieve Configuration Source (RTVCFGSRC) command to retrieve the configuration source for the ECS line, you can create a member in your designated file that is the source file listing for a CL program for recreating the ECS line, controller, and device descriptions. You only need to compile and run the program. For example:

1. Enter the RTVCFGSRC command to create a CL source file:

```
RTVCFGSRC CFGD(QESLINE) CFGTYPE(*ALL) SRCFILE(MYLIB/QCLSRC)
```

2. Use SEU (Source Entry Utility), or an editor of your choice, to view or edit the source file. The example shown below is a listing of the source file member that is created by the command in step number 1.

```
Columns . . . :   1  80                          Browse    BISEL/QCLSRC
 SEU==>                                                     QESLINE
 FMT **  ...+... 1 ...+... 2 ...+... 3 ...+... 4 ...+... 5 ...+... 6 ...+..
 *************** Beginning of data ********************************
 0000.01 /*       QESLINE          08:32:06 */                  950308
 0000.02 CRTLINSDLC LIND(QESLINE) RSRCNAME(LIN071) ONLINE(*NO) ROLE(*SEC) +
 0000.03           INTERFACE(*RS232V24) CNN(*SWTPP) VRYWAIT(*NOWAIT) +
 0000.04           AUTOCALL(*NO) EXCHID(056A0031) NRZI(*YES) MAXCTL(1) +
 0000.05           CLOCK(*MODEM) LINESPEED(2400) MODEM(*V54) +
 0000.06           MODEMRATE(*FULL) SWTCNN(*DIAL) AUTOANS(*NO) +
 0000.07           AUTODIAL(*YES) DIALCMD(*V25BIS) CALLNBR(*NONE) STNADR(1C) +
 0000.08           MAXFRAME(521) THRESHOLD(*OFF) DUPLEX(*HALF) MODULUS(8) +
 0000.09           MAXOUT(7) INACTTMR(300) POLLRSPDLY(0) LINKSPEED(9600) +
 0000.10           COSTCNN(128) COSTBYTE(128) SECURITY(*NONSECURE) +
 0000.11           PRPDLY(*TELEPHONE) USRDFN1(128) USRDFN2(128) USRDFN3(128) +
 0000.12           DSRDRPTMR(6) AUTOANSTYP(*DTR) CTSTMR(25) RMTANSTMR(60) +
 0000.13           CMNRCYLMT(2 5) TEXT(*BLANK)
 ***************** End of data ********************************



 F3=Exit   F5=Refresh   F9=Retrieve   F10=Cursor   F12=Cancel
 F16=Repeat find        F24=More keys
```

MULTI-POINT COMMUNICATION LINES

Depending on the number of users, amount of traffic, and other factors, you may be able to tune multi-point communication by adjusting the priority of one or more remote controllers. There are three parameters associated with the controller descriptions.

POLLPTY	Each controller on a multi-point line is placed in a polling list. The system polls each controller once as it cycles through the list. If you have four controllers (A, B, C, and D) and you set the POLLPTY of controller B to *YES, after the system polls all four controllers once, it goes back and polls controller B again before cycling through the original list. This gives controller B two polling opportunities for each polling cycle. The devices on controller B have more opportunity to obtain CPU resources (e.g., high-speed printing).
POLLLMT	The POLLLMT default value is 0, but it can be set as high as 4. If set higher than 0, then the controller gets another block of frames for each poll. This block of frames is for input and output.
OUTLMT	The OUTLMT parameter is similar to the POLLLMT parameter, except that the limit applies to the outbound (from the host) transactions only. Transactions usually involve more blocks for outbound transactions than for inbound. For example, an interactive transaction sending only a few bytes of data to the host may receive an entire screen of data from the host.

On multi-point lines, you might be able to improve the performance of one or two controllers in a network of several by adjusting these parameters. However, there is no substitute for higher speed lines or point-to-point lines.

PERFORMANCE TIPS FOR THE ASCII WORK STATION CONTROLLER

These performance tips are for PCs and PS/2s using the ASCII WSC method of attachment.

- Configure the 5150 device description with a minimal NRM Poll Timer value. The default vale is 0.3 seconds (sec). Set the NRM Poll Timer to 0.2 sec, which causes the ASCII WSC to use 0.0 sec for this value. This could enhance throughput by 15 to 20 percent.

- Both the AS/400 and the PC Configuration default to 8 data bits per byte. Do not change this unless you have to. The only reason to change the word length is for a modem or an asynchronous data network that does not support 8 data bits with no parity. This may be a requirement of old hardware. Configured for 7 data bits, there is extra overhead associated with things such as stripping a bit from each byte, building a suffix byte to inform systems about the word length change, and hiding ASCII control characters. The 7-bit data transfer is about 40-percent slower than an 8 data bit connection.

- Load and run PC programs (including Client Access) from the hard disk whenever possible. Accessing shared folders when using the ASCII WSC is much slower than using the hard disk.

Using the **WRKHDWRSC** Command

You can configure multiple line descriptions for a single communication line resource. You can not use more than one of those line descriptions at a time. For example, most systems have a communication resource, LIN011. IBM provides two communication line descriptions that use this resource, QTILINE and QESLINE.

Whenever you configure a new line description, you must know the name of the communication resource you intend to use. And, whenever you intend to use a line description, you must make sure that no other line is varied on that uses the same communication resource.

The WRKHDWRSC command is very useful for configuring new line descriptions or determining which lines use a particular communication resource. Invoke the command by entering:

```
WRKHDWRSC TYPE(*CMN)
```

*(The *CMN indicates you want the communication resource information.)*

The example below is typical of the display that you will be presented.

```
                       Work with Communication Resources
                                              System:       APACHE
Type options, press Enter.
  2=Edit    4=Remove    5=Work with configuration descriptions


Opt  Resource       Type  Text
     CMB01          9152  Combined function IOP
_     LIN01         2612  Comm Adapter
5      LIN011        2612  V.24 Port Enhanced
_     LIN02         2612  Comm Adapter
_      LIN021        2612  V.24 Port Enhanced
_    CMB02          2619  Combined function IOP
_     LIN03         2619  LAN Adapter
_      LIN031        2619  Token-Ring Port
_    CMB03          2617  Combined function IOP
_     LIN04         2617  LAN Adapter
_      LIN041        2617  Ethernet Port



                                                            Bottom
F3=Exit   F5=Refresh   F6=Print   F11=Display resource addresses/statuses
F12=Cancel
```

If you use option 5 (in my example on the LIN011 resource), you get to the screen that allows you to work with the configuration descriptions for that resource.

```
                    Work with Configuration Descriptions
                                          System:      APACHE
Resource name  . . . . . . . :   LIN011
Text . . . . . . . . . . . :     V.24 Port Enhanced

Type options, press Enter.
  1=Create    5=Work with description    8=Work with configuration status


Opt     Description
  _     QESLINE
  _     QREMOTESPT
  _     QTILINE
  _     Q1PLIN
  _     TUCSONW



                                                           Bottom
F3=Exit   F5=Refresh   F6=Print   F12=Cancel
```

TIPS FOR USING THE IBM-SUPPLIED COMMUNICATION CABLES

When you order communication adapters for the AS/400, you have a choice of
two cables: the EIA 232/V.24 Enhanced Cable or the plain vanilla EIA 232/V.24
cable. Make sure that the cable and the modem you intend to use match. Some
modems provide some automatic diagnostic loop-back functions (CCITT V.54).
These loop-back functions are initiated from the system by raising pin 18 for local
loop back or pin 21 for remote loop back on the V.24 interface. The AS/400
supports these loop backs for Problem Analysis.

Before CCITT V.54 was defined, some modems used pin 18 for the Signal
Quality Detect function. For V.54, pin 18 is driven from the system to the
modem; for Signal Quality Detect, pin 18 is driven from the modem to the
system. Hence, if a system that supports local loop back is connected to a
modem that uses pin 18 for Signal Quality Detect, both devices try to drive the
signal. In some cases, this causes a power check on the system.

The "unenhanced" cable has no connection on pins 18, 21, or 25. The enhanced
cable connects these three pins, thus enabling the V.54 diagnostics. Check your
modem documentation to see if the modem supports V.54 tests or uses pin 18
for Signal Quality Detect. If the modem does neither, then it makes no difference
which cable you use. If it uses pin 18 for Signal Quality Detect, then **DO NOT**
use the enhanced cable. If the modem supports CCITT V.54 (as IBM modems
do), then use the enhanced cable.

CONFIGURING THE ASCII WORK STATION CONTROLLER FOR PORT SHARING

ASCII port sharing allows you to have different ASCII displays (such as a
personal computer or an ASCII terminal), with different device types and physical
parameters, share the same port at different times without needing to manually

create a configuration description for each new display. This is especially useful when using dial-in work stations.

ASCII port sharing works by having the system determine the device type, line speed, parity, and word length of the connecting work station. Then the system updates the configuration record for that device automatically.

ASCII port sharing consists of the following functions, which may be used together or separately:

- Automatic detection of incoming line speed, parity, and word length.
- Automatic detection of device type.

To enable port sharing, create your device description using the *CALC parameter. In the following example, a display device is created for port 1 on the ASCII Work Station Controller. This device will allow a PC running ASCII terminal emulation, a PC running Client Access/400, or an ASCII terminal using a modem to dial in to the AS/400:

```
CRTDEVDSP DEVD(xxx) DEVCLS(*LCL) TYPE(*CALC) MODEL(*ASCII) PORT(1)
    ATTACH(*MODEM) CTL(CTL05) LINESPEED(*CALC) WORDLEN(*CALC)
    PARITY(*CALC) STOPBITS(1)
```

SECURITY

Several security considerations were discussed earlier in this book. You may want to review the Performing New Installations and Upgrades section on page 15. To review a few of the major points:

- Set security to level 30, 40, or 50 (refer to Security System Values on page 25).
- Understand the significance of the system values:
  - QSECURITY
  - QLMTSECOFR
  - QPWDEXPITV
  - QALWOBJRST (V3R1)
- There are a few others but these are the most important.

`V3R1`

What else should you be doing? Well, before you begin adding user profiles, setting up libraries, and generally managing your system, you should gain a solid understanding of how security works on the AS/400. A good understanding now saves you a lot of work later, makes your system operate at higher levels of efficiency, and makes your job managing the system a lot easier.

Here is some recommended reading:

AS/400 Security — Basic manual

AS/400 Security — Reference

AS/400 Security and Auditing Considerations

OfficeVision/400 Version 2 Technical Tips and Techniques

BASIC SECURITY RECOMMENDATIONS

As a point for your consideration, when you are implementing a security policy on the AS/400, avoid dealing with many individual objects. Try to implement your policies so that you can implement and maintain your system security with a SIMPLE solution. There are, of course, unique considerations; but if you take the time now to learn and understand how security is implemented, you lighten your workload later. Try to make extensive use of group profiles, authorization lists, adoptive authority, and other measures available to make your job easier.

The following are some basic recommendations:

> *When implementing your security design, you must consider your design with respect to ease of maintenance and impact on performance. The recommendations that follow are made with respect to ease of maintenance. For a discussion on performance considerations, refer to Security Design for Performance Recommendations on page 196.*

- Systems programmers. Suggest giving them *ALLOBJ authority by giving them a user class of *SECOFR. If you do not have systems programmers, then this does not apply.

- Application programmers. Do not give them *ALLOBJ, *SERVICE, *SECADM, or *SECOFR authority. Use library authorities to prevent access to production libraries. Create programmer libraries and have a program that "adopts" authority to copy selected production data to programmer libraries for testing.

- Group user profiles. Establish group profiles as soon as possible after system installation. Do not use individual profiles as group profiles. Consider the individual user and the group profiles as entities. As such, no one should sign on to the system using the group profile. One way to enforce this is to set the group profile password to *NONE.

  When you create individual user profiles, there is a parameter whereby all objects created by the individual are owned by another userid. Consider assigning ownership of objects created by individuals to the group profile. This allows all users in the group to have access to the objects and make system maintenance easier.

  Refer to Suggestions for Using V3R1 Multiple Group Profiles on page 177 for a discussion on group profiles.

- Naming Conventions. Establish and enforce a naming convention for objects on the AS/400. Use descriptive names.

- User/group profile names. Do not create any profile names starting with the letter Q.

  If you use other systems (e.g., TSO, VM/CMS), define userids with seven characters so that the same userid can be used on all other systems.

  Group profiles should **ALWAYS** have a name that suggests it is a group profile.

- Library security. Design libraries so that all objects within the library have identical or similar protection requirements.

- Object security. Specific object authority should only be defined to handle exceptions.

- Menu security. Avoid limiting a user's capability to menus. Use library and object security instead.

- Individual versus group authorization. Create groups that reflect job functions and use group authorization generally.

- Individual versus group ownership. Recommend group ownership over individual ownership for objects. As users are added to a group, they immediately have access to all the objects owned by the group. Also, when users are removed from the group, access is revoked.

- Authorization lists. Where possible, use authorization lists. They offer performance advantages over specific object authorizations.

- Logical files. For access to critical files, use logical files. This way, the owner of the file can authorize access by other users to specific fields or records rather than to the entire physical file.

- Passwords for IBM-supplied user profiles. Refer to Change Passwords for IBM-Supplied User Profiles on page 45.

RECOMMENDATIONS FOR NAMING USER PROFILES

The following recommendations are from the *AS/400 Security — Reference* manual.

- A user profile name can be up to 10 characters long. Both the OfficeVision/400 Licensed Program and some communications methods limit the user ID to eight characters. The Add User display also limits the user profile name to eight characters.

- Use eight characters or less if you use the OfficeVision/400 Licensed Program or communications now or plan to in the future. Use seven characters or less if you plan to use other systems (e.g., TSO, VM/CMS) and want consistent user IDs across all systems.

- When you use the OfficeVision/400 Licensed Program, you send mail to a person's user ID. Use a naming scheme that makes user IDs easy to remember.

- The system does not distinguish between uppercase and lowercase letters in a user profile name. If you enter lowercase alphabetic characters at your work station, the system translates them to uppercase characters.

- The displays and lists you use to manage user profiles list them in alphabetical order by user profile name.

- Avoid using special characters in user profile names. Special characters may cause problems with keyboard mapping for certain work stations or with national language versions of the OS/400 Licensed Program.

RESTORING SECURITY-SENSITIVE OBJECTS

 If you use V3R1 or later, the QALWOBJRST system value determines whether objects that are security-sensitive may be restored to your system. Use this command to prevent anyone from restoring a system state object or an object that adopts authority.

The shipped value for QALWOBJRST is *ALL. This value is necessary to install your system successfully.

> **WARNING: It is important to set the QALWOBJRST value to *ALL before performing some system activities, such as:**
> - **Installing a new release of the OS/400 Licensed Program.**
> - **Installing new licensed programs.**
> - **Applying PTFs.**
> - **Recovering your system.**

These activities may fail if the QALWOBJRST value is not *ALL. If you have set the system value QALWOBJRST to a value other than *ALL, then make sure you set it to *ALL for the above circumstances. Then return the value to your normal setting after completing the system activity.

Possible values for the QALWOBJRST system value:

*ALL   Any object may be restored to your system by a
                   user having the proper authority.

*NONE   Security-sensitive objects, such as system state
                   programs or programs that adopt authority, may
                   not be restored to the system.

*ALWSYSST   System state objects may be restored to the
                   system.

*ALWPGMADP   Objects that adopt authority may be restored to
                   the system.

The *AS/400 Security — Reference* manual recommends setting this value to
*NONE for normal operations. I recommend against that as it is too easy to
forget about it. Then, when the value must be set to *ALL to perform an
important system function, you run into problems. Most installations do not need
to have this level of security and should leave it at the shipped value of *ALL.

SECURITY SYSTEM VALUE RECOMMENDATIONS

Consider three operational environments: simple, medium, and complex.

Simple   Small sites, no program development, and packaged
                software. Little information on the system is confidential.
                System is stand-alone. An example is an educational
                institution that uses the system for tutorial purposes only.

Medium   Major programming done by contractors. Bulk of users use
                these contracted applications or other IBM applications such
                as Query/400 or OfficeVision/400. Some information on the
                system is restricted or confidential. There may be
                communication activities with personal computers or other
                systems. Most small and medium-size companies with
                systems that store company data belong in this category.

Complex   Substantial in-house application development. System may
                be part of complex network of PCs and other systems. Most
                of the information is highly confidential or very sensitive. A
                financial institution is an example of this environment.

I believe that most installations fall into the medium security environment.
System security for simple environments is not adequate for any business that
has important data on their computer system. The following are my
recommendations for the minimum security implementation on your AS/400.

Recommendations for Medium-Security Environments

The recommended security implementation for medium-environment systems is:

- Library security for general access to libraries.
- Additional object security over library content.
- Enroll users and give them limited capability.
- Authorization list over system objects.
- Authorization lists for office objects.
- Use of audit journal for some tracking of security events.
- Use of system values shown in the following table.

SYSVAL	Recommended Value	Comments
QALWOBJRST	*ALL	Determines whether objects that are security-sensitive may be restored to your system. Use this command to prevent anyone from restoring a system state object or an object that adopts authority. Values other than *ALL may prevent vital system maintenance activities. Refer to Restoring Security-Sensitive Objects on page 173.
QAUDLVL	*AUTFAIL *SECURITY	Security-related events and authorization failures should be logged.
QAUTOVRT	0	The more available the virtual devices are, the more exposure your system has. For example, if an unauthorized remote user reaches the maximum number of sign-on attempts on one virtual device, he or she may have access to other virtual devices.
QDSPSGNINF	1	Encourage each user to keep track of their own user ID to see whether anyone has tried to misuse it.
QINACTITV	30 minutes	Any time longer than 30 minutes normally indicates that the user is physically away from the terminal.
QINACTMSGQ	*DSCJOB	Allows user to resume work on the system at the point where interruption occurred.

SYSVAL	Recommended Value	Comments
QLMTDEVSSN	1	This enforces individual accountability. It is one way to alert a user who already has a session active. The terminal may have been left unattended.
QLMTSECOFR	0	It is not critical to limit the Security Officer or users with *ALLOBJ authority to certain work stations as long as user IDs and passwords are securely protected.
QMAXSIGN	3	This number should be high enough to allow possible typing errors, but not high enough to allow attempts to guess the password.
QPWDEXPITV	30	Changing the password regularly prevents accidental "leaks" from being active forever.
QRMTSIGN	*FRCSIGNON	There are normally quite a substantial number of remote users; thus the system is more prone to exposure.
QSECURITY	30	Any production system should be at least at level 30. There may be cases that require systems to move to level 40 or 50.

GROUP PROFILES

A group profile is created exactly like a user profile. The system does not recognize it as a group profile until you associate user profiles to it. When you are planning system security, I strongly recommend that you use group profiles for a number of reasons. Among them, ease of administration and potential performance gains.

Although I have included some recommendations here, this is not a complete discussion of group profiles or security. I recommend that you become familiar with the AS/400 manuals *AS/400 Security — Basic* and *AS/400 Security — Reference*.

Suggestions for Using Group Profiles

When planning the use of group profiles, give thought to the logical organization of your enterprise. The group profiles should be logically organized in much the same way as your company is organized. Consider departmental and job responsibilities when you are setting up your design. Refer to the following list for practical suggestions for using group profiles.

- You can manage authority more efficiently and reduce the number of individual private authorities for objects. However, if you misuse group profiles, you may cause a negative impact on system performance because of excessive authority checking.

- Use the password *NONE for group profiles.

- For users who are members of group profiles, consider assigning object ownership to the group profiles rather than to the user profiles. Use the OWNER parameter in the user profile. When you create a user profile, set the OWNER to *GRPPRF, rather than the default of *USRPRF.

- If you discover that a user has authorities that should belong to a group of users, do the following:

  1. Create a group profile.
  2. Use the GRTUSRAUT command to give the user's authorities to the group profile.
  3. Remove the private authorities from the user, because they are no longer needed. Use the RVKOBJAUT or EDTOBJAUT command.

- For each group profile, consider creating a job description for each user group, or optionally, creating a library for each group.

Suggestions for Using V3R1 Multiple Group Profiles

| V3R1 | A user may be a member of up to 16 groups. A group may have private authority to an object, or it may be the primary group for an object.

The first group in the user profile is referred to as the Group Profile (GRPPRF parameter in the user profile). The remaining 15 groups are referred to as supplemental groups (SUPGRPPRF parameter in the user profile).

Authority from one or more of the user's groups may be accumulated to find sufficient authority for the object being accessed. The rules regarding accumulated authority are:

- Special authority accumulates from the user and all group profiles.

- If the user profile does not have individual authority to an object, then authority is accumulated for all the group profiles of which the user profile is a member.

- If the user profile has individual authority to an object, then that authority overrides the object authorities of the group profiles, even if the group(s) authority is higher.

The following are suggestions for using multiple group profiles:

- Use multiple groups in combination with primary group authority, and eliminate private authority to objects.

- Because individual object authority overrides group authority to the object, avoid assigning individual authorities. If individual authorities are used, avoid assigning authorities that are less than the group's authority.

- Carefully plan the sequence in which group profiles are assigned to a user. The user's first group should relate to the user's primary assignment and the objects used most often. Use supplemental groups for tasks or assignments that the user performs less often.

- According to the *AS/400 Security — Reference* manual, the sequence in which private authorities are specified for an object has no effect on authority-checking performance. However, security and performance experts suggest keeping the following points in mind to minimize the impact on performance when using multiple group profiles.

  - Minimize the number of supplemental group profiles.

  - Within each user profile, list the supplemental group profiles in order from most authority to least authority.

- If you plan to use multiple groups, gain an understanding of the authority-checking process described in the *AS/400 Security — Reference* manual.

- Be sure you understand how using multiple groups in combination with other authority techniques, such as authorization lists, affects system performance.

SYSTEM KEYLOCK OR MODE SWITCH

The keylock switch (or mode positioning buttons on Advanced Series models) is used to physically secure the system and to enable or disable certain functions. The most common position is Normal, which prevents users from turning off the system manually. Place in the Normal position and remove the key. In this position, the power switch is totally deactivated. The following table lists the functions performed using each switch or mode setting.

System Function	KEYLOCK OR MODE POSITION			
	Manual	Normal	Auto	Secure
Use Dedicated Service Tools	Yes	No	No	No
Load system from tape	Yes	No	No	No
Change IPL source	Yes	No	No	No
IPL via switch	Yes	Yes	No	No
Remote IPL	No	Yes	Yes	No
PWRDWNSYS from work station	Yes	Yes	Yes	Yes
Off via power switch	Yes	No	No	No

The AS/400 Advanced Series model has a front panel that differs from the original model. Instead of a keylock switch, a series of function buttons is used to set the mode of operation. The mode corresponds to the keylock position. If you have a model 3xx system, you must first insert the system security key into the slot before changing the mode.

MONITORING SECURITY

The following information can also be found in the AS/400 Security manuals.

You can and should monitor security periodically at various levels. The first step you need to perform before starting a monitoring program is to make sure that you have performed the basics. The following is a simple checklist of the basic security implementation that you should have configured. Look this over and see if you comply, then proceed with the remainder of this subsection on monitoring. Limit this review to answering general questionnaires, analyzing the system status, verifying security requirements, or including statistical analysis of the requirements.

- Passwords have been changed for IBM-supplied user profiles.
- The number of users with special authorities is reasonably small.
- Multiple sign-on with the same user ID is prohibited.
- Password changes are required and enforced at appropriate intervals (e.g., 60 days).
- Group profiles have PASSWORD(*NONE) specified.
- An organization chart exists for all system users.

- The administration of user profiles is adequately organized.
- The limited capability (LMTCPB) parameter on the Create User Profile (CRTUSRPRF) or Change User Profile (CHGUSRPRF) command is set to *YES.

Monitor Programs That Adopt Owner's Authority

List all programs with adopted authority. Do an analysis of the subprograms and library arrangement for programs that run under the authority of users with special authority.

```
DSPPGMADP USRPRF(user-profile-name) OUTPUT(*PRINT)
```

Monitor Job Descriptions

If a user profile name is used as a value for the USER parameter in the job description, all jobs submitted with this job description are executed with attributes taken from that user profile. In this way, an unauthorized user can violate security. Use the Display Job Description (DSPJOBD) to look at the USER parameter. If a user profile is specified, verify that this is necessary and analyze the authorities of the user profile.

Procedures for Monitoring Security Periodically

Three important areas that require periodic monitoring are user profile definitions, library inspection, and application programs. Some suggestions and tips for monitoring these objects follow:

User Profile Inspection

Produce output of all defined user profiles and optionally produce output for any specific profiles:

```
DSPAUTUSR SEQ(*GRPPRF) OUTPUT(*PRINT)
DSPOBJD OBJ(*ALL) OBJTYPE(*USRPRF) OUTPUT(*PRINT) +
    DETAIL(*BASIC)
DSPUSRPRF USRPRF(name) TYPE(*BASIC) OUTPUT(*PRINT)
DSPUSRPRF USRPRF(name) TYPE(*ALL) OUTPUT(*PRINT)
```

You don't need to list IBM-supplied user profiles in detail. Good planning involves group profiles, authorization lists, and use of the Public Authority parameter. Few users need large profiles (e.g., objects owned).

Potential exposures:
- How many people have special authorities.
- How many people own large number of objects.
- What types of objects are owned.
- Understand any exposures.

Library Inspection

List the names of all libraries, objects in the libraries, and the authorities for the libraries.

```
DSPOBJD OBJ(*ALL) OBJTYPE(*LIB) OUTPUT(*PRINT)
DSPLIBF LIB(lib_name) OUTPUT(*PRINT)
DSPOBJAUT OBJ(lib_name) OBJTYPE(*LIB) OUTPUT(*PRINT)
```

Potential exposures:

- Overview of libraries.
- Understand any exposures.

Audit Programs

It is not practical to inspect all programs in the system.

```
DSPPGMADP USRPRF(user_name) OUTPUT(*PRINT)
DSPOBJAUT OBJ(libname/objname) OBJTYPE(*PGM) +
    OUTPUT(*PRINT)
DSPOBJD OBJ(libname/objname) OBJTYPE(*PGM) +
    OUTPUT(*PRINT) DETAIL(*FULL)
```

Potential exposures:

- Examine aspects of users with special authority.
- List programs owned by these users that adopt owner's authority.
- Inspect any program owned by user with *ALLOBJ authority that adopts owner's authority.
- Verify public authority of the program that adopts owner's authority to see which users can call the program.

Monitor History Log

The following commands can be used to help isolate specific events from the history log. Most security-related messages have message numbers in the range CPF2201 to CPF2299. The message number CPF2200 causes all messages in this range to be selected.

```
DSPLOG LOG(QHST) PERIOD((*AVAIL 010190) (*AVAIL 020190)) MSGID(CPF2200)
```

The following command displays all occurrences of someone trying to get at an object file without correct authority:

```
DSPLOG LOG(QHST) PERIOD((0000 010190) (*AVAIL *END)) MSGID(CPF2218)
```

Monitor Security Officer Actions

You may want to monitor the actions of the Security Officer or users with *ALLOBJ (all object) authority — particularly if several people have access to the Security Officer password (not a good idea), or if several people have *ALLOBJ authority. Use the following procedure to monitor the use of commands used by the Security Officer or users with (*ALLOBJ) special authority.

1. Create a journal to log Security Officer's actions.

```
CRTJRNRCV JRNRCV(SECLOG01) AUT(*EXCLUDE) +
    TEXT('SECOFR Receiver')
CRTJRN JRN(SECLOG) JRNRCV(SECLOG01) AUT(*EXCLUDE) +
    TEXT('Log SECOFR Actions')
```

2. Make QCLSECOFR the initial program or menu option for the Security Officer and users with *SECOFR authority.

3. Create the CL program SECLOG. See CL Program to Record Commands in a Security Journal, below.

4. Change the user profile of QSECOFR and users with *SECOFR authority to LMTCPB(*YES) so that commands can be entered only through the program that logs the requests.

CL Program to Record Commands in a Security Journal

```
/******************************************************/
/* SECLOG - This program will present the Command Entry*/
/* display and allow a user to issue commands.  The    */
/* commands that are run are recorded in the journal   */
/* SECLOG/OUTPUT - The entry in the journal receiver   */
/* associated with the security log has three possible */
/* forms                                               */
/*      *ERROR * command - error detected when running */
/*      *ENDRQS* command - end request during command  */
/*       running command BLANK - normal completion of  */
/*          command                                    */
/* RECOMMENDATIONS - Potential use is to record the    */
/* actions of an *ALLOBJ user such as the QSECOFR.     */
/* To prevent the enter of commands on other command   */
/* lines, define the user profile as LMTCPB(*YES)      */


/******************************************************/
SECLOG: PGM
            DCL     VAR(&MSG) TYPE(*CHAR) LEN(512)
            DCL     VAR(&KEYVAR) TYPE(*CHAR) LEN(4)
            DCL     VAR(&RTNTYPE) TYPE(*CHAR) LEN(2)
RECEIVE:/******************************************************/
   /* Receiving a request message shows command entry. */
   /******************************************************/


            RCVMSG   PGMQ(*EXT) MSGTYPE(*RQS) +
                     RMV(*NO) +
                     KEYVAR(&KEYVAR) MSG(&MSG)
                     RTNTYPE(&RTNTYPE)
            MONMSG    MSGID(CPF2415) EXEC(RETURN)
   /*                 F3(Return)                    */
   /*  F4 - PROMPT RTNTYPE = '10'    */
            IF    (&RTNTYPE = '10') CHGVAR &MSG   +
                  ('?' *CAT &MSG)
   /* F4(Prompt)       */
```

```
/**********************************************************/
/* Syntax check and allow prompting if requested          */

/**********************************************************/
          CALL QCMCHK (&MSG 512)
          MONMSG CPF0000 EXEC(GOTO RECEIVE)
/**********************************************************/
 /* Remove old request and replace with new request       */
   /* The new request includes values from prompting       */

/**********************************************************/
          RMVMSG    PGMQ(*EXT) KEYVAR(&KEYVAR)    +
                      CLEAR(*BYKEY)
          SNDPGMMSG TOPGMQ(*EXT) MSGTYPE(*RQS)    +
                      MSG(&MSG)
          RCVMSG PGMQ(*EXT) MSGTYPE(*RQS) RMV(*NO)
          CALL QCMEXC (&MSG 512) /*  RUN CMD  */

/**********************************************************/
    /*  Issue command and log in SECLOG                    */

/**********************************************************/
          MONMSG    MSGID(CPF1907) +
                      EXEC(CHGVAR &MSG +
                      ('*ENDRQS* ' || &MSG) )
          /*  ENDRQS  */
          MONMSG    MSGID(CPF0000) +
                      EXEC(CHGVAR &MSG +
                      ('*ERROR* ' || &MSG) )
          SNDJRNE JRN(SECLOG) ENTDTA(&MSG)
          MONMSG CPF0000 EXEC(SIGNOFF *LIST)
          GOTO RECEIVE
        ENDPGM
```

Auditing Security Using System-Provided Journals

You can audit security statistics in the system-provided security journal QAUDJRN. Refer to the **AS/400 Security — Reference** manual for a discussion on how to set up the security auditing journal and how to audit using the journal.

HOW TO LIST ALL USER PROFILES, SORTED BY GROUP PROFILE

Here are a couple of ways:

```
DSPAUTUSR SEQ(*GRPPRF) OUTPUT(*PRINT)
   — or —
DSPUSRPRF *ALL OUTPUT(*OUTFILE) OUTFILE(libname/filename)
```

Then use your favorite query facility to generate a report.

CHANGING OBJECT OWNERSHIP

The CHGOBJOWN command allows you to change the object ownership from one user to another, but you can only do this one object at a time. If you want to change object ownership of a group of objects, you can use the CHGLIBOWN command, part of QUSRTOOLS (refer to QUSRTOOL Library on page 307), or try using the following CL program.

CL Program CHGOWNER — Program to Change Object Ownership

```
            PGM         PARM(&OLDOWNER &NEWOWNER)
            DCL         VAR(&OLDOWNER) TYPE(*CHAR) LEN(10)
            DCL         VAR(&NEWOWNER) TYPE(*CHAR) LEN(10)
            DCLF        FILE(QSYS/QADSPUPO)
            DSPUSRPRF   USRPRF(&OLDOWNER) TYPE(*OBJOWN) +
                          OUTPUT(*OUTFILE) +
                          OUTFILE(QUSRSYS/QUSROBJ)
            OVRDBF      FILE(QADSPUPO) TOFILE(QUSRSYS/QUSROBJ)
BEGIN:      RCVF
            MONMSG      MSGID(CPF0864) EXEC(GOTO CMDLBL(STOP))
            IF          COND(&OOTYPE *EQ '*DOC') +
                          THEN(GOTO CMDLBL(DLO))
            CHGOBJOWN   OBJ(&OOLIB/&OOOBJ) OBJTYPE(&OOTYPE) +
                          NEWOWN(&NEWOWNER) CUROWNAUT(*REVOKE)
            MONMSG      MSGID(CPF2298)
            MONMSG      MSGID(CPF2981)
            GOTO        CMDLBL(BEGIN)
DLO:        CHGDLOOWN   DLO(*SYSOBJNAM) NEWOWN(&NEWOWNER) +
                          CUROWNAUT(*REVOKE) SYSOBJNAM(&OOOBJ)
            MONMSG      MSGID(CPF2981)
            GOTO        CMDLBL(BEGIN)
STOP:       DLTF        FILE(QUSRSYS/QUSROBJ)
            MONMSG      MSGID(CPF2105)
            ENDPGM
```

The syntax for running the program is:

```
    Call libname/CHGOWNER  old_owner  new_owner
```

If there are Office objects involved, or if the old owner is listed in the system directory, then the new owner must be an OfficeVision user or be listed in the system directory.

Another way to change object ownership is to delete the old user profile. In Version 2, when you delete a user profile, you can specify that any objects owned are transferred to another user.

OUTPUT QUEUE SECURITY

If you wish to restrict access to certain output queues, then create the queue with OPRCTL(*NO). The default value is *YES. By setting this value to *NO, you must specifically grant authority to selected users. This protects the queue and its contents from being manipulated, viewed, or otherwise accessed by unauthorized users.

There is one exception. Users who have *SPLCTL (spool control) special authority have unlimited control over spool files, including output queues specified with OPRCTL(*NO). Normally, only users who have security officer profiles have *SPLCTL special authority. However, I have seen some instances where the system operators were given *SPLCTL authority in addition to their normal system default authorities. Make sure you understand the implications of this authority and ensure that there is valid justification for its use.

For example, suppose you have an overnight batch payroll job that spools the check writing output to an output queue. In the morning, you intend to print the checks. As you can see, there is a window of vulnerability from the time the checks are spooled and placed in an output queue and the time the checks are printed. You may have unauthorized persons viewing — or worse, printing — the checks. So, not only should you be using the OPRCTL(*NO) for output queues, you may want to consider putting particularly sensitive output queues into more secure libraries than QGPL or QUSRSYS.

SYSTEM PASSWORD

Beginning with Version 2, Release 2, of OS/400, support is added to detect processor model changes on the 9404 and the 9406 AS/400 systems through the use of a system password. The system password identifies all model changes to:

- Maintain the quality and integrity of the AS/400.
- Ensure that IBM is paid the applicable charges due for the use of its licensed programs, including those having processor-based charges.
- Ensure the protection of IBM's intellectual property, including IBM Licensed Internal Code.

If a new software release is installed from tape, the system password is generated automatically and stored in the system. A new system password is required for each subsequent model change, and is provided with all IBM-supplied model changes starting with the general availability of V2R2. New systems are shipped from IBM with the system password installed. Model upgrades supplied by IBM are shipped with the system password, which must be entered when the upgrade is installed.

IBM recommends that, after installing V2R2 on a system, the system password be recorded in case it is needed by an IBM Service Representative. To obtain the system password from the machine, use the Work with Hardware Products (WRKHDWPRD) command, after the installation of V2R2, to print the system configuration list for the 9404 system unit and the rack configuration list for the 9406 system unit. The print out contains the system password and is the only way to view the installed system password. Keep the printout in a safe place.

As of V2R3, the system password can not be displayed. IBM decided that users never have a need to know the system password, so they removed the ability to display or print it. The system password is still required for upgrades, but IBM provides the password with the upgrade.

If the correct system password is unavailable and is required either for a model upgrade or some rare service condition, a temporary system password bypass can be selected to allow time for the correct system password to be obtained through a customer request to an IBM Marketing Representative. The Marketing Representative obtains the correct system password using a system password RPQ order. If the correct system password is not entered before the bypass time ends, the system will not complete the next IPL until the correct system password is installed. During this bypass time, system console messages warn that the system is in bypass and give the remaining bypass time.

The following is a list of things to consider:

- If you have multiple AS/400s and are creating a distribution tape from the central site for distribution to DSLO (Distributed Software License Option) systems, the code in OS/400 generates a unique password for each system on which it is loaded. This occurs when you actually load the software on the DSLO system, not when you create the tape. If the target system does not have a password, then one is created. Each system retains its individual password until a model upgrade is performed. When a model upgrade is ordered, a new password is sent with the upgrade itself.

- It is possible to distribute software using DASD. This involves loading software on a system, then removing all the DASD and installing it in a target system. IBM Rochester does not recommend distributing software in this fashion. If, however, you have a burning desire to flagellate yourself, contact your IBM Customer Engineer or send an IBMLink note to RCHVMP(ENTITLE) for further instructions.

- System password RPQ orders with invalid system serial numbers are rejected and a CE call is required to correct the system serial number.

- With V2R2, the ability to display or change the system password via DST option 10 is not supported, although the screens display the option. The screens have been updated since that release.

- The ability to display the system password is provided on V2R2 systems only through the print support provided by the WRKHDWPRD command. The ability to enter the correct system password is provided by IPL in Manual mode.

- If you need a new system password, order RPQ Number S40345 from IBM. You will be asked a few embarrassing questions (Why do you need a new password? Do you have a legitimate MULIC tape? Have you paid your bill?) and on approval of your request, you will be given a new password. If you have any questions, send an IBMLink note to RCHVMP(ENTITLE). Refer to Sending E-mail on IBMLink on page 302 for instructions on how to send IBMLink notes.

PREVENTING REMOTE DDM COMMANDS

To prevent remote users from issuing a DDM (Distributed Data Management) request or to prevent PC Support (or Client Access) users from issuing a remote command from their PCs, change the DDM access parameter in the Network Attributes:

```
CHGNETA DDMACC(*REJECT)
```

— or —

```
CHGNETA DDMACC(pgmname)
```

If you use *REJECT, then all requests are rejected. If you wish to be selective as to which requests are honored, then create a program that runs each time a remote DDM request is issued, and use the program name as the DDMACC parameter. Refer to the *Distributed Data Management* manual for more information.

Refer to Controlling Use of Client Access Functions on page 188 and Using PC Organizer When There is No Command Line on AS/400 on page 270 for additional information.

CLIENT ACCESS/400 CONVERSATION SECURITY

Client Access applications consist of a PC requester and an AS/400 server. The program that controls the links is called the Client Access Router. Each time you start the router, it asks for a user ID and a password. When the link is initiated, the router sends this information to the AS/400 for security verification. If you do not specify a user ID and password when starting the router, the system checks the communication entry in the subsystem to see if it allows a default user. If the subsystem allows it, the start request is accepted. This might be a security exposure. To avoid this, add a communications entry in the subsystem that handles the PC router requests, and add a new communication entry without a Default User. An example of this new communication entry in comparison with the default communications entry is:

Communications Entry	Device	Mode	Job	Default User	Max. Active
Original CMNE	*ANY	*ANY	*USERPRF	QUSER	*NOMAX
New CMNE	*ANY	QPCSUPP	*USERPRF	*NONE	*NOMAX

The default subsystem for handling PC router requests is QCMN. Use the command DSPSBSD to determine how the subsystem is defined. The command to be used for the add communication entry operation is ADDCMNE (Add Communications Entry).

```
ADDCMNE  SBSD(subsystem-description-name) DFTUSR(*NONE)  MODE(QPCSUPP)
```

This new communications entry forces the user to give a user ID and password to access data in the AS/400.

Password Substitution

V3R1

A new feature of V3R1 prevents unauthorized disclosure of passwords by monitoring the communication line. Passwords are transmitted using an algorithm of password substitution.

This method of protecting passwords can only be passed from intelligent work stations, such as personal computers, to the AS/400, or between systems that each support password substitution.

In order for a PC connection to take advantage of password substitution, you must bypass the AS/400 sign-on screen. If you enter the userid and password at the AS/400 sign-on screen from either a PC or a nonprogrammable terminal, the password will be sent in the clear and thus subject to monitoring. To avoid disclosure through monitoring the communication line, you must bypass the sign-on screen. This is true for PCs running Client Access/400 or terminals performing a display station passthrough session.

Pipelining Client Access User ID and Password

Another security exposure is the use of the "pipeline" facility to pass the user ID and password to the router automatically. This is an obvious security exposure as it allows anyone to sign on to the router automatically and thus gain access to the system. And, this procedure is not guaranteed to work between new releases.

Controlling Use of Client Access Functions

All of the Client Access/400 servers support user-written exit programs. These programs help ensure that your data is both secure and correct. Your exit program can determine if users have authority to perform a particular operation and what data they can access on the AS/400 system.

Network Attributes

There are two network attributes that control the use of Client Access functions:

PCSACC	Virtual printer File transfer Shared folders Type 2 Client Access messaging Data queues Remote SQL
DDMACC	Shared folders Type 0 and Type 1 Submit remote command

The following information comes from the *Client Access/400 for DOS and OS/2 Technical Reference* manual. The valid values for the PCSACC parameter are:

V3R1	***REGFAC**	The Registration Facility is new with V3R1. The Client Access/400 servers use the OS/400 Registration Facility function to determine the exit program to call for the data queue, license, message, transfer, remote SQL, shared folders, and virtual print functions. Based on the return value from the program, the server determines if the PC request should be rejected. If the return code indicates the request should be rejected, or if an error occurs, an error message is sent to the personal computer.
	*REJECT	The Client Access/400 servers reject every request from the personal computer. They send an error message to the PC application.
	*OBJAUT	The Client Access/400 servers verify normal object authorities. For example, they verify authority to retrieve data from a database file for a transfer request. This is the default value.
	User-written program	The Client Access/400 servers call the program name you supply and, based on a returned value from the program, determine if the PC request should be rejected. If the return code indicates the request should be rejected, or if an error occurs, an error message is sent to the personal computer.

The default for PCSACC and DDMACC is *OBJAUT, which means that a user has access to the Client Access functions for which the user has authority. You can also specify *REJECT if you do not want to allow **ANY** Client Access users. Note that DDMACC controls DDM access as well as the Client Access functions shown above.

Client Access Exit Programs

You can create a user-written exit program to enhance security. An exit program determines whether the user has authority to use a particular Client Access function.

If an exit program is used, a return code and a data string are sent to the exit program when any of the Client Access functions are called. Your exit program then must evaluate whether the user is allowed access to the function.

> *Using exit programs may adversely affect system performance because of passing data and the authorization checking that the exit program performs.*

The return code is a character string set to either 0 or 1. A code of 0 rejects the function and 1 allows it. The data string contains information on the user profile, application name, requested function, and other information, depending on the type of request. Refer to the *Client Access/400 for DOS and OS/2 Technical Reference* manual for additional information.

Here is an example of a CL program that can be used to reject Client Access Remote Command requests. In this case, I would indicate the name of the program in the DDMACC network attribute.

Example CL Program to Control Access of Client Access/400

```
PGM PARM(&RTNCODE &DATA)
DCL VAR(&DATA)  TYPE(*CHAR)  LEN(30)
DCL VAR(&RTNCODE)  TYPE(*CHAR)  LEN(1)
DCL VAR(&FUNC)  TYPE(*CHAR)  LEN(10)

/* We are only checking to see if the submit remote /*
/*  command function is called.  We could also      /*
/*  perform a validation against the user profile    /*
/*  as well.  The User Profile name is contained in /*
/*  the first 10 characters of the &DATA field       /*

CHGVAR    VAR(&FUNC)  VALUE(%SST(&DATA 21 10)
    IF        COND(&FUNC = 'COMMAND    ')  THEN(CHGVAR +
                VAR(&RTNCODE)  VALUE('0')
    ELSE    CMD(CHGVAR VAR(&RTNCODE)  VALUE('1')
ENDPGM
```

The program is called each time a user sends a request that is checked by the DDMACC parameter. We set the return code to 0 if the requested function is SBMRMTCMD (Submit Remote Command).

> If you intend to use the Client Access Organizer functions, you must either allow remote commands or construct a procedure to get the organizer function started on the AS/400. Refer to Using PC Organizer When There is No Command Line on AS/400 on page 270 for instructions on how to do this.

If you wish to use PCSACC programs, things get a bit more complicated because the information passed in the data field differs according to the requested function. For example, if you wish to restrict the transfer function to only certain users or restrict certain libraries, then you have to validate the user and/or library name of the request. Normally, securing the libraries or objects suffices, but some installations want to restrict the ability of users to transfer data to a PC, yet allow them access to data in their normal applications.

Restrict Usage of Client Access Server Programs

You can control Client Access functions by restricting the use of Client Access server programs. The following table lists the server programs and their functions.

Program	Library	Description
QCNPCSUP	QSYS	Authority checking
QXFINIT	QIWS	Shared folders Type 2
QPWSSTPO	QSYS	V3R1 file server (original DOS, DOS extended and OS/2 clients; shared folders Type 2)
QCNTEDDM	QSYS	DDM (shared folders Type 0 and 1, Remote Cmd.)
QTFDWNLD	QIWS	Transfer facility
QVPPRINT	QIWS	Virtual printer
QMFRCVR	QIWS	Messaging receiver
QMFSNDR	QIWS	Messaging sender
QRQSRVX	QIWS	Remote SQL
QHQSRV0	QIWS	Remote SQL
QHQSRV1	QIWS	Remote SQL

If you secure any of these programs, you secure the respective Client Access function. Merely set the public authority to *EXCLUDE. Now, only the Client Access users who have private authority or *ALLOBJ authority are able to use the function. When the user attempts to use an unauthorized function, they receive the following message:

```
5056 Security error occurred for system nnn.
```

There is also a message in QSYSOPR message queue:

```
Program start request received on communications device YYY was
             rejected with reason codes 709, 1506.
```

After changing the public authority to the programs to *EXCLUDE, grant private authority to those users who need access to any particular function.

Client Access Exit Program Registration Facility

With V3R1, you can use the new OS/400 Registration Facility. The registration facility is a service that provides storage and retrieval operations for OS/400 and non-OS/400 "exit points" and "exit programs." An exit point is a specific point in a system function or program where control may be passed to one or more specified exit programs. An exit program is a program to which control is passed from an exit point. This registration facility repository allows multiple programs to associate with a given system function or application function.

The registration facility APIs provide the capability to:

- Register and deregister exit points with the registration facility.
- Add and remove exit programs to and from the repository.
- Retrieve exit point and exit program information from the repository.
- Designate the order in which exit programs should be called.

A program exit point can call one program, a fixed number of programs, or all programs associated with an exit point. The exit program number associated with each exit program should be used to determine the sequence in which the exit programs are run.

The Work with Registration Information (WRKREGINF) command allows you to designate the program that is evoked for specific exit points. The following is an example of the display. Use option 8 from this screen to designate an exit program for the function listed.

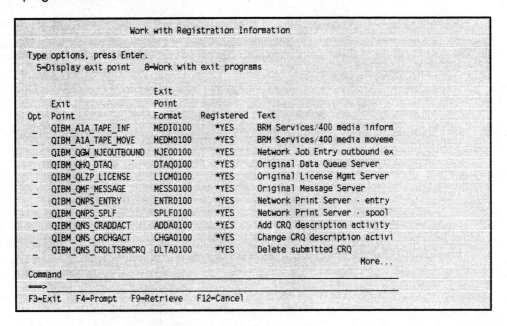

```
                         Work with Registration Information

Type options, press Enter.
  5=Display exit point    8=Work with exit programs

                          Exit
          Exit            Point
Opt  Point               Format     Registered  Text
  _  QIBM_A1A_TAPE_INF    MEDIO100    *YES       BRM Services/400 media inform
  _  QIBM_A1A_TAPE_MOVE   MEDMO100    *YES       BRM Services/400 media moveme
  _  QIBM_QGW_NJEOUTBOUND NJEOO100    *YES       Network Job Entry outbound ex
  _  QIBM_QHQ_DTAQ        DTAQO100    *YES       Original Data Queue Server
  _  QIBM_QLZP_LICENSE    LICMO100    *YES       Original License Mgmt Server
  _  QIBM_QMF_MESSAGE     MESSO100    *YES       Original Message Server
  _  QIBM_QNPS_ENTRY      ENTRO100    *YES       Network Print Server - entry
  _  QIBM_QNPS_SPLF       SPLFO100    *YES       Network Print Server - spool
  _  QIBM_QNS_CRADDACT    ADDAO100    *YES       Add CRQ description activity
  _  QIBM_QNS_CRCHGACT    CHGAO100    *YES       Change CRQ description activi
  _  QIBM_QNS_CRDLTSBMCRQ DLTAO100    *YES       Delete submitted CRQ
                                                                       More...
Command
===>
F3=Exit   F4=Prompt   F9=Retrieve   F12=Cancel
```

Refer to the following manuals for additional information for using exit programs and registration information — including several example programs and complete descriptions of the fields contained in the data string:

- ***Client Access/400 for DOS and OS/2 Technical Reference***
- ***AS/400 System API Reference***
- ***OS/400 Server Concepts and Administration***

SECURITY CONSIDERATIONS WHEN USING OFFICEVISION/400

If you have OfficeVision/400, refer to OfficeVision/400 on page 281.

LIBRARY AND OBJECT SECURITY

I recommend that, when you create a library, you give special consideration to the security of the objects in that library. Earlier, I pointed out that you try to design libraries so that objects within the library have the same or similar protection requirements. Let's look at what happens when you create a library and then create new objects within that library.

When you create a library, you use the Create Library command (CRTLIB). For example, if you wish to create a new library:

```
CRTLIB LIB(library_name) TYPE(*PROD) TEXT(*BLANK)
```

The TYPE and TEXT parameters are optional; I show the defaults. There are some additional parameters to be aware of. These parameters are only presented to you if you press the F10 key (Additional Parameters) when you are using the CRTLIB command:

AUT   The authority the public has to the library itself. Default is *LIBCRTAUT. Other values are *CHANGE, *ALL, *USE, and *EXCLUDE.

ASP   The ASP in which you place the library. Default is ASP #1.

CRTAUT   The default public authority that newly created objects within this library have. Default is *SYSVAL. Other values are *CHANGE, *ALL, *USE, and *EXCLUDE.

Whenever you create any object, the parameter AUT dictates public authority for that object. The default value for AUT is *LIBCRTAUT; that is to say, the default public authority is the value of CRTAUT of the library in which the object is placed. You can display this value by entering:

```
DSPLIBD LIB(library_name)
```

All libraries are objects in the QSYS library, so a new library's public authority is the same as the CRTAUT parameter of QSYS, which, by default, is set to *SYSVAL. *SYSVAL is *CHANGE by default. So, if your system is set to all the defaults, the public has, by default, *CHANGE authority to any new library that you create.

Now, when you create new objects and place them into your library, the authority specified by the CRTAUT parameter of the library is the default public authority for access to new objects. In this example, it is *SYSVAL. The *SYSVAL in this case is the system value QCRTAUT. As stated above, the default (or shipped value) for QCRTAUT is *CHANGE.

As you can see, if you group objects within a library to have similar or the same security requirements, it is fairly easy to provide the level of access you need. Set the CRTAUT parameter of the library to be the public access level you want. But, if your system is set up with the shipped defaults, and you create libraries and objects without regard to the security, then the public has change authority to the library and the objects within the library.

All is not lost if you have been creating libraries and objects with public authority of *CHANGE and you want something different. For example, if you have a library called TEST created with *CHANGE public authority and you want the public access to be *USE, then do the following:

```
RVKOBJAUT OBJ(TEST/*ALL) OBJTYPE(*ALL) USER(*PUBLIC) +
    AUT(*CHANGE)
GRTOBJAUT OBJ(TEST/*ALL) OBJTYPE(*ALL) USER(*PUBLIC) +
    AUT(*USE)
CHGLIB LIB(library_name) CRTAUT(*USE)
```

> *The last command (CHGLIB) changes the create authority to
> *USE, but this only affects newly created objects. It does not
> change the authority of existing objects in that library.*

You might think that you always want to create new libraries with a public
authority of something different than *CHANGE. You could change the
parameter CRTAUT of library QSYS. If you do this, then any new objects
created in QSYS assume the new public authority. This includes device
descriptions that are auto-configured. And, the public must have *CHANGE
authority to these device descriptions in order to use them. So, I recommend
that you leave QSYS alone.

SECURITY DESIGN FOR PERFORMANCE

How you implement security on the AS/400 can affect system performance
significantly. If you understand how security is implemented on your system and
how this can affect performance, then you can design you system's security
accordingly. This is, of course, only one aspect of system performance, but it
should not be overlooked. The following helps you understand how you can
better design security with regard to maintaining or improving system
performance.

First, let's examine some terms and procedures that are available to control
Resource Security.

Group Profiles	A group of similar users can share the same authority to objects.
Primary Group Profile `V3R1`	New feature of V3R1. Allows you to designate primary group profile authorities for objects. Improves performance because the primary group profile authority is stored in the object header. Refer to Primary Group Profile Authority below.
Authorization Lists	Objects with similar security needs can be grouped on one list. Authority can be granted to the list rather than to the individual objects.
Object Ownership	Every object on the system has an owner. Objects can be owned by an individual user profile or by a group profile. Proper assignment of object ownership helps you manage applications and delegate responsibility for the security of your information.
Library Authority	Put files and programs that require protection into a library and restrict access to that library. This is often simpler than restricting access to each individual object. To protect critical objects, secure both the object and the library.

Object Authority	In cases where restricting access to a library is not specific enough, restrict authority to use individual objects, such as files.
Public Authority	For each object, you can define what kind of access is available for any system user who does not have any other authority to the object. Public authority is an effective means for securing objects that are not confidential and it provides good performance.

Primary Group Profile Authority

The Primary Group Profile (PGP) authority for an object may provide better performance than private group authority when checking authority to an object. The information for the PGP authority is stored in the object header along with *PUBLIC authority and the owner's authority to the object. Thus, reducing the system resources required to validate a user's authority to an object.

A user profile must be a group profile to be assigned as the primary group for an object. The same profile cannot be the owner of the object and its primary group.

When a user creates a new object, parameters in the user profile control whether the user's group is given authority to the object and the type of authority given. The Group Authority Type (GRPAUTTYP) parameter in a user profile can be used to make the user's group the primary group for the object. The default value for GRPAUTTYP is *PRIVATE.

Use the Change Object Primary Group (CHGOBJPGP) command or the Work with Objects by Primary Group (WRKOBJPGP) command to specify the primary group for an object. To change the authority of the primary group, use the Edit Object Authority display or the grant and revoke authority commands.

Because system performance may be improved using the PGP authority, you may want to change all user profiles to use the this authority. Change the GRPAUTTYP to *PGP. You may also want to change the Create User Profile (CRTUSRPRF) command default to the PGP authority. To change the command default, use the Change Command Default command:

```
CHGCMDDFT CMD(QSYS/CRTUSRPRF) NEWDFT('GRPAUTTYP(*PGP)')
```

For additional information, refer to the *AS/400 Security — Reference* manual.

Authority Lookup

An authority lookup operation is performed whenever a user profile attempts access to an object. This is also referred to as an "access check." The purpose is to determine whether to allow or deny access to the object. You can think of authority lookups or access checks as a guard at the door that checks each person to determine if they should be allowed to enter. The more authority lookups that the system has to perform per second, the more CPU resources are expended, and there is a corresponding decline in performance. You can determine how many lookups your system performs by using Performance Tools/400.

Your objective in designing security for performance is to maintain appropriate security for all objects on the system while minimizing the number of authority lookups the system must perform when users attempt to access objects. The recommendations list below help you accomplish that goal.

Security Design for Performance Recommendations

The following table lists some recommendations to help you implement security with respect to system performance.

Recommendation	Comments
Do not secure objects unless required.	Just as you would not put a lock on every room in your home, you should not secure every object on your system. Whenever possible, make the *PUBLIC access adequate for operations.
Do not give any users less authority than *PUBLIC access.	If you give any user less access than *PUBLIC, the system performs individual access checks for every user. This is like putting a guard at the door to check every user to prevent a single user from entering. It is better to reduce the *PUBLIC access to lowest common denominator rather than giving a few users less than *PUBLIC access.
Use private authorities, not authorization lists, to grant users more than *PUBLIC access.	When an object has an authorization list, there is a check of every user on the list. If you give users private authority to the object, then only that user's authority is checked when access is attempted. This tends to conflict with recommendations stated earlier. Here I am talking about designing for performance. Earlier, the recommendation to use authorization lists was made with respect to maintenance and save times. Private authorities tend to require fewer access checks. You have to weigh the advantages of authorization lists versus the performance hits. You may find that there is a small hit on performance, so the advantage of ease of maintenance and save times of authorization lists overrides the performance issues.

Recommendation	Comments
Use either authorization lists or private authority to secure objects, not both.	If you use both, this is like telling the guard at the door to check everyone's badge and check a list to determine if people are allowed to enter. If you only use the list, then the guard need not check the badge. Similarly, do not force the system to perform access checks of both private authority and the authorization list when only the list is required. This reduces the number of authority lookups when a user attempts access to a secured object.
Group objects in a library and secure the library.	If you place objects with similar security requirements in the same library, you can restrict access to the library while allowing *PUBLIC access to the objects it contains. This is like placing a lock on the front door of your house. If you have a key to the house, you do not need keys to gain access to the rooms in the house. Library Security restricts access to users authorized to the library, improves performance by limiting authority lookups to the library, and simplifies security management by protecting multiple objects within a single library.
Use *LIBL instead of specific library names.	When a library is placed on the library list (*LIBL), the system checks user's right to access the library and stores the authority in the library pointers on the library lists. This eliminates the authority lookup operations when these *LIBL pointers are used.
Group profiles should own objects.	If an object is owned by a group profile, then group members have access to the object based on the group profile. If the group profile owns the object, then that information is contained in the object header. Those users who are then members of the group profile assume owner rights and there is no authority lookup when they access that object. If you set the *PUBLIC authority to *EXCLUDE, then other users who are not members of the group are denied access.

Recommendation	Comments
The same user profile should own an object and the program that adopts authority to it.	When you have programs that adopt authority to another object, you can reduce the number of authority lookups that the system performs when checking for access authority. Make the owner of the object the same as the owner of the program that adopts authority to it. The owner's authority is thereby stored in the object's header. Thus, the system can take advantage of this information, thereby reducing the lookup time.
Use the Primary Group Profile authority feature.	If you are at V3R1, the primary group profile (PGP) authority can provide better performance because the PGP authority is stored in the object header. Refer to Primary Group Profile Authority on page 195.

V3R1

WORK MANAGEMENT AND PERFORMANCE

It is important that you have a basic understanding of work management topics. You may need a very thorough understanding if your environment is complex. You system's environment is probably considered complex if it exhibits some or all of the following characteristics.

- Large number of interactive users with different job functions or priorities.
- Multiple batch jobs running at the same time.
- Multiple remote users.
- PCs on local area networks attached to the AS/400.

INITIAL POOL SIZES FOR BATCH-TYPE JOBS

Pool size refers to the main memory on your AS/400. Your main memory is divided into "memory pools." This allows you to customize the pool with characteristics that optimize the type of work to be performed in that pool. For example, interactive users have different job characteristics than longer-running batch jobs.

You can let the system make adjustments to the memory pools for you. In fact, when the AS/400 ships, it is set up to do this. But if you plan to manually "tune" your system, then you must allocate the memory pool sizes manually.

If you intend to adjust pool sizes manually, the following batch subsystem guidelines may be of interest.

Batch Job Type	Suggested Initial Storage Allocation	Comments
Short-running Job	350K to 500K	May require as much as 750K.
Long-running Job	500K to 750K	May require as much as 1000K.
Compiles	750K to 1000K to 2000K	Larger compiles will run better in 3000K of memory.
Queries	500K to 4000K	Amount of memory to use depends on size of query.
Reformat (Sorts)	1000K to 2000K	Larger sorts may need as much as 3000K.
Save/Restore Operations	1000K to 2000K	Some save operations may need as much as 3000K.

Refer to the *AS/400 Work Management* manual for further discussion on this topic.

SPOOLING PERFORMANCE OF ADVANCED FUNCTION PRINTING

If you are using Advanced Function Printing, or AFP, and your printing performance is not satisfactory, then check the setting of Spool Subsystem Pool size (subsystem QSPL). Increasing the pool size, up to 2MB, helps cut down on paging and increases performance. The following table can be used as a guideline to set up the memory pool size for Advanced Function Printing.

Number of Writers	Memory Pool Size (KB)	Memory Pool Activity Level
1	1,500	1
2	1,700	2
3	1,900	3
4	2,100	4
>4	2,300	5

LIMITING ABILITY TO CHANGE POOLS/ACTIVITY LEVEL

When using the WRKSYSSTS (Work with System Status) command, users can easily change pool sizes and activity levels. This is a nice feature, but it also creates a security concern. If you have spent time tuning your system, you probably do not want unauthorized people changing it for you. You may want to exclude system operators from attempting to tune the system. You can revoke authority to the CHGSHRPOOL, CHGSYSVAL, and CHGSBSD commands. This allows a user to use the WRKSYSSTS command but NOT modify the pool sizes or activity level.

```
GRTOBJAUT  OBJ(CHGSHRPOOL)  OBJTYPE(*CMD)  USER(*PUBLIC)  AUT(*EXCLUDE)
GRTOBJAUT  OBJ(CHGSYSVAL)   OBJTYPE(*CMD)  USER(*PUBLIC)  AUT(*EXCLUDE)
GRTOBJAUT  OBJ(CHGSBSD)     OBJTYPE(*CMD)  USER(*PUBLIC)  AUT(*EXCLUDE)
GRTOBJAUT  OBJ(CHGSHRPOOL)  OBJTYPE(*CMD)  USER(goodguy)  AUT(*USE)
GRTOBJAUT  OBJ(CHGSSYSVAL   OBJTYPE(*CMD)  USER(goodguy)  AUT(*USE)
GRTOBJAUT  OBJ(CHGSBSD)     OBJTYPE(*CMD)  USER(goodguy)  AUT(*USE)
```

SUBMITTING JOBS TO BATCH

There are many jobs that, due to the their nature (e.g., long-running or heavy resource user), should run in a batch mode and not interactively. Examples are save/restore jobs, clearing output queues, and query jobs.

By submitting these kinds of jobs to run in the batch environment:

- Your job does not compete with shorter-running interactive jobs.
- You do not have to wait for the job to end before you regain the use of your terminal.

The command to submit a job to batch is **SBMJOB**. Enter this command and press F4 to prompt for parameter entry display. Enter the command you want to run (e.g., CLROUTQ) and press F4 to prompt for this command. Enter the parameters, press Enter to return to the initial prompt screen, and press Enter again to submit the job. You can check the status of your jobs by entering the command WRKSBMJOB (Work with Submitted Jobs).

USING SETOBJACC WITH BATCH JOBS

The Set Object Access (SETOBJACC) command can load a database file, a database index, or a program into a storage pool. The storage pool can be a private pool, the pool the job is running in, or one of the system's shared pools.

If a private pool contains only the preloaded data, the data stays in memory until the object is explicitly purged (using SETOBJACC), overlaid with another file as a result of another SETOBJACC (not recommended), or the pool is cleared using the Clear Pool (CLRPOOL) command.

With SETOBJACC, if the file fits and there are no jobs active in the pool, the system loads it into the pool and does not purge the data thereafter. This provides very efficient application processing regardless of how the file is accessed by the application. Because much of the I/O for random processing is eliminated, it can eliminate the need to sort or reorganize the data for files that fit in a pool.

The SETOBJACC command has the following characteristics:

- Loads data in main memory. When loaded in main memory, access is much faster than disk I/O.
- The pool size should be large enough to contain all the data.
- Reduces I/O operations, especially for random access file operations.
- Can be used with batch or interactive jobs, but size of files usually restricts use to batch environments.
- Does not affect the performance of write operations.
- Can use shared memory pools (if dynamic tuning is turned off) or private pools.
- The should be no jobs running in the selected pools.
- The selected pool should be cleared using the CLRPOOL command.

Refer to the *AS/400 Work Management* manual for additional information.

CHECKING THE STATUS OF USER JOBS

Here are some basic techniques you can use to check the status of user jobs, batch and interactive.

WRKSBMJOB   Check the status of jobs submitted by you or another user. This command only checks on batch jobs — not interactive jobs.

WRKUSRJOB   Shows status of all jobs. The default varies depending on your assistance level. The *BASIC assistance level is particularly useful when using this command. Shows status of jobs and recommended action. Tells you what job queue the job is in, and allows you to change the job priority. This command is particularly useful for checking on any user's jobs.

WRKJOBQ   Can also be accessed by F22 key from the WRKUSRJOB display. The F14 key includes or excludes jobs waiting to run.

WRKACTJOB   You can select all active jobs in any subsystem you like. The problem with this command for checking on user jobs is that it only checks on active jobs. If a user's job is already complete, you do not see it.

SETTING UP AND MANAGING USER AUXILIARY STORAGE POOLS

Most users have only a single auxiliary storage pool on their system. System administration and maintenance are usually easier with only a single ASP. The system must have at least one ASP — called the System ASP. User-defined ASPs are generally used because they allow you to isolate objects on one or more specific disk units. This may reduce the loss of data due to a disk failure. In most cases, only data stored on disk units in the affected ASP is lost. However, when a disk unit fails, the entire system is unusable until the disk unit is repaired, unless the failed unit is protected by device parity protection (i.e., RAID-5) or mirrored protection.

Here are some considerations and reasons to set up User ASPs.

- Provide dedicated resources for frequently used objects, such as journal receivers.
- Hold save files. Objects can be backed up to save files in a different ASP. It is unlikely that both the ASP containing the object and the ASP containing the save file will be lost.
- Create different ASPs for objects with different recovery and availability requirements. For example, you can put critical database files or documents in an ASP that has mirrored protection or device parity protection.

- Create an ASP to place infrequently used objects, such as large history files, on disk units with slower performance.

- Use ASPs to manage recovery times for access paths for critical and noncritical database files using system-managed access-path protection.

- Objects and applications located in an ASP are largely self sufficient, not dependent on objects located elsewhere.

- You must configure enough space to accommodate object growth over time.

- You must configure enough disk arms in each ASP so you don't cause a performance bottleneck.

- Certain system objects must reside in the System ASP and cannot be moved to a user ASP.

- If user ASPs are configured wisely with the proper data, applications, and protection scheme, you significantly reduce the amount of time required to recover from a disk drive failure.

Beginning with V2R3, you can mix levels of disk protection within a single ASP. This reduces the complexity of managing multiple ASPs. For example, you can have both RAID-5 (Redundant Array of Independent Disks) disk protection and mirroring within the same ASP. One thing you should **NOT** do, however, is to mix protected DASD and unprotected DASD in the same ASP. You are defeating the purpose of the protection and exposing yourself to significant restoration times.

An example of using multiple ASPs and different levels of protection follows. Suppose you have your system ASP mirrored but you have many history files and archived data that you wish to keep online, but they are not so important as to require mirroring. You could place these in a user ASP that is unprotected (i.e., no mirroring or RAID-5 protection). If a drive fails in this unprotected ASP, your system stops. But once the disk is repaired, you reload that ASP only (which takes less time than a complete system reload) and you are off and running. Alternatively, you could protect the user ASP with RAID-5 protection, which is less expensive than mirrored protection, yet provides high disk availability.

Restrictions

There are some restrictions to and considerations for setting up user ASPs.

- Objects That Can be Moved to a User ASP:

    - Application programs

    - Physical files

    - Logical files (same ASP as physical files)

    - SQL tables

    - SQL views

    - SQL indexes

    - Save files

- Job queues

- Output queues

- Journals and journal receivers — the journals must reside in same ASP as the journaled files, the journal receivers can be in a different ASP.

- Objects That Cannot be Moved to a User ASP:

  - SQL collections

  - QTEMP library

  - IDDU dictionaries

  - Documents and folders (Client Access and OfficeVision/400) if you are at V3R0.5 or earlier. Beginning with V3R1 you can move documents and folders into user ASPs

  - Spool files

  - Authority lists

  - Configuration descriptions

  - Jobs

Tips on ASP Management

The following are some guidelines you may find useful when planning and setting up user-defined ASPs.

- Consider naming standards for your libraries to reflect the ASP in which they are located. This helps operators know where to restore objects when the system has been segmented into several user ASPs.

- Inform the authors of any applications developed outside your shop of your ASP strategy. They need to know where user data is located and where the application is to be located.

- To move objects from one ASP to another, do not use the MOVOBJ (Move Object) command. This only moves the object pointers and links. You must save the objects (to tape or save file) and restore them to a library that resides in the target ASP.

- Set the ASP overflow threshold using STRSST. Also consider establishing a never-ending CL program in an autostart job entry. The program monitors for message CPI0953 to detect the ASP storage threshold exceeding the set limit, and then to send a break message to key operations personnel. You want to avoid an overflow condition.

- The QUSRTOOL library offers several tools to assist with day-to-day operations:

  - Print ASP Use command (PRTASPUSE)

  - Print ASP Library command (PRTASPLIB)

  - Display Overflowed ASP function (DSPOVASP)

  - Check Database Dependencies command (CHKDBD)

- Beginning with V2R2 of the Operating System, if you have sufficient storage within an ASP, you can delete disk units from the ASP without destroying the contents (and thus requiring a reload of that ASP). Prior to V2R2, deleting disk units from an ASP requires that the ASP be reloaded.

PERFORMANCE TUNING GUIDELINES

Nearly all of the material in this section is found in the *AS/400 Work Management* manual. Do not try using these guidelines without first understanding the basic underlying aspects of performance. If performance tuning is new to you, set up the system to make the adjustments dynamically (refer to AS/400 Dynamic Tuning, below). If, later, you decide to manually tune your system, first make note of how the system is performing in the "automatic" mode so you will know if you are doing any better in the manual mode.

Your AS/400 has limited resources. You have a finite amount of memory, disk space, and communications resources. In order to achieve efficient performance, you have to balance your system resources. Those resources are:

- Main memory
- CPU
- Disk storage
- Communication lines

Unfortunately, there isn't a simple "cookbook" method to accomplish this resource balancing. As the system administrator, you have to understand what these resources are and what affects their efficient utilization.

There are several things you can do to better understand system tuning. IBM and other companies offer classes on the subject. There are self-paced education tools and several books written on the subject. The *AS/400 Work Management* manual is a good resource. Another excellent reference for you is the Redbook, *AS/400 Performance Management, V2R2*.

As you gain confidence and knowledge, you reach a point where you want to investigate system tuning. When you do this, keep in mind that you have to monitor your AS/400 closely and understand what factors within your environment affect performance. Each system is somewhat unique. Factors that affect your AS/400's performance may not affect the system down the street. As you begin to swim in the memory pools (little joke, eh?) you should be documenting your system performance each time you make a change. That way you can identify the effect your changes have on overall system performance.

AS/400 Dynamic Tuning

For most installations, dynamic tuning provides the best level of overall performance. However, as your system becomes larger — and in all likelihood, more complex — you may find that manual tuning is superior. I recommend trying dynamic tuning to determine which method is better.

- Some dynamic tuners are better than others in handling change. If your workload changes frequently during the day, and these changes are small, some dynamic tuners will make too many adjustments and be unable to provide an average level of performance equal to manual tuning. If the changes are major changes, then dynamic tuning may be best. In either case, try both tuning methods to determine the one best suited for your environment.

- The IBM-provided dynamic tuning works only with shared pools. If you are using private storage pools in any of your subsystems, dynamic tuning has no effect. If you have already defined private storage pools, you have to change those subsystem descriptions.

- Dynamic tuning changes the following performance values:
  - *MACHINE pool size
  - *BASE pool activity level
  - *INTERACT pool size and activity level
  - *SPOOL pool size and activity level
- *SHRPOOL1 to *SHRPOOL10 pool size and activity level

- Depending on the version of the Operating System, dynamic tuning may not properly set the machine pool if you are using Client Access/400 on your system. This should have been corrected with V3R1, but monitor the faulting rate during periods of high Client Access activity to determine if the machine pool faulting rate is acceptable.

- Set the System Value QPRFADJ to 3.

- Set up a journal to record the changes made to the system by dynamic tuning. Refer to the *AS/400 Work Management* manual.

MANUAL SYSTEM TUNING

Dynamic tuning is recommended for most situations. However, many users have found that they prefer manual tuning. Some reasons why you may wish to consider manual tuning are outlined below.

Workload Environment	Characterized By
Complex environment	Multiple subsystems or memory pools. Requires tighter control than automatic adjustment can provide.
Changes in workload are rapid or extensive	Automatic adjustment may not be able to cope with too-rapid changes in workload.
Workload variance is deterministic with respect to time of day	May require major system changes to accommodate the changes. Big swings in job priority. For example, daytime interactive versus evening batch environments.

Workload Environment	Characterized By
Private Memory Pools	Dynamic tuning only works with shared memory pools. If you use private pools, then you must manage them manually.

Manual Performance Tuning — Getting Started

When you set up your system for manual tuning, you should refer to the *AS/400 Work Management* manual for initial pool sizes and activity levels. You also need an understanding of performance terminology. In particular, you need to gain an understanding of:

- Database and non-database faults and the effect on system performance
- Machine pool size requirements
- Shared memory pool, *BASE
- Activity levels and effect on faulting rate
- Memory pools and effect on faulting rate

The table below is a short list of the preparatory items to do and some references. This table assumes that you are using the following memory pools:

- Machine pool for system jobs.
- *BASE memory pool for batch, communications, and other system jobs.
- QSPL memory pool for printing.
- QINTER memory pool for interactive jobs.

> If you have tailored your system to include pools other than the above, the IBM manual referenced above should be consulted for additional information on setting the size of the pools and the activity levels.

Item	Comments
System Value QACTJOB:	System value that controls amount of auxiliary storage allocated to active jobs. Refer to QACTJOB on page 23 and to the *AS/400 Work Management* manual.
System Value QTOTJOB:	System value that controls amount of auxiliary storage allocated to total jobs on the system. Refer to QTOTJOB on page 24 and to the *AS/400 Work Management* manual.
System Value QPFRADJ	System value that controls dynamic tuning. Set this value to 0 when you are doing manual tuning. Refer to QPFRADJ on page 21 and to the *AS/400 Work Management* manual.

Item	Comments
Initial size of the machine pool:	The *AS/400 Work Management* manual has a complete discussion on setting the initial size of the machine pool. If you want a quick tip, set the system value QPFRADJ to 3 and leave it for a few hours, then return the value to 0 for manual tuning. This turns dynamic tuning on for a while and the system makes several adjustments using an algorithm that follows the guidelines documented in the *AS/400 Work Management* manual.
Initial size and activity level of the *BASE memory pool:	The initial size and activity level of *BASE is set according to the total amount of main memory and processor size of your AS/400. The *AS/400 Work Management* manual has further information. This value is a starting point only and you will likely have to adjust it for optimum performance. You cannot directly adjust the memory size of *BASE. Whatever memory is left over after adjusting the size of all other memory pools is allocated to *BASE.
Size and Activity Level of the QSPL memory pool:	These values also vary. The amount of memory you need is small. Refer to the *AS/400 Work Management* guide for a more complete discussion, but for a quick-and-dirty start, set the memory size to 350KB with an activity level of 5. If you are using the advanced function printing facilities, then refer to Spooling Performance of Advanced Function Printing on page 200.
Initial size and activity level of the QINTER memory pool:	After you have determined the initial size of the other memory pools, allocate the remainder of the memory to QINTER. Set the pool size and look up the activity factor in the *AS/400 Work Management* manual. Divide the total memory in QINTER by the activity factor. The result is the initial value of the activity level of QINTER. Once again, this is a starting point and you will likely have to adjust the memory size and activity to gain optimum performance.

Other topics are also important. Several articles and books have been written on performance tuning. It is not my intent to cover all aspects of tuning in this book. If you embark on manual performance tuning, I am assuming that you have a basic understanding of the terminology.

Main Memory and CPU Utilization — Tuning Roadmap

Balance your main memory and CPU utilization by allocating the available memory and setting the job activity levels in your storage pools on your system.

Refer to the *AS/400 Work Management* manual for the initial set up of your memory and activity level. The following quick reference helps you tune the AS/400 (with regard to balancing the main memory and CPU utilization).

> *If you are using the auto-tune functions of the AS/400, then do not use this method. However, it is still a good exercise in how to tune the system and it helps you understand some of the issues and guidelines. Refer to the **AS/400 Work Management** manual before you begin.*

Use this roadmap to guide you through the steps to make and evaluate memory pool and activity level adjustments.

V3R1

The tuning guidelines used here were taken from the V3R1 *AS/400 Work Management* manual. The faulting rate guidelines may be different if you are at a different version or release of the Operating System.

> *This tuning roadmap uses the activity state as the primary tuning indicator and the faulting rate as the secondary tuning indicator. Some people may prefer to reverse the tuning indicators and use the faulting rate as the primary indicator and the activity state as the secondary. I really do not think there is much difference as the end result will be about the same.*

1. Enter the command WRKSYSSTS. You see something similar to the following screen:

```
                        Work with System Status          APACHE
                                                         07/17/94  16:26:56
% CPU used . . . . . . . :        42.5   Auxiliary storage:
Elapsed time . . . . . . :    00:00:02     System ASP . . . . . . :    19671 M
Jobs in system . . . . . :         335     % system ASP used . . :    11.5733
% addresses used:                          Total . . . . . . . . :    22243 M
   Permanent . . . . . . . :      5.116     Current unprotect used :     2017 M
   Temporary . . . . . . . :      2.208     Maximum unprotect . . :     2026 M

Type changes (if allowed), press Enter.

System   Pool    Reserved    Max    -----DB-----   ---Non-DB---
 Pool   Size (K) Size (K)  Active  Fault  Pages  Fault  Pages
   1     30000    15360      +++     .0     .0     .9     .0
   2     65584        0       3      .0     .0    1.8     .0
   3      1024        0       2      .0     .0     .0     .0
   4    100000        0      70      .0     .0    6.7     .0

                                                               Bottom
Command
===>

F3=Exit   F4=Prompt        F5=Refresh   F9=Retrieve   F10=Restart
F11=Display transition data   F12=Cancel   F24=More keys
```

---

a. Press F10 to make sure that statistics are reset.

b. Wait 3 to 5 minutes, then press F5 to refresh the display.

While waiting, observe the following:

Percent CPU used   If high (greater than 70 percent), then try to gain an understanding of the mix of batch versus interactive jobs. You want less than 70-percent interactive or performance begins to suffer.

Number of jobs in system   This includes spool files that have not been printed. If the number of jobs is much more than the total active jobs in system, look for reasons. If it is because of spool files, consider deleting old spool files.

Auxiliary storage   How much do you have and what percent is used. If approaching 80 percent used, then your performance begins to degrade

2. Is the MCHPOOL Non Data Base faulting rate within guidelines (see Table for Step 2, below)?

a. Yes. go to step 3.

b. No. Adjust MCHPOOL size (System Pool #1).

1) -50K if = 0.

2) +50K if > 3.0.

3) Press F10 to reset and go to step 1.

3. Wait 3 to 5 minutes, then press the F5 key. Is the Wait to Ineligible job transition state = 0?

a. Yes. Reduce Activity Level by 2, press F10 to reset, and repeat step 3.

b. No. Go to step 4.

4. Is the Active to Wait state 10 times the Activity Level ?

a. Yes. Go to step 5.

b. No. System not heavily used or complex application mix. Go to step 3.

5. Is the Wait to Ineligible state within guidelines (see Table for Step 5, below)?

a. Yes. Go to step 6.

b. No. Is the Database Fault + Non-database Fault < 15 to 20?

1) Yes. Increase activity level by 1, press F10, and go to step 3.

2) No. Increase pool size by 50K, press F10, and go to step 3.

6. Is the Total Fault rate for **each** pool within guidelines (see Table for Step 6, below)?

a. Yes. Go to step 7.

b. No. Go to step 5.b.2.

7. Is the Total Fault rate for **all** pools within guidelines (see the Table for Step 7 below)?

    a. Yes. Go to step 8.

    b. No. Go to step 5.b.2.

8. Activity level probably OK. Tuning exercise complete. Continue to monitor performance.

Use the following guidelines at steps 2, 5, 6, and 7.

<table>
<tr><td>

Table for Step #2
Machine Pool Non-database
Fault Rate

Good:	< 2
Acceptable:	2 to 5
Poor:	> 5

</td><td>

Table for Step #5
Ratio of Wait to Ineligible
and Active to Wait States

Good:	< 10%
Acceptable:	10% to 20%
Poor:	> 25%

</td></tr>
</table>

Table for Step #6
Sum of Database and Non-database Faulting Rate
in Each Pool Except Machine Pool

Model	Good	Acceptable	Poor
B10, B20, B30, B35, C04, C06, C10, D02, D04, E02	< 10	10 to 15	> 15
B40, B45, C20, C25, D06, D10, D20, D35, E04, E06, E10, F02, F04, 200/2030	< 15	15 to 25	> 25
B50, B60, B70, D25, D45, D50, D60, E20, E25, E35, E45, E50, E60, F06, F10, F20, F25, F35, F45, F50, 20S/2010, 100, 200/2031, 200/2032, 300/2040, 300/2041, 300/2042	< 25	25 to 50	>50
D70, D80, E70, E80, F60, F70, 30S/2411, 30S/2412, 135, 140, 310/2043, 310/2044, 320/2050	< 50	50 to 100	> 100
E90, E95, F80	< 100	100 to 200	> 200
F90, F95, F97, 320/2051, 320/2052	< 150	150 to 350	> 350

Table for Step #7 Sum of Database and Non-database Faulting Rate in All Pools Except Machine Pool			
Model	**Good**	**Acceptable**	**Poor**
B10, B20, B30, B35, C04, C06, C10, D02, D04, E02	< 15	15 to 25	> 25
B40, B45, C20, C25, D06, D10, D20, D35, E04, E06, E10, F02, F04, 200/2030	< 25	25 to 40	> 40
B50, B60, B70, D25, D45, D50, D60, E20, E25, E35, E45, E50, E60, F06, F10, F20, F25, F35, F45, F50, 20S/2010, 100, 200/2031, 200/2032, 300/2040, 300/2041, 300/2042	< 35	35 to 60	> 60
D70, D80, E70, E80, F60, F70, 30S/2411, 30S/2412, 135, 140, 310/2043, 310/2044, 320/2050	< 80	80 to 130	> 130
E90, E95, F80	< 180	180 to 300	> 300
F90, F95, F97, 320/2051, 320/2052	< 250	250 to 440	> 440

Refer to the *AS/400 Work Management* manual for a complete listing of faulting rates.

> *When tuning your system, it is important to change only one thing at a time and to determine the effect the change has before changing something else. Record the before and after data when you change something. You might want to keep notes or print the screen on the WRKSYSSTS display. If you don't, you could end up with a system that is not optimized or you might actually make matters worse.*

Additional Performance Tuning Considerations

Some additional things you need to consider when tuning your system are:

- Separate subsystems could prove useful in situations where you need to differentiate certain jobs or tasks from others for reasons such as control or critical jobs. For example, you may have "critical" batch jobs running in one subsystem and unplanned or "ad hoc" batch jobs in another subsystem.
- Consider grouping interactive jobs into separate subsystems based on their connectivity to the system or association with separate applications. For example, you could have the interactive jobs originating from the nonprogrammable terminals connected on twinaxial cabling running on one subsystem and jobs originating from personal computers on another.

- Separate batch jobs from all other jobs on the AS/400. Consider creating a separate subsystem for batch jobs and use a separate storage pool rather than *BASE. Refer to Moving Batch Jobs Out of *BASE Memory Pool on page 216.
- For batch work with active job queues:
  - For each batch thread, have one subsystem fed from one job queue with maximum active jobs = 1. Use private memory pool or *SHAREPOOLx.
- For batch work with sporadically used job queues, use one of following:
  - Set up single subsystem with multiple job queues. Each job queue with maximum active jobs = 1. Use *BASE memory pool or other shared memory pool.
  - Set up multiple subsystems, each with one job queue. Each subsystem with maximum jobs = 1. Use *BASE memory pool or other shared memory pool.
- If dedicated batch work (e.g., long-running night jobs):
  - Set single job queue per memory pool.
  - Make pool large enough so faulting rate is low.
  - Use PURGE(*NO); set this in the class description.
  - Set timeslice to 999999; also set in the class description.
- Consider running all batch jobs in a memory pool other than *BASE. Refer to Moving Batch Jobs Out of *BASE Memory Pool on page 216.
- Separate interactive work according to priority. For each interactive priority category:
  - Set up separate interactive subsystem for each category of interactive work.
  - Each interactive priority should have its own storage pool.
  - Create a class for each interactive priority with correct execution priority.
- Create a nighttime run environment for batch jobs that run at night. During these times, your interactive needs are most likely less than during daytime hours. It is during these periods that many shops run their resource-intensive and long-running batch jobs. Make sure these jobs have the resources they need. Create a simple CL command or program to change the subsystem description so that the system has the best use of resources possible. Of course, remember to change back to daytime environment before the sun comes up again.
- If you have many Client Access jobs, or if you use a lot of line transmissions that seem to take an unusually long time to complete, consider creating an additional memory pool for the subsystems with communications jobs (e.g., subsystem QCMN). Refer to Routing Client Access Communication Jobs to a Separate Memory Pool on page 217 and Using Subsystem Routing Entries for Communication Jobs on page 220

  The reason for a separate memory pool is that, even though communications jobs need only a small amount of memory at a time, they must access the memory before a time-out limit is reached. Failing to do so leads to error recovery procedures that tend to use a large amount of system resources. One way to find information on time-outs is to start the Service Tool (STRSST command) and search for communications errors in the error log.

- Look for memory pools that have the highest faulting rate. Target these pools first for tuning.
- Look for unusual causes for faulting. For example:
  - Program compiles in wrong pool.
  - Large queries running simultaneously.
  - Large queries running in interactive memory pools.
  - Interactive save/restore operations.
- Determine if causes for high faulting are likely to recur regularly.

Tips to Improve Memory/CPU Utilization

The following tips may help you improve memory or CPU utilization:

- Use native AS/400 RPG methods — not old ones such as S/36 RPG.
- Reduce disk I/O.
- Don't use CANCEL/FREE with SHARE(*NO).
- Increase storage pool size. Use shared pools and dynamic tuning. I believe that dynamic tuning works best in situations where you have significant, but infrequent, changes in the workload during the day. If your workload is steady, then you may not see any difference between dynamic and manual tuning. Dynamic tuning is easy to use, so if you do not see a significant difference between manual and dynamic tuning, stick with dynamic tuning. If you do not use dynamic tuning, be prudent in your use of shared pools or you may find that your response time is variable. If you need certain jobs (e.g., interactive order entry) to maintain a relatively steady response time, then you do not want these users to share a pool with, say, the programmers.

  One other note on dynamic tuning. I have seen many situations where performance was not as good with dynamic tuning as with manual tuning. These situations seem to be characterized by frequent and rapid changes in the workload. Refer to AS/400 Dynamic Tuning on page 205 for additional information.

- Make sure your batch jobs are separate from your interactive jobs. Most experienced tuners recommend that you single-thread your batch jobs to have only one batch job running per storage pool. One way you can do this is to have multiple batch subsystems with one JOBQ per subsystem. If the JOBQ and subsystem are used all the time, then allocate a private storage pool to that subsystem. If the JOBQ and subsystem are used sporadically, then use a shared pool or *BASE. Once again, use of the dynamic tuning function and shared pools may work really well here.

- Check the time slice value in the CLASS description. Rick Turner, considered one of IBM's best performance experts, recommends this rule of thumb: set the time slice value equal to three times the average CPU cycle per job. If you have one of the faster CPU-model AS/400s, you may find that the default time-slice value is too long. Monitor how many of your jobs reach time-slice end (TSE). You don't want more than 5 percent. If you have more, then your time-slice value is probably too short. If you have set the system value QTSEPOOL equal to *BASE, then, when your jobs reach TSE, they are transferred to pool *BASE for execution. You may have to experiment to determine which value is best for QTSEPOOL. My recommendation is to adjust the time slice so no more than 5 percent of the jobs reach TSE and set QTSEPOOL = *BASE.

- Use odd-length packed fields for decimal arithmetic.
- Make your infrequent routines subroutines to reduce the "dead" code and the paging requirements.
- Use shared open data paths.
- If you have a lot of main storage and have interactive jobs with lots of transactions or use a lot of processing time, specify PURGE(*NO).
- Install more main memory.
- Increase CPU power.

Disk Storage Utilization Guidelines

After you have performed the basic tuning described above and in the **AS/400 Work Management** manual, observe the disk status. Enter the command WRKDSKSTS. When viewing the Work with Disk Status display, observe the percent-busy data (not the percent used). Each unit (actuator) should be less than 40-percent busy. If each unit is between 40 and 60 percent, you may experience variable response times. If each unit is more than 60-percent busy, there are not enough actuators to provide good performance.

If the actuator is in a user ASP, then the 40-percent rule does not necessarily apply. Also, you might exceed the 40-percent rule during periods with a large amount of batch activity — this is not necessarily cause for alarm.

> *An exception to the 40-percent rule is the 6502 IOP card. The 6502 IOP is a "combo" card with the IOP function and disk controller function on the same card. The guideline for the 6502 is 70 percent. That is, the 6502 reaches saturation when the WRKDSKSTS display indicates 70 percent — not 40 percent as for other disk IOPs. If percent busy is greater than 70 percent on the 6502 IOP, you will likely experience performance degradation.*

The percent of each actuator used does not have as much effect on performance as does the percent busy. As you approach 90-percent used, your disk I/O performance degrades. I advise users to keep below 80-percent used. Refer to the **AS/400 Work Management** manual for additional information.

Tips to Improve Disk I/O Performance

The following tips may help improve your disk I/O performance:

- Eliminate unnecessary database operations like generic searches.
- Reorganize high-use programs to keep active routines together.
- Use join files to bring records from multiple physical files together rather than using multiple reads.

- Use externally described printer files.
- Limit sign-on/sign-off activity. Encourage the use of DSCJOB.
- Reduce batch activity during the times that compete with interactive jobs.
- RGZPFM more frequently.
- Install more disk arms.

Communications I/O Utilization Guidelines

When you collect and analyze performance data (using AS/400 Performance Tools), you can print a report that displays the communication I/O utilization. Each communication I/O should be below 40-percent utilization — this includes your work station controllers. If utilization of any communication I/O is greater than 40 percent, you are likely to experience higher response times.

Tips to Improve Communication I/O Utilization

Communication performance is frequently dependent on variables that may be outside of your control. The following tips may help improve the communication I/O utilization:

- Concentrate printers on the same communication line to free other lines for interactive users.
- Rank the users according to activity, and balance the communication lines so that not too many highly active users are on the same line.
- Get more or faster communication lines.

MOVING BATCH JOBS OUT OF *BASE MEMORY POOL

The default location for running batch jobs is in the *BASE memory pool. This pool is a shared memory pool. Typical jobs running in *BASE are:

- Batch jobs
- Subsystem monitors
- System transients
- Pool switching jobs
- Other machine jobs

The batch jobs generally run at a lower priority than the other jobs. Under normal circumstances, this may not be a problem (with the exception of pool switching jobs). But, if you remove the batch jobs from *BASE, you ensure that they do not compete with the other jobs.

To separate the batch jobs from the *BASE memory pool, do the following:

1. Hold the job queue QBATCH — and any other job queues that feed subsystem QBATCH:

```
HLDJOBQ JOBQ(QGPL/QBATCH)
```

Proceed to the next step when all batch jobs that are running have completed.

2. End the subsystem QBATCH. If at V3R1, this is not necessary.

   ```
   ENDSBS SBS(QBATCH) OPTION(*IMMED)
   ```

3. If a second memory pool is not defined, add a shared memory pool to subsystem QBATCH:

   ```
   CHGSBSD SBSD(QBATCH) POOLS((1 *BASE) (2 *SHRPOOL1))
   ```

4. Check the sequence numbers of the routing entries in QBATCH and then select option 7:

   ```
   DSPSBSD SBSD(QBATCH)
   ```

5. Change the routing entries associated with each sequence number noted in step 4:

   ```
   CHGRTGE SBSD(QBATCH) SEQNBR(xxxx) POOLID(2)
   ```

6. Restart subsystem QBATCH if it is stopped, and release the job queue:

   ```
   STRSBS SBSD(QSYS/QBATCH)
   RLSJOBQ JOBQ(QGPL/QBATCH)
   ```

7. Tune the system. You have to adjust the memory pool size and activity levels for *BASE and *SHRPOOL1 (that you created in step 3).

   You need less memory and activity level in *BASE now that you have removed the batch jobs.

ROUTING CLIENT ACCESS COMMUNICATION JOBS TO A SEPARATE MEMORY POOL

If you have a large number of Client Access jobs, you can separate the communication jobs (in QCMN and QSERVER subsystems) from other jobs. Typically, the QCMN and QSERVER jobs run in the *BASE memory pool. If you move these jobs into their own memory pool, you can help minimize conflicts that may occur in *BASE. This may improve the performance of Client Access and lessen conflicts with other jobs running in *BASE.

V3R1 The QCMN subsystem is used for communications jobs. The QSERVER subsystem is new for V3R1. The file server (previously called the shared folder Type 2 server) and the database server must run in this subsystem. Prior to V3R1, all shared folder Type 2 jobs ran in a subsystem called QXFPCS. This subsystem is not used in V3R1 and is replaced with the QSERVER subsystem.

> *If you are not running V3R1, then substitute QXFPCS for QSERVER in the following procedures.*

Use the following procedure to place the Client Access/400 jobs in QCMN and QSERVER in a memory pool other than *BASE.

1. If you are at V3R1, you can make changes to subsystems while they are active. Otherwise, you must first end the subsystems. To end the subsystems, issue the following commands:

```
ENDSBS SBS(QCMN) OPTION(*IMMED)
ENDSBS SBS(QSERVER) OPTION(*IMMED)
```

2. Configure the subsystems with an additional memory pool. For example, you could configure an unused shared memory pool:

```
CHGSBSD SBSD(QCMN) POOLS((1 *BASE) (2 *SHRPOOL3))
CHGSBSD SBSD(QSERVER) POOLS((1 *BASE) (2 *SHRPOOL3))
```

3. Add some memory and an activity level to the shared memory pool. If you have auto-tuning turned on, it makes any necessary adjustments when activity starts in the pool. If you are manually tuning the system, then you have to adjust this for optimum performance later.

```
CHGSHRPOOL POOL(*SHRPOOL3) SIZE(500) ACTLVL(5)
```

4. Print a copy of the QCMN and QSERVER subsystems description:

```
DSPSBSD SBSD(QCMN) OUTPUT(*PRINT)
DSPSBSD SBSD(QCMN) OUTPUT(*PRINT)
```

5. Change the routing entries in the QCMN and QSERVER subsystems that control Client Access/400 jobs. There are several routing entries that you need to change. Refer to the tables below for a listing of the routing entries and the print outs (from Step 4) of the QCMN and QSERVER subsystems descriptions for the sequence numbers. The syntax for changing the routing entry is:

```
CHGRTGE SBSD(QCMN) SEQNBR(nnn) POOLID(2)
CHGRTGE SBSD(QCMN) SEQNBR(nnn) POOLID(2)
```

where: *nnn* is the sequence number for the routing entry you are changing.

The following format is used for the routing data that is compared using a routing entry in a subsystem:

Position	1	9	19	29	37	47
Value:	Mode	Device	UserID	PGMEVOKE	Program Name	Library Name
Default Value:	QPCSUPP	none	none	PGMEVOKE	Depends on Client Access function	QSYS

Client Access Function	Subsystem	Routing Data	QCMN Job Name	Class
Communication Jobs using modes QCASERVR and QPCSUPP	QCMN and QSERVER	QCASERVR QPCSUPP	APPC Device APPC Device	QCASERVR QWCPCSUP
5250 Display Emulation	QCMN	None	APPC Virtual Device Name	QBATCH
5250 Printer Emulation	QCMN	None	APPC Device Writer Name	QBATCH
Virtual Printer Writer	QCMN	QVPRINT	APPC Device Writer Name	QWCPCSUP
Remote Command	QCMN	None	APPC Device	QWCPCSUP
File Transfer	QCMN	QTFDWNLD	APPC Device	QWCPCSUP
Remote SQL	QCMN	QRMSQL	APPC Device	QWCPCSUP
License Management	QCMN	QLZPSERV	APPC Device	QWCPCSUP

Message Function
    Sender
    Receiver
	QCMN	
		QMFRCVR
		QMFSNDR
			
			APPC Device
			APPC Device
				
				QWCPCSUP
				QWCPCSUP

Original Data Queue Server	QCMN	QHQTRGT	APPC Device	QWCPCSUP

File Server
    Initial Job
    Autostart Job
    Server Job
	
	QCMN
	QSERVER
	QSERVER
		
		None
		QSTART
		QSRVR
			
			APPC Device
			QSERVER
			QPWFSERV
				
				None
				QPWFSERVER
				QPWFSERVER

Database Server	QSERVER	QZDAINIT	QZDAINIT	QPWFSERVER
Optimized Data Queue Server	QCMN	QZHQTRG	APPC Device	QCASERVR
Network Print Server	QCMN	QNPSERVR	QNPSERVR	QCASERVR
Central Server	QCMN	QZCSERVR	QZCSERVR	QCASERVR
Remote Command / Distributed Program Call	QCMN	QZCSERVR	QZCSERVR	QCASERVR

If you have other Client Access jobs that are not covered in the table above, or you have other communication jobs that you want to move out of the *BASE memory pool, you can modify the subsystem description with routing entries. Use compare values for the jobs you wish to capture. Refer to Using Subsystem Routing Entries for Communication Jobs, below.

USING SUBSYSTEM ROUTING ENTRIES FOR COMMUNICATION JOBS

A communications job is a batch job that is started by a program start request from a remote system (e.g., a personal computer running Client Access/400). The job processing involves a communication request and appropriate specifications.

For a communications batch job to run, a subsystem description containing a work entry for communications jobs must exist on the system. The communications work entry identifies to the subsystem the sources for the communications job it will process. The job processing begins when the subsystem receives a communications program start request from a remote system and an appropriate routing entry is found for the request.

To provide special routing for any communications job, you must first identify the jobs you want to route. Use the WRKACTJOB command. Find the job and use option 5 to work with it. Let's use an example where we want to run a job called ALASCOM in a memory pool other than *BASE. Issue the WRKACTJOB command and locate the job. Take option 5 as shown below:

```
                        Work with Active Jobs                      APACHE
                                                         05/04/95  07:20:28
CPU %:     .0      Elapsed time:   00:00:00    Active jobs:   110

Type options, press Enter.
  2=Change  3=Hold  4=End  5=Work with  6=Release  7=Display message
  8=Work with spooled files  13=Disconnect ...

Opt  Subsystem/Job  User      Type  CPU %  Function       Status
  _    QBATCH        QSYS      SBS    .0                   DEQW
  _    QCMN          QSYS      SBS    .0                   DEQW
  5    ALASCOM       CAMPBELL  EVK    .0   * -PASSTHRU     EVTW
  _    DT2           SEFRASER  EVK    .0   * -PASSTHRU     EVTW
  _    DT2           SFRASER   EVK    .0   * -PASSTHRU     EVTW
  _    JBNU77        QSECOFR   EVK    .0   * -PASSTHRU     EVTW
  _    JBNU77        QSECOFR   EVK    .0   * -PASSTHRU     EVTW
  _    JLSEWALD      SEWALD    EVK    .0   * -PASSTHRU     EVTW
  _    NEIL          CAMPBELL  EVK    .0   * -PASSTHRU     EVTW
                                                              More...
Parameters or command
===>
F3=Exit     F5=Refresh   F10=Restart statistics   F11=Display elapsed data
F12=Cancel  F23=More options   F24=More keys
```

On the Work with Job screen (example shown below), take option 11 to display the call stack.

```
                            Work with Job
                                              System:   APACHE
Job:   ALASCOM      User:   CAMPBELL     Number:   188390

Select one of the following:

     1. Display job status attributes
     2. Display job definition attributes
     3. Display job run attributes, if active
     4. Work with spooled files

    10. Display job log, if active or on job queue
    11. Display call stack, if active
    12. Work with locks, if active
    13. Display library list, if active
    14. Display open files, if active
    15. Display file overrides, if active
    16. Display commitment control status, if active
                                                        More...
Selection or command
===> 11
F3=Exit    F4=Prompt    F9=Retrieve    F12=Cancel
```

Make a note of the first program or procedure in the call stack. An example screen is shown below:

```
                         Display Call Stack
                                              System:   APACHE
Job:   ALASCOM      User:   CAMPBELL     Number:   188390

Type options, press Enter.
  5=Display details

       Request  Program or
Opt    Level    Procedure       Library   Statement      Instruction
                QWTPIPPP        QSYS                      00A6
_                                                        
                QPAPAST2        QSYS                      02E4
_



                                                          Bottom
F3=Exit         F10=Update stack   F11=Display activation group   F12=Cancel
F16=Job menu    F17=Top   F18=Bottom
```

The first program or procedure shown in the call stack is the job you use in the subsystem routing entry. As shown in the above screen, we need to create a routing entry for the QWTPIPPP program.

Job routing of communications jobs is determined by the program start request that is received from the remote system. When a program start request is processed on the target system, a fixed-length data stream that is used as routing data is created. Position 29 of the routing data always contains PGMEVOKE for communications requests. Subsystem routing entries that specify a compare value of PGMEVOKE in position 29 typically have *RTGDTA as the program name. This means that the program name specified in the routing data (from the remote system's program start request) is the program to run. The last routing entry in the QCMN subsystem is generally the PGMEVOKE routing entry.

If a special processing environment is required for certain communications jobs, you can add a routing entry to the subsystem description, specifying a compare value whose starting position is 37. This compare value should contain the program name for the program start request. The routing entry must have a sequence number lower than the routing entry that uses PGMEVOKE as the compare value.

In our example, assume that you want to route the QWTPIPPP job to run in a memory pool other than *BASE using a class we have defined for run priority and time slice. We would need to add a routing entry for the QWTPIPPP job. This routing entry must come before the routing entry that uses PGMEVOKE as the compare value, and it must use starting position 37:

```
ADDRTGE SBSD(QCMN) SEQNBR(nnn) CMPVAL('QWTPIPPP' 37) PGM(*RTGDTA)
        CLS(classname/libname) POOLID(2)
```

The next time QWTPIPPP program is evoked, it should run in POOLID(2) of the QCMN subsystem, with the class name we would indicate in the routing entry.

Defining Subsystem Pools

When you create subsystems, if you decide to run jobs in the *BASE pool, create the subsystem with two pools — each one in *BASE. Then, if you decide to run the jobs in a different pool, you can make the change to the subsystem while it is active. The first defined memory pool is used to run the subsystem monitor job. The subsequent pools (if any) are used to run other subsystem jobs. If no other pools are defined, then all subsystem jobs run in the single memory pool. All subsystem monitor jobs should run in the *BASE memory pool. Remaining jobs can run in a pool of your choosing. Refer to Subsystems for Communication Lines and Remote Locations on page 161 for an example of creating a subsystem description.

Job Priority in System Pools

Run jobs of like priority in one pool. If you run jobs of different priorities in the same pool, you could impact throughput.

A common mistake users make is to run batch-type jobs interactively. For example, performing a SAVLIB. If the library is large and the user runs the SAVLIB command, the job runs at the same priority and in the same pool as other interactive jobs. A better way is to use the Submit Job (SBMJOB) command to force the job to run in batch mode.

OFFICEVISION/400 PERFORMANCE TUNING

If you believe that your OfficeVision/400 performance is suffering, consider the following in addition to the performance tuning tips presented elsewhere in this book.

- Pool switching. You can force the movement of long-running interactive transactions from their initial subsystem (most likely running in the *INTERACT memory pool) to the system's *BASE pool.

  Change the system value QTSEPOOL to *BASE. Refer to Tips to Improve Memory/CPU Utilization on page 214 for additional information.

- Have users perform long-running Office functions in batch mode. The corresponding function, menu, and menu option are shown in the following table.

Function	Menu Name	Menu Option	Command Interface
Data Text Merge and Printing	Print Options	Place on job queue	PRTDOC
Spell Check	Work with Documents in Folders	Option 11	CHKDOC
Pagination	Work with Documents in Folders	Option 13	PAGDOC
Search for Documents	Search for Documents	Wait for Completion = N	QRYDOCLIB

The command interface can be used with the SBMJOB (submit job) command to run in batch mode.

- If immediate delivery of mail is not required, you may be able to improve interactive office work by changing the priority of the QDIALOCAL job. This job is queued whenever a user sends, forwards, or replies to a note. The default priority is 20. If you change the default to priority 25, the mail function slows down a bit, but your other interactive jobs may improve. Change the class of QDIALOCAL:

  ```
  CHGCLS CLS(QGPL/QDIALOCAL) RUNPTY(25)
  ```

- If you do a lot of data/text merges, consider running them in their own memory pool.

- Unless necessary, avoid using the "confirmation of notes delivery." Set the default to Off. To change the default, press the F13 key at the Send Note menu, then go to the Change Defaults menu.

- When distributing a large document for review, rather than sending the document, place the document in a common shared folder accessible to everyone. Then send them a note or message to access the folder and review the document. This eliminates the need for the system to track the document for multiple users.

- If you have custom menus that incorporate Office functions and local applications, avoid using the STROFC x options. A better approach (for performance reasons) is to use the OfficeVision-supplied menu and then use option 50 to get to local applications.

  Using the STROFC x command requires much greater system resources than simply taking the option from the OfficeVision menu.

  To use option 50, specify a program name when creating or changing enrollment information. The program you specify could then lead to further menus for local applications.

- Keep OfficeVision objects cleaned up. Refer to Housekeeping on page 101 for additional information.

EXPERT CACHING

V2R3 introduced a self-tuning dynamic storage pool caching algorithm, also known as "expert caching." Expert caching changes the way the AS/400 manages data transfers by automatically tuning or adjusting the amount of data read from DASD into memory and then varying the length of time the changed data stays in memory. This expert cache is implemented as a part of storage management. It selectively enhances storage I/O performance using main memory already present on the machine. Expert caching manages the caching for the jobs within the memory pools defined on the system. Its artificial intelligence caching algorithm continuously monitors physical and logical storage activity, dynamically adjusting the caching parameters for a given pool.

When you implement expert caching, the system automatically determines the best approach for handling data in the storage pool. When many jobs are running in a small storage pool, the system limits the amount of memory that each job uses. When the storage pool has enough memory for the number of jobs that are running, the system determines how much data to bring into the storage pool.

> Controller-based read caching may be implemented for some disk devices. If you have this kind of disk caching, it may conflict with expert caching. You do not want both types of caching to be active simultaneously.

Considerations for Using Expert Caching

Dynamic storage pool paging (aka Expert Caching) can improve performance, depending on how it brings objects into memory.

- If many jobs are running in a small storage pool, the system limits the amount of memory used by each job.

- If the storage pool for those jobs has enough memory, the system determines (object by object) how much data to bring into the storage pool.

- If objects are referred to sequentially, the system brings larger blocks of data into memory and delays writing changes of the data. This reduces the number of I/O operations issued by the job and reduces the contention for disk drives. In turn, this reduces the time that jobs wait on I/O requests.

- If objects are referred to randomly, the system does not bring in large blocks of data because that does not reduce the number of I/O operations.

> *If expert caching is enabled, and the system abnormally ends, the recovery time could be longer than it would be if expert caching was disabled.*

The following are guidelines for using dynamic storage pool paging (expert caching):

- Expert caching uses main memory. A bit of extra main memory is a good thing.
- Expert caching works best:
  - For applications that spend most of their time waiting for disk I/O.
  - For applications with lots of updates or add activities.
  - For jobs that are not optimized for performance.
- Expert caching runs only in the shared memory pools. Turn it on in one pool at a time, let it run for a few days, then evaluate results.
- After turning on expert caching, vary the amount of memory in the shared pool to evaluate the impact of the change. Try adding memory, but not too much. After a point, performance is not helped by more memory.
- If your applications access data in an extremely random manner, expert caching may not help — may even hinder — performance. Turn it off if this is the case.
- Compare performance data before and after expert caching. You should see fewer disk I/O operations and less CPU time per job.
- Don't worry too much if the overall CPU utilization increases after implementing expert caching. This may be the ability of the CPU to accomplish more work in a given unit of time due to the expert caching. Do not make the mistake of presuming that an increase in CPU utilization is necessarily bad.

Activating Expert Caching

Expert caching works on shared memory pools only. Control is at the individual memory pool level, not the object or system level. Batch jobs using expert caching may read more data into memory than interactive jobs.

To activate, set the paging option in the shared memory pool to *CALC. For example, if want to change the *BASE memory pool to expert caching, enter the following command:

```
CHGSHRPOOL  POOL(*BASE)  PAGING(*CALC)
```

You can also use the WRKSHRPOOL command to make changes or to verify which shared pools have expert caching enabled. Enter the command WRKSHRPOOL. You see a screen similar to the one below. The two columns labeled "Paging Option, Defined and Current" provide the current state of expert caching. *FIXED indicates that expert caching is disabled and *CALC indicates it is enabled. The fields that are underscored can be changed. For example, the memory pools size, maximum activity, and paging option.

```
                              Work with Shared Pools
                                               System:   APACHE
Main storage size (K)   . :        196608

Type changes (if allowed), press Enter.

              Defined    Max   Allocated   Pool  -Paging Option--
Pool          Size (K)  Active  Size (K)    ID   Defined  Current
*MACHINE        30500     +++     30500      1   *FIXED   *FIXED
*BASE           31084      10     31084      2   *CALC    *CALC
*INTERACT       84000      15     84000      4   *FIXED   *FIXED
*SPOOL           1024       5      1024      3   *FIXED   *FIXED
*SHRPOOL1       50000      10     50000      5   *CALC    *CALC
*SHRPOOL2        5000       1                    *FIXED
*SHRPOOL3           0       0                    *FIXED
*SHRPOOL4           0       0                    *FIXED
*SHRPOOL5           0       0                    *FIXED
*SHRPOOL6           0       0                    *FIXED
                                                           More...
Command
===>
F3=Exit   F4=Prompt   F5=Refresh   F9=Retrieve   F11=Display text
F12=Cancel
```

DISCONNECT JOB

Signing on and off the system uses system resources. This is not a problem unless you have many users. Minimize the system impact when signing on and off by using the DSCJOB command instead of the SIGNOFF command. When you disconnect using the DSCJOB command, the system maintains your job in the wait state (it is not using system resources) and displays the normal sign-on screen on your display station. If you later sign-on to the same display, you pick up the job where you left off. The big advantage is that the system does not use as much resource getting you there. The DSCJOB can be entered on the command line or by using the Operational Assistant.

You may want to create a command that is easier for your users to remember. For example, you could create a command called BYEBYE, which would execute the system command DSCJOB.

AUTOSTART JOBS

Autostart jobs are batch jobs that start whenever the associated subsystem starts. Generally, autostart jobs are used to perform repetitive work or one-time initialization work that is associated with a particular subsystem.

Think of autostart jobs as personal computer AUTOEXEC.BAT files for the AS/400. For example, use an autostart job associated with the controlling subsystem to start up other subsystems. Or create a special batch subsystem with an autostart job that performs various unique and specialized tasks associated with that subsystem.

You can have multiple autostart job entries. When the subsystem starts, all the autostart jobs start. Typically, autostart jobs start when the subsystem starts and end when the subsystem ends.

EXAMPLE OF CREATING SUBSYSTEM AUTOSTART JOBS

The autostart job can be any program or command that you want to execute whenever the subsystem is started. Autostart jobs have six requirements:

1. A program or command to be executed whenever the subsystem starts.
2. A job queue to be submitted to.
3. A subsystem to run In wlth the appropriate job queue enlry.
4. A routing entry in the associated subsystem.
5. A job description.
6. An autostart job entry in the subsystem.

Taking each requirement in turn, the steps you need to take are as follows:

1. Create a program or command to be executed when the subsystem starts. The program or command to be run can be any program. You can create your program using any programming language. There are no limitations, except that the program has to run in batch mode. Let's assume that you have a program called MYPROGRAM that you wish to run as an autostart job for a new subsystem that you are going to create.

2. Create a job queue to submit your autostart job. All batch-type jobs must be submitted to job queues. If you are using an existing subsystem, then more than likely that subsystem already has job queues that you can use for autostart jobs. If you are creating a new subsystem, then you will likely create job queues for the subsystem. A single job queue can be associated with multiple subsystems, but this is not recommended. Suppose you are going to create a new subsystem called GEORGE. You may want to create a job queue called GEORGE just to be consistent.

   ```
   CRTJOBQ JOBQ(libname/GEORGE) TEXT(JOBQ GEORGE)
   ```

3. Now create a subsystem description and add a job queue entry.
   ```
   CRTSBSD SBSD(libname/GEORGE)  POOLS((1 *BASE))
       TEXT(Subsystem George)
   ```

   > There are several other parameters that you could enter. Refer to the **AS/400 Work Management** manual for additional information. In this example, the subsystem uses the *BASE memory pool.

   ```
   ADDJOBQE SBSD(libname/GEORGE) JOBQ(libname/GEORGE)
       MAXACT(1) SEQNBR(10)
   ```

> *The subsystem uses the sequence number to select the job queues from which to pull jobs.*

V3R1

Prior to V3R1, most subsystem description changes must be made with the subsystem ended. With V3R1, you can make many changes with the subsystem active.

4. You need to add a routing entry to the subsystem. This is an easy step, but somewhat confusing to newer users. A recommended routing entry for your autostart batch job is:

```
ADDRTGE SBSD(libname/GEORGE)  SEQNBR(xx)  CMPVAL(AUTOSTART)  PGM(QCMD)
    CLS(QBATCH)
```

The following are explanations of the parameters used in the ADDRTGE command.

SBSD   This constitutes the library and subsystem names.

SEQNBR   Generally a low sequence number is used. Use lower numbers for specific tasks and higher numbers for tasks that are more general in nature. Use the DSPSBSD command to check for existing routing entries and use an entry that isn't already used.

CMPVAL   The compare value can be anything you like. Choose a value that is specific and not likely to be used in other jobs. Make it something meaningful to you. Use this value for the routing data in the job description (below).

PGM   When a new job starts with routing data equal to the CMPVAL(value), this program starts. The QCMD program is a general-purpose program that retrieves messages from the job's message queue and interprets the messages as if they were commands.

CLS   The class contains information such as run priority and time slice. For most batch-type jobs, the QBATCH class is fine.

5. You need a job description. Create a separate job description for each autostart job. Let's say that the job description is the same as the subsystem and job queue names.

```
CRTJOBD JOBD(libname/GEORGE)  JOBQ(libname/GEORGE)
    USER(username)  RTGDTA(AUTOSTART)
    RQSDTA('CALL MYPROGRAM')
```

The following are explanations of the parameters used in the CRTJOBD command.

JOBD	This constitutes the library and job description names.
JOBQ	You already created the job queue earlier. Put in the name here.
USER	You must have a valid user profile here. You cannot use the default value (*RQD) when creating a job description because the job is not submitted by a user, so it cannot pick up the user's information. Make sure the user profile used has enough authority to run the job. Consider creating a specific user profile for this purpose with a password of *NONE so no one can sign on using the profile.
RTGDTA	The value you use here must be the same as the value used in the routing entry above.
RQSDTA	This must be enclosed within apostrophes. This is the command you wish to run. In the above example, you intend to run a program called MYPROGRAM, so you must precede the program name with a CALL statement. If you were executing a command, then you would not need the CALL statement. This data is sent to the job's message queue where QCMD (see routing entry) interprets the character string as a command to be executed.

6. Add the autostart job entry to the subsystem description.

```
ADDAJE SBSD(libname/GEORGE)  JOB(KICKOFF)  JOBD(libname/GEORGE)
```

The following are explanations of the parameters used in the ADDAJE command.

SBSD	The library and subsystem names.
JOB	You can use any job name you like. The name KICKOFF is purely arbitrary.
JOBD	This is the job description you created.

Now, here's how it all works. When you start the subsystem, the sequence is:

1. The system checks for any autostart job entries in the subsystem description. It finds the entry and gives it the job name KICKOFF. It also provides the job with the job description GEORGE.

2. The system checks job description GEORGE, and obtains the routing data (AUTOSTART) and request data (CALL MYPROGRAM).

3. The system compares the routing data it found in the job description with the routing entries (in sequence) in the subsystem description. When it finds a match, it executes the program using the class indicated in the subsystem routing entry —in this case, the program QCMD and the class QBATCH.

4. The program QCMD checks the job's message queue and discovers the request data, CALL MYPROGRAM, which was passed there by the job description. It interprets this as a command, so it issues the CALL command to run the program called MYPROGRAM — which runs in batch mode with a priority and time slice indicated in the QBATCH class.

5. When you end the subsystem, the autostart job ends, if it hasn't already ended.

ALLOCATING DEVICES TO SUBSYSTEMS

By default, the subsystem QINTER allocates all devices by work station type — not by name. The purpose of this is to capture and allocate all devices regardless of the naming convention used. As you go about configuring your system, you may wish to allocate work stations to subsystems other than QINTER. The following information can be found in the *AS/400 Work Management* manual.

- When a subsystem starts, it attempts to allocate all work station devices in the subsystem description. There is no hierarchy regarding device names versus device types.

- If the device is varied off, the subsystem cannot allocate it. The system arbiter (QSYSARB) holds a lock on all devices that are varied off.

- If the device is varied on, and is not allocated by another subsystem, then the subsystem can allocate it and display the Sign On Display.

- If the device is allocated by another subsystem and is at the Sign On Display (i.e., no active job), the second subsystem can allocate the device from the first subsystem.

- If the device is varied off and all subsystems have started before you vary on the device, and if more than one subsystem could potentially allocate the device, it is unpredictable which subsystem will actually allocate it.

To avoid the situation of unpredictability, you can do one of the following:

- Do not use work station-type entries in any subsystem — use only work station name entries. This means removing the work station-type entries from the IBM-supplied subsystem descriptions. You can enter work station name entries using generic prefixes (e.g., DSP*).

- Vary the work station on when the system is started by specifying ONLINE(*YES) in the device description for the work station. The subsystem that allocates the device is determined by the order in which the subsystems start.

- You can add work station entries to a subsystem description, which causes the subsystem to allocate the device or not allocate the device.
  - To INCLUDE the device:

        ADDWSE SBSD(lib-name/sbsd) WRKSTN(dev-name)
            AT(*SIGNON)

  - To EXCLUDE the device:

        ADDWSE SBSD(lib-name/sbsd) WRKSTN(dev-name)
            AT(*ENTER)

The *AT(*ENTER)* parameter keeps the subsystem from allocating the device at subsystem startup, but allows you to use the TFRJOB command to transfer the job after subsystem startup.

REMOTE CONSOLE USING ASCII WORK STATION CONTROLLER

There are two requirements to make a display device a console on the AS/400:
- The device must be a "dumb" terminal or a PC running terminal emulation. You cannot use a PC that relies on a communications router to establish the connection to the AS/400.
- The device must be allocated by the controlling subsystem. In most cases, this is subsystem QCTL.

If you sign on to the AS/400 and meet the first requirement, you can temporarily move your job to the controlling subsystem — thus, satisfying the second requirement. Enter the command:

    TFRJOB JOBQ(QCTL)

This transfers your current job to the QCTL job queue, which immediately routes it to the active controlling subsystem (in this case QCTL). Once your current job is allocated by the controlling subsystem, you have console capability. You can end all subsystems, do system saves, and perform other functions that require the system to be in a restricted state. You can even do this if you are using a PC attached to the ASCII Work Station Controller running ASCII terminal emulation software. However, once you sign off, your job run time attributes return to the original state.

Many users want a permanent solution for the devices attached to the ASCII WSC. For example, you can configure modem-attached PCs running ASCII terminal emulation software to be console devices every time they dial in.

The following procedure was written to describe adding a work station entry that is used on an ASCII Work Station Controller, but you can use the procedure to add any work station entry to the controlling subsystem.

The standard procedure is:

1. Change the system value for the controlling subsystem.
2. IPL the system.
3. Make changes to the disabled controlling subsystem.
4. Change the system value for the controlling subsystem back to the original setting.
5. Perform a second IPL.

The procedure below is a bit easier and less time consuming.

If you have an ASCII WSC, you might want to have console capability for a remote user. This gives you the ability to dial-in to your AS/400 and perform functions restricted to the console, such as place the system into a restricted state, perform system saves, or end communications. The requirements are:

- You must have an ASCII WSC.
- You cannot use PC Support/400, Client Access/400, or similar programs that use a communications router.
- You must have an ASCII terminal or a PC ASCII terminal emulation program.

The steps you need to follow are:

1. Create a modem-attached device description on the ASCII WSC. This can be any ASCII device but you will not be able to use Client Access as a console device. Suggested devices are 3151/3161 ASCII terminals or a VT100 terminal. If you have a PC, you can use a communication program that emulates VT100 or 3151/3161 terminals.

   You can use the device description with Client Access — you just can't use Client Access as a true console because you may have to end the QCMN subsystem. (A Client Access/400 PC can be used as a console, but not in a remote configuration. Refer to Configuring a Client Access/400 Personal Computer as a Console on page 245.) To use the device description with Client Access *as well as* an ASCII terminal or emulation program, configure the device as TYPE=*CALC.

2. If you are at V3R1 or later, skip directly to step 4; otherwise sign on at a terminal that is allocated by any subsystem **except QCTL**. Do not use your system console terminal as it is usually in QCTL. Make sure there are no active jobs in subsystem QCTL. If QBASE is your controlling subsystem (not recommended), then substitute QBASE for QCTL in these instructions.

3. If you are at a system level lower than V3R1, you must end the subsystem to add a work station entry to a subsystem. To end the controlling subsystem, perform an IPL to end it. Then you can add a work station entry to the controlling subsystem. Notify your users that you are about to conduct an IPL, then issue the command:

```
PWRDWNSYS OPTION(*CNTRLD) DELAY(*NOLIMIT)
```

V3R1

> *Make sure you issue the PWDWNSYS with the *CNTRLD option, otherwise the IPL will occur immediately. By using the *CNTRLD option, the IPL process begins, but pauses while waiting for all jobs to end — in this case, your interactive session on the work station. The controlling subsystem, QCTL, shuts down "far enough" for you to make modifications to the subsystem description. At this point, do not sign off your work station or you will have to start all over.*
>
> *You do not want to use a device attached to QCTL because, as soon as you attempt to perform a PWRDWNSYS, the system attempts to end the QCTL subsystem. If there is an active job in that subsystem, it does not "end enough" for you to add a work station entry.*

4. Add a work station entry to the QCTL subsystem description. If you are at V3R1 or later, you can do this while the subsystem is active.

    ```
    ADDWSE SBSD(QCTL) WRKSTN(dev-name) AT(*SIGNON)
    ```

5. If you are at V3R1 or later, you are finished. Otherwise, you must complete the IPL process. When the system has finished the IPL, the device description created in step 1 should be a named work station entry in the controlling subsystem. You could just sign off the system and the IPL would proceed from the command entered in step 3. Or you could issue the command:

    ```
    PWRDWNSYS OPTION(*IMMED) RESTART(*YES)
    ```

Now when you dial up the ASCII WSC into the port configured as a console-attached device (i.e., Subsystem QCTL or QBASE), your device description is allocated by the controlling subsystem. You are able to perform all the functions that you could perform from a console such as SAVSYS or ENDSBS *ALL. However, you are unable to vary off the ASCII WSC. If you IPL your system, you lose your dial-in connection.

SETTING UP AN UNATTENDED NIGHTTIME ENVIRONMENT

The following information can also be found in the *AS/400 Work Management* manual.

You may have jobs that can be run in an unattended nighttime environment. You could submit these jobs throughout the day to be processed by a special subsystem. To set up this environment:

```
CRTSBS  SBSD(QGPL/NIGHTQ)  POOLS((1 *BASE)) +
    TEXT('Nighttime Jobs')
CRTJOBQ  JOBQ(QGPL/NIGHTQ)  TEXT('Nighttime JOBQ')
ADDJOBQE  SBSD(QGPL/NIGHTQ)  JOBQ(QGPL/NIGHTQ)
    MAXACT(1)
```

```
ADDRTGE  SBSD(QGPL/NIGHTQ)  SEQNBR(10)  CMPVAL(*ANY)  +
    PGM(QSYS/QCMD)  CLS(QGPL/QBATCH)
```

Then create a job description that specifies the job queue QGPL/NIGHTQ.

When you are ready to start the NIGHTQ subsystem:

1. End all active subsystems except the controlling subsystem.

```
ENDSBS
```

2. Start the NIGHTQ subsystem.

```
STRSBS NIGHTQ
```

3. Change the QSYSOPR message queue to place it in default mode so any
   messages requiring a response receive a default reply.

```
CHGMSGQ MSGQ(QSYSOPR) DLVRY(*DFT)
```

4. Submit a job to power down the system with a job priority of 9 to the
   NIGHTQ job queue. This priority places the job at the end of the queue so
   the system is powered down when all other jobs have been processed.

```
SBMJOB  JOBD(QBATCH) JOBQ(QGPL/NIGHTQ) JOBPTY(9) +
    CMD(PWRDWNSYS *IMMED)
```

USING WRKACTJOB AND WRKSYSACT COMMANDS

The Work with Active Jobs (WRKACTJOB) and the Work with System Activity
(WRKSYSACT) commands are useful to get an indication of system
performance. However, the WRKACTJOB command tends to use a fair amount
of system resources. Avoid using this command if you are trying to troubleshoot
a particularly busy system. Another command that does not use as much
system resource is WRKSYSACT (Work with System Activity). You must have
Performance Tools installed on the system to use the WRKSYSACT command,
but it does not use nearly as much of the system resource as WRKACTJOB, and
it runs at a very high priority. Remember, though, that only one person can use
the WRKSYSACT command at time.

Automatic Refresh — WRKSYSACT

If you intend to use the automatic refresh capability of the WRKSYSACT
command, remember the following methods to exit from this mode:

- Press the Attn key.
  - Only works if you have disabled keyboard buffering (also referred to as
    the "type-ahead" function).
  - If using a PC, the Attn key is usually mapped to the Esc key.
- Use the System Request function.
  - If using a PC, this function is usually mapped to the Alt+Print Screen
    key.

You can toggle off/on keyboard buffering:

- On a nonprogrammable terminal:

  ```
  Press Alt-Hex, then press K
  ```

- On a PC, this can vary. If you are using Client Access/400 or PC Support/400:

  ```
  Press Alt+F7, then press K
  ```

On newer IBM terminals, the type-ahead symbol appears on the bottom of the screen next to the Message Waiting indicator. It looks like two hash marks (»). On PC Support/400 or Client Access/400 displays, the type-ahead (or keyboard buffering) symbol is indicated by KB at the bottom of the screen.

IS A BATCH PROGRAM RUNNING?

Often, it is necessary to know if a batch job is running. For example, you may like to have a batch job that is submitted automatically each day to power down the system at a standard time, but provide a command to override the batch job at any time during the day. Before the new power down job is submitted, you want to cancel the old job. But how do you find the fully qualified job name of the batch job? And is it still running? This technique is a simple way to do this in a CL program.

The technique is based around having a data area that contains the fully qualified job name. Of course, the name of this data area must be known by both programs involved. The procedure is as follows:

1. The first thing that the batch job does is create the data area with its job name in it. Note that the data area could already exist. If this is the case, recreate it or change the data in it.
2. If the data exists, then any other program can check for its existence, and the status of the job whose name is in the data area.
3. The final action of the batch job, just before it completes, is to delete the data area.

These steps are documented below in CL program fragments.

Batch Job Coding

This first CL program is used to create the data area, then execute whatever function or program you wish, followed by deleting the data area. The CL code to set up the data area in the batch job is shown below.

Batch Job Status CL Program — Create Data Area

```
/*----------------------------------------------------------*/
      /*  Declare the variables that we will need.        */
/*----------------------------------------------------------*/
            DCL       VAR(&JOBNAM) TYPE(*CHAR) LEN(10)
            DCL       VAR(&JOBUSR) TYPE(*CHAR) LEN(10)
            DCL       VAR(&JOBNUM) TYPE(*CHAR) LEN(6)
```

```
                    place the first executable statements here        .

        /*-----------------------------------------------------------*/
                /* Set up the data area with the job name.   */
        /*-----------------------------------------------------------*/
                RTVJOBA    JOB(&JOBNAM) USER(&JOBUSR) NBR(JOBNUM)
                CRTDTAARA  DTAARA(library/data-area) TYPE(*CHAR)
                             LEN(26) VALUE(&JOBNAM *CAT &JOBUSR +
                             *CAT &JOBNUM) +
                             TEXT('Job name of important batch +
                                 job')
                MONMSG     MSGID(CPF0000) EXEC(CHGDTAARA +
                             DTAARA(library/data-area)   +
                             VALUE(&JOBNAM *CAT &JOBUSR +
                             *CAT &JOBNUM))
        /*-----------------------------------------------------------*/
        /*  Now go and do the real stuff that the job should do.  */
        /*    Place your CL program, calls, or other things here  */
        /*-----------------------------------------------------------*/

        Just before the program ends, the data area is deleted:

        /*-----------------------------------------------------------*/
                /*  Now go delete the data area and end     */
        /*-----------------------------------------------------------*/
        ENDPROGRAM: DLTDTAARA  DTAARA(library/data-area)
                    RETURN
                    ENDPGM
```

Finding Batch Job Status

This CL program is used to check for the existence of an active batch job. It does this by searching for the data area (created in the previous CL program) and then do whatever you think should be done based upon what you find.

Batch Job Status CL Program — Check Existence of Active Batch Job

```
        /*-----------------------------------------------------------*/
                /*  Declare the variables that we will need.  */
        /*-----------------------------------------------------------*/
                DCL        VAR(&BCHJOB) TYPE(*CHAR) LEN(26)
                DCL        VAR(&JOBNAM) TYPE(*CHAR) LEN(10)
                DCL        VAR(&JOBUSR) TYPE(*CHAR) LEN(10)
                DCL        VAR(&JOBNUM) TYPE(*CHAR) LEN(6)
                .
                .    now within the program . . . . . . . .
                .
        /*-----------------------------------------------------------*/
                /*  Now, what is the batch job?              */
        /*-----------------------------------------------------------*/
                RTVDTAARA  DTAARA(library/data-area) +
                             RTNVAR(&BCHJOB)
```

```
        MONMSG    MSGID(CPF1015) EXEC(GOTO CMDLBL(NOJOB))

        /* The data area gave me a name - unstring it */

        CHGVAR    VAR(&JOBNAM) VALUE(%SST(&BCHJOB  1 10))
        CHGVAR    VAR(&JOBUSR) VALUE(%SST(&BCHJOB 11 10))
        CHGVAR    VAR(&JOBNUM) VALUE(%SST(&BCHJOB 21  6))

        /*        See if the job is still there      */

        CHGJOB    JOB(&JOBNUM/&JOBUSR/&JOBNAM)
        MONMSG    MSGID(CPF1321) EXEC(GOTO CMDLBL(NOJOB))

        /* Now do something to the job              */

           Here we do whatever has to be done if the
                batch job is running

        GOTO      CMDLBL(NEXTSTEP)

NOJOB:  /* Here we do whatever should be done if the batch */
        /*        job  is not running                       */

NEXTSTEP:
```

TIPS FOR PERFORMANCE TOOLS

Performance Tools is an IBM program product. It provides a collection of tools that includes performance analysis and capacity planning. The following tips are provided to assist you with the use of these tools.

Allocating Trace Table Size

The collection of trace data by the Performance Monitor stops when the trace table (the area allocated for it) is full. This can happen in as little as two hours on a heavily used system. To change the size of this table, do the following:

1. Start System Service Tools (STRSST).
2. Take option 1 — Start a service tool.
3. Take option 2 — Trace vertical licensed internal code.
4. Take option 1 — Allocate trace tables.
    At this point, you can set the trace table size from 2K to 16M.

Once the data has been dumped (using DMPTRC or the option on STRPFRMON), it can be processed by the Transaction Report.

QPGMR Profile and Performance Tools

Do not change the IBM-supplied QPGMR user profile. To do so could affect the performance monitor program.

CHANGING SYSTEM AND USER LIBRARY LIST

The system part of the library list is controlled by the system value QSYSLIBL. The user part of the library list is controlled by the system value QUSRLIBL. All users pick up these lists whenever they sign on to the system. Refer to Library List System Values on page 23.

Also, the individual user library lists can be customized by creating a job description with the parameter INLLIBL set to the value(s) you choose. The default job description for user profiles is QDFTJOBD. Do not alter this job description for the purpose of adding libraries to the library list (refer to Job Descriptions below). Rather, create a new job description for this purpose. You can base the new job description on the default job description. Add this new job description to the user's profile.

JOB DESCRIPTIONS

A job description collects a specific set of job-related attributes. The same job description can be used by multiple jobs. Thus, if you use a job description, you do not need to specify the same parameters repeatedly for each job. You can create job descriptions to describe batch jobs or interactive jobs. You can create unique descriptions for each user of the system.

As stated in this book, a common use of the job description is to specify job logging levels, select libraries for the job's library list, and route printed output. For a detailed discussion, refer to the *AS/400 Work Management* manual.

One word of caution — with the exception of the recommendations in this book, be very cautious when making any changes to the IBM-supplied job descriptions Qxxxxxx. An inappropriate change could cause serious problems. For example, if you change the job description to add a user library to the library list, and later you delete the library, then any user profile where that job description was specified, will be unable to sign on to the system.

AUTOMATIC IPL AFTER SYSTEM SHUTDOWN

You can IPL the system automatically at a specified date and time by setting the system value QIPLDATTIM. This value causes the system to IPL if it is not running (i.e., it is in a shutdown state) when the date and time occur. The initial value is *NONE. Assuming your date format is MDY, the following example shows how to change the IPL date and time to August 16, 1990, at 10:00:00.

```
CHGSYSVAL SYSVAL(QIPLDATTIME) VALUE('081690 100000')
```

You can also perform this function by using the Operational Assistant functions in the POWER menu. Refer to Power Off and On Schedule on page 96.

TEMPORARY ADDRESS SPACE

Temporary addresses are used when temporary objects are created (e.g., spaces, open data paths). As these temporary objects are created, address space is used on the system. If the temporary address space reaches 100 percent (i.e., 0 percent available), the system stops. As temporary objects do not persist across IPLs, you can recover the temporary address space by performing an IPL. Monitor the percent used of temporary addresses with the WRKSYSSTS command. If you notice the temporary address space approaching 80 to 90 percent, perform an IPL as soon as you can. Routinely monitor how fast address space is used so you can estimate how often you need to IPL. If you believe that you must IPL too frequently, notify your Systems Engineer. You may have a problem and IBM development in Rochester might be able to help.

LOCKING DEVICES OUT WHEN PERFORMING BACKUPS

There are times when you do not want anyone to sign on to the system; yet, as soon as users see the sign-on screen on their display terminal, they begin signing on anyway. Here is an idea you can use to prevent users from signing on even though they do have a sign-on screen.

1. Create a display file that says something like, "The System is Unavailable." Use this display file as the sign-on display file for a new subsystem. Refer to Appendix C: Customizing Your Sign-On Display on page 327 for instructions.

2. Create a subsystem description that is similar to the regular interactive subsystem. Call it something like NOINTER. Set the maximum jobs (MAXJOBS) parameter to 0. Also, change the SGNDSPF parameter to reflect your newly created display file. When you create this new subsystem, it's probably easier to copy the existing subsystem description. Make sure that all the work stations that can be allocated in the original subsystem can be allocated in this new one.

3. Start the new subsystem. When completely started, end the original subsystem. All work stations allocated by the original subsystem are now allocated by the new one. The sign-on display says the system is unavailable, and if a user tries to sign on, they are not allowed to because MAXJOBS = 0.

SECURITY IMPLEMENTATION AND IMPACT ON PERFORMANCE

How you implement security can have an impact on performance. Poorly designed object security and access to objects can degrade performance. Develop an understanding of how security is implemented on the AS/400. Refer to Security Design for Performance on page 194 for a discussion of this topic.

When performing save and restore operations from tape, most users accept the system defaults when using the save and restore commands. This could have an impact upon the system's interactive performance.

Factors That Affect Tape Save/Restore Performance

Tape save and restore performance can be affected by the following factors:

- Size and activity level of the storage pool.
- Run priority of the save or restore job. Most users run save and restore operations using interactive commands. This can degrade overall interactive system interactive performance.
- Size of the system, processor, and memory.
- Size of the machine pool.
- Size of the data being saved.
- Type of data being saved. Some objects are more complex and take longer per megabyte to save.
- Number of objects saved. Saving many small objects takes longer than saving a few large objects, even if you are saving the same number of megabytes of data.
- The current state of the system. Placing the system in a restricted state improves performance because the system does not need to check object locking or compete with other users for resources.
- Authority of user running the job. If the user has *SAVSYS or *ALLOBJ special authority, the system does not need to check authority for each object.
- Speed of the save device.
- Other activity on the system, which can cause the system to compete for resources and to wait for locks to be released.
- Using the save-while-active function, which increases the total time the save operation requires, but decreases the amount of time that the objects being saved are unavailable.
- Use of the OUTPUT parameter. Creating output while saving extends the time it takes to do a save.
- Software data compression, which degrades performance because it requires more processor cycles. It does reduce the amount of media that is used.
- Hardware data compression, which improves performance.

Performance of Streaming Versus Start/Stop Tape Drives

The AS/400 system supports streaming tape drives and start/stop tape drives. Examples of start/stop tape drives are

- 2440
- 3430

- 3422
- 3480
- 6341

Examples of streaming tape drives are:
- 2440
- 9348
- 9347
- 9346
- 6346

A start/stop tape drive can stop and restart movement of the tape between reading or writing blocks of tape data. A streaming tape drive cannot. If the next request does not reach the device fast enough, the tape drive overruns its position on the tape and must stop and backup before it can run the next command. Repositioning takes time and can cause additional stress to the device and the tape.

The AS/400 save and restore operations are designed to keep the tape in streaming mode as much as possible. On heavily used systems, its ability to maintain streaming mode is reduced. This increases the save or restore time. When possible, limit save and restore operations on streaming tape drives to times of lower system activity.

Before you purchase a tape drive, determine which type of tape drive best suits your needs and make your decision accordingly.

Data Compaction and Data Compression

The AS/400 system supports data compression and data compaction.
- Software data compression is performed by the Operating System.
- Hardware data compression is performed by the AS/400 I/O adapter.
- Hardware data compaction is performed by the tape unit. It is supported on:
  - 3480 and 3490 tape units (if the tape unit has the compaction feature).
  - 7208 Model 12 tape unit when using the 5GB format.

Tuning Save/Restore Operations in a Nonrestricted Environment

Beginning with V2R3, the save and restore functions were changed so that some of the performance benefits from running a save operation or a restore operation in a restricted state are now seen in a nonrestricted environment. Depending on circumstances, you may be able to achieve up to a three-fold improvement in performance. This improvement is also available as a Program Temporary Fix (PTF 13301) for Version 2, Release 2.

To achieve the maximum save/restore performance, the size of the pool in which the save job is running, and its activity level, must be set correctly. Set the ratio of pool size to activity level at a factor of 6,000 (6MB). If you make this ratio higher than 6,000 you will not see performance gains.

Before choosing the values to use, you must consider:
- Tape device
- Types of objects being saved
- Processing unit being used
- Memory available
- Priority of the save or restore operation

Setting the Memory

Keep the following in mind when adjusting the memory for your save and restore jobs:
- Run your save or restore operation in batch mode. This is most easily accomplished by issuing the SBMJOB command to submit the save or restore operation to batch mode.
- Adjust the memory allocation/activity level ratio in the batch subsystem to 6,000:1. Do this by adding memory or changing the activity level.
- Set the priority of the save or restore job lower than that of the interactive users on the system.
- Save and restore operations use no more than half of the available memory in any one pool.
- The maximum amount of memory you can allocate is 6MB. Allocating more does not help performance.

PC SUPPORT AND CLIENT ACCESS/400

PC Support/400 was the original name given to IBM's solution for personal computer connectivity. When V3R0.5 was announced, IBM changed the name to *Client Access/400* to reflect the broader connectivity requirements for a range of clients including:

- Apple Macintosh
- Personal computers running DOS
- Personal computers running DOS with extended memory
- Personal computers running Microsoft Windows
- Personal computers running OS/2
- UNIX work stations
- Future operating environments

Also, beginning with V3R0.5, IBM announced that there would be no further enhancements for personal computers that do not support DOS extended memory. This includes the family of personal computers that use the Intel 8086/8088 processors. Most computers sold today use the Intel 80486 or Pentium processors running DOS+Windows. The tips in this section concentrate on these clients.

In this section, I use the term Client Access/400 when referring to either the PC Support/400 or Client Access/400 application programs. References to manuals are the V3R1 manuals for Client Access/400. I also use the terms Windows client, DOS client, or OS/2 client when referring to Client Access/400 for Windows, for DOS with extended memory, and for OS/2.

MIGRATING TO CLIENT ACCESS/400 FOR WINDOWS 3.1

If you are upgrading your system software to V3R1, the installation diskettes for Client Access/400 are optional. That is, unless you specifically include the Client Access/400 installation diskettes with your software upgrade order, you will not get them. I strongly advise that you order the Client Access/400 installation diskettes, as the upgrade process from the DOS client to the Windows client is a difficult and time-consuming process.

If you do not have Client Access/400 for Windows installation diskettes, you can migrate one or more of your existing PCs from the DOS client. The following steps are required to migrate to the Windows client. Refer to the *Client Access/400 for Windows 3.1 Getting Started* manual for additional information.

1. Install the Client Access/400 Family on the AS/400. Make sure you have the following options installed:

    a. Client Access/400 for Windows 3.1

    b. RUMBA for Windows

c.   PC5250 for Windows

d.   Client Access/400 PC Tools Folder

2. Install the latest cumulative PTF package. The migration program is included in the cumulative PTF package.

3. Create a directory in QDLS. On the AS/400, enter:

```
MD DIR('/QDLS/CAMIGRAT')
MD DIR('/QDLS/CAMIGRAT/MRIxxxx'
```

> where: *xxxx* is the number for your national language. For example, English is 2924.

4. Copy Client Access/400 for Windows to the directory. On the AS/400, enter:

```
CPY OBJ('/QPWXCWN/*.*') TODIR('/QDLS/CAMIGRAT')
CPY OBJ('/QPWXCWN/MRIxxxx/*.*)
    TODIR('/QDLS/CAMIGRAT/MRIxxxx')
```

5. Start a PC and attach it to the AS/400 using Client Access/400 for DOS. Use shared folders and assign a network drive to the AS/400 system.

6. On the PC, access the QIWSTOOL directory on the shared folders network drive.

7. At the PC DOS command prompt, enter the command **IWSTOOL** to display a list of tools in the QIWSTOOL directory.

8. Select CAMIGRAT from the list and press Enter. A description of the CAMIGRAT migration program appears.

9. Go to the end of the description and copy the CAMIGRAT program to the PC or to an AS/400 directory as follows:

a.   To copy the program to the PC, enter the path name for the PC directory that contains PC Support/400 or Client Access/400 (e.g., c:\pcs).

b.   To copy the program to an AS/400 shared folder directory, enter the path name for the AS/400 directory.

10. Start Microsoft Windows.

11. Select Run from the File pull-down menu in Windows Program Manager.

12. Enter:

```
drive:\path\camigrat.exe
```

in the Command Line text box where drive and path specify the PC or AS/400 directory that contains the migration program.

13. Follow the instructions in the migration program. The migration program creates the configuration files for Client Access/400 for Windows 3.1 from your current configuration files and stores the new files in the directory you specify.

When this is complete, the migration program starts the Client Access/400 for Windows Installation Program. The values from the existing configuration files appear as defaults in the installation dialog boxes.

14. When the installation is complete, the installation program directs you to restart Windows. However, you must restart the PC for the migration to succeed. During this restart, make sure that PC Support/400 does not start.

15. Reboot your PC and start Windows. After the migration has completed, start Client Access/400 for Windows. You should now be able to access the AS/400 using the Windows client.

16. Once you have successfully attached to the AS/400, go to the Client Access/400 group and select the Administration icon. Follow the instructions for creating a set of installation diskettes for Client Access/400 for Windows. Use these diskettes to migrate the remaining PCs — unless you enjoyed the migration procedure above.

After migration to Client Access/400 for Windows is complete, follow these steps to clean things up.

1. Delete the migration program from the PC or from the AS/400 directory.

2. Delete the files from the directories that you created in the QDLS directory on the AS/400:

```
DEL OBJLNK('/QDLS/CAMIGRAT/MRIxxxx/*.*')
DEL OBJLNK('/QDLS/CAMIGRAT/*.*')
```

3. Remove the CAMIGRAT and MRIxxxx directories on the AS/400:

```
RMVDIR DIR('QDLS/CAMIGRAT/MRIxxxx')
RMVDIR DIR('QDLS/CAMIGRAT')
```

COMMUNICATION SECURITY USING CLIENT ACCESS

A new feature of V3R1 is the use of password substitution. This prevents disclosure of the password if someone is monitoring the communication line. There are some limitations to this feature. Refer to Password Substitution on page 188.

CONFIGURING A CLIENT ACCESS/400 PERSONAL COMPUTER AS A CONSOLE

Client Access/400 console support enables a personal computer to function as the AS/400. The PC used as the console is attached to the AS/400 using a console cable (IBM feature code 9026 or 9027). The cable connects the serial port of the PC to the 2609 or 2612 I/O adapter on the AS/400.

The PC used as the AS/400 console must be running the PC5250 emulation feature of Client Access/400.

For additional information, refer to IBM announcements and sales information.

RESOLVING PC HARDWARE IRQ, MEMORY, AND BASE I/O CONFLICTS

One of the most common problems users encounter when configuring their PC for attachment to the AS/400 is resolving memory conflicts when installing the adapter cards required to establish the connection. Most adapters have on-board ROM (Read Only Memory) and RAM (Random Access Memory) modules required for the adapter's operation. The ROM module contains adapter diagnostic routines and function code. The RAM module is used as a buffer for communications with the PC's CPU. Problems are encountered from conflicts when two or more devices compete for the same system resource, such as memory, DMA channel, or IRQ.

Personal computers use a combination of IRQs, DMA channels, memory addresses, and base I/O addresses to perform unique functions, maintain pointers and instructions, and communicate with peripheral devices. When you install additional hardware or adapter cards, you frequently must set one or more of these parameters. Unless you understand these parameters, you may cause conflicts, thereby disabling the new device or adapter or the PC itself.

Commonly Used Hardware Interrupt Levels

IRQs are used by PC hardware devices, such as printers and modems, to let the system board know that they need attention. When an interrupt is invoked, the CPU puts its other work "on hold" and services the needs of the interrupting device. An Ethernet card or 5250 emulation card, for example, may cause the CPU to load the card's device driver when the interrupt signal is given. Modern PCs have 16 IRQs.

Hardware interrupts are related to specific physical wires on ISA systems and cannot be shared by multiple devices. This is not true of EISA systems or IBM Micro Channel systems. It is essential, therefore, to configure new devices so that they do not attempt to use IRQs already assigned.

If you are installing a new device or adapter card, you may have to designate an IRQ. You must choose one that is not already used The following table lists the commonly used hardware IRQs.

IRQ	Description
0	System timer.
1	System keyboard.
2	Used in AT systems as a gateway to IRQ 9 to 15. Occasionally used for EGA/VGA video.
3	Sometimes used for COM2. May be good choice for network adapter or emulation card if COM2 is not used.
4	COM1 serial port.
5	LPT2 parallel port. Good choice for an adapter or emulation card for use with Novell NetWare if LPT2 is not used.
6	Usually used for floppy diskette controller.

IRQ	Description
7	LPT1 parallel port.
8	System clock.
9	Redirected as IRQ 2.
10	Available.
11	Available.
12	Available.
13	Sometimes used for math coprocessor.
14	Usually used for hard drive controller.
15	Available. Often used for second hard drive controller.

There are actually two banks of IRQs, each a bank of eight. Generally, IRQ 2 is used to link the first bank of eight to the second bank of eight. This would suggest that IRQ 2 is unavailable for assignment. Some devices can only address the first bank (IRQ 0 to 7). To avoid losing the use of a first bank IRQ, IRQ 9 is addressed as IRQ 2. This relationship is called "cascading." Therefore, when IRQ 2 is in use, do not give an assignment to IRQ 9.

Commonly Used DMA Channel Numbers

The purpose of Direct Memory Access (DMA) channels is to save time by allowing certain devices to write data straight to the system's memory without intervention of the CPU. AT-type systems have eight DMA channels. Earlier XT-type machines have only four.

As with IRQs, some of these channels may be preassigned to standard devices. Other devices, like network cards, may require one of the remaining DMA channels.

The following table lists the commonly used DMA Channels.

DMA Channel	Description
0	Dynamic RAM refresh
1	Hard disk controller
2	Floppy controller
3	Available on all PCs
4, 5, 6, 7	Available on AT and Micro Channel PS/2s

PC Hardware I/O Addresses

The I/O address, sometimes called the Base I/O, is a range of addresses in memory reserved by the CPU. It serves as a mail stop for devices that need to communicate with the processor chip. Each device has memory space reserved. If two devices attempt to use the same memory space, conflicts can result. If required, network adapter manufacturers normally give you a set of choices for using I/O addresses.

The following table lists commonly used I/O addresses on most personal computers.

I/O Address	Description
000 to 0FF	Reserved for system
1F0 to 1F8	Hard disk drive
200 to 207	Game port
278 to 27F	Parallel port, LPT2
2F8 to 2FF	Serial port, COM2
378 to 37F	Parallel port, LPT1
3F0 to 3F7	Floppy diskette controller
3F8 to 3FF	Serial port, COM1

Hardware Base Memory Addresses

Some peripheral boards have jumpers that allow you to move the start address of the card's ROM to avoid conflicts. This can be risky because some controller software may be expecting the standard addresses.

On computers that have upper memory available, most memory managers detect and exclude the adapter's ROM memory addresses range. RAM address conflicts are not generally detected, therefore, the memory manager has to be informed not to use conflicted RAM addresses.

The following table lists common Base Memory Addresses on most personal computers.

Base Memory Address Range	Description
F000 to FFFF	System BIOS
E000 to EFFF	Used on AT-type systems
D000 to D7FF	Combination of system memory and memory available for add-in ROM
C000 to C7FF	CGA video or Super VGA video displays
B800 to BFFF	MDA-Hercules video display or Super VGA video displays
B000 to B7FF	Monochrome display
A000 to AFFF	VGA video display
0000 to 9FFF	System memory

Generally, if nothing else is occupying the space, a safe address range to try using for configuring a network adapter or emulation adapter is CA00 to DFFF. Use the exclude statement in your memory manager.

Hardware Memory Addresses for Various Adapter Cards

The following table lists hardware memory addresses for some adapter cards that you might use to connect personal computers to the AS/400.

Hardware	Memory Address	Comments
VGA adapter	A000 to BFFF	Consider excluding this entire address in the EMM386 statement in your CONFIG.SYS file.

Hardware	Memory Address	Comments
Token-Ring network adapter	D800 to DBFF	May conflict with VGA adapter on some systems.
Ethernet adapter	D000 to D3FF D400 to D7FF	May conflict with COM2, Extended DOS programs, or LPT2.
IBM Micro Channel 5250 emulation adapters	DC00 to DFFF	Use the reference diskette to change the interrupt level to level 7.
IBM ISA bus 5250 emulation adapters	CC00 to CFFF	Edit the STARTPCS.BAT file to add the /L7 parameter. The line should read: E5250AH /L7
Other (non-IBM) 5250 emulation adapters	Check with manufacturer to determine where adapter handler loads in memory. Or use the DOS command MEM /D to determine the beginning address and exclude to end of the segment. For example, if the adapter loads at beginning of address A800, then exclude the range from A800 to AFFF.	Check with the manufacturer to determine how to change the adapter handler interrupt.

EXPANDED MEMORY

The *Client Access for DOS Extended Memory — Setup* manual and the Redbook, *AS/400 PC Support Under DOS,* both have good discussions about expanded memory. Refer to those sources. In the meantime, try the following for a quick start.

Expanded memory page frame should be allocated 64K of contiguous memory. Recommend memory locations for IBM Client Access using expanded memory support are:

PC/AT and PS/2 Mod 30   Page Frame = D000

Token-Ring ROM = CC00

Token-Ring RAM = C400

5250 Emulation RAM = CC00

Micro Channel PS/2s
Page Frame = C000
Token-Ring ROM = D0000 to D1FFF
Token-Ring RAM = D8000 to DBFFF
5250 WSE RAM = DC000 to DFFFF
Fixed Disk Controller = D400

MEMORY CONFLICTS WHEN MIXING ADAPTER CARDS

Depending on the manufacturer of your PC and your installed adapters, you may experience problems with memory address conflicts, which causes a problem getting Client Access up and running. You may have to change the interrupt and memory addresses of the adapter board. The conflicts could be between your adapter board, the video addresses, the use of high memory, and other adapters you have installed (e.g., Non-IBM 5250 emulation cards, FAX cards, LAN adapter cards). I don't have any tried-and-true method to resolve these conflicts. You have to map your memory and use any of a number of memory management techniques or programs to reformat everything.

You change the interrupt level on your IBM Enhanced Emulation Card by manually editing the STARTPCS.BAT to add the interrupt level parameter to the E5250AH statement. The method of changing non-IBM emulation cards may be different.

E5250AH /Ln   where: *n* is the interrupt level.

Check the documentation that comes with your emulation card to help determine the appropriate interrupt level to use. Refer to Commonly Used Hardware Interrupt Levels on page 246 for additional information.

WORK STATION CONFIGURATION TOOLS

Generally, system configuration is done by using system software and is maintained in a special chip called the CMOS. Older PCs may have used DIP switches.

The setup program that specifies the configuration in CMOS is often accessed by a keystroke combination. For example, to access the setup function of an IBM ValuePoint, press the F1 key during the memory check portion of the power on cycle. You use the setup program to specify date, time, drive types, memory type/size, and display parameters.

Some computers, notably IBM Micro Channel PS/2s, and EISA bus systems, provide reference diskettes, which let you configure expansion cards without conflicts. Some ISA systems also provide reference diskettes, but most do not. On those systems that do not provide reference diskettes (the majority), you must manually configure expansion cards. This can occasionally be a daunting task, and various work station configuration tools can be very useful.

The following are examples of some work station configuration tools. This does not represent a recommendation, nor is it an all inclusive list.

Tool Name	Supplier	Comments
Microsoft Diagnostics (MSD)	Microsoft Corporation	Included at no cost with Microsoft Windows (see box note below). Provides limited information on system configuration.
Check It Pro and Win Check It	TouchStone Software Corporation	Very comprehensive tools. Many options available provide very detailed information on your system configuration.
Manifest	Quarterdeck Office Systems	Part of the QEMM Expanded Memory Manager program. Provides memory, interrupt levels, and other information about the systems and adapters. Running TECHSUP.BAT creates detailed report on your system configuration.
PC Tools	Central Point Software	Suite of tools for performing various PC-system-related functions. Very comprehensive. Includes tools for backup and recovery, disk compression, and other utilities.
TOKEN.EXE	IBM Corporation	Tool used to query the hardware settings of Token-Ring adapter. Located in the AS/400 QIWSTOOL shared folder.
XIINFO Package	IBM Corporation	The XIINFO utility, part of the APARHELP package available through the IWSTOOL shared folder. This tool provides information on memory usage and system configuration.

Tool Name	Supplier	Comments
QCONFIG	IBM Corporation	Tool supplied with IBM DOS 6 and DOS 7. Provides information on adapters, memory addresses, and other technical information. Running QCONFIG /D /P provides information on all adapter addresses.

> *The Microsoft Diagnostics tool is included at no additional cost with Microsoft Windows. It is located in the WINDOWS directory and is executed by entering the command, MSD at a DOS prompt. Although simplistic, it may be all that you need to determine IRQs and memory addresses.*
>
> *You can create a detailed system report using MSD by entering the command:*
>
> ```
> MSD  /F  <filename>
> ```

CLIENT ACCESS/400 FOR WINDOWS 3.1 AND PCMCIA 5250 ADAPTERS

If you are using Client Access/400 for Windows 3.1 on personal computers with PCMCIA 5250 emulation adapters, perform the following steps:

1. Install Client Access/400 for Windows using the installation diskettes. Refer to Migrating to Client Access/400 for Windows 3.1 on page 243. **DO NOT** attempt to connect to the AS/400 after installing.

2. Exit Windows.

3. Determine the interrupt level, memory address, and I/O port address used by the 5250 emulation PCMCIA adapter.

   a. If using an IBM 5250 Emulation PCMCIA adapter, do step 1) or 2):

      1) View the CFG5250.DAT file using any PC editor. If you ran the installation program from a diskette, the file is on the diskette. If you ran the program from the hard drive, the file is located in hard file directory — most likely the C:\ENB5250 directory.

      Note the following values by looking at the Enabler User Selection:

E_PORT=	This is the I/O port address.
E_MEM=	This is the on-card memory address.
E_INT=	This is the interrupt level.

      2) Or you can run the enabler program (ENB5250.EXE) and it tells you all the parameters.

b. If you are using a non-IBM PCMCIA 5250 emulation adapter, check the manufacturer's documentation to determine how to find the information. There may be a configuration program that could tell you what you need to know.

4. Change the interrupt address, memory address, and I/O port address:

Use an editor to change the file C:\CAWIN\PCSTDLC.DAT. Find the [Enh5250EMAdapter] section. Generally toward the end of the file.

```
[Enh5250EMAdaper]
IntLevel=xx
MemAddrr=yy
IOAddr=zz
```

Change the values for xx, yy, and zz according to the information you noted in step 3 (above) and the tables below:

Interrupt Level Valid Addresses Values for xx
02
03
04
05
06
07

Memory Address Table	
yy	On-Card RAM Address
00	Auto setting
5C	5C000 to 5DFFF
6C	6C000 to 6DFFF
7C	7C000 to 7DFFF
8C	8C000 to 8DFFF
9C	9C000 to 9DFFF
CC	CC000 to CDFFF
DC	DC000 to DDFFF

I/O Address Table	
zz	I/O Port Address
40	240n
41	241n
:	:
7F	27Fn
01	011n (PCMCIA only)
02	021n (PCMCIA only)
03	031n (PCMCIA only)
04	041n (PCMCIA only)

5. Insert the following line in the AUOTEXEC.BAT file before you start Windows. This executes the enable program each time you start your PC.

```
C:\ENB5250\ENB5250
```

EDIT THE PATH STATEMENT IN YOUR AUTOEXEC.BAT FILE

If you have Client Access/400 or RUMBA/400 installed on your PC, it is a good idea to edit the AUTOEXEC.BAT to include the directories in your PATH statement. See Sample AUTOEXEC.BAT File on page 256.

SAMPLE PERSONAL COMPUTER CONFIGURATION FILES

The following sample configuration files may be helpful. I added comment lines for additional explanation.

Sample CONFIG.SYS File

```
DEVICE=C:\DOS\HIMEM.SYS

REM  The following line loads DOS into high memory and enables the use of
Upper Memory Blocks.

DOS=HIGH,UMB

REM  The FRAME=NONE parameter in the EMM386 line provides
REM    access to upper memory area without allocating a 64KB
REM    page frame for expanded memory use.  This enables the
REM    use of extended memory and allows DOS TSRs and device
REM    drivers to load into high memory.
REM    Exclude address is for an IBM Micro Channel Token Ring
REM    adapter card.

REM  Any memory excluded in the EMM386 statement must also be
REM    excluded in the [386Enh] section of the
REM    C:\WINDOWS\SYSTEM.INI file.
REM    The format is. EMMExclude=mmmm-nnnn

DEVICE=C:\DOS\EMM386.EXE FRAME=NONE X=D800-DFFF
DEVICEHIGH=C:\DOS\SETVER.EXE
FILES=40
BUFFERS=10
DEVICE=C:\DOS\SMARTDRV.EXE /DOUBLE_BUFFER

REM  Some memory managers will recommend using STACKS=0.0 to
REM    conserve memory.  Using 0.0 may cause problems with
REM    Client Access/400.  If you use 0.0 and have problems.
REM    then try using 9.256 to see if it helps.
```

```
STACKS=9,256

REM  The following two lines load the IBM LAN Support Program
REM   device drivers for the Token-Ring adapter

DEVICEHIGH=C:\LSP\DXMA0MOD.SYS 001
DEVICEHIGH=C:\LSP\DXMC0MOD.SYS N 40008580AA03,D800,0,0,0
SHELL=C:\DOS\COMMAND.COM C:\DOS /P

REM  The following line is required in most NetWare environments

LASTDRIVE=Z
```

Sample AUTOEXEC.BAT File

```
@REM  Make sure that the directory for SMARTDRV.EXE is same
@REM   as the directory used in the CONFIG.SYS file.  Do not
@REM   mix the DOS and WINDOWS programs for SMARTDRV.
@REM   Do not use the LOADHIGH prefix to load SMARTDRV into
@REM   high memory.  It will not work.

C:\DOS\SMARTDRV.EXE
@ECHO OFF
PROMPT $P$G

@REM  It is a good idea to add the C:\PCS directory to your
@REM   path statement in the AUTOEXEC.BAT file.

PATH=C:\WINDOWS;C:\DOS;C:\PCS;C:\RUMBAPCS
SET TEMP=C:\DOS
C:\DOS\MOUSE.COM

@REM  Try loading DOS TSR type programs in high memory using
@REM   the LOADHIGH (LH) prefix.  For example, DOSKEY in the
@REM   following line is loaded high.

LH C:\DOS\DOSKEY
CD\PCS

@REM  The following line uses the CALL command to invoke the
@REM   STARTPCS.BAT file and then return control to this batch
@REM   file to continue to execute any remaining commands.
@REM   In this case, to start Windows.

CALL C:\PCS\STARTPCS.BAT
C:\WINDOWS\WIN
```

Sample SYSTEM.INI File

The following changes to the SYSTEM.INI file of Microsoft Windows are highly recommended. These changes are found the [386Enh] section. Add or change the following entries.

```
[386Enh]
:
:
VirtualHDIrq=OFF
32BitDiskAccess=Off
IRQ9Global=On
EMMExclude=D800-DFFF
TimerCriticalSection=1000
InDOSPolling=Off
:
:
```

(The EMMExclude memory address is for example purposes only. It matches the exclude range in the CONFIG.SYS example, above.)

Refer to the IBM Redbook, *V2R3 PC Support/400 and Microsoft Windows 3.1 Advanced Topics*, for a complete explanation of the above changes.

USING EIMPCS PROGRAM

Beginning with V2R3 of the Extended DOS client, the EIMPCS program was changed from a .SYS file to a .EXE file. This allows you to invoke EIMPCS from the STARTPCS.BAT file rather than the CONFIG.SYS file.

The only function that requires EIMPCS is the Work Station Function (WSF) printer emulation. If you do not use printer emulation on your work station, you can remove this function from the STARTPCS.BAT file. Use any DOS editor to REMark out the line. Removing EIMPCS may help with memory constraints.

RUNNING WORK STATION FUNCTION IN RESTRICTED MODE

When you run WSF, you have several options — one of which is run WSF in the restricted mode. The restricted mode disables the ability to "hot key" to a DOS session. In Windows, this restriction has no effect because you can still open a DOS prompt window. In DOS, because you are in restricted mode, you cannot hot key to a DOS application.

The restricted mode was developed to address some problems when running WSF under Windows. These problems are characterized by PC-to-host communication link failures and internal PC processing failures (system hangs). These problems are caused by conflicts between the way WSF and Microsoft Windows handles system resources. If you experience the symptoms described when running WSF under windows, IBM recommends that you run WSF in the restricted mode.

Configuring WSF to Run in Restricted Mode

To configure the Work Station Function to run in restricted mode, edit the batch file that invokes the WSF.EXE program. When running under Windows, this file is the PCSWWSF.BAT file. When running under DOS, the file is normally STARTPCS.BAT.

Look for the lines (there are two of them) that invoke WSF. Add the optional parameters /NODOS and /D. The lines should read:

```
WSF   /NODOS /D
```

The /NODOS parameter specifies that the WSF in the Windows environment runs in restricted mode. Because the personal computer is in restricted mode, you cannot hot key to a DOS session. In Windows, this restriction has no effect because you can open a DOS prompt window. In DOS, because you are in restricted mode, you cannot hot key to a DOS application.

The /D parameter is an optional parameter to the NODOS. This allows you to hot key one time (and one time only) to DOS to allow the personal computer organizer to run.

Removing WSF When Running in Restricted Mode

Because the hot key to DOS is disabled, you can not run the STOPWSF or RMVPCS commands. To remove WSF from memory, press the key combination Ctrl+Alt+End. This is not the reboot key combination Ctrl+Alt+Del.

If you are running under Windows, the PCSWWSF.BAT file contains a line that invokes COMMAND.COM. If you are running WSF in restricted mode, REMark out this line. Otherwise, you will have to enter EXIT at the DOS prompt after pressing Ctrl+Alt+End.

Using the WFXWSF Utility

You can use the utility WFXWSF to quickly edit the batch file used to invoke WSF to switch between native and restricted modes. The syntax is:

```
WFXWSF [filespec] [options]
```

The *filespec* specifies the location, name, and extension of the file that WFXWSF should change according to the specified parameters. If no file is specified, the default is PCSWWSF.BAT.

The /r option restores the Work Station Function to its native operating mode. Running the WFXWSF tool with no option changes the batch file, which invokes WSF.EXE to start the work station function in restricted mode.

For example, if you enter the command:

```
WFXWSF
```

the C:\PCS\PCSWWSF.BAT file is changed to invoke WSF with the /NODOS /D parameters. To restore the PCSWWSF.BAT file to invoke WSF in the native mode, enter:

```
WFXWSF /R
```

> *Administered users who need the Work Station Function restricted mode can run the WFXWSF tool on their own personal computers. However, these changes are lost the next time PCSUPDT updates the administered configuration of those users. To permanently change the configuration, the administrator must run the tool against the PCSWWSF.BAT file within the administered subdirectories in I:\QIWSADM\USER.*

CHANGING CLIENT ACCESS WINDOWS PIF FILES

PIF files are used to define how non-Windows applications should run when executed within the Microsoft Windows environment. IBM provides several PIF files with Client Access for the DOS based clients. If you change these PIFs on your PC, then make a backup of your changes. These PIFs may be updated during software upgrades and PTF installation, and any changes you may have made will be lost.

CHANGING SUBSYSTEM DESCRIPTION QCMN

If you have a large number of PCs attaching to the AS/400, consider changing the memory pool assignment in subsystem description QCMN. Refer to Additional Performance Tuning Considerations on page 212 for additional information.

COMMON CLIENT ACCESS/400 STARTUP PROBLEMS

Some common startup problems and solutions are described in the following table.

Error Message	Potential Problem	Corrective Measures
4028 Access Denied	Files in shared folder may have been saved using the STG(*FREE) command, which clears everything except the header information. The files look like they are there, but in reality, they aren't.	Verify that the folder was saved using STG(*FREE). If saved, then perform a RSTDLO.
5044 Router Not Connected	Error in system name of connection-specific information at PC install time. Router has been stopped or connection lost.	Verify installation parameters. Use WRKCFGSTS to check status.
5056 Security Error Occurred	User profile does not exist or has special authority *ALLOBJ. User signed on with wrong password. Journal QAOSDIAJRN in QUSRSYS not active.	Sign-on with correct userid and password; reenter STARTPCS. Create user profile if it does not exist. If you want user profile to have *ALLOBJ authority (e.g., QSECOFR), then explicitly authorize it to the automatically created display device using GRTOBJAUT command. Start journal QAOSDIAJRN in QUSRSYS.
5064 or PC Hangs When Starting WSF	Either QBASE or QCMN subsystems not active.	Start QBASE or QCMN subsystems. Check QSYSOPR MSGQ for CPF1269; note reason code.

Error Message	Potential Problem	Corrective Measures
5118 Adapter Cannot be Opened	AS/400 system not active. Hardware problem or connection. Line/Controller/Device varied off. Address already in use.	Check hardware and connections (e.g., cables). Do not use address 0 of first port of any WSC for PCs. Use WRKCFGSTS to check status of AS/400 and subsystems. Verify installation parameters. Verify that auto-configuration is on. Verify that PS/2 emulation card is properly seated in PS/2.
5119 Link Connection Failure	See 5118 error. Configuration problem exists.	Use WRKACTJOB and WRKCFGSTS to check status. Check QSYSOPR message queue, cross check AS/400 versus PC parameters.
5122 No More Links Available	Twinaxial link already established or all Token-Ring links in use.	Stop PCS Router (STOPRTR) and restart AS/400 Client Access.
5140 Connection Failed	Entries in CONFIG.SYS incorrect.	See error 5119.
5227 Host Installation or Client Access Not Complete	Client Access not initialized or installed. Client Access folder QIWSFLR is missing or incomplete, or Library QIWS is corrupted. Problem with QCMN subsystem.	Run the INZPCS command. Restore QIWSFLR or reload Client Access.

Error Message	Potential Problem	Corrective Measures
5251 Unable to End Due to Active Conversations	Client Access has active conversations with AS/400.	FSPC RELEASE * — to release shared folders. STOPMSG — to end messaging. STOPWSF n — to end WSF sessions. STOPRTR /F — to force termination of PCS. RMVPCS ALL /F — to terminate and release memory.
5952 Access Denied	User not enrolled in system directory. Damaged folders. User not authorized to QIWSFLR.	Use ADDDIRE to add user profile to system directory. Perform RCLDLO *INT. Grant user authority to QIWSFLR.
6957 System software does not follow VCPI or DMPI specifications	Expanded memory error.	Sometimes occurs when configuring EMM386.EXE with the NOEMS parameter. Remove NOEMS parameter from EMM386 statement in the CONFIG.SYS file.

DISPLAYING THE ERROR LOG

Besides the common error messages listed above, there are several other possible messages. You can display the error log and obtain additional Help information on error messages using one of the following:

- Select the option to View the Error Log from the PCS menu.
- Click on the Error Log icon if using MS Windows.
- Enter the command:

```
C:\PCS\PCSLOG
```

from the DOS command line.

The most current error message is at the bottom of the display with the cursor resting on it. Several options are available through the Help key or the action bar at the top of the display. Refer to the *Client Access/400 for DOS Extended Memory User Guide* for additional information.

When you configure Client Access/400, it is a very good idea to place the Error Log function on the PC hard disk. Use the Client Access configuration utility, which you can access from the PCSMENU, to copy the program objects from the AS/400 shared folder to the PC.

SHARED FOLDERS

The AS/400 system uses folders to store information such as text documents, mail, and data. Client Access/400 shared folders function allows you to access and share members in folders on the AS/400 system. It also allows you to store personal computer files in folders. The documents in a folder on the AS/400 system can be used by both AS/400 system users and personal computer users. A folder can be accessed by more than one AS/400 system user or personal computer user at a time. Shared folders are similar to directories on your personal computer. You can assign a drive letter to one folder on the AS/400 system, or you can assign a drive letter to all of the folders on the AS/400 system. Up to eight drives can be assigned with the shared folders function.

Types of Shared Folders

There are four types of shared folders: Type 0, Type 1, Type 2, and an extended DOS version. Type 0 uses the simplest memory cache and can be used with any release of Client Access or PC Support. The performance may not be as good as other shared folder types. Type 1 uses a more sophisticated memory cache than Type 0 and its performance is better. However, it uses more memory. Type 2 offers all the features of Type 1 with improved performance, but, once again, requires more memory. The extended DOS version of shared folders is similar to Type 2, but uses extended DOS. To use Type 1 or Type 2 folders, you must have the statement STARTFLR in your STARTPCS.BAT file. The following table has some guidelines on which type of shared folder you may want to use.

Folder Type	When to Use
Type 0	Not enough memory to run other types. Satisfied with current performance.
Type 1	Want improved performance and memory is available. Want option to remove shared folder function from PC memory when not using it. Need to connect to S/36. Need to connect to AS/400 earlier than V1R3.

Folder Type	When to Use
Type 2	Want improved performance with more sophisticated file server and have enough memory to run with other applications. Want option to remove shared folder function from PC memory when not using it. Have V1R3 on your AS/400.
Extended DOS Type	If you have extended memory. Have V1R3 or later on your AS/400. Want to use the CHKFIL command to check files in and out of a folder. This is the recommended type to use. It is also the default when you install Client Access for DOS extended memory or Client Access for Windows 3.1

Shared Folder Subsystem — QXFPCS

The subsystem QXFPCS in library QIWS starts automatically when the first work station using shared folder function Type 2 or Extended DOS version of shared folders, is started. You can start this subsystem manually faster than letting it start automatically:

```
STRSBS QIWS/QXFPCS
```

You may want to place that command in your startup program. Monitor this subsystem for performance. Refer to Work Management and Performance on page 199.

Controlling Shared Folder Memory

This discussion applies only to PC Support/400 for DOS and Client Access/400 for DOS. The memory control function does not apply to Client Access/400 for DOS extended memory or Client Access for Windows 3.1. As most personal computers sold today fully support extended memory, this topic may not apply to you.

Type 0 shared folders use 78K of memory, Types 1 and 2 use 94K. Without EMS, the Type 0 shared folder uses 78K with no reserved cache. You can control the installed cache by using the B = nn parameter:

```
DEVICE=C:\PCS\FSDD.SYS B=nn
```
where: nn = 0 to 34 (each number represents 1880 bytes).

If you have EMS, then the Type 0 program is split between conventional and expanded memory (30K/64K).

With Types 1 and 2 folders, you can control memory use by altering the C:\PCS\CONFIG.SYS file. The easiest way to do this is by using the Client Access Configuration Program. This program updates your CONFIG.SYS, CONFIG.PCS, and STARTPCS.BAT files with the necessary device and file entries automatically. You can access the Client Access Configuration program by entering the following command:

> `d:\path:\PCSMENU`   where: *d:* = the drive specification.
> *path* = the directory on that drive.

If you do not have the PCS menu migrated to your hard drive, you can access the PCS menu by entering the following command after you have started shared folders:

> `I:\QIWSFLR\PCSMENU`

The following entries control shared folders in the CONFIG.PCS file. If you use the Client Access Configuration Program, you do not need to worry about editing this file.

MCAC nnn   Conventional memory caching. Value nnn can be set from 3 to 360 (3K to 360K). If there is no MCAC entry, then there is no caching.

CBSZ nn   Communication buffer size for conventional memory. Allowable values for nn are from 2 to 32 (2K to 32K). The default is 14K. The communication buffer allows the AS/400 and shared folders to exchange information for moving files between the PC and the AS/400. The larger the buffer, the faster your PC applications run.

FEMU n,n,n,n   Controls if shared folder functions are loaded into conventional or expanded memory. The value for n can be either 1 or 2. The parameters are positional:

> n1   loads shared folders programs.
> n2   loads communication buffers.
> n3   loads memory cache buffers.
> n4   loads memory cache tables.

If $n = 1$ (or if you do not specify an entry), then the function loads into expanded memory; if $n = 2$, then the function loads into conventional memory.

MCAE nnnn   Expanded memory cache buffer size. Where *nnnn* = 0 or a value from 32 to 4096. If *nnnn* = 0, then no caching.

Shared Folder Memory Recommendations

If you have expanded memory, use Type 1 folders. Load as much as you can into expanded memory. For example, you want Type 1 folders and have plenty of expanded memory. You could place the following commands in your CONFIG.PCS file:

```
FEMU 1,1,1,1
MCAE 4096
```

If you do not have expanded memory, do not use any caching. You must decide if you want to use Type 0 folders (78K of memory) or Type 1 or Type 2 folders (94K). Type 1 and Type 2 folders allow you to use the RMVPCS command; Type 0 does not. If you have a 286 or a 386 processor and extended memory, then use Client Access for DOS extended memory.

Something else to consider, regardless of folder type, is to place all your PCS code on your PC hard disk. This is especially important if your PC is remotely attached with an SDLC, a 5394, or an ASYNC connection. Loading the PCS code on the hard disk:

- Allows the PCS code to load more quickly.
- Minimizes the need for shared folders to only perform file transfers and run the occasional PC program.
- Minimizes the need for any caching because all your PCS code is on the PC hard disk.

Refer to Copying Client Access Functions to the PC on page 274 for a discussion on migrating Client Access/400 functions to the PC.

Shared Folder Security

Shared folders are often thought of as a logical disk drive located on the AS/400. As such, you can use many DOS commands to do such things as copy and delete files or invoke programs. You can also create directories using the DOS commands MKDIR or MD. This, in effect, creates a shared folder. You can place PC objects (such as executable programs, data files, and text files) in this directory (shared folder).

When a user creates a directory (shared folder) on the AS/400 using the DOS or OS/2 commands, other users, by default, are excluded from access to the directory (shared folder) and the objects contained therein. The only method for controlling security to shared folders is from the AS/400.

The following is an example of controlled authority to shared folders. Assume that I have created a shared folder called APIPA. To work with the folder security, enter the command:

```
WRKFLR FLR(*ALL)
```

You should use the *ALL parameter (which is the default) to get the highest level list. The list presented includes only those folders you have the authority to access. This allows you to take the option to work with the folder authority as shown in the example of the Work with Folders screen, below:

```
                              Work with Folders

Folder . . .     /_____
Position to . . . . . .  _____ Starting characters

Type options (and Folder), press Enter.
    1=Create         3=Next level      4=Delete        5=Work with documents
    7=Rename         8=Details        14=Authority

Opt  Folder        Opt  Folder        Opt  Folder        Opt  Folder

  __  AFP000          __  CKSTMT##.##    __  INTRO02        __  JMULLINS
  __  AHOMER          __  COTTON         __  INTRO03        __  LANSAVES
  14  APIPA           __  DEWAR          __  INTRO04        __  MAPICS##.##
  __  ASHLEY          __  DRUM           __  INTRO05        __  MILLER
  __  BAILEY          __  DT22B6         __  INTRO06        __  NEWSOME
  __  BISEL           __  FAC08          __  INTRO07        __  OFFICE
  __  BRANCH          __  FAC12          __  INTRO08        __  OVPCLASS
  __  CAMIGRAT        __  FEECLASS       __  INTRO09        __  PAPERVU
  __  CAMPBELL        __  INTRO01        __  INTRO10        __  QACWC
                                                                  More...
F3=Exit                 F5=Refresh        F6=Print list     F9=Work with
F11=Display descriptions  F12=Cancel       F13=Previous level
```

Taking option 14 (Authority) brings up the following screen. On this screen you can change the public authority access or work with individual user access using the F13 (Change authorized users) and F6 (Add new users) keys.

```
                          Change Folder Authority

Folder . . . . . . . . . . . . . :    APIPA
  In folder . . . . . . . . . . :      *NONE


Owner . . . . . . . . . . . . . :    BISEL
Primary Group . . . . . . . . . :    *NONE

Type changes, press Enter.

    Authorization list . . . . . .    *NONE_____  Name

    Sensitivity . . . . . . . . . .   1            1=None, 2=Personal
                                                   3=Private, 4=Confidential

    Public authority . . . . . . .    *EXCLUDE     *ALL, *CHANGE
                                                   *USE, *EXCLUDE, *AUTL



F3=Exit   F6=Add new users   F12=Cancel   F13=Change authorized users
F15=Change access codes   F24=More keys
```

Now, at this point, you have defined user access to the shared folder itself. Any new objects placed into the folder will have user access set to the authority of the folder itself. But, you have not defined user access to any objects already contained in the folder. You can go back to the folder display level and take option 5 to work with the documents, then take option 14 on each object in the folder to define user's access, or you can use the Change DLO Authority

(CHGDLOAUT) command. For example, if I wanted to allow all users to access the objects in the APIPA folder (from the example screens above), I would enter the command:

```
CHGDLOAUT DLO(*ALL) FLR(APIPA) USRAUT((*PUBLIC *USE))
```

It is easier to enter CHGDLOAUT and then press F4 (Prompt) than it is to enter the full command on the command line, but you get the idea.

PC TEXT ASSIST AND OFFICEVISION/400

Some functions on the AS/400 require the use of Text Assist (e.g., OfficeVision/400). There are two types of Text Assist, Type 0 and Type 1. Type 0 is the original Text Assist provided in Version 1, Release 1, of PC Support/400. Type 1 Text Assist provides additional functions of cursor draw, sorting, and notepads. Type 1 uses more memory. When you start the PC Organizer, Text Assist loads automatically. You can, however, control which type is used by using the PCOM command in the CONFIG.PCS file. Once again, you can configure the text assist function from the Client Access Configuration Program (recommended), or by using an editor to modify the CONFIG.PCS file.

You can enhance the organizer functions with the optional command PCOM in your CONFIG.PCS file. The record entry in the CONFIG.SYS has the following syntax:

```
PCOM HOTKEY,LOADTA,TA1
```

The parameters are positional. If you omit one, keep the commas. For example:

```
PCOM,,TA1
```

HOTKEY	Specifying HOTKEY lets you toggle between DOS and any work station session while the Organizer is running. You must first invoke the DOS session by using option 6 or the STRPCCMD command.
LOADTA	Indicates you want the Text Assist function to be DOS resident. If you leave it blank, the system loads Text Assist dynamically when you need it and unloads it when you exit the editor. If you make Text Assist resident, you use 136K of memory for Type 0 Text Assist and 190 for Type 1. If you do not make it resident, there is a delay while the code loads.
TA1	Specifies Type 1 Text Assist, which allows cursor draw, sorting, and notepads. Leaving this entry off loads Type 0 Text Assist, which is the same as Version 1, Release 1.2. There is no TA0 entry.

ETHERNET AND CLIENT ACCESS

Ethernet support (IEEE 802.2) was announced with V1R3 of PC Support. There are a few things you should know before you configure your network:

- Verify that the Ethernet cards you want to use will, in fact, work with Client Access. Many of the older Ethernet cards don't and some of the newer ones don't either. Check with IBM or the card manufacturer to verify that the card in question is one of the "supported" cards. Some "unsupported" cards work, but check with the manufacturer of the card.

- When installing Client Access, I recommend that you change the CONFIG.PCS to add the following statement:

      TRMF 1496

   This sets the maximum frame size to 1496. The default is 1994 and this is too large as the maximum frame size allowed for Ethernet adapters used in this environment is 1496.

- You must be using LAN Support Program Version 1.2 or later.

- You may have to convert the device addresses when you configure the work stations. Refer to the *Client Access/400 for DOS Extended Memory — Setup* manual.

NOVELL NETWARE, MICROSOFT WINDOWS, AND CLIENT ACCESS

IBM regularly publishes Redbooks, which are designed as supplemental manuals to the standard documentation. Three Redbooks are useful when dealing with Client Access/400 and coexistence with Microsoft Windows and Novell NetWare. These books do not cover Client Access/400 for Windows Version 3.1, but they do apply to the V3R1 DOS-based Client Access/400 products.

- *PC Support/400 Coexistence with Novell NetWare and Microsoft Windows 3.0*. This is a very good reference to use when configuring Client Access with Novell or Microsoft Windows.

- *Using DOS PC Support/400 with Novell NetWare 3.11 and NetWare for SAA 1.3*. This Redbook supersedes the one above. The first one is still available on CD-ROM.

- *Client Access/400 for DOS Extended with Novell NetWare 3.12 and NetWare for SAA 2.0*. This Redbook picks up where the previous one left off. (This is yet to be released by IBM.)

- *V2R3 PC Support /400 and Microsoft Windows 3.1 Advanced Topics*. Very well written book. Covers many advanced DOS and Windows related topics.

- *Inside Client Access/400 for Windows 3.1*. This Redbook covers many topics that you will not find in the IBM manuals.

For information on ordering these Redbooks, refer to Frequently Called IBM Telephone Numbers on page 321 for a list of IBM Support Telephone numbers.

Here is some additional information and tips for using Novell NetWare and Client Access/400:

1. If using Novell NetWare for SAA:

   a. Recommend using Version 1.3b for Client Access/400 for DOS.

   b. You must use version 2.0 for Client Access/400 for Windows.

   c. You will have better results if you use VLM (NDIS drivers) rather than NETX.

2. If you are directly connecting the work stations to the AS/400 and require coexistence with Novell NetWare:

   a. Use NetWare 3.12 or 4.1.

   b. Use VLM (NDIS drivers) rather than NETX.

PROBLEM DETERMINATION WHEN USING MICROSOFT WINDOWS AND CLIENT ACCESS

Refer to Appendix K: Checklist for Using CA/400 with Microsoft Windows on page 375 for additional tips and restrictions when using Microsoft Windows and Client Access/400.

IBM also maintains an informational PTF that you can download entitled, *PC400-DOS Configuration and Setup Tips for Running PC Support/400 (Client Access/400) with Windows.* It outlines some of the more common methods of solving Client Access/400 and Windows coexistence problems.

- To order the PTF, do the following:

   ```
   SNDPTFORD PTF(II06590)
   ```

- When you get the PTF, you can print the PTF information by doing:

   ```
   DSPPTF LICPGM(INFODLS) SELECT(II06590) COVERONLY(*YES) OUTPUT(*PRINT)
   ```

Other informational PTFs are available. Refer to PTF Information on page 124.

USING PC ORGANIZER WHEN THERE IS NO COMMAND LINE ON AS/400

Under normal circumstances, the Client Access organizer function on the PC issues a remote command to execute the AS/400 organizer. This requires a command line on the AS/400 to execute. This presents a problem when there is no command line available on the AS/400. For example, when using OfficeVision/400.

The organizer gets started by the PCO.EXE command on the PC. By default, this command issues two remote commands to the AS/400:

   ```
   STRPCO
   GO PCOMNU
   ```

If the user were an OfficeVision/400 user, the default value for the initial program in the user profile is QOFC/QOFINLPG. This starts OfficeVision and initiates the main office menu as the first user menu, but it does not provide for a command line on the OfficeVision/400 main menu. Many end-user applications use this approach as well (i.e., do not provide a command line for user's menus).

Without a command line, the default commands do not get executed, therefore, the Organizer never completely starts. When you sign off the AS/400, the Organizer does not end and control does not pass back to the PC to allow further execution of the batch file that may have originally evoked the Organizer function.

If you have excluded a command line from the user's first menu screen, then the Organizer is unable to start on the AS/400, and the results are not likely to be as you expected. If you wish to continue to provide users with menus that omit the command line, you can still fully execute the PC Organizer function by using one of the following methods:

> *If you have excluded remote commands by setting DDM access parameter to *REJECT (refer to Preventing Remote DDM Commands on page 187).*

Use a PCOP Entry to Start the Initial AS/400 Program

This first method is the easier to configure. Perform the following procedure:

1. **DO NOT** have an initial program entry in the user profile. Users who are using Client Access and the PC Organizer should have this parameter deleted from their user profile.

2. Add the following two lines to the C:\PCS\CONFIG.PCS file using the Client Access Configuration Program. The remote commands specified in the PCOP entries are executed in the order that they appear in the CONFIG.PCS file. The first entry should always be the STRPCO command.

```
PCOP 1, STRPCO
PCOP 1, CALL lib_name/pgm_name
```

If you wanted to start OfficeVision/400, the second entry would be to call QOFC/QOFINLPG.

Now when the user starts their personal computer, the STARTPCS.BAT file initiates the PC Organizer function. The two PCOP entries start the organizer on the AS/400 and initiate the program to bring up the OfficeVision/400 main menu or other main menu as the initial menu for the user. When the user signs off the system, the organizer ends and control is passed back to the personal computer.

Create a CL Program for the Initial Program in the User Profile

This method is more secure than the first method described above. The end user could easily change the CONFIG.PCS file.

1. Create a very simple CL program that does two things: first, it starts the organizer function on the AS/400, and then it executes the program that you want for the initial program. Call this program anything you like. For now, let's call it INITIAL in library QUSRSYS.

```
PGM    */  Initial Program to Start Office    /*
    STRPCO
    CALL  PGM(QOFC/QOFINLPG)
ENDPGM
```

2. Indicate that this CL program is to be the Initial Program in the User Profile.

3. Add a single PCOP entry in the CONFIG.PCS file. This is optional (but recommended), because you have already included the STRPCO command in the CL program.

    ```
    PCOP 1, STRPCO
    ```

    When the user starts their PC, the PCO command starts the organizer on the PC. Also, the STRPCS command in the CL program starts the organizer on the AS/400, immediately followed by the program that you want to be the initial program.

AUTOMATICALLY END CLIENT ACCESS/400 WHEN USING THE ORGANIZER

If a user signs off the AS/400 after the PC Organizer has been invoked, the Organizer ends and the user is presented with the main sign on screen. If the user signs on again, the Organizer does not restart unless the user toggles to the DOS session and invokes the Organizer from the DOS command line using the command PCO.

You can force the end of session and remove the Client Access function from PC memory by using one of the following methods:

*   Issue a command to end all Client Access functions from the STARTPCS.BAT file immediately following the statement that invokes the Organizer.

*   Issue a command to end only the Work Station Function from the STARTPCS.BAT file immediately following the statement that invokes the Organizer. Also, create a batch file to start the Work Station Function and the Organizer that the user can use to restart after signing off. This batch file ends the Work Station Function when the user signs off.

Refer to the following topics:

*   Using PC Organizer When There is No Command Line on AS/400 on page 270.

*   Automated Stop Client Access Program on page 272

AUTOMATED STOP CLIENT ACCESS PROGRAM

Before turning off your personal computer, "gently" end the Client Access session. This prevents the AS/400 from "seeing" the PC going down abruptly and, as a result, going into error recovery. The following files perform this shutdown procedure. Create each file and place them in the PCS subdirectory. Run the program SIGNOFF.BAT to end your session. The file CONFIG.RLS is a configuration file so you can release the virtual printers.

SIGNOFF.BAT — Personal Computer Batch File

This is the format for stopping Client Access functions and removing them from PC memory.

```
@REM STOP THE WORKSTATION SESSIONS
STOPWSF 1 /F
STOPWSF 2 /F
STOPWSF 3 /F
STOPWSF 4 /F
STOPWSF 5 /F

@REM RELEASE VIRTUAL PRINTERS
CFGVPRT CONFIG.RLS

@REM RELEASE SHARED FOLDERS
FSPC RELEASE *

@REM STOP THE ROUTER
STOPRTR /F

@REM REMOVE PCS FUNCTIONS FROM MEMORY
RMVPCS ALL /F
@ECHO ON
```

> The SIGNOFF.BAT file is written under the assumption that you have copied the WSF, RMVPCS, RMTCMD, and Virtual Printer functions from the I:\QIWSFLR (or I:\QIWSFL2) folder into the C:\PCS subdirectory.
>
> Use the **Location of Client Access Functions** under the **General Options** in the **Configure Client Access** option of the **Client Access menu (PCSMNU)**.

CONFIG.RLS Configuration File

This configuration is used as the target for the CFGVPRT command in the SIGNOFF.BAT file.

```
@REM This file lists the three VPRT ports without any
@REM assignment
@REM   in effect, releases the virtual printer
@REM   assignments when the CFGVPRT command is run.
PRNT 1
PRNT 2
PRNT 3
```

COPYING CLIENT ACCESS FUNCTIONS TO THE PC

When configuring Client Access using the PCSMENU program, you can specify where you want the Client Access functions to reside (on the PC or the AS/400). If you specify the PC, then the configuration program copies the selected functions from the AS/400 to your PC hard drive and modifies the STARTPCS.BAT to reflect that it can be invoked directly from the PC's hard disk.

The best (and easiest) way to copy Client Access functions to your personal computer is to use the **Location of Client Access Functions** under the **General Options** in the **Configure Client Access** option of the **Client Access menu (PCSMNU).**

This method assures that all components are copied to the hard disk and that the appropriate batch and configuration files are modified.

AUTOMATICALLY UPDATING USER FILES

Client Access uses the update function to maintain files located on the PC at the same level as files on the AS/400. This is performed using the PCSUPDT command, which, by default, is included in the STARTPCS.BAT file. Whenever you start Client Access, the PCSUPDT utility is invoked. If the files on the AS/400 have a different date/time stamp than corresponding files on the PC, then the files on the AS/400 are copied to the PC.

The PCSUPDT update utility is not limited to Client Access use. You can use this utility for your own file maintenance. For example, you may want to automatically maintain files:

- An AS/400 and individual PCs.
- An AS/400 and a NetWare file server.
- A NetWare file server and individual PCs.
- Two or more NetWare file servers.

Client Access/400 uses an UPDT entry in the CONFIG.PCS file to define the source and target for the update function. If you choose, you may add additional UPDT entries to define the additional sources and targets for your own files. You can also create you own unique configuration files or include the source and target as optional parameters when you invoke the PCSUPDT utility.

As an example of using PCSUPDT, let's assume that you want to maintain files on user's PCs at the same level as files on a NetWare file server. Let's assume a NetWare directory defined as F:\ACCOUNT\DATA is the source and the target is a PC directory of the same name. Rather than using a configuration file to define the source and target, invoke PCSUPDT, including the source and target as optional parameters. The syntax for invoking PCSUPDT would be:

```
PCSUPDT F:\ACCOUNT\DATA C:\ACCOUNT\DATA
```

When PCSUPDT is invoked, it looks for the existence of a trigger file, called UPDATE.PCS, in the source directory. If found, it checks the date and time stamp of the trigger file on the source and target. If the date and time are the same, no update occurs. If different, then PCSUPDT checks for any package files and processes information found in the file. If there is no trigger file, then PCSUPDT checks the date and time stamp of the package file(s) on the source and target. If the date and time stamp of the package files are different, then PCSUPDT processes the information in the package file(s). If trigger files and package files are not used, then each file on the source is checked against the file of the same name on the target. If the date and time stamps are different, then each file is processed (i.e., copied from the source to the target).

The trigger file, mentioned above, is merely any file that has a date and time stamp. Typically, you create or edit a trigger file with some information that is meaningful to you. The package files are text files with an extension of .PKG. They define which files are to be included in the update. Information in the package file must be inserted in a specific format.

For a complete discussion on using the PCSUPDT utility, refer the *Client Access/400 for DOS Extended Memory — Setup* manual.

ELIMINATE SECOND SIGN-ON IN CLIENT ACCESS

If you want to avoid signing on twice when using Client Access (once at the Enter Common User ID prompt and then again at the Work Station Function Signon Screen, do the following and you only have to enter the Common User ID and password when you start the router:

1. Set the system value QRMTSIGN to *VERIFY.
2. Modify the master work station profile to *Bypass the pre sign-on display.*
3. Modify the session profile to *Bypass the AS/400 sign-on display.*

VALUE OF MAXCTL IN THE TOKEN-RING LINE DESCRIPTION

The default value for MAXCTL in the Token-Ring Line Description is 40. If you have been adding personal computers or other AS/400s to the Token-Ring network, be sure that you have not exceeded the value for MAXCTL. You can check the current value by:

```
DSPLIND line-description-name
```

If the value for MAXCTL is less than the number of controllers you wish to attach to the Token-Ring line, then do the following:

```
VRYCFG CFGOBJ(line-description-name) CFGTYPE(*LIN) STATUS(*OFF)
CHGLINTRN line-description-name MAXCTL(max-number-controllers)
VRYCFG CFGOBJ(line-description-name) CFGTYPE(*LIN) STATUS(*ON)
```

Using the ASCII Work Station Controller with Client Access

The ASCII Work Station Controller translates 5250 data streams to ASCII data streams and vice versa. The ASCII Work Station Controller emulates twinaxial work stations for the ASCII work stations it supports to allow them to take advantage of the AS/400 programs and the AS/400 interactive operations.

Special Cable Required to Attach Modem to ASCII WSC

The cable used to connect a modem to a PC or PS/2 is commonly referred to as a "PC Serial Cable." This type of cable has all the pins on one connector directly wired to the corresponding numbered pins at the connector at the opposite end. You cannot use this cable to attach a modem to the ASCII Work Station Controller.

A special cable is required to attach a modem to the ASCII WSC. I have listed the part numbers and included an illustration of the wiring diagram for this cable. If you don't wish to purchase the special cable, you can have one made for you.

IBM Modem Cable:
- PN: 69X7016 (USA)
- PN: 21F2671 (Germany)
- PN: 21F2674 (Japan)

The wiring diagram shown below is that used for the IBM cable. You can use this diagram to make your own cable or cable adapter.

Direct Connection Cable for Connecting a Modem to the ASCII Work Station Controller

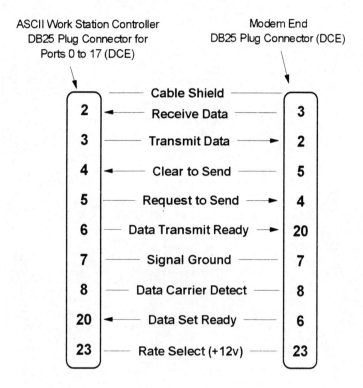

ASCII Work Station Controller
DB25 Plug Connector for
Ports 0 to 17 (DCE)

Modem End
DB25 Plug Connector (DCE)

	Cable Shield	
2	Receive Data	3
3	Transmit Data	2
4	Clear to Send	5
5	Request to Send	4
6	Data Transmit Ready	20
7	Signal Ground	7
8	Data Carrier Detect	8
20	Data Set Ready	6
23	Rate Select (+12v)	23

Configuring the ASCII WSC for Personal Computers

The ASCII Work Station Controller can be configured to allow port sharing among different ASCII devices. Refer to Configuring the ASCII Work Station Controller for Port Sharing on page 168.

Performance Tips When Using ASCII WSC

Refer to Performance Tips for the ASCII Work Station Controller on page 166 for some performance tips when using the ASCII WSC with Client Access.

PERSONAL COMPUTER CONNECTIVITY OPTIONS

This table has the IBM part numbers and other useful information that you need to connect PCs to the AS/400. I think everything is correct, but these things change from time to time.

AS/400 Connection Options	Micro Channel PS/2 Model 50 and Higher	Non-Micro Channel Personal Computers
Local Twinaxial Attachment or through a 5394 USING AS/400 Client Access	36/38 Work Station Emulation Adapter PN: 69X6279 FC: 6279 T-Connector for 69X6279 PN: 69X6293 FC: 6293	5250 Emulation Card - Convenience Kit (Adapter, T-Connector, no software) PN: 92G5022 FC: 5022
Local Twinaxial Attachment or through a 5394 Includes 5250 Emulation Software for DOS	36/38 Work Station Emulation Adapter Convenience Kit (Adapter, T-Connector, & DOS Software) PN: 69X6287 FC: 6287	5250 Emulation Adapter Convenience Kit (Adapter, T-Connector, and DOS Software) PN: 92G5022 FC: 5022
Local Twinaxial Attachment or through a 5394 Included 5250 Emulation Software for Windows	36/38 Work Station Emulation Adapter Convenience Kit (adapter, T-Connector, and Windows software) PN: 11H0764	5250 Emulation Adapter Convenience Kit (adapter, T-Connector, and Windows software) PN: 11H0763
Remote SDLC Attachment of a Single PC USING AS/400 Client Access	Multi-Protocol Adapter PN: 6451003 FC: 3043 Modem cable (standard serial cable) PN: 1502067 FC: 2067 7855 or 5853 synchronous modem at each end	SDLC Adapter Card PN: 1501205 FC: 1205 Modem Cable (standard serial cable) PN: 1502067 FC: 2067 7855 or 5853 synchronous modem at each end
Remote Attachment of a Single PC WITHOUT AS/400 Client Access	Multi-Protocol Adapter PN: 6451003 FC: 3043 Modem cable (standard serial cable) PN: 1502067 FC: 2067 Remote 5250 Emulation Software 2.0 PN: 92X0718 FC: 3255 7855 or 5853 synchronous modem at each end	SDLC Adapter Card PN: 1501205 FC: 1205 Modem Cable (standard serial cable) PN: 1502067 FC: 2067 Remote 5250 Emulation Software 2.0 PN: 92X0718 FC: 3255 7855 or 5853 synchronous modem at each end

AS/400 Connection Options	Micro Channel PS/2 Model 50 and Higher	Non-Micro Channel Personal Computers
Remote ASCII attachment through an ASCII WSC Using Client Access or DIAL/3X RPQ 5799-PCE	Serial port is standard on PS/2s 7855 or 5853 asynchronous modem (or equivalent) at each end Modem Cable at PS/2 end (standard serial cable) PN: 1502067 FC: 2067 Special modem cable at ASCII WSC end, or PN: 69X7016 (USA) PN: 21F2671 (Germany) PN: 21F2674 (Japan) Make your own cable for ASCII WSC, see Special Cable Required to Attach Modem to ASCII WSC on page 276 for wiring diagram.	If serial port not installed, get Serial/Parallel adapter for PS/2 Mod 25-40 (not L40): PN: 6450215 FC: 0215 7855 or 5853 asynchronous modem (or equivalent) at each end Modem Cable at PS/2 end (standard serial cable) PN: 1502067 FC: 2067 (ATs have 9-pin serial connector, you will need adapter for modem cable) Special modem cable at ASCII WSC end, or PN: 69X7016 (USA) PN: 21F2671 (Germany) PN: 21F2674 (Japan) Make your own cable for ASCII WSC, see Special Cable Required to Attach Modem to ASCII WSC on page 276 for wiring diagram.
Token-Ring Attachment with AS/400 Client Access	16/4 Token-Ring Adapter/A, or PN: 16F1133 FC: 1133 Token-Ring Adapter/A PN: 69X8138 FC: 4790 Token-Ring Attachment Cable PN: 6339098 FC: 3390 LAN Support Program V1.2 PN: 96X5678 FC: 5678	16/4 Token-Ring Adapter PN: 25F7367 FC: 7367 Token-Ring Adapter PN: 25F9858 FC: 9858 Token-Ring Attachment Cable PN: 6339098 FC: 3390 LAN Support Program V1.35 PN: 96X5678 FC: 5678
Ethernet Attachment with AS/400 Client Access	3Com's Etherlink/MC (Model 3C523) or Western Digital's Ethercard Plus/A (Model WDLAN-EP/A-F0001) Newer models may be available; other vendors provide Ethernet adapters as well.	3Com's Etherlink II (Model 3C503), or Western Digital's Ethercard Plus* (Model WDLAN-EPR-F0001) Newer models may be available; other vendors provide Ethernet adapters as well.

Personal Computer Keyboard Stickers

You can order personal computer keyboard stickers for 5250 emulation from IBM.

- Keyboard stickers for enhanced keyboards (101/102 keys): Publication Number SX21-9861.

- Keyboard stickers for PC, XT, and AT keyboards — 5250 style: Publication Number SX21-9000.

- Keyboard stickers for PC, XT, and AT keyboards — PC style: Publication Number SX21-9825.

Transferring a Spool File to the PC

You can easily transfer a spool file to the PC by first performing a CPYSPLF (Copy Spool File) to a physical file. Then use the File Transfer function of Client Access to transfer the physical file to the PC, converting it to ASCII text along the way.

Predefining the Library List for File Transfers

When you perform file transfers in Client Access, you frequently may need to predefine a list of libraries that are commonly used to keep a listing of the physical files you are accessing. It would be nice to allow the users to press the F4 key to prompt for this list. The default list of libraries is the user part of the system library list. You can customize this list by creating a special job description for the user that is identical to the normal JOBD used, except the library list contains a list of libraries as the library list.

Uppercase Letters When Using the IBM ODBC Driver

When you are defining AS/400 objects when using the IBM ODBC (Open Data Base Connection) driver, it is a good idea to use uppercase letters. There have been instances where using lowercase letters has caused problems.

Using Multiple Member Files with IBM ODBC Driver

The IBM ODBC driver does not support multiple member database files. This limitation may be removed in future releases of OS/400, but as of this writing, only the first member is accessible. If you intend on using the ODBC driver to access data in physical files, you should consider using only single member database files.

OFFICEVISION/400

OfficeVision/400 consists of a base product (including the document library services, administration, and personal directories functions) and optional functions (the calendar, mail, text search, and word processing functions).

OFFICEVISION/400 BACKUP CONSIDERATIONS

There are several things to consider when saving OfficeVision objects. Refer to OfficeVision/400 Backup Considerations on page 56 and the *AS/400 Backup and Recovery — Basic* manual for additional information.

OFFICEVISION/400 SECURITY

There is a very good discussion of OfficeVision/400 security in the Redbook, *OfficeVision/400 Version 2 Technical Tips and Techniques*. You can order this book. Refer to Frequently Called IBM Telephone Numbers on page 321.

You should have a good understanding of security when setting up and administering users in OfficeVision/400. In addition, there are a few useful commands to keep in your toolbag. Mostly, these deal with document security. Users often create documents in their folders, but they want others to have access to those documents or other items. The following is a list of handy document library object (DLO) commands to help you manage security and give the user the flexibility required.

DLO Command	What It Does
ADDDLOAUT (Add Document Library Object Authority)	Authorizes access of a user, a group profile, or an authorization list to one or more DLO.
CHGDLOAUT (Change DLO Authority)	Changes a user's, a group profile's, or an authorization list's authority to DLOs.
RMVDLOAUT (Remove DLO Authority)	Deletes a user's, a group profile's, or an authorization list's authority to DLOs.
DSPDLOAUT (Display DLO Authority)	Displays authority specifications such as owner, name, authorization list, and personal status.

DLO Command	What It Does
EDTDLOAUT (Edit DLO Authority)	Displays same information as DSPDLOAUT, and permits you to change, add, and delete authorities.
CHGDLOOWN (Change DLO Ownership)	Transfers ownership of DLOs from one user to another. You can also revoke the original owner's authority to the DLO.
DSPAUTLDLO (Display Authorization Lists DLOs)	Lists the DLOs whose security is specified by the authorization list parameter.
DSPUSRPMN (Display User Permission)	Lists users who can work on behalf of a user, or users on whose behalf a user can work.
GRTUSRPMN (Grant User Permission)	Gives a user permission to handle DLOs or perform OV/400-related tasks on behalf of another user.
RVKUSRPMN (Revoke User Permission)	Removes a user permission to handle DLOs or perform OV/400-related tasks on behalf of another user.

CLIENT ACCESS AND OFFICEVISION/400

There are special considerations when using Client Access and Text Assist in OfficeVision/400. Refer to PC Text Assist and OfficeVision/400 on page 268.

OFFICEVISION/400 — SPELLING AID DICTIONARIES

Refer to Select Spelling Aid Dictionary on page 32 for information on specifying spelling aid dictionaries in the text profiles.

CALENDAR ALARM PROGRAM — QALARM

Refer to Autostart Job Entry for OfficeVision/400 on page 32 for information about the QALARM job, which is used for automatic appointment reminders and job scheduling.

PRINTING CALENDARS

When users select the option to print their calendar, there is a field to select the printer device. When first installed, the OfficeVision default printer device is *WRKSTN, which directs the output to the device defined in the work station device description. Each user can change the printer device and the system remembers the setting. You can select any printer by name, or select the value *USRPRF. Refer to Printed Output Routing Figure on page 148 for an example of printed output routing.

SAVING AND RESTORING CALENDAR ENTRIES

A simple way to save only calendar entries is to use the SAVCAL command. Type **SAVCAL** and press F4 to prompt you for required parameters.

If you need to restore calendar entries, use the CL command RSTCAL. This, of course, implies that you have calendar entries saved on tape. Type the command **RSTCAL** and press F4 to prompt you for parameters. It is self explanatory.

It is a good idea to check the Cleanup options in the Operational Assistant to determine if the number of days to keep calendar items suits your needs. Type **GO ASSIST** and take the option to view/change cleanup options.

SIZING CONSIDERATIONS IN OFFICEVISION/400

The following may help you size OfficeVision/400. The data is not exact. It is provided as a guideline only.

Planning Considerations

The following items must be considered when planning size and performance for OfficeVision/400:
- Number of users
- Calendars
  - Number of calendars
  - How many calendars per user
- Documents and folders
  - Average pages per document
  - Number of documents per user
  - How long kept online
- Mail
  - Length of time kept online
  - Number of mail items sent each day

- Number of sent items that require confirmation
- Average number of recipients per distribution list
- Personal directory
  - Number of directories
  - Number of entries
  - All users have personal directories or only a few

Estimating Size for OfficeVision/400

The following example assumes that you have 50 users enrolled in OfficeVision/400.

Disk Space (for 50 Users)

Use the following table to estimate the amount of disk space for each "enrolled" user.

OfficeVision/400 Function	Assumptions	Disk Space Per User (KB)	Total if 50 Users (MB)
Enrollment Data	Fifty "enrolled" users.	1.3	0.065
Calendar	Ten resource calendars with 650 entries per user.	1,400.0	70.000
Documents and Folders	Twenty 3-page documents and two folders per user.	700.0	35.000
Mail	One hundred outgoing per user (75 with confirmation). Average mail three pages. Two recipients per mail item.	3,000.0	150.000
Directory and Distribution Lists	Fifty directory entries with department names and six optional fields. Twenty distribution lists of 15 users each.	2.0	0.100

OfficeVision/400 Function	Assumptions	Disk Space Per User (KB)	Total if 50 Users (MB)
Personal Directory	One directory with 500 entries per user.	2.0	0.100
Work Space when Active	Fifty users signed on and in OV/400 at same time.	125.0	6.250
	Total Disk Space	5,230.3KB	261.500 MB

Memory Requirements (for 50 Users)

Use the following table to estimate the amount of main memory for each *active* user.

OfficeVision/400 Function	Assumptions	Memory Per User (KB)	Total if 50 Users (MB)
System/Office Base	Fifty "active" users.	160	8.0
Each Active User	One active calendar, editing documents, and working with mail.	500	25.0
	Total Memory	660KB	33.0MB

SYSTEM PERFORMANCE TUNING FOR OFFICEVISION/400

Refer to OfficeVision/400 Performance Tuning on page 223 for information on performance tuning in an OfficeVision/400 environment.

OMITTING NAMES ON DISTRIBUTION LISTS

Users from the Professional Office System (PROFS) world have an imbedded command to omit the names of recipients in distribution lists and substitute a phrase in the TO: field of outgoing notes. This is handy, particularly in instances where there are many users receiving a note. OfficeVision/400 does not have this feature, but you can do something similar if you use the following.

- The default shell document for sending notes is QNOTE in the QWPDOCS folder. Copy this shell document, name it something meaningful, like DISTLIST, and place it in the same folder.

- Revise the shell document just created. Delete the edit instruction code in the TO: field. Either leave it blank or enter a phrase like, To Distribution.
- Educate users to use the change defaults option F13 **BEFORE** they begin to type the body of their note.
  - From the Send a Note screen, press F13 to change defaults.
  - Move the cursor to the Shell Document field and press F4 to list the shells.
  - Select the new shell from the list presented.
  - Press Enter to return to the Send a Note screen.

Once the user defaults are changed (but not saved as permanent), the user types the note and sends it out. People on the receiving end do not see the names of recipients.

SENDING/RECEIVING MAIL TO/FROM SMTP USERS

You can send and receive mail to/from a system that uses SMTP (Simple Mail Transfer Protocol), which is part of TCP/IP. The method for setting this up is explained in the *TCP/IP Configuration and Reference.* The steps you need to take to accomplish this are:

1. Add a routing entry to the QSNADS subsystem description.
2. Create a distribution queue.
3. Update the QSNADS routing table.
4. Update the system distribution directory.
5. Update the system SMTP alias table.
6. Change the SMTP attributes.

There are some restrictions. My purpose for including this tidbit is to inform you that this can be done. The procedure is explained fully in the *TCP/IP Configuration and Reference* manual.

DAMAGED OFFICEVISION/400 OBJECTS

As the number of users increases, the likelihood of damaged objects occurring on the system also increases. These damaged objects can be such things as mail items, userids, calendars, and authorization lists. Objects can become damaged in any number of ways, such as power or equipment failures. Normally, the damaged objects don't cause any problems, but there is a likelihood that they could manifest themselves into problems such as unusually high system activity. So, users may want to run the Reclaim Storage (RCLSTG) command from time to time to clean up these damaged objects. The *AS/400 Backup and Recovery — Basic* manual has a good discussion on the use of this command. Also, refer to Reclaiming Storage (RCLSTG) on page 73 for some ideas on using RCLSTG.

I have also found that the INZSYS command can "repair" some damaged objects. Some users have reported that running the INZSYS (which takes less time than the RCLSTG command) is a useful command to try.

One easy way to find damaged objects — although it does not guarantee that you will catch all of them — is to do the following.

> This procedure may take some time to execute.

1. Display the descriptions of all objects on the system, routing the output to an outfile.

    ```
    DSPOBJD OBJ(*ALL/*ALL) OBJTYPE(*ALL)
        OUTFILE(library_name/outfile_name)
    ```

2. Run a query over the outfile looking for ODOBDM *EQ '1'. This returns a list of the damaged objects identified by the system.

SUBSYSTEM QSNADS

Subsystem QSNADS must be running for OfficeVision/400 distribution to work. If you fail to start QSNADS, you get an error message when you attempt to send a note. Place the command STRSBS QSNADS in the system startup program QSYS/QSTRUP. Also, refer to Adding Communication Entries to Subsystems on page 163 for information regarding communication entries.

COMMAND LINE IN OFFICEVISION/400

The OfficeVision/400 main menu does not offer a command line. Users frequently use option 10 to get to a command line, but you can provide a command line by assigning a function key or option to call the program:

```
CALL QUSCMDLN
```

This brings up a command line window. For example, you could assign option 50 to issue this command. Option 50 is easily assigned as part of the OfficeVision enrollment process.

FORCING UPPERCASE ON DATA MERGED IN OV/400 DOCUMENT

OfficeVision/400 has no facility to force the contents of a character field to uppercase. Therefore, if you have a character data field in a file that potentially contains lowercase characters, you are unable to use OV/400 to force the shifting of this field to uppercase. However, you can use the facilities of the AS/400 relational database to accomplish this task.

One of the functions available in defining a field through DDS is the ability to pass the contents of the field through a translation table before the field is processed by a program. Therefore, you can specify that a character field be passed through a translation table that translates characters from lowercase to uppercase. Fortunately, the AS/400 even provides the lowercase-to-uppercase translation table in library QSYS.

Take the example of a physical file called PEOPLE, which contains five fields as follows:

```
R PEOPLEREC
    LASTNAME     25 A
    FIRSTNAME    15 A
    CITY         10 A
    STATE         2 A
    ZIPCODE       9 A
```

Create a logical file that allows us to work with all of these fields, plus an uppercase-only version of LASTNAME and FIRSTNAME.

The logical file is called PEOPLELF.

```
R PEOPLERECL              PFILE(PEOPLE)
    LASTNAME
    FIRSTNAME
    CITY
    STATE
    ZIPCODE
    LASTNAMEUC            RENAME(LASTNAME)
                          TRNTBL(QSYS/QSYSTRNTBL)
    FRSTNAMEUC            RENAME(FIRSTNAME)
                          TRNTBL(QSYS/QSYSTRNTBL)
```

When doing a data/text merge into an OV/400 document, use the logical file PEOPLELF. If you make a reference to LASTNAME or FIRSTNAME, then the results in the merging of the field will not be modified from its original value in the physical file. However, if you use the fields LASTNAMEUC and FRSTNAMEUC, then the results will be merged from the logical file, which uses the translate tables to convert the original lowercase characters in the physical file to uppercase in the merging of the data.

USING THE OPERATIONAL ASSISTANT IN OFFICEVISION/400

The Operational Assistant functions are useful, not only for system functions, but also for the OV/400 user. Some functions in the Operational Assistant will impact the users (e.g., deleting old calendar entries).

Attention Key Handling

OfficeVision/400 uses its own attention key handling program, which conflicts with using it for the Operational Assistant. The best way to give office users access to the Operational Assistant is through option 50 on the OfficeVision/400 menu. Refer to the *AS/400 System Operation* manual for instructions.

Calendar Items

The Operational Assistant can be set up to delete calendar items older than a specified age (in days). Refer to Operational Assistant on page 83.

OFFICE DOCUMENT TIPS

Refer to Document Library Objects on page 291 for additional information.

A GOOD IBM REDBOOK TO GET

There is an IBM Redbook, *OfficeVision/400 Version 2 Technical Tips and Techniques*, which has some good information for the OfficeVision/400 Administrator. Refer to Frequently Called IBM Telephone Numbers on page 321 for some handy telephone numbers — in particular, the phone number for ordering publications.

DOCUMENT LIBRARY OBJECTS

The following are important points about Document Library Objects (DLOs):

- OfficeVision/400 uses DLOs.
- Personal computer files are most commonly stored as DLOs. If you are using the Integrated File System feature of V3R1, then you can place PC files in the "root" file system. Refer to Integrated File System on page 52.
- Client Access/400 for Windows 3.1 files are stored in IFS root system.
- All DLOs are stored in shared folders in library QDOC or library QDOCnnnn (refer to Version 3, Release 1, and DLOs, below).

A good discussion of shared folders can be found in the *Office Services Concepts and Programmer's Guide*. This is a good reference source for your library. You can obtain this Redbook from IBM.

VERSION 3, RELEASE 1, AND DLOS

Prior to V3R1, all DLOs were in library QDOC in the system ASP. Beginning with V3R1, a QDOCnnnn library exists for each user ASP that contains DLOs. The library for DLOs in the system ASP remains as QDOC (same as in versions prior to V3R1). The library for DLOs in other ASPs is:

QDOCnnnn   where: *nnnn* = 0001, 0002, etc.

RECLAIM DOCUMENT LIBRARY OBJECTS

Refer to Reclaim Documents and Folders on page 74.

REORGANIZE DOCUMENT LIBRARY OBJECTS

Refer to Reorganize Document Library Objects (RGZDLO) on page 104 for information on using the RGZDLO command to reduce your disk space use.

OFFICE DATA STORAGE MANAGEMENT

Don't allow your system to become overcrowded with too many documents or your folders to become too large. The term "large" is somewhat subjective as it depends on the number of users and the size of the system.

Develop a strategy for saving (offline) those documents and folders that are not often needed. One method is to assign an expiration date to your document(s), then save all documents that are past the expiration date and delete them from the system. (This requires discipline as the user must enter an expiration date when a new document is created.)

If you write a little CL program, you can accomplish the same thing using the following steps. These steps presume that the CL program is run daily.

1. Use the QRYDOCLIB command to create a file that contains all documents with a creation date equal to the current date.

2. For each document in the file created in step 1, change the document expiration date using the CHGDOCD command (e.g., current date plus 90 days).

3. Run the QRYDOCLIB command to create a file that contains all documents with an expiration date within, say, three days of the current date.

4. For each document in the file created in step 3, send the owner a message stating that these documents will be saved to tape and deleted from the system in three days.

5. When you run the SAVDLO command to save and delete the documents, use the *SEARCH parameter to select those documents that have expired. See Archiving Documents on page 293 for a sample CL program using the QRYDOCLIB command.

COPY FROM/TO PC DOCUMENTS

You can copy data in a PC document to a system database file, or copy a member of a database file to a folder in PC format. Use Client Access or the following CL commands.

To copy a PC document to a database file:

```
CPYFRMPCD FROMFLR(flrname) FROMDOC(pcdoc) +
    TOFILE(filename/pcdoc)
```

(The physical file or source physical file must be created before doing this.)

To copy a database file member to a PC document:

```
CPYTOPCD FROMFILE(libname/filename) FRMMBR(mbrname) +
    TOFLR(flrname) TODOC(pcfile.ext)
```

(If the PC document does not exist, it is created.)

USING STG(*FREE) WHEN SAVING DOCUMENTS

You can free up some disk storage space if you save DLOs using the STG(*FREE) option. This saves the document, deletes the data, and retains the header information. You have to maintain a tape log so you know where the documents are. System users see the list of documents in their folder, but when they attempt to access the document, they receive an error message. The document must be restored before the user can work with it.

Be careful using the STG(*FREE) option when saving the DLOs because the data in a folder saved in this manner is not accessible until it is restored. This includes all personal computer files, even the files in the Client Access shared folders.

Refer to the **AS/400 CL Reference** manual for further information on using the SAVDLO command.

ARCHIVING DOCUMENTS

If you have a lot of documents on your system, you may be interested in an archiving technique to free up some storage. You can use the SAVDLO with STG(*FREE) — refer to Using STG(*FREE) When Saving Documents on page 292 — or you can use the Mark for Off-line Storage indicator, which users can use to indicate the disposition of their documents when a SAVDLO is performed. The Off-line Storage Mark is part of the document description header.

I have written a CL program to help you archive documents. This CL program demonstrates the use of the Off-line Storage Mark and the QRYDOCLIB command.

Sample CL Program for Archiving Documents

```
/*    CL PROGRAM  --  SAVDOCS                               */

/***************************************************************/
/* SAVDOCS PROGRAM CHECKS TO SEE IF ANY DOCUMENTS HAVE NOT  */
/* CHANGED SINCE A GIVEN DATE AND SAVES THE DOCUMENTS USING */
/* THE MARKED FOR OFFLINE STORAGE MARK TO DETERMINE IF IT   */
/* SHOULD BE KEPT, DELETED, OR DELETE THE CONTENTS          */
/*                                                          */
/***************************************************************/

        PGM     PARM(&CHGDATE &FLR)

/* The program expects the parms to be character values.   */
/* The first parm should be in the form 'mm/dd/yy' and the */
/* second parm should be in the form of 'foldername' or    */
/* '*ALL'                                                   */

        DCL     VAR(&FLR) TYPE(*CHAR) LEN(10)
        DCL     VAR(&CHGDATE) TYPE(*CHAR) LEN(8)
        DCLF    FILE(QSYS/QAOSIQDL)

/* If folder name begins with a 'Q', then halt processing as /
/* we do not want to attempt to process any IBM-supplied   */
/* documents or files ...                                   */

        IF      COND((%SST(&FLR 1 1) *EQ 'Q') *OR +
                (%SST(&FLR 1 1) *EQ 'q'))
                THEN(GOTO CMDLBL(QERROR))

/*  All documents with a last change date less than &CHGDATE*/
```

```
/* will be listed in the outfile.                          */

         QRYDOCLIB  QRYDFN(*IF  ((*CHGDATE *LE &CHGDATE))) +
                    FLR(&FLR) OUTFILE(QGPL/DOCLIB)    +
                    OUTMBR(*FIRST *REPLACE)
         OVRDBF     FILE(QAOSIQDL)  TOFILE(QGPL/DOCLIB)


/* Read the next record from the DOCLIB file created above */
BEGIN: RCVF
       MONMSG MSGID(CPF0864) EXEC(GOTO  CMDLBL(SAVDLO))
/*           /This would be the last record                */

/* We need these tests for Q* folders because we could put */
/* in the parameter *ALL for the folder name ....          */

         IF       COND(%SST(&QDLFLR 1 1) *NE 'Q') +
                  THEN(GOTO CMDLBL(NEXT))

         IF       COND((%SST(&QDLFLR 1 1) *EQ 'Q') *AND +
                  (&QDLAHV *EQ '0')) +
                  THEN(GOTO CMDLBL(BEGIN))
/*            Don't take any action if the folder name      */
/*            begins with a 'Q'.  IBM supplied folders      */
/*            begin with a 'Q', such as the Client          */
/*            Access folders                                 */

/* Set the offline storage mark to 'unmarked' for any       */
/*  documents in folders                                    */
/*  that begin with Q ...                                   */

         CHGDOCD DOC(&QDLDNM) FLR(&QDLFLR) MARK(*NO)
         GOTO    CMDLBL(BEGIN)



/* Check the value of the OFFLINE STORAGE mark.  If = 0,    */
/* then this means that the user has neglected to mark the  /
/* document and the document has already met the age        */
/* criteria ... so we change the offline storage mark       */
/* to delete the document after the next SAVDLO ...         */

NEXT:    IF       COND(&QDLAHV *EQ '0') THEN(CHGDOCD +
                  DOC(&QDLDNM) FLR(&QDLFLR) +
                  MARK(*YES *RMVALL))
         GOTO    CMDLBL(BEGIN)



/* Go through the folder(s) using the offline storage mark */
/* as the criteria for document disposition. The offline   */
/* storage mark can indicate KEEP, DELETE CONTENTS, or     */
/* DELETE DOCUMENT after SAVDLO. Users who have marked     */
/* their documents, will have made the decision for you for*/
/* the action to be taken ...                              */
SAVDLO: IF       COND((&FLR *EQ '*ALL') +
```

```
                    *OR (&FLR *EQ '*all')) +
                    THEN(CHGVAR VAR(&FLR) VALUE('*ANY'))
         SAVDLO   DLO(*SEARCH) FLR(&FLR) DEV(TAP01)   +
                    ENDOPT(*LEAVE) CHKFORMRK(*YES)    +
                    OUTPUT(*OUTFILE) OUTFILE(QGPL/SAVRECORD) +
                    OUTMBR(*FIRST *ADD)

/* You must make sure that you have not changed the OFFLINE */
/* STORAGE mark for objects in the Q* folders.  The default */
/* value is to NOT mark these objects.  If the offline      */
/* storage mark is 'unmarked', then the SAVDLO command using*/
/* the CHKFORMRK(*YES) will ignore those unmarked objects   */
/* if you are uncomfortable about this, then modify the     */
/* program to disallow the folder name *ALL (*ANY in the    */
/* SAVDLO command) ...                                      */

         MONMSG   MSGID(CPF9055) /* Doc successfully stored */

         SAVOBJ   OBJ(SAVRECORD) LIB(QGPL) DEV(TAP01)   +
                    ENDOPT(*REWIND)

/*  At this point, you may want to delete QGPL/SAVRECORD    */
/*   and/or QGPL/DOCLIB, on the other hand, you may want to */
/*   keep them on the system to perform queries.  You can   */
/*   even use these file to extract the the owner name and  */
/*   send that person a message stating which files were    */
/*   saved and the disposition of those files.              */

         GOTO     CMDLBL(END)

QERROR: SNDPGMMSG  MSG('You have attempted to use the +
                    SAVDOCS program specifying a +
                    folder beginning with ''Q''.  IBM +
                    supplied folder begins with ''Q'' +
                    and should not be saved using +
                    this program.  Program SAVDOCS +
                    terminating.  Retry again with +
                    different named folder or *ALL.) +
                    TOMSGQ(*QSYSOPR)


END:     ENDPGM
```

TAPE MANAGEMENT

Too many users ignore basic tape management principles. The tips presented here can save you a lot of trouble if you take the time to understand them. Remember, the most important time for you to have reliable tapes is when you need to restore something. If your business depends on a successful restoration of data, you don't want to have a failure occur because you didn't follow good tape management practices.

MAGNETIC TAPE

There is a videotape available that covers tape handling, the importance of tape labeling, how the AS/400 can help evaluate tapes, and other information. Order the videotape from IBM, Publication Number SV31-3405. Another publication you might want to review is the quick reference card, *Managing Your AS/400 Tape Library.*

Keep Your Tape Drives Clean

Keep the tape drive heads and tape path clean. Follow the instructions that came with the tape drive. Always clean the heads and tape path before any system save, installation of new releases, or any lengthy tape operation. Refer to the *AS/400 System Operation* manual for more information, but common sense prevails here — keep it clean and it will work better.

Handling Reel-to-Reel Tapes

Here are some rules for handling reel-to-reel tapes:
- Do not squeeze outer flanges of tape reels when handling tapes. Hold the tape in your palms evenly around the outer edge.
- Store tapes vertically (recommended) unless you use stacking rings.
- Always keep the reel protected with a locking collar when not in use.
- Always secure the end of the tape with a tape fastener to keep the tape from unwinding.
- **NEVER** transport tape without tape fastener.
- Regularly clean the tape head and tape path — particularly before an install or major backup/restore.
- Acclimate tapes by removing them from shipping containers and placing them in the computer room for 24 hours before processing.

Handling ¼-inch Cartridge Tapes

The ¼-inch cartridge tapes require some special handling considerations. **ALWAYS** use either the *UNLOAD or *REWIND option before removing the tape cartridge. **NEVER** use the *LEAVE option before removal. If you use the *LEAVE option, you will probably have tape wound on both the take-up and rewind spools of the cartridge, thus exposing an area of tape used for data recording to dust, other airborne contaminants, and uneven stretching.

You may have noticed that, when you first insert a cartridge tape, the tape fast forwards to the end, then rewinds to the beginning before you are allowed to use the tape. This tensioning procedure is necessary because the drive does not have dual capstans, which would otherwise maintain a constant tension. You can hasten this process if you use the *UNLOAD option before removing cartridges. This sets up the cartridge with all the tape on the take-up spool so that the tensioning procedure only has to wind the tape in one direction the next time you insert it.

AS/400 Evaluation of Tape Media

The AS/400 logs the media errors as tapes are used. You can use one of the following procedures to look at or print the tape errors.

Use System Service Tools

1. To begin, enter **STRSST** on the command line.
2. Enter 1, Start a Service Tool.
3. Enter 1, Work with Error Log.
4. Enter 4, Work with Tape/Diskette Statistics.
5. Enter 1, Display, and 1, Lifetime.
6. Select the type of media to be evaluated.

Use the PRTERRLOG command:

Enter the command **PRTERRLOG *VOLSTAT** *(Also accessible through the GO CMDSRV menu.)*

Errors can be either permanent (hard) errors or recoverable (temporary or soft) errors. If any permanent read or write errors are recorded in the error log, immediately discard that tape. The acceptable error rates for recoverable errors are shown in the following table. An excessive number of recoverable errors indicates the tape is worn out and should be removed from your tape library.

Acceptable Tape Media Errors

The following table lists the media errors that are considered acceptable. The read and write errors are defined as kilobits (Kb).

Tape Media and Device Type	Acceptable Write Errors	Acceptable Read Errors
1/2-inch Reel 9347	One temporary write error per 4,500Kb written.	One temporary read error per 50,000Kb read.
1/2-inch Reel 9348/2440	One temporary write error per 5,000Kb written at 1,600 bpi. One temporary write error per 8,500Kb written at 6,250 bpi.	One temporary read error per 100,000Kb read.
1/2-inch Reel 3422	One temporary write error per 8,500Kb written.	One temporary read error per 144,000Kb read.
1/2-inch Cartridge 3480/3490	One temporary write error per 160,000Kb written.	One temporary read error per 50,000,000Kb read.
1/4-inch Cartridge 6346/9346	One temporary write error per 1,250Kb written.	One temporary read error per 12,500Kb read.
All tapes	No hard write errors acceptable.	No hard read errors acceptable.

ELECTRONIC CUSTOMER SUPPORT

The AS/400 system has an integrated set of functions that are designed to help service and support your system. These functions are referred to as AS/400 Electronic Customer Support, or ECS, and include:

- Hardware and software problem analysis, reporting, and management.
- Copy screen image.
- Question and answer support.
- IBM technical and product information access.

AS/400 Electronic Customer Support provides a connection to the IBM service system following problem analysis and isolation procedures on the AS/400 system. For more information on how this works, see the information on reporting problems that are detected by the system in the *System Startup and Problem Handling* manual.

IBM PRODUCT INFORMATION — IBMLINK

Using IBM product information, you can obtain additional information about the AS/400, enroll in IBM education offerings, view IBM announcement information, use a subset of PROFS to send/receive mail to/from other IBMLink users (including your IBM Marketing Representatives and Service Engineers), and other IBMLink functions. I find that the IBMLink PROFS services provide excellent E-mail functions for customers and their IBM support personnel. To use these functions:

1. Enter **WRKPRDINF** on any command line, or use the options found through the User Support options on the Main menu.

2. Enter your account number, user ID, and password (refer to your AS/400 Welcome Pack), and press the Enter key.

3. A 3270 emulation display appears (the connection might take a minute or two).

Keep one thing in mind when you use the WRKPRDINF command — you automatically start a 3270 printer emulation job called QIAPRT in subsystem QBATCH. If your QBATCH subsystem is single-threaded (the shipped default), then as long as you are signed on to IBM, no other batch jobs are able to run in QBATCH. You can get around this problem by doing the following:

1. Create a duplicate of job description QBATCH. Call it PRTEML.

   ```
   CRTDUPOBJ OBJ(QBATCH) FROMLIB(QGPL) OBJTYPE(*JOBD) TOLIB(QGPL)
      NEWOBJ(PRTEML)
   ```

2. Change this job description so jobs run in a different job queue. The QSPL job queue is a good choice.

   ```
   CHGJOBD JOBD(PRTEML) JOBQ(QSPL)
   ```

3. Create a duplicate of the STRPRTEML command in a library ahead of QSYS in the system library list. Refer to Changing IBM Commands on page 316.

```
CRTDUPOBJ OBJ(STRPRTEML) FROMLIB(QSYS) OBJTYPE(*CMD) TOLIB(USRCMDS)
```

4. Finally, change the job description used by the STRPRTEML command in the library ahead of QSYS (Library USRCMDS in example above).

```
CHGCMDDFT CMD(USRCMDS/STRPRTEML) NEWDFT('JOBD(PRTEML)')
```

Now when you are using WRKPRDINF, the printer job is running in subsystem QSPL and you are not impacting the other user jobs trying to run in QBATCH.

PRINTING IBMLINK INFORMATION ON YOUR AS/400

If you plan to print IBMLink information on your designated AS/400 system printer, take the following steps to update your printer options on IBMLink.

1. On IBMLink Main menu, type **PROFILES 1** and press Enter.
2. On the Output Profile display:
   a. Type **P** after the CHANGE CODE.
   b. Type **DIAL** after the 328X ID prompt.
   c. Type **3** after the DISPLAY prompt.
   d. Press Enter.

The printed output profile governs printing of information when the PRINT key is pressed from any IBMLink application, and during electronic note printing. The output is routed to the AS/400. The AS/400 routes it according to criteria such as your user profile or job description. Normally, the printed output goes to the OUTQ or DEVICE specified in your user profile. See Printed Output Routing Figure on page 148 for a schematic of printer routing on the AS/400.

SENDING E-MAIL ON IBMLINK

One of the more useful options available to IBMLink users is the ability to send E-mail and transfer files to other IBMLink users and IBM support personnel (e.g., your Marketing Representative or Systems Engineer). If your IBM support personnel have given you their node and userid (if not, ask them), you can send notes to them and vice versa. This is an especially efficient means for your support personnel to keep you informed of system management topics, education offerings, birthday greetings, and other useful bits of information.

To send a note or open incoming mail on IBMLink, select User Functions on the main IBMLink menu, then select Electronic Note on the User Functions menu. In the To: field, address your note using the format:

```
node(userid)
```

You can also use the fastpath command NOTE to get the note screen, and OPENMAIL to open incoming mail. Refer to the ECS User Guide and your IBMLink Welcome Pack for additional information.

ORDERING PUBLICATIONS ON IBMLINK

Customers can access the IBM publication ordering facility through IBMLink. The following features are available:

- Publication search and order
- Online confirmation of order acceptance
- Order status query
- Same-day cancellation

The application is accessible from the IBMLink OrderLink Main menu or the fastpath command PUBORDER. PUBORDER provides the capability to enter orders for both billable and nonbillable IBM publications. Unit and total order prices are displayed during order entry.

The prerequisite for using PUBORDER is that the customer's IBMLink registration must reflect this capability. If necessary, customers should contact their IBM Marketing Representative to have the IBMLink branch office coordinator update their registration.

IBMLINK FASTPATH COMMANDS

Several fastpath commands are available. You can view a list of all the fastpath commands by entering **A** on the command line. Some useful commands follow:

ANNOUNCEMENT	Access IBM announcements
EDUCATION	Access IBM education offerings
NICKNAME	Process your nickname files
NOTE	Send a note
NOTELOG	Work with your notelogs
NOTES	Access E-mail menu
OPENMAIL	Open your E-mail
PRICE	Get the price of IBM hardware or software
PUBORDER	Publication orders
SALESMANUAL	Access the IBM Sales Manual menu
SUPPORTLINK	Technical information search

DIAL ACCESS TO IBMLINK AT 9600 BPS

On August 15, 1991, IBM announced customer access to IBMLink at 9600 bps at no additional charge over the 2400 bps service. If you have 9600 bps capability (e.g., you are using an IBM 7855 modem), then you can obtain AS/400 system and printer IDs and instructions for 9600 bps dial connectivity on the AS/400 by sending an IBMLink note to AM00190 at HONE83.

REPORTING PROBLEMS

You can report problems to your service representative by using:

- The Analyze Problem (ANZPRB) command.
- The Work with Problems (WRKPRB) command.
- The Send Service Request (SNDSRVRQS) command to report the problem(s) from the problem log.
- The function key to analyze a new problem from the problem log.
- A telephone.
- A facsimile machine.

V3R1
- The automatic problem notification and reporting function (V3R1). Refer to Automated Problem Management and Reporting on page 33.

Whenever possible or practical, use the ECS method of reporting problems because:

- Component information is included with the report. This enables the IBM Customer Engineer to come equipped with a new part if necessary.
- You have the opportunity to include remarks with your report.
- If the problem is software related, the report is dispatched directly to Level 2 support.
- If the problem is software related and you have included remarks (highly recommended), then you can give the IBM Service Representative much, if not all, of the information he or she needs to help you with your problem. This not only helps the service representative, but decreases the time to resolve the problem.
- If the problem is hardware related, the report is dispatched directly to the service representative's portable terminal (this is faster than using the telephone to report the problem).

Here is how to do it:

1. Enter the WRKPRB (Work with Problem) command and press Enter.
2. Move the cursor next to the problem you want to report, and enter option 8 (Work with Problem).
3. Select option 2 (Report Problem) and follow online instructions. If you want to add some remarks, select option 12 (Enter Notes).

COPYING SCREEN IMAGES

You can copy the screen image of one user onto another user's display, or copy the screen image of your own display to a spool file for printing. User-to-user copy screen is useful when performing tasks such as trying to help someone through a series of commands while on the phone. Copying your screen image to a spool file might be useful when creating an instruction manual or the like.

To copy screen images to another user:

```
STRCPYSCN SRCDEV(source_display) OUTDEV(display_name)
```

Enter the source device name (e.g., DSP12) and the name of your display.

The source display (if not your own) receives a message stating that the request has been made. The user at the source must answer the message allowing the copy screen function. Once the copy screen function starts, the receiving display stays one screen behind the sending display.

To copy screen images to an outfile:

```
STRCPYSCN SRCDEV(source_display) OUTFILE(libname/filename)
```

Enter the source device name (e.g. DSP12) and the name of the file to receive the images. You can have multiple members. Define the member when you start the copy screen command. You can then print the outfile, include it in an OfficeVision/400 document, or download it via PC Support for inclusion into a PC based text processor.

To end the copy screen images:

1. From the sending display, type **ENDCPYSCN** on the command line and press F4 to prompt. Type the parameter value for the display station that requested the copy screen and press Enter.

2. From the receiving display, get to a System Request screen (Alt+SysReq, or Shift+SysReq), then enter **ENDCPYSCN** and press the Enter key.

PTF MANAGEMENT

I have included some tips on PTF management in the section on System Management. Refer to PTF Management on page 122.

QUSRTOOL LIBRARY

Many of the examples in the AS/400 library are contained in the optionally installable library QUSRTOOL. This library provides access to various example programs that you can enable or revise for your use.

Library QUSRTOOL contains only the source for these examples. The creation and management of the objects is left to you as the user. If you modify the source, it is recommended that you first copy the source to a user library. This ensures that your modifications are preserved when the QUSRTOOL contents are changed by IBM.

The contents of QUSRTOOL are not integrated system functions, are not considered part of the OS/400 licensed program, and may change from release to release. See member AAAMAP in source physical file QATTINFO in library QUSRTOOL for more information about this library.

WHAT ARE QUSRTOOLS?

The AS/400 ships with a library called QUSRTOOL. This library contains miscellaneous tools and information not otherwise found in other program products.

There are two general categories of tools in QUSRTOOLs:
- TAA Tools. System management and programming tips and techniques. These tools share a common "create" technique. They make up the majority of the tools.
- Non-TAA Tools. Unconnected tools. Each has its own create process.

Here is a sampling of the QUSRTOOL commands that I think you will find useful. There are many more, and I recommend that you become familiar with them.

QUSRTOOL Command	What It Does
CHGLIBOWN	Change owner of library and objects within the library. Only objects owned by a specific owner are changed.
CHKSAVRST	Check save/restore job log for important Save/Restore messages.
CHKSAVTAP	Check Save tape format to see if the system can read it.
DLTOLDSPLF	Delete old spooled files based on a date from an output queue or all output queues.

QUSRTOOL Command	What It Does
PRTLIBANL	Print a library analysis of one or all libraries for summary totals of object types and a breakdown of file and program types.
PRTSYSSUM	Print a summary of the important system information such as size and last PTF package applied.
SCNSRC	Scan a source file for a value string. If you have AS/400 Application Development Tools, you can use the scan function included with the Source Entry Utility command FNDSTRPDM.

VIEWING QUSRTOOL DESCRIPTIONS

Before using tools contained in the QUSRTOOL library, view or print the documentation contained in the physical file QUSRTOOL/QATTINFO. The first member, AAAMAP, is the Introduction and Overview of QUSRTOOL. Print this information using one of following methods (in order of output quality):

Using OfficeVision/400

Create a document called AAAMAP and use the GET option in OfficeVision to copy the member AAAMAP of QUSRTOOL/QATTINFO into your document, then print it.

Using the Source Entry Utility (SEU)

```
STRSEU SRCFILE(QUSRTOOL/QATTINFO) SRCMBR(AAAMAP) OPTION(6)
```

Using the Copy File Function

```
CPYF FROMFILE(QUSRTOOL/QATTINFO) TOFILE(*PRINT) +
    FROMMBR(AAAMAP)
```

Use the DSPTAATOOL Command

Create the tool DSPTAATOOL (Display TAA Tool) command. Once you create this command, you can use it to display a tool's description by specifying:

```
DSPTAATOOL TOOL(toolname)
```

You can also use the tool to print the tool's documentation by using the OUTPUT parameter:

```
DSPTAATOL TOOL(toolname) OUTPUT(*PRINT)
```

The general members in the QATTINFO source file are:

AAAMAP	Detailed overview and general instructions of QUSRTOOL.
AAAAREADME	Lists changes in the current release QUSRTOOL.
AAAUPDATE	Lists changes in the current release for TAA Tools.
TAASUMMARY	Summary of the TAA tools by category and alphabetically within each category.

CREATING THE QUSRTOOLS

Use the techniques described above to read about the tools and gain an understanding of what they do. Then follow the steps below to create the tools you want.

> *Typically, QUSRTOOLs are program objects. Many of the tools are CL programs. The CL compiler is included with the Operating System. However, some tools will require RPG, COBOL, or C compilers. Review the documentation to determine if you need a compiler other than what is on your system.*

1. Create a library called TAATOOL.

    ```
    CRTLIB LIB(TAATOOL) TEXT('TAA Tools Library')
    ```

2. Create the CL program TAATOLAC in the TAATOOL library:

    ```
    CRTCLPGM PGM(TAATOOL/TAATOLAC) SRCFILE(QUSRTOOL/QATTIC)
    ```

3. Change your current library to TAATOOL (this also adds the TAATOOL library to your library list):

    ```
    CHGCURLIB LIB(TAATOOL)
    ```

4. Call the CL program TAATOLAC to create the CRTTAATOOL command. Make sure you haven't omitted the previous step to change your current library.

    ```
    CALL TAATOLAC
    ```

    You must specify the library for the TAA tool commands and a library to hold the data files that some TAA tools create. I recommend that you specify the TAATOOL library in each case.

5. Modify any backup programs and procedures to include the TAATOOL library in your regularly backed up library list.

6. Use the CRTTAATOOL command to create additional tools. You can use this command to create a single tool or all of the tools at once. To create a single tool, issue the command:

    ```
    CRTTAATOOL  TOOL(toolname)
    ```

7. Then issue the following command to create all the tools:

```
CRTTAATOOL TOOL(*ALL) CRTFILELIB(libname)
```

UPDATES TO QUSRTOOLS

IBM does not issue PTFs to QUSRTOOLs; however, they do issue updates from time to time. To determine if you have the current update, display the TAATOOL data area:

```
DSPDTAARA  TAATOOL/TAATOOL
```

If the TAATOOL data area exists, the release information is displayed. If no information displays, you don't have an update.

To get the latest update, contact your IBM Representative. If the Representative does not have a copy, ask the Representative to send a note to RCHASA04(QUSRTOOL).

MISCELLANEOUS INFORMATION

This section contains tips that I could not clearly place in other sections.

USE SMALL BITS OF SOAP IN YOUR SHOWER

When your soap bar gets so small that you have just a tiny piece, it begins to get soft and mushy or breaks up into itty, bitty pieces. When the soap bar becomes a sliver of its former self, simply grab a new bar, wet it down, and press the old bar onto the top. When it dries, the two bars of soap are welded together to form a single bar.

PERFORMING AN IPL FROM THE SYSTEM CONTROL PANEL

When you have occasion to perform an IPL from the system control panel, use the following procedure. Use the control panel switch or push button to make your selections as follows:

1. Place the system in the Manual mode.
2. Press the Select switch or push button (increment or decrement) until 02 is displayed in the Function display or Function/Data display on the control panel.
3. Press the Enter push button on the control panel.
4. Press the Select switch or push button (increment or decrement) until the character that represents the storage area or device you want to use for your IPL source (A, B, or D) appears in the Data or Function/Data display.
   A   Storage area A
   B   Storage area B
   D   Alternate IPL device (tape drive)
5. Press the Enter push button on the control panel. The character disappears from the Data or Function/Data display.
6. Press the Select switch or push button (increment or decrement) until 03 is displayed in the Function display or Function/Data display on the control panel.
7. Push the Enter push button to start the IPL.
8. Switch the system to Normal mode if you wish to continue the IPL in Normal mode. If left in Manual mode, do the following:
   a. Sign on to the system when the Sign On display appears.
   b. On the IPL Options display, select the option you wish to perform during the IPL steps.

TESTING THE INTERNAL BATTERY ON 9402/9404 AS/400 SYSTEMS

> The following method does not provide meaningful results on 9406 systems. If you wish to have the battery tested on 9406 systems, ask your IBM Service Representative for assistance.

Many AS/400 systems have an internal battery. The 9406 systems use this internal battery to save a copy of the main memory map to disk in the event of electrical failure. The 9404 and 9402 systems use the internal battery to keep the system active for a short period of time in the event of power failure, before saving the main memory to disk and shutting down the system. You can test the internal battery on 9402 and 9404 systems as follows:

1. Perform a manual IPL and bring the system up in Dedicated Service Tools.
2. When at the DST screen, unplug the electrical power to the system from the wall outlet.
3. Wait 15 seconds or so and plug in the system. If the battery is in reasonable shape, when power is restored to the AS/400 your display will return to DST. You can then resume the IPL. If the battery is weak, you just killed the system.

If you do kill the system **WHILE IN DST**, it is of no consequence. If you perform this test while the Operating System is active, even if there is no activity on the system, you could cause damage to objects. You **DO NOT** want that to happen.

USING CL COMMAND CRTDUPOBJ ON LIBRARY OBJECTS

Take care when using the CRTDUPOBJ command on library objects. There are even some objects (e.g., Save Files) on which you cannot use CRTDUPOBJ even though you can use the command on libraries. Using the CRTDUPOBJ is not recommended for use on libraries. If there are database files in the libraries, they have access paths (either shared or created). Using the CRTDUPOBJ command does not duplicate these access paths. There may even be cases where using the CRTDUPOBJ on the library will not create true copies of objects within the library. The best way to copy a library (and its contents) is to use the SAVLIB and RSTLIB commands. You can save the library to tape or to a save file. SAVLIB "copies" all objects in the library, and RSTLIB creates the necessary access paths.

USING THE COMMAND ENTRY SCREEN

As you become more familiar with the AS/400, you will use commands more frequently, relying less on the menus. If you are entering commands more often than using the menus, you may want to take advantage of the Command Entry processing program. Enter the command:

```
CALL QCMD
```

on the command line. This brings up the Command Entry display. Initially, it is blank. Below is an example of how it may look after you have entered several commands from the command line.

```
                          Command Entry                        APACHE
                                                 Request level:   4
Previous commands and messages:
  > wrkhdwrsc *cmn
  > wrkusrprf *all
  > CRTDEVDSP DEVD(NEWDSP) DEVCLS(*LCL) TYPE(*CALC) MODEL(*ASCII) PORT(5) ATT
    ACH(*MODEM) CTL(CTL05) LINESPEED(*CALC) WORDLEN(*CALC) PARITY(*CALC) STOP
    BITS(1) TEXT('Test device for ASCII WSC')
    Description for device NEWDSP created.
  > dspusrpfr
    Command DSPUSRPFR in library *LIBL not found.
    Error found on DSPUSRPFR command.




                                                               Bottom
Type command, press Enter.
===> dspusrpfr_____



─────────────────────────────────────────────────────────────
F3=Exit   F4=Prompt   F9=Retrieve   F10=Include detailed messages
F11=Display full      F12=Cancel    F13=Information Assistant   F24=More keys
```

The Command Entry display allows you to enter commands to be processed by the system. Previous commands you have entered along with messages from the running of those commands are displayed in the history area above the command line. Any commands that end in an error are automatically retrieved and displayed on the command line.

By positioning the cursor on a command or its associated messages in the history area and pressing the F4=Prompt function key, the prompt screen for the selected command is displayed. Retrieve previous commands that were run by pressing the F9=Retrieve function key. Select a specific command to be run again by placing the cursor on that command or its associated messages and pressing the F9=Retrieve function key. Commands that may have rolled off the top of the display can be retrieved by using the Page Up key.

The online help information for a specific command can be displayed directly from the command entry display by typing a command on the command line and pressing the F1=Help key or the Help key while the cursor is still on the command line.

Commands may be longer than a single line. Commands that are too long for this command line can be processed using the full-screen command entry display or by using the F4=Prompt function key. You can also use the F11=Display full key to bring you to the full command entry display.

GO COMMANDS

There are several useful GO commands on the AS/400. GO commands are used to call up menus. You can access these menus from the menu system on the AS/400; but as your familiarity with the system grows, you will probably find yourself using the fastpath more frequently. The following GO commands (not an all-inclusive list) are useful.

ASSIST	Operational Assistant
BACKUP	Backup actions
CMDSEC	Security commands
CMDSAV	Save commands
CMDSRV	Service Tools menu
CMDTAP	Tape commands
CMDWRK	Lists all the "Work with" commands
CMN	Communications commands
FILE	File commands
JOB	Job commands
LICPGM	Menu for working with Licensed Programs
MAJOR	Menu of major command groups
PERFORM	AS/400 Performance Tools
POWER	System power on/off menu
PRINTER	Printer commands
PROBLEM	Problem handling
PROBLEM2	Additional problem handling
PTF	PTF commands
RESTORE	Main restore menu
RJE	Remote Job Entry commands
SAVE	Main save menu
SETUP	System setup menu
STATUS	Status commands
TAPE	Tape commands

GETTING A POP-UP WINDOW COMMAND LINE

Refer to Command Line in OfficeVision/400 on page 287 for information on getting a command line in OfficeVision/400. This technique can be used in any program.

ADDING A MEMBER TO A MULTI-MEMBER LOGICAL FILE

If you experience a lock condition when attempting to add a member to a multi-member logical file (e.g., attempting to do an ADDLFM), try this solution.

1. Create a single-member logical file over the physical file member using the exact same keys used for your multi-member logical file. This single-member logical file is locked while building the access path, but that causes no problems. Other jobs can be accessing your usual multi-member logical file while this is going on.

2. Do the ADDLFM on you original multi-member logical file. This takes no longer than if it were done over an empty physical file member because the access path exists. You get message CPI3210 advising you that the path is shared.

3. Delete the single-member logical file. The access path becomes owned by the multi-member logical file.

USE QUERY/400 TO VIEW OR PRINT PHYSICAL FILE DATA

Query/400 is a very effective and simple means to view, and optionally print, physical file data. I find it much more functional than using DFU (except you cannot change the data). You can also use Query/400 in conjunction with the CL commands. Many CL commands have an OUTPUT(*OUTFILE) parameter. If you haven't used Query/400 to view these outfiles, you might find it really useful. Not only can you view the entire outfile, but you can be selective in what you view and optionally print. This technique can be much easier than using DFU or PDM.

For example, you have obtained a list of all user profiles, but you only want the profile name and the print device or output queue:

```
DSPUSRPRF *ALL OUTPUT(*OUTFILE) OUTFILE(libname/filename)
```

Now start Query/400 (STRQRY) and use the menu interface to select the file and the records you want.

RENAMING DEVICE, CONTROLLER, OR LINE DESCRIPTIONS

With Version 2 of the operating system, you can rename device, controller, or line descriptions. The object must be varied off first, then you can use the WRKDEVD, WRKCTLD, WRKLIND, or RNMOBJ commands. This is especially handy when installing new displays and printers. If you don't like any of the default AS/400 naming conventions, you can allow the system to auto-configure the device, then rename it. This way, you are sure that the display or printer is configured correctly.

If you use the WRKCFGSTS command and select the *BASIC assistance level, you don't even have to vary the device off before changing the name. Use option 9 to rename the object and the Operational Assistant varies the device off, renames the object, and then varies the device on again.

CHANGING IBM COMMANDS

One of the most common reasons users change IBM commands is because they prefer different defaults than those supplied by IBM. You can change the defaults of any command (IBM- or user-created) by using the CHGCMDDFT command.

You must be cautious when changing IBM-supplied commands. Whenever a new release or version of the Operating System is installed, there is a possibility that any changes you made to IBM commands will be lost. This is because the old commands may be overwritten by the new. I mentioned earlier that you can place a copy of the original object in the CHGSYS library. Here is another technique that some users employ.

1. Create a library to hold all user commands (include those that you create yourself).

    ```
    CRTLIB USRCMDS
    ```

2. Place this library ahead of QSYS in the system library list. Use the following command:

    ```
    WRKSYSVAL SYSVAL(QSYSLIBL)
    ```
    then take option 2.

3. Enter the same sequence number that QSYS now has, type in the library name **USRCMDS**, and press the Enter key. Verify that the library USRCMDS is immediately ahead of QSYS.

4. Use the CRTDUPOBJ command to place a copy of the command you are going to change into library USRCMDS.

5. Change the command that is in library USRCMDS.

Now you have two commands of the same name. However, the library USRCMDS is searched first, so that is the command that is used. You can be assured that, if you fully qualify any IBM commands with the original library and command name, you are using the IBM-supplied command defaults. Also, if the old command in library QSYS is replaced during the installation of a new release or version, your changes are not affected because you have placed them in a different library.

MINIMIZE SWIRL MARKS WHEN WAXING YOUR CAR

Some car waxes and polishes have abrasives to remove oxidized paint or imperfections. If you use these compounds, the resulting swirl marks left in the paint are more pronounced than if you use nonabrasive waxes. Only use abrasive compounds if you need to remove oxidized paint. Otherwise, use a nonabrasive product.

After applying the nonabrasive car wax, let it dry. Then, sprinkle a very small amount of cornstarch on the car. Buff the car using a soft cotton cloth or toweling. The cornstarch helps to remove or minimize the swirl marks caused during the buffing.

ENDING A DISPLAY STATION PASSTHROUGH SESSION

If you have multiple AS/400s connected together, then you are probably using the display station passthrough function. After you set up communications between the AS/400s, you can start a passthrough session using the command STRPASTHR. When you are ready to signoff the remote AS/400, use ENDPASTHR (end pass-through), rather than merely signing off the system using the SIGNOFF command or option 90 from the main menu. If you are using V2R3, you can issue the SIGNOFF command specifying:

```
SIGNOFF ENDCNN(*YES)
```

(This ends the remote connection and has the same effect as the ENDPASTHR command.)

If you do not end pass-through (or end connection in the SIGNOFF command), then you are presented with the sign-on screen on the remote system rather than returning to your home system. Then you must sign on to the remote system again and perform either the ENDPASTHR or the SIGNOFF ENDCNN(*YES) command to end the connection and return to your home system.

Consider this alternative. Copy the SIGNOFF command to a library ahead of QSYS in the system library list *(refer to Changing IBM Commands on page 316)*. Then change the default value for ending the connection of the copied SIGNOFF command from ENDCNN(*NO) to ENDCNN(*YES). Now, if you issue the SIGNOFF command or take option 90 from the Main menu, your display passthrough session ends because the connection is terminated and you are returned to your home system. If you are not in a passthrough environment, the ending of the connection parameter is ignored.

To change the SIGNOFF command to end connection of passthrough sessions, do the following:

1. Copy the SIGNOFF command to a library ahead of QSYS in the system library list.

   ```
   CRTDUPOBJ OBJECT(SIGNOFF) FROMLIB(QSYS) OBJTYPE(*CMD) TOLIB(USRCMDS)
   ```

2. Change the command default of the copied command.

   ```
   CHGCMDDFT CMD(USERCMDS/SIGNOFF) NEWDFT('ENDCNN(*YES)')
   ```

> *I have seen instances where using the ENDCNN(*YES) parameter causes a session to hang (for example, in asynchronous dial-up APPN connections). If this occurs on your system, then change the SIGNOFF command back to the shipped default.*

FULL-SCREEN VERSUS WINDOW VIEW OF HELP SCREENS

The default settings on the AS/400 provide a window view any time you press Help. You can then press F20 to get a full-screen view. Some users prefer a full-screen view each time they press the Help key. You can accomplish this by changing the user profile.

```
CHGUSRPRF USRPRF(user_profile_name) USROPT(*HLPFULL)
```

CHANGING ENTRIES IN THE SYSTEM DIRECTORY

Sometimes, after you have enrolled a user in the System Directory, you may need to change the entry. You can always go into the directory and edit an entry description, address parameter, or other information. Prior to V2R2, you could not rename an entry. The commands used for changing and renaming are CHGDIRE and RNMDIRE.

The RNMDIRE is a long-running command. I recommend you run this command in batch mode (i.e., use the SBMJOB command). The command also requires that you "quiesce" (stop) most or all distribution functions that use the directory (e.g., SNADS, X.500).

REFERENCING AND ACCESSING IBM INFORMATION

I have included this section to help AS/400 users who either are not familiar with IBM's business structure or are unsure of the recent changes within IBM.

SYSTEMS ENGINEERING SUPPORT

In years past, whenever you purchased a major piece of equipment from IBM (such as a midrange system), you could expect to receive system engineering support at no cost. IBM maintained a large and sophisticated staff of System Engineers whose mission was to provide technical support to IBM's Marketing Representatives and customers. Regrettably, this support has declined. In order to remain competitive, IBM has reduced the profit margin on the products they sell. One result is that IBM can no longer afford to provide this "no cost" Systems Engineering support for routine operational issues and skill transfer.

The Systems Engineer is gone, but there still exists the Operational Support Specialist and the System Operational Support Specialist. Most often, these people are former System Engineers and are available to help with defect support, problem determination, and fee-based operational services. Should you have a defect in software and believe you may need an IBM advocate to help, call upon these resources. You can also contract these local resources as a service team to help with operational services.

AS/400 SUPPORT FAMILY

AS/400 users in need of common, day-to-day usability help are encouraged to use IBM's Support Family of services. These service offerings can provide you with everything from operational support to specific consulting engagements. I recommend that you become familiar with this suite of offerings.

This form of remote support should be high on your list for operational support. Most local IBM offices are not providing personnel for routine operational support except on a fee basis. If you haven't tried the Support Family of services, consider doing so.

I particularly recommend the following as a minimum for most AS/400 sites. Contact your local IBM office or the Support Family Services marketing line for additional information.

AS/400 SupportLine   Choose either the monthly or hourly subscription. If you need assistance infrequently, then consider the hourly subscription. Monthly subscription costs are based on processor size.

Regardless of which service you choose, you receive a subscription to electronic access of the IBM Q&A database.

AS/400 Alert   This is a very reasonably priced service to alert you to HIPER PTFs. This relieves you of the task of reviewing the Preventive Service Planning Report (PTF SF98vrm) on a regular basis. AS/400 Alert provides a notification service (FAX or mail) to alert you to the HIPER PTFs that are important to your installation.

For additional information, refer to the phone number list under Frequently Called IBM Telephone Numbers on page 321.

PROCEDURE FOR CALLING IBM DEFECT SUPPORT

> *Beginning January 1, 1995, you need to have a SupportLine Contract in order to gain access to any telephone voice support, including defect support. If you do not have a SupportLine Contract, your means of contacting IBM is through Electronic Customer Support, FAX, or mail.*

When you experience a hardware or software problem, be prepared when you call for service or assistance. Have this basic information available:

- Your IBM Customer Number.
- Your system type and model (e.g., AS/400 Type 9406, Model E60).
- The name, Version, and Release of your Operating System — this is always OS/400. You should know your version and release numbers.
- For a hardware problem, try to be as descriptive as you can. If you know the feature code of the problem or any error codes that you have noticed, be sure to tell your support person.
- For a software problem, it is helpful if you know can identify the software component (e.g., OS/400, PC Support).
- Make a note of all correspondence (oral or written) that deals with your problem, including the problem number. IBM uses the problem number to track your problem.

Refer to the phone list below for the appropriate number to call (i.e., software or hardware defect).

FREQUENTLY CALLED IBM TELEPHONE NUMBERS

Here is a list of frequently called IBM telephone numbers. You may want to make a note of these for future reference.

IBM Service or Function	Telephone Number
Hardware service	1-800 IBM-SERV (426-7378)
Obtain microcode diskettes for IBM 5394 and 5494 remote work station controllers	1-800-334-1089
Obtain microcode diskettes for 3812 and 3816 printers	1-800-247-7118
Software warranty service	1-800-237-5511
New license software and hardware products (AS/400 catalog sales)	1-800-IBM-CALL (426-2255)
AS/400 CD-ROM sales	1-800-926-0364, option 3
AS/400 Support Family (includes SupportLine and marketing support)	1-800-274-0015
IBM Solution Manager	1-800-426-4260
IBM software version release upgrades and publications	1-800-879-2755
IBM education	1-800-IBM-TEACh (426-8323)
IBM direct, to order supplies	1-800 IBM-2468 (426-2468)
IBM publications	1-800-879-2755
IBM FAX information service	1-800-IBM-4FAX 426-4329
Lexmark printer technical support	(606) 232-3000
Certified Psychics Hotline (Group of palm readers and tarot card dealers who can predict when your next disk outage will occur)	1-900-888-4467

APPENDIX A: INITIAL INSTALLATION CHECKLIST

Use the following basic checklist to help you perform an initial installation of your AS/400 system.

Description	Comments	X
Install console terminal and system printer.	Only install console and system printer. Do not install any other devices until finished with initial installation procedures.	

Confirm delivery, all hardware and software installed. Use following commands to help:
   GO LICPGM - Licensed Programs
   DSPSFWRSC - Print List of Software
   WRKHDWPRD - Rack Configuration
	Print copy of rack configuration and installed Licensed Programs.
	
	Start a System Log Book.	

Verify your alternate IPL tape device.	Make sure that the designated alternate IPL tape device is correct for your MULIC or FULIC tape media.	
Decide if you are to configure Checksum or user ASPs.	Configure checksumming or user ASPs now, before continuing.	

Set system values. At least check the following:
   QDATE
   QTIME
   QAUTOCFG - ON or OFF
   QALWOBJRST - set to *ALL
   QCMNRCYLMT - set to 2 5
   QCTLSBSD - QBASE or QCTL
   QDEVNAMING
   QSPCENV - S/36 or Native
   QLMTSECOFR - 1 or 0
   QSECURITY - 10, 20, 30, or 40
	Many system values can be accessed and changed using the SETUP menu. Enter the command **GO SETUP.**
	
	Refer to the first section of this book, **AS/400 Power Tips & Techniques,** and the **AS/400 Work Management** manual for additional information.	

Change passwords of IBM-supplied user profiles.	Use the SETUP menu. Enter the command **GO SETUP.** Refer to Change Passwords for IBM-Supplied User Profiles on page 45.	

Description	Comments	X
Verify Network Attributes. Ensure that you have set the following: System Name Local Net ID Local Control Point Name Local Location Name	Use the command **CHGNETA.**	
Verify Electronic Customer Support contact information is set up.	Use the command **WRKCNTINF.**	
If you have OfficeVision/400 installed, follow the initialization procedures.	Refer to the **AS/400 Managing OfficeVision/400** manual.	
Set up the Operational Assistant including: Administration (enroll users) Auto-cleanup Backup list	Take appropriate options on the Operational Assistant menu. Use the Help key and the **AS/400 System Operation** manual. Access menu with the **GO ASSIST** command.	
Apply Cumulative PTF Package.	Refer to **AS/400 System Operation** manual for instructions.	
Save the entire system: Access the save menu **GO SAVE.** Take option 21.	Place the QSYSOPR message queue in break mode before running the save: **CHGMSGQ QSYSOPR DLVRY(*BREAK)**	
IPL the system.	Use the POWER menu. Enter the command **GO POWER.** Take option 4.	

APPENDIX B: SOFTWARE UPGRADE CHECKLIST

Checklist for Planning for your New Release. The following information is available in the **AS/400 Software Installation** manual. I advise that users refer to this manual in preparation for software installation or upgrade.

The following list contains tasks that can be done days, or even a few weeks, before you schedule the time to install the new release on your system. For a complete description of each task, refer to the **AS/400 Software Installation** manual.

Task	Level of Importance	When to Complete
Review information.	Recommended	When convenient
Verify your order and release level.	Recommended	When you receive the release
Prepare to install AS/400 softcopy manuals.	Recommended	When convenient
Check media integrity.	Optional	When you receive the release
Permanently apply PTFs.	Optional	When convenient
Check disk storage space requirements.	Recommended	1 to 2 days before installation
Choose automatic or manual installation.	Required	When convenient
Estimate installation time.	Recommended	When convenient
Save and delete changes to IBM-supplied objects.	Recommended	1 to 2 days before installation
Verify entries in the system distribution directory.	Recommended	Same day as installation
Gather performance information.	Optional	1 to 2 weeks before installation
Order the current cumulative PTF package.	Recommended	1 to 2 weeks before installation
Evaluate the release level interoperability for systems in a network.	Recommended	When convenient
Save the system.	Recommended	1 to 2 days before installation
Prepare the tape drive.	Recommended	Same day

APPENDIX C: CUSTOMIZING YOUR SIGN-ON DISPLAY

To customize and use a sign-on display file, copy and then modify the IBM-supplied source code for the sign-on display that is shipped with your system. Before you attempt this, you should be familiar with application tools such as Screen Design Aid (SDA)and Source Entry Utility (SEU).

1. Copy the QDSIGNON member from QGPL/QDDSSRC file to a new source file, such as QDDSSRC in your own library. Give it a new name, such as, NEWSIGNON.

    ```
    CPYF FROMFILE(QGPL/QDDSSRC) TOFILE(libname/QDDSSRC) FROMMBR(QDSIGNON)
         TOMBR(NEWSIGNON) MBROPT(*ADD) CRTFILE(*YES)
    ```

2. Use SDA or SEU to add whatever code you wish to the NEWSIGNON source member. The code you add should come **AFTER** the IBM-supplied code. You may change the **LOCATION** of the IBM-supplied fields, but you **MUST NOT** change the **ORDER**, the **SIZE**, or the **NAMES** of the fields.

3. Create the display file. I suggest using the same name as the new source member NEWSIGNON and that you place your new sign-on display file in library QGPL. Do not name the new sign-on display QDSIGNON.

    > *The IBM-supplied display file QSYS/QDSIGNON, must be left alone. DO NOT DELETE IT, DO NOT REPLACE IT.*

    > *When you create the display file, specify **MAXDEV(256)** rather than the default (1).*
    >
    > *If you fail to do this, you could bring the system to its knees because message queues fill up at an alarming rate and you will not be a happy camper.*

4. Test your new sign-on display.

    a. Change the subsystem description to use the new sign-on display. Usually, this is either QBASE or QINTER, but it could be any subsystem on your AS/400.

        ```
        CHGSBSD QINTER SGNDSPF(QGPL/NEWSIGNON)
        ```

    b. End the subsystem and restart it to use the new sign-on display. If the subsystem QBASE is the controlling subsystem, you must IPL the system. If you paid attention to earlier suggestions in this book, then your controlling subsystem is QCTL, which will allow to end and restart subsystem QINTER.

        ```
        ENDSBS QINTER
        STRSBS QINTER
        ```

APPENDIX D: ADDING A "NEWS LINE" TO THE SIGN-ON SCREEN

One advantage to a customized sign-on screen is the ability to add a single line of "site news." This could advise users of scheduled system downtime or other information that changes frequently enough that you don't want to change the sign-on screen DDS for it. This feature is implemented by adding a MSGID entry to the DDS, which can appear anywhere on the screen. In testing, the same position as the IBM field QSNERROR was used. The following line was added at the end of the DDS, using SEU:

```
A N02   MSGLINE    80A  0 24  1MSGID(USR0001
    QGPL/USRMSGF)
A                            DSPATR(HI)
```

> **CAUTION**: *Do not change the original IBM source code. As stated in the instructions for Customizing Your Sign-On Display, you should be working with a copy of the original source code. Refer to Appendix C: Customizing Your Sign-On Display on page 327.*

As the QSNERROR field uses indicator 02 to turn it on, the program uses the negated indicator (N02) to allow the two fields to use the one screen location. The effect of this entry is to cause the first-level text of message USR0001 from message file USRMSGF in library QGPL to display on line 24, starting at column 1, unless indicator 02 is on. The DSPATR(HI) keyword highlights the line.

To create the message file and message text, the following commands are used:

```
CRTMSGF MSGF(QGPL/USRMSGF) TEXT('Test message file for +
    signon screen')
ADDMSGD MSGID(USR0001) MSGF(QGPL/USRMSGF) +
    TEXT('This line of text will appear on the +
    signon screens')
CRTDSPF FILE(QGPL/SIGNON) SRCFILE(QGPL/QDDSSRC) +
    MAXDEV(256)
```

For this test, we named the sign-on DDS source member SIGNON. The next step is to change the sign-on file for QINTER:

```
CHGSBSD SBSD(QGPL/QINTER) SGNDSPF(QGPL/SIGNON)
```

This change takes effect when QINTER is restarted. To change the one-line message, all that is required is to use the CHGMSGD command:

```
CHGMSGD MSGID(USR0001) MSGF(QGPL/USRMSGF) +
    TEXT('Here is some new text')
```

The change occurs as soon as the change command is processed. Note that this does not change the display on screens already showing the sign-on screen, but the new message is picked up when the screen is next displayed. Also note that the sign-on screen does not support the second-level text of the message description.

OTHER USES FOR A NEWS LINE ON THE SIGN-ON DISPLAY

This method could be used to provide a number of different messages on the sign-on screen. Different fields, each with a different message ID, could be used for different categories of messages, such as operating hours or coming events. However, it is not possible to change the appearance of the message (e.g., color, highlighting) without altering the display file. The main disadvantage with having to change the display file is that the new file is not displayed until the subsystem is restarted, which means that all users have to sign off. Changing the message description can be done without affecting work on the system.

Depending on local requirements, the news message could be placed anywhere on the screen. In that case, there is no need to qualify the field with the N02 indicator as in the example above.

APPENDIX E: AS/400 JOB LOGS AND OUTPUT QUEUE UTILITY

The procedures in this appendix step you through the creation of an automated output queue utility for AS/400 job logs.

AS/400 JOB LOGS

All jobs that run on the AS/400 — be they interactive sessions, batch jobs, or subsystem monitors — produce a job log. A job log is a spooled output file, containing:

- The commands in the job.
- The commands in a CL program if the CL program was created with the LOG(*YES) option (or other methods of achieving the same effect).
- All messages (first- and second-level message text) sent to the requester and not removed from the program message queue.

These job logs are useful tools in determining the cause of a problem, either programming errors or some problem deeper within the system. However, they can easily accumulate on the system if not managed.

REASONS FOR JOB LOG MANAGEMENT

There are several reasons to prevent the number of job logs from accumulating within the system.

- Reducing the number of jobs within the system. Whenever a job has spooled output, OS/400 must keep track of that job. Therefore, keeping job logs for longer than necessary impacts system performance.
- Reducing the number of spool files. By keeping unnecessary spool files, the amount of space occupied by spooling is greater than really needed.
- Speeding access time to spooled job logs. The more output files spooled on an output queue, the longer commands such as WRKOUTQ take to execute.

There are a number of reasons why job logs should not be allowed to accumulate on the system. Likewise, there is no reason why they should be printed as a matter of course. This is a waste of system resources and paper.

The only time it is necessary to refer to the log of a completed job is when there is a problem: either a job did not work properly or, in the analysis of a system problem, you have been directed to look at the job log. It is important in this situation that the job logs contain as much information as possible, and that the correct log can be found quickly. Note that, while a job is running, the job log can be examined by the DSPJOBLOG command. This is often a good means of testing programs during the debugging phase.

LOG PARAMETER ON JOB DESCRIPTIONS

You can control the information written to the job log. The LOG parameter on the job description consists of three values:

- Message level
- Message severity
- Message text level

See the *AS/400 Work Management* manual for more information.

The first value, message level, ranges from 0 (no data is logged) to 4 (all requests and all messages greater than the specified severity level).

The second value, message severity, specifies the minimum severity level that causes error messages to be written to the log, and varies from 0 to 99.

The third value, message text level, specifies the level of message text that is entered in the log. *NOLIST is a good choice here, as no job log is produced if the job ends normally. If the job end code is 20 or greater, a log is produced with the first- and second-level message text included.

The IBM-supplied job descriptions QBASE, QCTL, QINTER, and QPGMR all have a log level of LOG(4 0 *NOLIST).

WHERE DOES THE JOB LOG GO?

Job log printing is via the system-supplied printer file QPJOBLOG, in library QSYS. The OUTQ parameter specifies where the job log is queued when the job is completed. This can be overridden to any output queue.

When a job starts, a job log file is opened on the job log output queue. This can be examined using the DSPJOBLOG command. When the job finishes, this spooled output file is either deleted or kept. If the log level parameter on the job description specified *NOLIST, the log is deleted when:

- For interactive jobs, the default signoff on *NOLIST is used. (Note that an interactive job is deemed to end normally if the user enters a SIGNOFF command, irrespective of whether commands issued during the session may have ended in error.)
- For batch jobs, the job ended normally.

For an interactive job to keep its job log after the session finishes, either the user must SIGNOFF with *LIST, or the logging level must be changed using the CHGJOB command. A batch job keeps its job log if the job does not end normally.

THE OPERATIONAL ASSISTANT

With OS/400 there is a feature called the Operational Assistant, introduced with V1R3. The Operational Assistant provides, among other things, an automated cleanup of message queues, system journals, and logs based on defined values. When the Operational Assistant cleanup process is active, jog logs are directed to the output queue QEZJOBLOG in the library QUSRSYS, and all job logs older than a set number of days are deleted each time cleanup is run. If you are using the Operational Assistant, then you may elect to use it to clean up your job logs. On the other hand, the utility defined in this section offers some additional enhancements that you may want to incorporate. Refer to Operational Assistant on page 83.

WHAT THE UTILITY PROGRAM DOES

The Change Job Log Output Queue program CHGJOBLOGQ is designed to switch job log output queues to a separate queue for each day. There is one queue for each day of the week. After the seventh day, when the first day of the week recurs, the log is cleared before new logs are queued to it. This process continues for every day of the week. Therefore, only seven days' worth of logs are kept, and the size of each output queue is minimized as only one day's worth of logs are kept there.

The program uses a data area to ensure that it is run only once per day. Even if the system is restarted, the job logs from jobs that completed earlier in that day are not erased. The utility program RTVDAT is used to determine the name of the day, and that name is used to construct the output queue name. See Objects Used on page 336 for details of the objects used by CHGJOBLOGQ.

HOW TO ENSURE THE PROGRAM RUNS

There are a number of ways to ensure that CHGJOBLOGQ runs each day. The best way is to add a CALL JOBLOG/CHGJOBLOGQ to the existing autostart job for QCTL. Another way is to make it the initial program for QSYSOPR, if the system operator signs on each day, or submitting it to QBATCH automatically.

The QCTL autostart job is recommended as the best method, as this ensures that the program is called whenever the system is started, and that it runs as one of the first jobs on the system that day. This presumes that QCTL is restarted each morning.

Note that, if job logs are being managed as part of the Operational Assistant cleanup process, then the program does not change the QPJOBLOG printer file, create output queues, or clear any output queues. The Operational Assistant maintains a data area, QOADTAARA, in library QUSRSYS. This data area is created when the cleanup parameters are first specified. The values of interest in this data area are:

- Position 1. Y if cleanup is active.

- Positions 16 through 20. Number of days to retain joblogs; *NONE if job logs are not to be deleted automatically.

> **WARNING:** **Using this data area to obtain information about the Operational Assistant cleanup operations is an unsupported interface. While this works on V1R3, there is no guarantee that it will continue to work with future releases of OS/400.**

If the data area indicates that the Operational Assistant is managing job logs, then the program exits without changing any output queues, data areas, or the QPJOBLOG printer file. A program message is sent to the user stating this.

PROGRAM LISTING FOR CHGJOBLOGQ

The listing of the CL source code for the CHGJOBLOGQ program is shown below.

```
        PGM
/************************************************************/

/*   This program should form part of the normal daily     */
/*   "Startup" program, either as part of the controlling   */
/*   subsystem Autostart job, or manually started by the    */
/*   system operator.                                       */
/*                                                          */
/*   The aim of this program is to prevent joblogs from     */
/*   accumulating in the system, by having a different      */
/*   joblog                                                 */
/*   output queue for each day of the week, with the queue  */
/*   cleared at the start of each day. This program calls    */
/*   the utility "RTVDAT" to get the name of the day of the */
/*   week.                                                  */
/*                                                          */
/*   The program first determines whether the output queue */
/*   has already been changed that day, and if not, gets    */
/*   the day of week name using RTVDAT.                     */
/*   The new output queue is cleared, or created if it does */
/*   not exist. The system supplied printer file, QPJOBLOG, */
/*   is changed to point to this output queue. If all works,*/
/*   the data area containing the date is updated. This data*/
/*   area, JOBLOG/QCLSRTDAT is created if it cannot be      */
/*   found. The output queues are named:                    */
/*            HKOQxxxJOB   in library QUSRSYS               */
/*   where "xxx" is the first three characters of the name  */
/*   of the day of the week.                                */
/*                                                          */
/*   If Operational Assistant is responsible for clearing   */
/*   up joblogs, the program will not change the joblog     */
/*   output queue.                                          */
```

```
/*                                                           */
/*                                                           */
/*---------------------------------------------------------*/
/***********************************************************/
          DCL       VAR(&SYSDAT) TYPE(*CHAR) LEN(6)
          DCL       VAR(&LSTDAT) TYPE(*CHAR) LEN(6)
          DCL       VAR(&SPLDAY) TYPE(*CHAR) LEN(3)
          DCL       VAR(&JLOUTQ) TYPE(*CHAR) LEN(10)
          DCL       VAR(&OADATA) TYPE(*CHAR) LEN(25)
/***********************************************************/
/*  Now see if Operational Assistant is looking after      */
/*  joblogs.                                                */
/***********************************************************/
          RTVDTAARA DTAARA(QUSRSYS/QOADTAARA (1 25)) +
                      RTNVAR(&OADATA)
          MONMSG    MSGID(CPF0000) EXEC(GOTO CMDLBL(CHKDATE))
          IF        COND((%SST(&OADATA 1 1) *EQ 'N') *OR +
                      (%SST(&OADATA 16 5) *EQ '*KEEP')) +
                      THEN(GOTO CMDLBL(CHKDATE))
          SNDPGMMSG MSG('Job log output queue not +
                      changed. Operational Assistant is +
                      managing job logs')
          GOTO      CMDLBL(ERROR)
                    /* Bypass rest of pgm    */
/***********************************************************/
/*     Now get today's date, & compare it to the value saved /
/*     in the data area QCLSTRDAT from the last execution.  */
/***********************************************************/
CHKDATE:  RTVSYSVAL SYSVAL(QDATE) RTNVAR(&SYSDAT)
          RTVDTAARA DTAARA(JOBLOG/QCTLSTRDAT) RTNVAR(&LSTDAT)
          MONMSG    MSGID(CPF0000) EXEC(DO)
          CHGVAR    VAR(&LSTDAT) VALUE('000000')
          CRTDTAARA DTAARA(JOBLOG/QCTLSTRDAT) +
                      TYPE(*CHAR) LEN(6) VALUE(&SYSDAT) +
                      TEXT('Last joblog output queue +
                      change date')
          ENDDO
          IF        COND(&LSTDAT *NE &SYSDAT) +
                      THEN(GOTO CMDLBL(GETDATE))
          SNDPGMMSG MSG('Job log output queue not +
                      changed. CHGJOBLOGQ has already +
                      run today')
          GOTO      CMDLBL(ERROR)   /* Bypass rest of pgm*/
/***********************************************************/
/* Construct output queue name from &SPLDAY, then clear the */
/* queue (creating it if it doesn't exist).                */
/***********************************************************/
GETDATE:  ADDLIBLE  LIB(TAATOOL)
          TAATOOL/RTVDAT DAY3U(&SPLDAY)
          RMVLIBLE  LIB(TAATOOL)
          CHGVAR    VAR(&JLOUTQ) +
                      VALUE('HKOQ' *CAT &SPLDAY *CAT +
                      'JOB')
```

```
              CLROUTQ     OUTQ(&JLOUTQ)
              MONMSG      MSGID(CPF3357) +
                            EXEC(CRTOUTQ +
                            OUTQ(QUSRSYS/&JLOUTQ) +
                            TEXT('Job logs for ' *CAT &SPLDAY))
/**********************************************************/
/*    Finally change QPJOBLOG, and update the data area.   */
/**********************************************************/
              CHGPRTF     FILE(QPJOBLOG) OUTQ(QUSRSYS/&JLOUTQ)
              MONMSG      MSGID(CPF0000) EXEC(DO)
              SNDPGMMSG   MSG('Error in CHGPRTF command')
              GOTO        CMDLBL(ERROR)
              ENDDO
              CHGDTAARA   DTAARA(JOBLOG/QCTLSTRDAT) +
                            VALUE(&SYSDAT)
              MONMSG      MSGID(CPF1015) EXEC(CRTDTAARA +
                            DTAARA(JOBLOG/QCTLSTRDAT) +
                            TYPE(*CHAR) +
                            LEN(6) VALUE(&SYSDAT) +
                            TEXT('Last joblog output queue +
                              change date'))

/**********************************************************/
/* Send a successful completion message before exiting.    */
/**********************************************************/
              SNDPGMMSG   MSG('Job log output queue ' +
                            *CAT &JLOUTQ *CAT ' cleared and +
                            QPJOBLOG print file + chaged.')
              GOTO        CMDLBL(ENDCHG)

/**********************************************************/
/*     Arrggghhh!  Something went wrong...                 */
/**********************************************************/
ERROR:        SNDPGMMSG   MSGID(CPF9898) MSGF(QCPFMSG) +
                            MSGDTA('Job log output queue not +
                            changed. See previous errors in +
                            job log') MSGTYPE(*ESCAPE)
/**********************************************************/
ENDCHG:       RETURN
              ENDPGM
```

OBJECTS USED

CHGJOBLOGQ uses a number of objects:

HKOQxxxJOB   Seven output queues, one for each day of the week. The
                 xxx is replaced by the first three characters of the day
                 name (e.g., HKOQMONJOB). The output queues are
                 kept in the QUSRSYS library, and are created if they do
                 not exist when first required.

QCTLSTRDAT   A data area, stored in the JOBLOG library, that contains the date when the program was last run. Used to prevent the output queues from being cleared twice in one day. Again, this data area is created if it is not found when accessed.

RTVDAT   Utility that provides the text representation for the day of the week. This is part of the QUSRTOOL library. Refer to QUSRTOOL Library on page 307 for information on using QUSRTOOL commands and functions.

APPENDIX F: AUTOMATED JOURNAL MANAGEMENT

If you are using the Operational Assistant, do not use this procedure to maintain the IBM-supplied system journals. You may run into conflicts. You should, however, maintain your own application journals and the IBM system journal QAUDJRN (security auditing journal).

This sample program was written back in Version 1 days. The names of the IBM journals have changed since then. Refer to Journals on page 106 for the current list of IBM system journals. The primary purpose for leaving this program in place is to provide an example for managing any journals. For example, you might want to use the program to manage your journals — just substitute the journal names used in the program with the journal names you want to manage.

JRNMGMT SAMPLE CL PROGRAM

Create the following CL Program. Call it JRNMGMT.

```
/* AUTOMATIC JOURNAL MANAGEMENT PROGRAM           */
/*                                                */
/*  PROGRAM NAME: JRNMGMT                         */
/*  DISCLAIMER:  Evaluate the applicability of this  */
/*  program in your environment.                  */
/*                                                */
/*  AUTOMATIC JOURNAL MANAGEMENT                  */

/*  WARNING: Do not try to use this program to    */
/*  manage system journals (QAOSDIAJRN, QSNADS,   */
/*  QDSNX, QSXJRN) if Operational Assistant       */
/*  "automatic cleanup" functions are started. The  */
/*   program will work for all user defined journals */
/*   which comply with the guidelines specified in  */
/*   the following documentation.                 */
/*                                                */
/*  For this program to work properly, you must have  */
/*  followed the instructions which are attached to  */
/*  the end of this program listing.  Please follow  */
/*  them before running this program.             */
/*                                                */
/*  This program monitors for message CPF7099     */
/*  (Journal Receiver threshold has been reached)  */
/*   in MSGQ: JRNMSGQ in QUSRSYS for any journal  */
/*   receiver.  When the message is received the  */
/*   journal is changed, saved to a save file in  */
/*   QGPL and the journal receiver is deleted.    */
/*                                                */
/*  The system JOURNAL RECEIVERS must be changed  */
/*  to a threshold value other than *NONE.  The   */
/*  system JOURNALS must have been changed to send  */
/*  the message to MSGQ: JRNMSGQ in QUSRSYS       */
```

```
          /****************************************************/
          PGM

          DCL       VAR(&JRN) TYPE(*CHAR) LEN(10)
/*                  Journal name */
          DCL       VAR(&JRNLIB) TYPE(*CHAR) LEN(10)
/*                  Journal library name        */
          DCL       VAR(&RCV) TYPE(*CHAR) LEN(10)
/*                  Journal receiver name        */
          DCL       VAR(&RCVLIB) TYPE(*CHAR) LEN(10)
/*                  Journal receiver lib name    */
          DCL       VAR(&MSGID) TYPE(*CHAR) LEN(7)
/*                  Message ID from JRNMSGQ MSGQ*/
          DCL       VAR(&STRING) TYPE(*CHAR) LEN(40)
/* String to hold message data (1-10) = Journal name */
/* 11-20 = Journal library name: (21-30) = Journal   */
/* receiver name: (31-40) = Journal recevier library */
/*   name)                                     */

/* Ensure JRNMSGQ exists in QUSRSYS                   */
          CHKOBJ    OBJ(QUSRSYS/JRNMSGQ) +
                    OBJTYPE(*MSGQ)
          MONMSG    MSGID(CPF9801) EXEC(CRTMSGQ +
                    MSGQ(QUSRSYS/JRNMSGQ) +
                    TEXT('MSGQ to receive +
                    JRNRCV threshold messages'))
/*    Create the message queue if not present         */

/* Examine messages which appear in JRNMSGQ           */
RCV:      RCVMSG    MSGQ(QUSRSYS/JRNMSGQ) +
                    WAIT(*MAX) MSGDTA(&STRING) +
                    MSGID(&MSGID)
          IF        COND(&MSGID *EQ 'CPF7099') +
                    THEN(DO)

/* CPF7099 - Journal receiver &RCV in &LIB threshold */
/* exceeded.  Processing will continue               */

/* If message is CPF7099 set values from &MSGDTA     */
          CHGVAR    VAR(&JRN) +
                    VALUE(%SST(&STRING 1 10))
          CHGVAR    VAR(&JRNLIB) +
                    VALUE(%SST(&STRING 11 10))
          CHGVAR    VAR(&RCV) +
                    VALUE(%SST(&STRING 21 10))
          CHGVAR    VAR(&RCVLIB) +
                    VALUE(%SST(&STRING 31 10))

/* Detach current receiver and attach a new one      */
          CHGJRN    JRN(&JRNLIB/&JRN) JRNRCV(*GEN)

/* Create a SAVF in QGPL with same name as journal    */
/*   receiver                                         */
```

```
            CRTSAVF    FILE(QGPL/&RCV)

/*  Save the journal receiver in the SAVF              */
            SAVOBJ     OBJ(&RCV) LIB(&RCVLIB)  +
                       DEV(*SAVF)  +
                       OBJTYPE(*JRNRCV)  +
                       SAVF(QGPL/&RCV) DTACPR(*YES)

/*  Delete the old journal receiver                    */
            DLTJRNRCV  JRNRCV(&RCVLIB/&RCV)

/*  Send instructions to QSYSOPR                       */
            SNDPGMMSG  MSG('Journal Receiver'  +
                       *BCAT &RCV *BCAT 'in'  +
                       *BCAT &RCVLIB *BCAT  +
                       'reached its threshold  +
                       value and was placed in a  +
                       save file named'  +
                       *BCAT &RCV *BCAT 'in library  +
                       QGPL.  You should now use  +
                       the SAVSAVFDTA command to  +
                       save the save file and  +
                       then delete it from QGPL.  +
                       Journaling continues for  +
                       journal' *BCAT &JRN *TCAT  +
                       '.') TOMSGQ(*SYSOPR)
        ENDDO

/*  Return to get next message from JRNMSGQ            */
            GOTO       CMDLBL(RCV)
            ENDPGM
```

SETUP INSTRUCTIONS FOR **JRNMGMT**

The CRTJRNRCV (Create Journal Receiver) command has a THRESHOLD value whose default is *NONE, which means the receiver keeps growing in size until someone manually does a CHRJRN command to "detach" the old receiver and "attach" a new one. The old receiver may then be saved and deleted to free up the space it was using on the system. This set of instructions and the associated program automate the journal management function and keep the size of these receivers from getting out of hand.

What to Do

Follow these instructions to prepare your system for automatic journal management.

1. Enter the CL source code on the AS/400 and compile the program called JRNMGMT.

2. Use the submit job command to run the program as a batch job. Check your batch subsystem description (e.g., DSPSBSD QBATCH options 1 and 6) to make sure the number of active jobs (MAXJOBS) is more than one and the

active jobs permitted to run from the JOBQ (MAXACT) is more than one. Make adjustments using the CHGSBSD and CHGJOBQE commands, as necessary.

```
SBMJOB    CMD(CALL PGM(JRNMGMT)) JOB(JRNMGMT)
```

3. Follow the instructions under Setting Up JRNMGMT as an Autostart Job, on page 346 so the program JRNMGMT (created in step 1) starts each time QBATCH starts.

How to Set Up Your System to Automatically Manage Journals

To set up automatic journal management, follow these steps:

1. Create a message queue called JRNMSGQ in library QUSRSYS.

```
CRTMMSGQ (QUSRSYS/JRNMSGQ) TEXT('MSGQ for CPF7099
    Jrnrcv threshold reached')
```

> This step is unnecessary if the JRNMGMT program has already been run because JRNMGMT creates a message queue named JRNMSGQ in QUSRSYS if the message queue does not yet exist.

2. Use the following command to get an idea of the size of your existing journal receivers. Write down the largest sizes for future reference. The xxxx is a four-digit number.

```
DSPOBJD    OBJ(-libname-/*ALL) OBJTYPE(*JRNRCV)
```

You can use *ALL for libname to see all journal receivers on the system. Ignore the system-supplied receivers in QUSRSYS named QAOSDIxxxx, QDSNXxxxx, QSNADSxxxx, and QSXJRNxxxx as these are maintained by the Operational Assistant.

This is an example of what the screen looks like (there is at least one screen for every library that contains a journal receiver).

```
  .......      Display Object Description ----   - Basic    --
                                                   Library 1 of 1
  Library:   -libname-                          ..............
  Type options, press Enter.                    ..............
    5=Display full attributes   8=Display service attributes
  Opt  Object      Type    Attribute  Freed   Size   Text
       ITEMMA0001  *JRNRCV             NO    630996   Item Master
       CUSTMA0002  *JRNRCV             NO  28532736   Customer Master
       PAYOUT0001  *JRNRCV             NO     65782   Accounts Payable




                                                        Bottom
  F3=Exit   F12=Cancel   F17=Top   F18=Bottom
```

3. Enter the following commands and write down the attached journal receiver name for each journal. Each receiver name has a four-digit number at the end (xxxx).

```
                                       Receiver name:
WRKJRNA    JRN(ITEMMAST)          _____
WRKJRNA    JRN(CUSTMAST)          _____
WRKJRNA    JRN(PAYOUT)            _____
```

The following is a sample screen for PAYOUT.

```
                       Work with Journal Attributes
   Journal . . . . . :   PAYOUT        Library . . . . . :  ACCTNG
   Auxiliary storage pool . . . . . . . :  1
   Message queue . . . . . . . . . . . :   QSYSOPR
     Library . . . . . . . . . . . . :      *LIBL
   Text . . . . . . . . :   JOURNAL FOR ACCTS PAYABLE
   Type options, press Enter.
     8=Display attributes
           --------Attached--------
   Option   Receiver      Library
            PAYOUT0001    ACCTNG




                                                       Bottom
   F3=Exit   F12=Cancel   F13=Display journaled files
   F14=Display journaled access paths  F15=Work with receiver directory
```

4. Use the following commands to create new journal receivers with a threshold level set. Notice that the sequential number on the end of the receiver name (xxxy) is one number higher than the attached receiver.

```
CRTJRNRCV   JRNRCV(ACCTNG/CUSTMA0002) THRESHOLD(1000) +
    TEXT('JOURNAL FOR CUST MASTER')
CRTJRNRCV   JRNRCV(ACCTNG/ITEMMA0003) THRESHOLD(1000) +
    TEXT('JOURNAL FOR PROBLEM DATA BASE')
CRTJRNRCV   JRNRCV(ACCTNG/PAYOUT0002) THRESHOLD(100) +
    TEXT('JOURNAL FOR ACCTS PAYABLE')
```

> *The threshold values (in kilobytes) specified in this example are arbitrary values based on the size of the receivers in step 2 (above). Adjust them according to your best "guess-timate" of how quickly you feel your receivers will fill up.*

5. Change the journal to attach to the new receiver you just created, and change the message queue parameter to send threshold messages to message queue JRNMSGQ.

> *Use the same values for xxxy as in step 4 (above).*

```
CHGJRN JRN(ACCTNG/CUSTMAST) +
    JRNRCV(ACCTNG/CUSTMA0002) +
    MSGQ(QUSRSYS/JRNMSGQ)
CHGJRN JRN(ACCTNG/ITEMMA0003) +
    JRNRCV(ACCTNG/ITEMMA0003) +
    MSGQ(QUSRSYS/JRNMSGQ)
CHGJRN JRN(QUSRSYS/QSNADS) +
    JRNRCV(ACCTNG/PAYOUT0002) +
    MSGQ(QUSRSYS/JRNMSGQ)
```

6. The "example" journals have now been modified to run under the automatic management program. You can save all the old receivers with these commands.

```
CRTSAVF FILE(QGPL/CUSTMAST)
SAVOBJ OBJ(CUSTMA*) LIB(ACCTNG) DEV(*SAVF) OBJTYPE(*JRNRCV)
    SAVF(QGPL/CUSTMAST) DTACPR(*YES)
CRTSAVF FILE(QGPL/ITEMMAST)
SAVOBJ OBJ(ITEMMA*) LIB(ACCTNG) DEV(*SAVF) OBJTYPE(*JRNRCV)
    SAVF(QGPL/ITEMMAST) DTACPR(*YES)
CRTSAVF FILE(QGPL/PAYOUT)
SAVOBJ OBJ(PAYOUT*) LIB(ACCTNG) DEV(*SAVF) OBJTYPE(*JRNRCV)
    SAVF(QGPL/PAYOUT) DTACPR(*YES)
```

7. At this point you could save the save-file-data (SAVSAVFDTA command) and then delete the Save files. Here is an example of the SAVSAVFDTA and DLTF commands.

```
SAVSAVFDTA SAVF(QGPL/CUSTMAST) DEV(-device name-)
DLTF FILE(QGPL/CUSTMAST)
```

8. Use the following to determine the names of the receivers that are not attached and are still on the system.

```
WRKJRNA JRN(ACCTNG/CUSTMAST)
WRKJRNA JRN(ACCTNG/ITEMMAST)
WRKJRNA JRN(ACCTNG/PAYOUT)
```

Press F15 (Work with Receiver Directory) for each of the WRKJRNA commands (above). These receivers were saved in step 6. Use option 4 to delete all receivers except the one that has a status of "attached."

If you receive message CPA7025 (Receiver rrrrrrrrr in QUSRSYS never fully saved), it means you have not saved this receiver yet. If you take the I option (ignore), it deletes the receiver anyway.

This is an example of the Work with Receiver Directory screen.

```
                    Work with Receiver Directory

Journal . . . . . :  PAYOUT        Library . . . . . :  ACCTNG
Total size of receivers . . . . . . . . . . . . . . . :  999424
Type options, press Enter.
  4=Delete   8=Display attributes

                                    Attach          Save
Opt  Number  Receiver   Library    Date    Status   Date
 _   01001   PAYOUT0001  ACCTNG    09/13/89 PARTIAL  11/11/90
 _   01002   PAYOUT0002  ACCTNG    12/05/89 ONLINE   12/15/90
 _   01003   PAYOUT0003  ACCTNG    12/05/89 ATTACHED 01/10/91          .




                                                     Bottom

F3=Exit   F5=Refresh   F11=Display size   F12=Cancel
```

Summary

Your system is now ready to handle each journal receiver automatically as it reaches its threshold. The system operator will be notified each time a CPF7099 message (Journal receiver threshold reached) is received. The only steps the operator needs to take are to save the save-file data (SAVSAVFDTA) to external media for the Save file specified in the message, and then delete the Save file (using the DLTF command) from QGPL.

This is a typical message that occurs in the QSYSOPR message queue:

```
                     Display Messages

                                 System:   SYS400C4
Queue . . . . . :  QSYSOPR       Program . . . . :   *DSPMSG
 Library . . . :   QSYS           Library . . . :
Severity . . . :  10             Delivery . . . :   *HOLD
 From . . . :  JWL      12/06/89   15:30:10
 Journal Receiver PAYOUT0002 in ACCTNG reached its threshold value and
   was placed in a save file named PAYOUT0002 in library QGPL. You
   should now use the SAVSAVFDTA command to save the save file and then
   delete it from QGPL. Journaling continues for journal PAYOUT.



                                                     Bottom

F3=Exit           F10=Display all      F11=Remove a message
F12=Cancel        F13=Remove all       F16=Remove all except unanswered
```

Setting Up JRNMGMT as an Autostart Job

Use the following to setup JRNMGMT as an autostart job:

1. Display the subsystem description menu for QBATCH.

    ```
    DSPSBSD    SBSD(QBATCH)
    ```

    > If you are using QBASE as the controlling subsystem, then substitute the name QBASE for QBATCH in these steps.

    Use menu options 1 and 6 to make sure the number of active jobs (MAXJOBS) is more than one and the active jobs permitted to run from the JOBQ (MAXACT) is more than one. Make adjustments using the CHGSBSD and CHGJOBQE commands, as necessary.

    This is an example of how to change the SBSD if MAXJOBS is set to 1 and the Job Queue Entry MAXACT is set to 1.

    ```
    CHGSBSD SBSD(QBATCH) MAXJOBS(2)
    CHGJOBQE SBSD(QBATCH) JOBQ(QBATCH) MAXACT(2)
    ```

    > You may have already done this when setting the environment to run JRNMGMT as a batch job.

2. Create a User Profile for Journal Manager Autostart Job Entry.

    ```
    CRTUSRPRF USRPRF(JRNMGR) TEXT('Journal Manager')
    ```

3. Create a Job Description for Journal Manager to use.

    ```
    CRTJOBD JOBD(SYSMGT/JRNMGMT) TEXT('Auto Journal Mgmt')
        USER(JRNMGR) RTGDTA(QCMDB) +
        RQSDTA('CALL SYSMGT/JRNMGMT')
    ```

4. Add an Autostart Job Entry to QBATCH SBSD for Journal Manager.

    ```
    ADDAJE SBSD(QBATCH) JOB(JRNMGMT) JOBD(SYSMGT/JRNMGMT)
    ```

5. Change Object Ownership of the current journal receivers to JRNMGR.

    a. Find out the names of the current journal receivers.

    ```
    DSPOBJD OBJ(*ALL/*ALL) OBJTYPE(*JRNRCV)
    ```

    The current receivers are those with the highest sequential number (suffix) shown as xxxx in this example.

```
                   Display Object Description - Basic
                                                  Library 1 of 1
Library:   ACCTNG
Type options, press Enter.
  5=Display full attributes   8=Display service attributes
Opt  Object     Type     Attribute  Freed   Size  Text
 _   CUSTMA0003  *JRNRCV              NO    667648  JOURNAL FOR CUST MA
 _   ITEMMA0004  *JRNRCV              NO     40960  JOURNAL FOR ITEM MA
 _   PAYOUT0002  *JRNRCV              NO     40960  JOURNAL FOR ACCTS P
                                                              Bottom


F3=Exit   F12=Cancel   F17=Top   F18=Bottom
                        (C) COPYRIGHT IBM CORP. 1980, 1989.
```

b. Change the object ownership to JRNMGR using the same suffixes (xxxx) you noted in step 5a.

```
CHGOBJOWN  OBJ(ACCTNG/CUSTMAxxxx) OBJTYPE(*JRNRCV) +
     NEWOWN(JRNMGR) CUROWNAUT(*REVOKE)
CHGOBJOWN  OBJ(ACCTNG/ITEMMAxxxx) OBJTYPE(*JRNRCV) +
     NEWOWN(JRNMGR) CUROWNAUT(*REVOKE)
CHGOBJOWN  OBJ(ACCTNG/PAYOUTxxxx) OBJTYPE(*JRNRCV) +
     NEWOWN(JRNMGR) CUROWNAUT(*REVOKE)
```

6. Give Journal Manager *ALL authority for the Journals.

```
GRTOBJAUT  OBJ(ACCTNG/CUSTMAST) OBJTYPE(*JRN) +
     USER(JRNMGR) AUT(*ALL)
GRTOBJAUT  OBJ(ACCTNG/ITEMMAST) OBJTYPE(*JRN) +
     USER(JRNMGR) AUT(*ALL)
GRTOBJAUT  OBJ(ACCTNG/PAYOUT) OBJTYPE(*JRN) +
     USER(JRNMGR) AUT(*ALL)
```

7. Give Journal Manager *USE authority for required commands in JRNMGMT.

```
GRTOBJAUT  OBJ(CHGJRN) OBJTYPE(*CMD) USER(JRNMGR) AUT(*USE)
GRTOBJAUT  OBJ(CRTSAVF) OBJTYPE(*CMD) USER(JRNMGR) AUT(*USE)
GRTOBJAUT  OBJ(SAVOBJ) OBJTYPE(*CMD) USER(JRNMGR) AUT(*USE) GRTOBJAUT
     OBJ(DLTJRNRCV)
OBJTYPE(*CMD) USER(JRNMGR) AUT(*USE) GRTOBJAUT OBJ(SNDPGMMSG)
     OBJTYPE(*CMD) USER(JRNMGR) AUT(*USE)
```

8. Start QBATCH subsystem, which starts JRNMGMT automatically.

```
STRSBS     SBSD(QBATCH)
```

APPENDIX G: SAMPLE UPS HANDLING PROGRAM

The following program causes the AS400 to power down in an orderly fashion if five or more power failures occur within three minutes or less. This program is for a FULL UPS. The source can be modified for use by a BASIC UPS by changing the messages that are checked by RCVMSG (a basic UPS uses MSGID CPI0994). You can test an UPS program without a real UPS by creating a simple CL program that performs a SNDPGMMSG for message IDs CPF1816 and CPF1817 (power failure messages).

Sample UPL Handling Program

```
PGM
    DCL     VAR(&MSGID) TYPE(*CHAR) LEN(7) /* MSGID recvd +
              from QUPSMSGQ */
    DCL     VAR(&WAIT) TYPE(*CHAR) LEN(5) /* Tell RCVMSG +
              how long to wait*/
    DCL     VAR(&RTNTYPE) TYPE(*CHAR) /* Used to make sure +
              that the blank message condition is not really +
              the result of SNDMSG                          */
    DCL     VAR(&COUNT)  TYPE(*DEC) LEN(2) VALUE(0) /* Used +
              to keep track of power failures              */
    DCL     VAR(&TIMEA)  TYPE(*CHAR) LEN(6) /* Current time */
    DCL     VAR(&TIMDIF) TYPE(*CHAR) LEN(5) /* Time +
              difference                                   */
    DCL     VAR(&TIMEX)  TYPE(*DEC) LEN(5) VALUE('60')
              /* Power failure time window                 */
    DCL     VAR(&FLUCT)  TYPE(*DEC) LEN(2) VALUE('5')
              /* Number funtions allowed in time window */
    DCL     VAR(&TIMEB)  TYPE(*CHAR) LEN(6)
              /* End of time window                        */
    DCL     VAR(&TIMER)  TYPE(*LGL) LEN(1) VALUE('0')
    DCL     VAR(&UPS)    TYPE(*LGL) LEN(1) VALUE('0')
    DCL     VAR(&AGAIN)  TYPE(*LGL) LEN(1) VALUE('0')

    ALCOBJ  OBJ((QGPL/QUPSMSGQ *MSGQ *EXCL))
    CLRMSGQ MSGQ(QGPL/QUPSMSGQ)
    CHGVAR  VAR(&WAIT) VALUE(*MAX)


/***************************************************************/
/* WAIT AT LABEL B: UNTIL A MESSAGE IS SENT TO QUPSMSGQ.     */
/* CPF1816 INDICATES THAT POWER FAILURE HAS OCCURRED. '     */
/* INDICATES THAT POWER HAS NOT BEEN RESTORED.  CPF1817     */
/* INDICATES THAT UTILITY POWER HAS BEEN RESTORED.          */
/***************************************************************/

B: RCVMSG MSGQ(QGPL/QUPSMSGQ) WAIT(&WAIT) MSGID(&MSGID) +
             RTNTYPE(&RTNTYPE)
    IF      COND(&MSGID *EQ 'CPF1816' *OR &MSGID *EQ +
              'CPF1817' *OR &MSGID *EQ '       ' *AND +
              &RTNTYPE *EQ '  ') THEN(DO)
```

```
RTVSYSVAL    SYSVAL(QTIME) RTNVAR(&TIMEA)
IF       COND(&TIMER) THEN(DO)
         IF       COND(&TIMEA *LT &TIMEB) +
                  THEN(TAATOOL/CLCTIMDIF +
                  FROMTIME(&TIMEA) TOTIME(&TIMEB) +
                     SECONDS(&TIMDIF))
         ELSE     (CHGVAR &TIMDIF VALUE('00000'))
         IF       COND(TIMDIF *EQ '00000') THEN(DO)
                  IF       &UPS THEN(DO)
                           SNDMSG MSG('Utility power has +
                           not returned.  The system is +
                           terminating.') TOUSR(DMA)
                           CHGVAR &AGAIN '0'
                           ENDO
                  ELSE     CMD(DO)
                           IF       COND(&COUNT *GE &FLUCT) +
                                    THEN(DO)
                                    SNDBRKMSG MSG('Power +
                                     fluctuations are +
                                     occurring.  Please sign +
                                     off your work station +
                                     immediately.') +
                                     TOMSGQ(DSP02)
                                    CHGVAR   &AGAIN '0'
                                    ENDDO
                           ELSE     DO
                                    CHGVAR   &TIMER '0'
                                    CHGVAR   &COUNT '0'
                                    CHGVAR   &WAIT  '*MAX'
                                    CHGVAR   &AGAIN '1'
                                    ENDDO
                           ENDDO
                  ENDDO
         ELSE     DO
                  IF       COND(&MSGID *EQ +
                            'CPF1816') THEN(DO)
                           CHGVAR   VAR(&COUNT) +
                              VALUE(&COUNT + 1)
                           CHGVAR   VAR(&UPS) +
                              VALUE('1')
                           ENDDO
                  ELSE     DO
                           IF COND(&MSGID *EQ +
                            'CPF1817) THEN(DO)
                              CHGVAR  &UPS +
                              VALUE('0')
                              ENDDO
                           ENDDO
                       CHGVAR   &WAIT VALUE(&TIMDIF)
                       CHGVAR   &AVAIN VALUE('1')
                       ENDDO
                  ENDDO
         ELSE     DO
```

```
                         CHGVAR  &TIMDIF VALUE(&TIMEX)
                         TAATOOL/ADDTIM  NBRSECS(&TIMEX) +
                           ENDTIM(&TIMEB)
                         CHGVAR  &COUNT VALUE(1)
                         CHGVAR  &TIMER VALUE('1')
                         CHGVAR  &UPS   VALUE('1')
                         CHGVAR  &WAIT  VALUE(&TIMDIF)
                         SNDMSG  MSG('Utility power +
                           failure has occurred.  If +
                           power is not restored within +
                           3 minutes, the system will +
                           shutdown.') TOUSR(D A)
                         ENDSBS  SBS(QINTER) +
                           OPTION(*CNTRLD) +
                           DELAY(*NOLIMIT) /* Prevent +
                             other users signing on. +
                             This may not be reqd in all +
                             environments.  */
                         MONMSG .MSGID(CPF1054)  /* It +
                             was not active */
                         MONMSG  MSGID(CPF1055)  /* It is +
                             terminating */
                         CHGVAR  *AGAIN VALUE('1')
                         ENDDO
               ENDDO
       ELSE    DO
               CHGVAR &AGAIN VALUE('1')
               ENDDO
       IF      &AGAIN GOTO B
       ELSE    DO
               SNDMSG  MSG('The system has now powered +
                   down') TOUSR (QYSOPR)   /* Test +
                   Message  */
               DCLOBJ  OBJ((QGPL/QUPSMSGQ *MSGQ *EXCL))
               PWRDWNSYS  OPTION(*CNTRLD) DELAY(30) +
                   RESTART(NO)
               ENDDO
ENDPGM
```

APPENDIX H: SYSTEM MANAGEMENT AND OPERATIONS CHECKLIST

Use the following auditing checklist to help you develop and maintain your system management and system operations procedures.

As you go through each checklist task description, evaluate its importance in your environment and assign a *weight* to the category. I recommend you use a scale of 1 to 5, where 5 is most important and 1 is least.

Once you have assigned a weight, evaluate the *use* In your environment. I recommend that you use a scale of 1 to 4, similar to rating the movies using the star system. A 1 indicates poorly done or not done at all and a 5 indicates the best with little improvement required.

Now, multiply the *weight* by the *use* to arrive at a *score*. Total the scores for each section and for the entire checklist. Use the scores to determine the areas where you should concentrate your attention for improvement.

Weight	Use	Score	Task Description
			1. BACKUP/RECOVERY
			1.1. User Aux Stg Pools (ASP) implemented
			1.2. Commitment control
			1.3. Checksum implemented
			1.4. DASD Mirroring (V1R3)
			1.5. Backup procedures
			Documented
			Correct MULIC Tape (location)
			SYSVALs
			Device configuration
			Updated for new/changed applications
			1.6. Manual procedures
			1.7. Recovery procedures
			Documented
			Tested
			1.8. Backup methods
			"Save" device? Alt-IPL device
			Save System (SAVSYS)
			Save all non-system libraries(SAVLIB *NONSYS)
			Save security data (SAVSECDTA)

Weight	Use	Score	Task Description
			Save document library objects (SAVDLO)
			Save changed objects (SAVCHGOBJ)
			Save While Active (QUSRTOOL or V2R2)
			Use of online save files
			Journaling
			File changes
			Access paths
			Dual systems (MIMICS, etc.)
			Review of SAVE job logs for failures
			1.9. External media standards
			Labeling
			Tape/Diskette management system
			Retention dates
			Media Rotation schedule
			Onsite storage methods
			Offsite storage methods
			Questionable-media purge procedures
			1.10. Log of PTFs installed
			Battery Backup (9402/4 or all "D" models)
			1.11. Uninterruptible Power Supply (UPS)
			1.12. Review process to ensure backup procedures are current
			2. CLEANUP
			2.1. Run Operational Assistant (covers '*' items below)
			2.2. *Delete unnecessary LIBs, Files, PGMs, DIR entries, USRPRFs, DOCs, FLRs, JOBDs
			2.3. *JOBLOGs, PGMDUMPs, JOBDUMPs (delete unneeded files)
			2.4. *MSGQs (delete old messages)
			2.5. Offline stg for seldom used objects
			2.6. *OUTQs... Print/Save/Delete (Save to DBF)
			2.7. *PRBLOG & RGZPFM assoc. physical files
			2.8. Purge "old" downloaded PTFs

Weight	Use	Score	Task Description
			2.9. Purge (*)system/user JRNRCVs
			2.10. *QHST files (save & delete)
			2.11. Reorganize physical file members
			2.12. Reuse deleted records (V2R1)
			2.13. Reclaim storage (RCLSTG - 50% faster on V2R1)
			2.14. Check "last used" field in obj. descriptions (V1R3)
			2.15. *Reclaim spool storage
			2.16. Automatic release of storage (V2R3)
			3. COMMUNICATIONS
			3.1. Alert handling procedures
			3.2. Distributed systems management procedures
			3.3. Documentation of network
			3.4. Network attributes
			SYSNAM
			LCLCPNAME
			LCLLOCNAME
			LCLNETID(APPN)
			3.5. Modem test procedures
			3.6. Monitor Line status w/ queries
			3.7. Network management
			3.8. SYSVAL: QCMNRCYLMT = '2 5'
			4. DOCUMENTATION
			4.1. Backup procedures
			4.2. Cable labels
			4.3. Cabling diagram
			4.4. Change log
			4.5. Communications configuration
			Local
			Remote
			4.6. Contact information
			IBM
			Other hardware/software vendors
			User personnel
			Suppliers

Weight	Use	Score	Task Description
			Remote locations
			4.7. Hardware configuration
			Local devices (PRTDEVADR)
			Remote devices
			Configuration object detail (LINDs, etc.)
			Recreate configuration program (RTVCFGSRC)
			Hardware devices and features (WRKHDWPRD)
			Model Unique Licensed Internal Code tape
			4.8. Network attributes
			4.9. Operations procedures
			4.10. Passwords
			Security Officer
			Customer Engineer
			Remote system(s)
			Software support
			4.11. PTF status
			4.12. Problem log
			4.13. Publication Library
			4.14. Security methods and controls
			4.15. Software configuration
			Software installed
			Release level currency
			PTF Levels
			4.16. Standards for software documentation
			Applications
			Files/Field Descr./Data Dictionary, Field ref. file, text descr., edit codes, col. headings, values, ranges, etc.
			Programs, Author, last modified, CALLed by, parameter descriptions, etc.
			Operations - run book
			4.17. System Values
			4.18. Text fields used on all objects
			5. EDUCATION

Weight	Use	Score	Task Description
			5.1. Overall education plan
			5.2. Discover Education (DE)
			5.3. Offsite classes
			5.4. Personal Learning Series (PLS)
			5.5. Sears tapes
			5.6. Tutorial System Support (TSS)
			5.7. Other vendors classes (software and hardware)
			6. ENVIRONMENT
			6.1. Air conditioning/humidity/temperature
			6.2. Isolation transformer
			6.3. Lightning/station protectors
			6.4. Raised floor
			6.5. Cabling specifications met
			Twinaxial
			Telephone twisted pair
			Fiber optic
			6.5. Electrical grounding
			6.6. Emergency Power Off (EPO) switch
			6.7. Fire alarm, smoke detectors, sprinklers, Halon
			6.8. Cleanliness
			6.9. Operations area organized efficiently
			6.10. Adequate files, cabinets, shelving
			6.11. Secured paper/forms storage area
			6.12. Power surge protectors
			6.13. Service clearances
			6.14. Plastic covers over panel buttons and switches
			7. HARDWARE MONITOR & MAINTENANCE
			7.1. Communications errors
			7.2. Device errors
			7.3. Maintenance calendar
			7.4. Monitor Statistical Data Recording (SDR) for tape/diskette media failures (*VOLSTAT)
			7.5. Error Log (PRTERRLOG)

Weight	Use	Score	Task Description
			7.6. Electronic Customer Support (ECS)
			7.7. Tape drive cleaning schedule
			7.8. Tape handling procedures
			8. JOB ACCOUNTING
			8.1. Journal cleanup (ACGJRN)
			8.2. Review and distribute reports
			9. OFFICE
			9.1. Autostart job entry for Office
			9.2. Omitting names on distrib. list
			9.3. Reorganize (cleanup) office database files
			10. OPERATIONS
			10.1. Log of events
			10.2. Operations manuals available & current
			10.3. Run book
			10.4. Shift change meetings
			11. PERFORMANCE
			11.1. Benchmark before and after system changes
			11.2. Performance monitor
			11.3. Performance tuning
			11.4. Program design for performance database, shared files, logical files, etc.
			11.5. Tuning values (Work Management)
			11.6. No high-priority batch jobs
			11.7. Console not used for application jobs
			11.8. Performance Analysis tool (V2R1)
			12. PERSONNEL RESPONSIBILITIES
			12.1. Backup operator
			12.2. Change coordinator
			12.3. Configuration control
			12.4. Help desk
			12.5. Preventive Maintenance coordinator
			12.6. Problem coordinator
			12.7. Publication control
			12.8. Q&A coordinator

Weight	Use	Score	Task Description
			12.9. Recovery coordinator
			12.10. Security administrator
			12.11. System Management manager
			12.12. Technical support contacts
			12.13. Overall interdepartmental communication
			13. RUNTIME CONSIDERATIONS
			13.1. System/36 Environment
			S36E values(CHGS36)
			Device Naming conventions (QDEVNAMING)
			Performance considerations
			13.2. Check completion codes in JOBLOGs
			13.3. Damaged objects on system
			13.4. DASD space monitoring
			By user (DSPUSRPRF)
			By library (DSPLIB)
			13.5. File record counts & # of increments
			13.6. IPL frequency (spool buckets, WCBT, addr. regen.)
			13.7. Run from 'B' side of Licensed Internal Code
			13.8. Message reply list
			13.9. Number of jobs on system
			13.10. Batch/Interactive job scheduling
			13.11. Operator checklist for task completion status
			13.12. System values
			QCTLSBSD = QCTL/QBASE
			QPFRADJ = '0' or '3'
			QPRTDEV = (printer name)
			13.13. QSTRUPPGM
			13.14. QSYSOPR MSGQ, delivery, severity
			13.15. Review JOBLOGs w/ sev40 (or greater) completion
			13.16. RGZPFM system files (use the Operational Assistant)
			13.17. RGZPFM user files

Weight	Use	Score	Task Description
			13.18. Routing of printer messages
			13.19. Routing of work station messages
			13.20. SAA conventions
			13.21. Separate library for saving system objects before making changes to them
			13.22. Special OUTQs QPJOBLOG, QPPGMDMP, SQPSRVDMP
			13.23. Temporary and Permanent address space (WRKSYSSTS)
			13.24. Use SAVLICPGM, RSTLICPGM, DLTLICPGM
			14. SECURITY
			14.1. Group profiles
			14.2. Authorization lists
			14.3. System values
			Invalid sign-on attempts (QMAXSIGN)
			Level 10,20,30,40,50 (QSECURITY)
			QSECOFR sign on to any work station (QLMTSECOFR)
			Password controls (see list of SYSVALs)
			14.4. Lmt. *PUBLIC to *USE auth. in IBM-supplied libraries
			14.5. Monitor violations (QSYSMSG MSGQ)
			14.6. QSECOFR, QSYSOPR, QPGMR SPCENV(*NONE)
			14.7. QSRV passwords secure and available to CE (24 hours a day)
			14.8. System keys
			14.9. Test libs. and UPDPROD(*NO) for Pgmrs.
			15. SUPPORT
			15.1. Use of Analyze Problem (ANZPRB) command
			15.2. CE manuals and equipment
			15.3. Use ECS to report Hardware problems
			15.4. Use ECS to report Software problems

Weight	Use	Score	Task Description
			15.5. Electronic Mail to IBM
			15.6. Help function
			15.7. Help Desk
			15.8. IBMLink
			15.9. Interactive Debug/Trace used by prgmrs., existence, status, circumvention, fix, recovery, resolution
			15.11. ODF for remote system users
			15.12. PTF management plan
			15.13. SNDPTFORD procedures
			15.14. Q&A for clients
			15.15. Q&A Local & Remote
			15.16. Search index
			15.17. Copy Screen Image (STRCPYSCN)
			For internal users
			For external consultants and contractors
			For support from IBM
			16. STANDARDS
			16.1. Naming conventions (configuration objects)
			16.2. User IDs & directory entries
			16.3. Libraries
			16.4. Files
			16.5. Programs
			16.6. Printers
			16.7. Other: DTAARAs, JOBDs, etc.
			17. SERVICE LEVELS (Objectives & Tracking)
			17.1. Reliability
			17.2. Availability
			17.3. Stability
			17.4. Responsiveness
			17.5. User Satisfaction
			17.6. User surveys
			17.7. Feedback to users

APPENDIX I: USING THE ECS LINE FOR REMOTE SUPPORT

To use the built commands STRRMTSPT and ENDRMTSPT to enable access from a remote system, you must first provide the necessary communications objects on the source system. The two commands above are used on the target system only.

The source code to create a CL command and a CL program, called REMOTE, appear at the end of this appendix. The CL command and CL program create the line controller and device descriptions on the source system so that a user can access the target AS/400. After creating the communication objects, AS/400 passthrough is initiated to the user on the source system to sign on to the target machine. When the ENDPASTHR command is executed, the REMOTE program deletes the communication objects on the source system and varies off the ECS line.

INSTRUCTIONS FOR THE TARGET SYSTEM

To initiate remote support, notify the user on the target system to do the following:

1. Check the System Value QAUTOVRT. It must be greater than zero (0).
2. Execute the command STRRMTSPT:

```
STRRMTSPT  DEVCLS(*VRT) DSPTYPE(5251) DSPMODEL(11) +
    STNADR(FE) USRPRF(usrprf) RSRCNAME(LIN011) +
    RMTLOCNAME(QREMOTE) LCLLOCNAME(QLOCAL)
```

- USRPRF should be an existing user profile. QPGMR is default.
- STNADR is the hexadecimal address for the display. Default is FE.
- Resource name is the one for ECS line Default is LIN011. If the resource name is other than this, make sure you select the correct one.

3. When the operator receives the message Remote Support Enabled, then proceed with Instructions for the Source System, below.

INSTRUCTIONS FOR THE SOURCE SYSTEM

After the user on the target system receives the message Remote Support Enabled, proceed with the following:

1. Execute the CL command **REMOTE**.
   a. This is a user-created command and is not part of OS/400. The source code for this command is at the end of this appendix. The command and CL program of the same name should be in library QGPL or other library in your library list.
   b. The parameters for the command are:
      PHONE: Target System's ECS Line Phone Number.
      PREFIX: The prefix used to gain access to outside line.

AREACODE:	Three-digit area code number (only used if long distance).
STNADR:	Hexadecimal Station Address. Default is FE. Must match target system's address.
RESOURCE:	Resource name used for ECS line. Default is LIN011.
LONGDIST:	Long distance, Yes or No (Y/N).

2. After entering the required parameters, a pass-through session is initiated and you are presented with the target system AS/400 sign-on screen. If you do not get this screen, check for errors to resolve the problem, and execute the command again.

3 If you want to initiate a passthrough session from the remote system to the local system, you can use the following command:

```
STRPASTHR  RMTLOCNAME(QREMOTE) MODE(LU62) RMTNETID(*NONE)
```

4. When you are finished, remember that you must end the passthrough session with the ENDPASTHR command — not SIGNOFF. If you use SIGNOFF, then sign on again and issue ENDPASTHR.

5. After the pass-through session ends, tell the user at the target system to execute the ENDRMTSPT (End Remote Support) command to disable remote support.

6. After you end the pass-through session, the REMOTE CL program deletes the communication objects created to enable the pass-through session. For your reference, all the communication objects (line description, controller description, and device description) are named QREMOTESPT.

SOURCE CODE FOR REMOTE CL PROGRAM

The following is the source for the CL program to create the line, controller, and device descriptions for the remote environment. After creation of the communication objects, the dial-up connection is initiated and the passthrough session is started. When finished with the passthrough session, the connection will be terminated and communication objects will be deleted.

CL Program for Remote Support

```
/*    PROGRAM SOURCE CODE FOR REMOTE CL PROGRAM           */

PGM        PARM(&PHONE &PREFIX &AREACODE &LONGDIST +
                 &STNADR &RESOURCE)

           DCL       VAR(&PREFIX) TYPE(*CHAR) LEN(1)
           DCL       VAR(&AREACODE) TYPE(*CHAR) LEN(3)
           DCL       VAR(&PHONE) TYPE(*CHAR) LEN(7)
           DCL       VAR(&LONGDIST) TYPE(*CHAR) LEN(1)
           DCL       VAR(&CNNNBR) TYPE(*CHAR) LEN(16)

/*  The CNNNBR is the inbound phone number for the ECS line */
/*  on the target system.  You will be prompted for this    */
```

```
/*   number during execution of the REMOTE command.  The    */
/*   operator at the remote (target) system must give you    */
/*   this phone phone number.                                */

          DCL        VAR(&STNADR) TYPE(*CHAR) LEN(2)
          DCL        VAR(&RESOURCE) TYPE(*CHAR) LEN(10)
          DCL        VAR(&REPLY) TYPE(*CHAR) LEN(4)
          IF         COND(&PREFIX = 'N') THEN(CHGVAR
                         VAR(&PREFIX) VALUE(' '))
          IF         COND(&LONGDIST = 'N') THEN(CHGVAR +
                         VAR(&CNNNBR) VALUE('SST' *CAT +
                         &PREFIX *TCAT ':' *CAT &PHONE))
          IF         COND(&LONGDIST = 'Y') THEN(CHGVAR +
                         VAR(&CNNNBR) VALUE('SST' *CAT +
                         &PREFIX *TCAT ':' *CAT '1' +
                         *CAT &AREACODE *CAT *PHONE))


/*   The SST: prefix will concatenated to the CNNNBR.        */
/*   This will turn on the modem speaker                     */


/*   This program will create the necessary line,            */
/*   controller, and device descriptions to perform support  */
/*   services on a remote system.                            */


/*   Make sure, on the remote system, that the system value, */
/*   QAUTOVRT, is not set to zero.  Have the operator run     */
/*   the command, DSPSYSVAL QAUTOVRT.  If it is zero, then    */
/*   run the command, CHGSYSVAL  SYSVAL(QAUTOVRT) VALUE('x')*/
/*               where x is greater than zero                */


/*   The remote system operator must run the following       */
/*     command on the remote system                          */
/*                                                           */
/*          STRRMTSPT  DEVCLS(*VRT) DSPTYPE(5251)   +        */
/*                     DSPMODEL(11) USRPRF(usrprf) +         */
/*                     RSRCNAME(LIN011) RMTLOCNAME(QREMOTE) + */
/*                     LCLLOCNAME(QLOCAL)                    */
/*                                                           */
/*   The STRRMTSPT command will create the line, controller, */
/*   device descriptions and enable the communications.  The */
/*   resource name used should be the resource name for the  */
/*   ECS line, default is LIN011.                            */
/*   The 'usrprf' name should be a user profile that already */
/*   exists on the target system.                            */


/*   When the user on the target system receives message that*/
/*     remote support is enabled, then you can run this       */
/*     program on the source system.                          */
/*   The following objects will be configured and varied on   */
/*     at the target system upon completion of STRRMTSPT      */


/*          QTIPASLIN ... SDLC Line Description              */
```

```
/*          QTIPASCTL ... APPC Controller Description      */
/*          QTIPASDEV ... APPC Device Description          */
/*          QTIVRTCTL ... Virtual Controller Description   */
/*          QTIVRTDSP ... Virtual Display of type specified */
/*                       in STRRMTSPT                       */
/*          QTIVRTDSPA .. Virtual Display Type 5251         */

/* When you are through providing support and have ended   */
/* the pass-through session, you should have the target    */
/* system operator perform the ENDRMTSPT command, which    */
/* will vary off and delete the objects created during     */
/* STRRMTSPT.                                               */

/* First, clean up line, controller, and device            */
/* descriptions that may be left over from a previous      */
/* session ...                                             */

             VRYCFG     CFGOBJ(QREMOTESPT) CFGTYPE(*CTL) +
                          STATUS(*OFF) RANGE(*NET)
             MONMSG     MSGID(CPF9999)
             DLYJOB     DLY(2)
             VRYCFG     CFGOBJ(QREMOTESPT) CFGTYPE(*LIN) +
                          STATUS(*OFF) RANGE(*OBJ)
             MONMSG     MSGID(CPF9999)
             DLYJOB     DLY(2)
             DLTLIND    LIND(QREMOTESPT)
             MONMSG     MSGID(CPF9999)
             DLTCTLD    CTLD(QREMOTESPT)
             MONMSG     MSGID(CPF9999)
             DLTDEVD    DEVD(QREMOTESPT)
             MONMSG     MSGID(CPF9999)

/* Now, attempt to create mode LU62, if mode LU62 exists.  */
/* then do nothing                                         */

             CRTMODD    MODD(LU62) MAXSSN(8) MAXCNV(8) +
                          LCLCTLSSN(4) PREESTSSN(4) +
                          INPACING(7) OUTPACING(7) +
                          MAXLENRU(*CALC) COS(#CONNECT)
             MONMSG     MSGID(CPF9999)

             CRTLINSDLC LIND(QREMOTESPT) RSRCNAME(&RESOURCE) +
                          ONLINE(*NO) ROLE(*PRI) CNN(*SWTPP) +
                          EXCHID(05600000) AUTODIAL(*YES) +
                          DIALCMD(*V25BIS) CALLNBR(*NONE) +
                          TEXT('Remote Support Line')

             CRTCTLAPPC CTLD(QREMOTESPT) LINKTYPE(*SDLC) +
                          ONLINE(*NO) SWITCHED(*YES) +
                          APPN(*NO) SWTLINLST(QREMOTESPT) +
                          MAXFRAME(521) EXCHID(05600000) +
                          CNNNBR(&CNNNBR) ROLE(*SEC) +
                          STNADR(&STNADR) +
```

```
                       TEXT('Remote Support Controller')

            CRTDEVAPPC DEVD(QREMOTESPT) RMTLOCNAME(QLOCAL) +
                       ONLINE(*NO) LCLLOCNAME(QREMOTE) +
                       RMTNETID(*NONE) CTL(QREMOTESPT) +
                       MODE(LU62) APPN(*NO) +
                       TEXT('Remote Support Device')

            VRYCFG     CFGOBJ(QREMOTESPT) CFGTYPE(*LIN) +
                       STATUS(*ON)
            DLYJOB  DLY(2)

            VRYCFG     CFGOBJ(QREMOTESPT) CFGTYPE(*CTL) +
                       STATUS(*ON)
            DLYJOB     DLY(2)

/*  I have discovered that the DLYJOB is required on some    */
/*    systems for reasons that I cannot determine.  It just  */
/*    seems to be necessary.  If you discover that if you    */
/*    manually run the commands and they work and they       */
/*    don't in the CL pgm, then put in a short delay.        */

            STRPASTHR  RMTLOCNAME(QLOCAL) MODE(LU62)

/*  If you want to passthrough from the remote system to     */
/*   the local system, the command to use on the remote      */
/*   system is: STRPASTHR  RMTLOCNAME(QREMOTE) MODE(LU62)     */
/*              RMTNETID(*NONE)                               */

/* After ending the pass-through session, the following      */
/* will clean up the objects created on the source system.   */
/* make sure the user on the target system runs the CL       */
/* command, ENDRMTSPT, to clean up the target system.        */

            VRYCFG     CFGOBJ(QREMOTESPT) CFGTYPE(*CTL) +
                       STATUS(*OFF) RANGE(*NET)
            MONMSG     MSGID(CPF9999)
            VRYCFG     CFGOBJ(QREMOTESPT) CFGTYPE(*LIN) +
                       STATUS(*OFF) RANGE(*OBJ)
            MONMSG     MSGID(CPF9999)

/*  Deleting the objects created earlier ...                 */

            DLTLIND    LIND(QREMOTESPT)
            DLTCTLD    CTLD(QREMOTESPT)
            DLTDEVD    DEVD(QREMOTESPT)

END:        ENDPGM
```

SOURCE CODE FOR REMOTE COMMAND

This command is used to initiate the variables and execute the REMOTE program created above.

CL Program for the Command Processor for Remote Support

```
CMD        PROMPT('Enable Remote Support')

           PARM      KWD(PHONE) TYPE(*CHAR) LEN(7) MIN(1) +
                     CHOICE('Enter Phone number (no +
                     dashes)') PROMPT('Phone Number')
           PARM      KWD(PREFIX) TYPE(*CHAR) LEN(1) +
                     RSTD(*YES) +
                     VALUES(1 2 3 4 5 6 7 8 9 0 N) +
                     MIN(1) +
                     CHOICE('Select 0-9 or N for None') +
                     PROMPT('Outside Line Prefix')
           PARM      KWD(AREACODE) TYPE(*CHAR) LEN(3) +
                     DFT(602) FULL(*YES) +
                     CHOICE('3 digit Area Code') +
                     PROMPT('Area Code')
           PARM      KWD(LONGDIST) TYPE(*CHAR) LEN(1) +
                     RSTD(*YES) DFT(N) VALUES(N Y) +
                     CHOICE('Select Y or N (Yes or No)') +
                     PROMPT('Long Distance')
           PARM      KWD(STNADR) TYPE(*CHAR) LEN(2) DFT(FE) +
                     FULL(*YES) CHOICE('Hex code for +
                     Station Address') PROMPT('Station +
                     Address')
           PARM      KWD(RESOURCE) TYPE(*CHAR) LEN(10) +
                     DFT(LIN011) MIN(0) +
                     CHOICE('Communication Resource Name') +
                     PROMPT('Communication Resource')
```

INSTRUCTIONS FOR LOADING AND COMPILING

The steps you need to take to create the program and command are:

1. Create CL source file for the CLP and CMD source.
2. Create a CL program QGPL/REMOTE from the CL source code.
3. Create a CL command QGPL/REMOTE from the CMD source code.

You're done.

APPENDIX J: COMMUNICATION MATCHING PARAMETER WORKSHEETS

Use the worksheets that follow as aids when configuring local and remote systems.

- AS/400 to AS/400
- S/36 to AS/400
- S/38 to AS/400
- S/370 to AS/400

AS/400 to AS/400 Matching Parameter Configuration Worksheet

Remote AS/400		Local AS/400
Line Descr: _____		Line Descr: _____
Ctrl Descr: _____		Ctrl Descr: _____
Device Descr: _____		Device Descr: _____

L	C	D	Remote AS/400	Value	Local AS/400	D	C	L
x			Data Link Role		Data Link Role		x	
x			Exchange ID		Exchange ID		x	
	x		Link Type		Link Type		x	
	x		APPN Capable		APPN Capable		x	
	x		RMTNETID		RMTNETID		x	
	x		Exchange ID		Exchange ID			x
	x		Data Link Role		Data Link Role			x
	x		Station Address		Station Address		x	
		x	Remote Location		Local Location	x		
		x	Local Location		Remote Location	x		
		x	RMT Network ID		RMT Network ID	x		
		x	Mode		Mode	x		
		x	Mode		Mode	x		
		x	Mode		Mode	x		
		x	Mode		Mode	x		
		x	Mode		Mode	x		
		x	APPN Capable		APPN Capable	x		

Legend:

L	Line Description
C	Controller Description
D	Device Description
x	Matching Value Parameter

S/36 to AS/400 Matching Parameter Configuration Worksheet

Remote S/36
Line Descr: _____
Subsys Descr: _____
Device Descr: _____

Local AS/400
Line Descr: _____
Ctrl Descr: _____
Device Descr: _____

L	S		Remote S/36	Value	Local AS/400	D	C	L
x			Protocol		Data Link Role		x	o
x			Line Type		Connection Type			x
x			Station Address		Station Address		x	
x			Exchange ID		Exchange ID		x	
x			Remote System		Local Ctrl Pt			
x			Remote Block ID		Exchange ID			x
	x		Subsystem Type		APPN Capable		x	
	x		Local Location		Remote Location	x		
	x		Remote Location		Local Location	x		
	x		Session Group		Mode	x		
	x		Session Group		Mode	x		
	x		Session Group		Mode	x		
	x		Session Group		Mode	x		

Legend:

L	Line Description (S/36 and AS/400)
S	Subsystem Description (S/36)
C	Controller Description (AS/400)
D	Device Description (AS/400)
x	Matching Value Parameter
o	Opposite Value Parameter

S/38 to AS/400 Matching Parameter Configuration Worksheet

Remote S38

Line Descr: _____
Ctrl Descr: _____
Device Descr: _____

Local AS/400

Line Descr: _____
Ctrl Descr: _____
Device Descr: _____

L	C	D	Remote S/38	Value	Local AS/400	D	C	L
x			Line Type		Link Type		x	.
x			Line Type		Date Link Role		x	
x			Connection Type		Connection Type			x
x			Data Rate		Linespeed			x
x			NRZI Decoding		NRZI Data Encod			x
x			Wire Link Type		Duplex			x
x			Non-IBM Modem		Modem Type Sup.			x
x			Exchange ID		Exchange ID		x	
	x		Type/Model		APPN Capable		x	
	x		Ctrl Unit Addr		Station Address		x	
	x		Exchange ID		Exchange ID			x
	x		Link Type		Data Link Role			x
		x	Device Type/Model		APPN Capable	x		
		x	Local LU Name		Remote Loc Name	x		
		x	Remote LU Name		Local Loc Name	x		
		x	Mode		Mode	x		
		x	Mode		Mode	x		
		x	Mode		Mode	x		
		x	Mode		Mode	x		

Legend:

L   Line Description
C   Controller Description
D   Device Description

S/370 to AS/400 Matching Parameter Configuration Worksheet

Remote S/370
Line Name: _____
PU Name: _____
LU Name: _____

Local AS/400
Line Descr: _____
Ctrl Descr: _____
Device Descr: _____

N	P	L	Remote S/370	Value	Local AS/400	D	C	L
			SSCPID		SSCPID		x	
	x		Address		Station Address		x	
		x	LU Name		Device Name	x		
		x	Locadr (Dec)		Loc Addr (Hex)	x		
		x	Logmode		Mode	x		
		x	Logappl		Remote Loc Name	x		
		x	Net Name (DFHTCT)		Local Loc Name	x		

Legend:

N	Line Description Name, S/370
P	Physical Unit Name, S/370
L	Logical Unit Name, S/370
L	Line Description Name, AS/400
C	Controller Description, AS/400
D	Device Description, AS/400

APPENDIX K: CHECKLIST FOR USING CA/400 WITH MICROSOFT WINDOWS

Use the following checklist to configure PC Support or Client Access for use with Microsoft Windows. This appendix applies to the DOS and DOS extended versions of PC Support and Client Access. It does not apply to the Client Access/400 for Windows 3.1 version.

Using Expanded Memory with PC Support

PS Support may not run with expanded memory in Windows. Try loading EIMPCS.SYS prior to loading the EMS device driver, or use the P=0 code on the EIMPCS.SYS command line of the CONFIG.SYS file if EIMPCS.SYS is loaded after the EMS device driver.

There is an incompatibility between PC Support and Microsoft EMM386.EXE expanded memory device driver. Use the P=0 parameter in the EIMPCS.SYS command line in the CONFIG.SYS file or the STARTPCS.BAT (depends on where you execute EIMPCS from).

Check Use of PCSWIN Command

PCSWIN must be loaded immediately after STARTRT.EXE in the STARTPCS.BAT file. PCSWIN allows PC Support communications buffers to be allocated out of conventional memory so they are not disturbed by Windows context switching. By default, 16K of buffer space is allocated for this purpose. You can specify a different value by using a command line parameter:

    PCSWIN /B=nn   where *nn* = as high as 64.

If many PC Support functions are starting simultaneously, you may need to increase the buffer above the default of 16K.

PC Support Hangs Up

Check the following:

- Token-Ring adapter or 5250 Emulation adapter RAM is excluded from Windows using EMMEXCLUDE entry in the SYSTEM.INI file. The format is EMMEXCLUDE=XXXX-XXXX. (For example, to exclude all upper memory code, use EMMEXCLUDE=A000-FFFF.) Memory excluded must match the memory excluded in the EMM386 statement in the CONFIG.SYS file.
- Verify that the TwinAxial Adapter Handler memory is excluded from Windows using the above EMMEXCLUDE entry.

There is a problem with Windows SMARTDRV.EXE in Windows 3.1. Try changing the CONFIG.SYS file:

```
DEVICE=C:\WINDOWS\SMARTDRV.EXE /DOUBLE_BUFFER
```

or try removing the line altogether. Another point here, do not load SMARTDRV high. It automatically loads into extended memory if available.

If you are using DOS 5 or higher, the DOS version of SMARTDRV may be newer than the Windows version. Use the latest version.

DOS/16M Error

This error occurs if DOS16M.386 is not located in the PCS subdirectory. DOS16M.386 is needed beginning with V2R1.1, and is part of the PCSWIN.PKG file.

Cannot Access IBM AS/400 Network Functions

This error (Error 7004) occurs if you start Windows but did not start PCS first, or you may have incorrect levels of PCSXI and PCSWIN. Verify that correct version and release of PCSXI and PCSWIN are loaded.

Problems with PC Support in Windows Enhanced Mode

The following tips may help if you are experiencing problems in Enhanced mode.

- Make the following changes to the SYSTEM.INI file if you are experiencing problems in 386 enhanced mode under Windows 3.1:

```
386ENH
VIRTUALHDIRQ=OFF
32BITDISKACCESS=OFF
IRQ9GLOBAL=TRUE
HIGHFLOPPYREADS=NO
EMMEXCLUDE=DC00-E000 (see note 1)
TIMERCRITICALSECTION=1000 (see note 2)
```

Note 1:   *EMMEXCLUDE range may vary. See above.*

Note 2:   *This should match the EMM386.EXE X= Parameter. Increments of 500 milliseconds.*

- Do not mix the Windows 3.1 version of HIMEM.SYS, SMARTDRV.EXE, and EMM386.EXE with the DOS-supplied files.

- If you are using a Microsoft mouse, make sure you are using Version 8.20 of the MS MOUSE.COM or higher. Erratic mouse problems may be remedied by changing the minimum time slice from the default of 20 to 5. Set the time slice value in the Windows Control Panel under 386 Enhanced.

- If you have a PC using AMI BIOS dated earlier than April 9, 1990, Microsoft recommends obtaining an updated chip.

- To check BIOS date, COM ports, TSR loading, etc., Microsoft has included a diagnostic tool. End Windows and get to a DOS prompt. Change to the WINDOWS directory and type MSD. This is similar to Quarterdeck's Manifest program.

Program Information Files (PIF)

PIF files used with PC Support should be configured as either Window or full-screen usage. Be sure to select Background or Exclusive. If you leave these blank, then the program will not multi-task.

Running PC Support from an icon

If you are running Work Station Function (WSF) from an icon and you are NOT running PC Organizer (highly recommended), then the batch file that starts WSF should contain the following:

```
CD C:\PCS
WSF /Z
COMMAND.COM
RMVPCS WSF /F
```

Hot Keying in Windows

Windows uses the Alt-Esc key combination as its default hotkey. Configure a new hotkey for PC Support or disable the Alt-Esc sequence in the PIF file that starts WSF.

6441 Errors When Starting WSF

If you get 6441 errors when starting WSF, try the following to solve the problem:

- A 6441 error can occur if folders are not being used and the controller is configured for switched disconnect *YES. Either configure the controller for SWTDSC *NO, or assign a shared folder to keep the router from disconnecting.

- The AS/400 should generate a job log for the 6441 error. Execute WRKSPLF against the user ID that received the 6441 error. For example:

```
WRKSPLF SELECT(user)
```

Using Virtual Print with Windows

Some tips when using the Virtual Print function in Windows:

- Virtual Printers assigned before starting Windows are available to Windows and non-Windows applications. If no physical printer was detected on the printer port being used for virtual printing when Windows was INSTALLED, then the printer must be defined using the Windows Control Panel in order to use Virtual Printers from Windows applications.

- If the assigned virtual printer is an emulated printer (e.g., an IBM LaserPrinter emulating a 3812), then use Data Type 4 (ASCII Data) so that PC printer output is not translated, and set up the Windows printer driver the same as the physical printer (e.g., IBM LaserPrinter).

- If the assigned Virtual Printer is an AS/400 system printer (e.g., a 4234 printer), then use Data Type 2 (ASCII to SCS), and the Windows printer driver should be the generic/text only.

- If the assigned Virtual Printer is an AS/400 AFPDS printer (e.g., 4028 printer), and you are using V2R2 of PC Support, then use Data Type 5 (AFPDS), and the Windows printer drivers should be AFPDS. This driver is shipped with V2R2 of PC Support.

- With V2R2 of PC Support, you can view the AS/400 Output Queues through the Windows Print Manager. If you are unable to do so, verify that the Virtual Printer code (VPRT.EXE) and the data queues code (LOADDQ.EXE) are being loaded prior to starting Windows.

Miscellaneous Tips and Restrictions When Using Windows and PC Support

Keep in mind these restrictions when using Client Access/400 for DOS in Windows:

- Don't use the Remove PC Support Function (RMVPCS) from within Windows on those functions that were started before Windows.

- If WSF is run in a windowed DOS session in Windows 386 enhanced mode, you must switch to full-screen mode (using Alt-Enter) before trying to hot key from DOS to a WSF session.

- Do not configure the WSF Master Profile to use the graphics buffer as a save area when running 386 enhanced mode. This only allows you to run your WSF session in a full-screen mode.

- If you are using V2R1.1 or earlier of PC Support, the extended DOS SDLC, Extended DOS ASYNCH, and DOS ASYNCH routers may not function. Try running Windows in Real or Standard mode.

- If you have a DEVICE=EMM386.EXE command in your CONFIG.SYS file, you may not be able to run Windows in Standard mode. Either remove EMM386, or run Windows in REAL or ENHANCED mode. This is a DOS 5.0 restriction.

- If you set STACKS=0,0, this may cause problems when using Windows in 386 enhanced mode on some PCs.

- Avoid starting functions that you would expect to be shared across multiple applications from within Windows, such as shared folders and Virtual Printers. Start these functions before starting Windows. If you start these functions from within a windowed session, then the function is usually only available to that window and not to other sessions.

INDEX

—D—

—E—

—F—

—G—

—Q—

—R—

—S—

Reader's Comment Form
AS/400 Power Tips & Techniques

Please use this form to identify any errors or to make any comments. As this is not an IBM document, the IBM Corporation does not take any responsibility for its content; however, I will attempt to maintain it and do my best to assure its accuracy. If you wish a reply, please indicate such in your comments.

Send To: Steve Bisel
c/o Midrange Computing
5650 El Camino Real, Suite 225
Carlsbad, CA 92008-7128
Attn: Book Editor
FAX (619) 931-9935

Or Internet E-mail to: Steve Bisel
75771.1123@compuserve.com

From: Name: _____

         Company: _____

         Address: _____

         _____

Comments: